Disaster Risk Management

About the Editors

Dr. Atanu Sarkar is an Assistant Professor of Division of Community Health and Humanities, Faculty of Medicine, Memorial University, St John's, Newfoundland and Labrador, Canada. He teaches environmental and occupational health.

Dr. Suman Ranjan Sensarma is an urban planner. He has more than 12 years of varied experiences in human settlement and habitat, urban planning, climate change and integrated risk management.

Disaster Risk Management

Conflict and Cooperation

Edited by

Suman Ranjan Sensarma

and

Atanu Sarkar

CONCEPT PUBLISHING COMPANY PVT. LTD.,
NEW DELHI-110059

ISBN-13: 978-81-8069-849-1

First Published 2013

Published and Printed by

Concept Since 1974

Concept Publishing Company Pvt. Ltd.
A/15-16, Commercial Block, Mohan Garden
New Delhi-110059 (India)
T: 25351460, 25351794, *F*: 091-11-25357109
E: publishing@conceptpub.com, W: www.conceptpub.com
Editorial Office: H-13, Bali Nagar, New Delhi-110 015, India.

Cataloging in Publication Data--*Courtesy:* D.K. Agencies (P) Ltd. <docinfo@dkagencies.com>

Disaster risk management : conflict and cooperation / edited by Suman Ranjan Sensarma and Atanu Sarkar.
p. cm.
Contributed articles.
Includes bibliographical references and index.
ISBN 9788180698491

1. Emergency management—Government policy. 2. Emergency management Government policy—India. 3. Risk management. 4. Risk management—India. I. Sensarma, Suman Ranjan. II. Sarkar, Atanu.

DDC 363.348 23

Foreword

Disaster risk management is a complex process that encompasses natural environment, social processes, psychological elements, cultural issues, historical matters, and political and economic ideologies. Much attention has been paid towards management of disaster risk since the 2005 initiative of the International Strategy for Disaster Reduction (ISDR) that defined the Ten Essentials in order to empower local governments and other agencies to implement the Hyogo Framework for Action until 2015. At its launch, the initiative was adopted by 168 governments and has been warmly welcomed by academics, practitioners, businesses, communities, and NGOs. The initiative emphasizes the importance of defining the numerous roles and responsibilities in disaster management and, therefore, strengthening the institutional support to society in general.

In the 21st century, our understanding of disasters that are caused by natural, technological, and/or human sources has improved significantly. Both, the developing and the developed worlds, have made considerable progress, within their capacity and limitations, towards the development of policies and mitigation measures to reduce future disasters. However, disasters continue to harm millions of people each year worldwide. Even though it is somewhat understood that unequal exposure to unsafe conditions as well as differential access to resources often leads to a more severe impact on some people than others, further research is required for us to gain a deeper understanding of the underlying causes of people's vulnerability. Identification and assessment of threats are crucial not only for sustainable development and resilience building, but also for the development of feasible risk reduction strategies and decision making processes. I find that all new publications in this field—articles, magazines, and books alike—are valuable, much needed, and enriching, but they are not enough.

When Dr. Sarkar requested me to write a foreword for his book, I felt truly honoured and privileged. This publication, entitled *Disaster Risk Management—Conflict and Cooperation,* edited by Suman Ranjan Sensarma and Atanu Sarkar, is quite unique in its approach on the subject matter. It examines various perspectives and methodologies; variety of geographic locations; urban versus rural analysis; global case studies; disaster insurance issues; political angle; conflict concerns; health impacts; role of media; and most importantly, engaging stakeholders. The chapter on local level cooperation addresses a very essential component required for an effective and efficient disaster risk management programme. A wide range of issues, from mitigation methods to the insurance market to disaster response and recovery, have been covered in this book, making it a remarkably comprehensive collection of scholarly writings.

I wish to thank the authors for their contributions to this book. I hope that researchers, teachers, practitioners, experts, and students around the globe will appreciate the content and see the merits of the book just as I do.

Prof. Dr. N. Nirupama

Disaster & Emergency Management
York University
Toronto, Canada

Foreword

Disaster studies and emergency management is a relatively young and emergent discipline. Over the past three decades the gap between practitioners and academics has been slowly closing as the core body of knowledge of disaster studies expanded and emergency management practices refined. Today universities around the world are delivering disaster studies and emergency management degree programmes replacing experience as the only path into the profession. It is in this dynamic and crucial context that this new book shines. The strength of *Disaster Risk Management – Conflict and Cooperation* lies in its diverse perspectives and topics.

The roots of disaster studies lie in the disciplines of earth sciences, geography and sociology with tendrils extending into political science, administrative studies, psychology and health studies. It is from this fertile mix of perspectives that our modern concepts of how disasters unfold and affect our communities have grown. This important work has helped us see disasters, as Quarantelli said, not as physical events but as social happenings. These ideas, that it is the affected society that matters more than the cause and that all disasters are an outcome of a complex interaction of socio-economic and physical factors, now form the heartwood of a discipline that continues to grow and branch out.

Disaster studies today remains entwined in the many disciplines that have contributed to its development and continues to make new connections with other evolving fields. Technical advances in disciplines such as engineering, remote sensing and computer science have found natural applications in hazard mitigation, community preparedness and disaster response and recovery. New approaches in social governance, planning and communication have also been easily translated into the same areas of practice. The fruit of this cross-fertilization is now producing a new crop of disaster research and improved emergency management practices.

Furthermore, as the professional practice of emergency management has applied the knowledge generated by this diverse research, it has created a feedback loop. Researchers now examine how hazards impact on society as well as how society creates, adapts to and manages those hazards. The value of such an academic-practice pairing, like urban studies and community planning or, perhaps more classically, biology and medicine, is apparent. Now the best practices in emergency management are driven by the best theories of disaster studies and researchers look to their practitioner colleagues for the real world applications that can motivate further inquires. This is generating a reflective cycle where the application of theory improves practice and the lessons from practice inform the development of theories. This is creating a metamorphosis in the discipline so there no longer a distinction between academics and practitioners.

Emergency management practices are also finding a foothold in other endeavours. Community planning is one such area that shows promise for mutually beneficial outcomes from greater integration of emergency management practice. In a rural or urban setting, in developed nations or in regions still growing their economies: the value of increasing resiliency through the development of social, economic and physical capital is being recognized. Other disciplines, from architecture to social work, are seeing how hazards and disasters can impact on their work in the community and how emergency management needs to be an integral part their activities. Disasters are contextualized by the at-risk society and, therefore, all components of society need to contribute to emergency management.

The range of hazards under consideration is also being stretched. The risks associated with geological and meteorological hazards have increased as population densities change and natural processes vary to expose more people to more severe events. However, new risks, from resurgent and emerging diseases to those born from our own technological creations, deserve further investigation. Each change in society carries with it the potential for benefits and harm: this is the true nature of risk. The challenge is in finding the balance between progress and protection. Researchers and practitioners must cooperate to achieve this.

The emergency management discipline has grown spatially as well as topically and relevant practices are being adopted around the world. Past efforts, such as the United Nation's International Decade for Natural Disaster Reduction in the 1990s, helped foster an exchange of ideas and promising initiatives. Now the international community has numerous formal arrangements and programmes and, possibly more importantly, an informal network of researchers and practitioners sharing their struggles and advances. This global approach continues to yield improvements and must be promoted and enhanced.

The future of the academic research in disaster studies and the profession practice of emergency management will involve several parallel but seemingly divergent processes. The core body of knowledge in disaster studies will continue to expand and the number of researchers dedicated to this area will grow correspondingly. Universities are creating separate departments aimed at developing and disseminating this knowledge through unique degrees. Concurrent with this focusing of effort there are more researchers in different fields who are contributing to the disaster studies body of knowledge so that greater specialization and wider diversity are occurring simultaneously.

The same forces are at work within the community of practice. Students are receiving educations with emergency management as the central or major topic of their degree as a first step into a career in emergency management. This is a new stage in the evolution of the profession which, in the past, has relied on skills sets gained through experience alone. Yet, while this new cohort of emergency managers is progressing forward, more practitioners in other fields, like health or planning, are taking on emergency management roles. So, as is the situation in the academic world, the practice community is dealing with more people who are emergency management specialists and more who are taking on roles tangent to their own speciality.

These processes, the simultaneous focusing and expansion of influence in research and practice of emergency management, are crucial. The editors of this volume, Dr. Atanu Sarkar and Dr. Suman Ranjan Sensarma, are to be commended for recognizing the value of this diversity of research and practice. They have brought together a collection of works from a global community of researchers. Each chapter presents a new perspective on a wide range of topics relevant to practitioners and of great interest to other academics. *Disaster Risk Management – Conflict and Cooperation*, as a whole, represents an excellent cross-section of this broadening discipline while the individual chapters contribute to various specific lines of inquiry.

This collection of pieces highlights the importance of fostering different points of view on the common issues facing communities. In drawing these together the editors have provided the reader with the opportunity to dip into single chapters as a resource or to read the book, in its entirety, to fully appreciate how each chapter complements the others. The chapters contain both fresh ideas as well as provide support for well-established concepts. As such every reader – those new to the field and those with experience, whether academic or practitioner – is sure to find something to excite their own thoughts and spur on further exploration.

John Lindsay
Assistant Professor
Applied Disaster and Emergency Studies
Brandon University
Canada

Foreword

In all millennia of recorded history, human societies have grappled with natural and man-made disasters: cyclone, tornado, hurricane, flood, tsunami, earthquake, volcanic eruption, forest fire, and many others. In recent times, climatic changes have resulted in life-threatening drought, famine, rainfall variations, and the shrinking of fresh watercourses. Newly emerging and re-occurring natural and man-made disasters, albeit differing in magnitude and scale, and also depending on the resilience of the affected society, have often resulted in loss of lives, destruction of sustainable livelihoods, unimaginable human suffering, and the total collapse of the core governance institutions and infrastructure of the affected society. Disasters have raised very complex human security challenges: breakdown of infrastructure, mass starvation and acute hunger, healthcare crisis, and lack of the other essential necessities of life. Disasters bring together the two components of human security: "freedom from fear" (as in the case of authoritarian regimes) where the State – by its actions or inaction – impedes humanitarian assistance from the international community, and "freedom from want" where natural disasters, even in a well-governed democratic nation-state, would still inevitably lead to hunger, disease, infrastructure collapse, and lack of the essential necessities of life and dignity. During disasters, the overwhelming burden of human security problems: disease, hunger, starvation, and death is borne by vulnerable groups who are least able to afford medical treatment and preventive measures, and whose governments have the least capacity to meet these urgent needs in an emergency.

Disaster risk management, and—by implication – "disaster diplomacy" has often been embedded in traditional top-down approaches which often relegate the affected local community to the margins of decision-making processes. This book seeks to address these gaps and challenges. By identifying the multiple actors needed for effective and sustainable disaster risk management framework, and focusing on the necessary local-national-regional-international policy framework and linkages, the contributors to this volume offer constructive discourse across disciplines. This discourse is aimed at disaster risk management policy reform.

As no human society is completely immune to disasters, examples of the devastation caused by disasters abound in every region of the world. In Japan, the Hanshin Earthquake ('Kobe earthquake' as it is commonly known outside of Japan) of 17 January, 1995, and the triple disaster (earthquake, tsunami, and the Fukushima Daiichi nuclear crisis) of 11 March, 2011 in the Tohoku region claimed thousands of lives, and devastated the livelihoods of societies at the epicentre of the disasters. Before these recent disasters in Japan, the Kanto earthquake of 1923 was estimated to have claimed about 140,000 lives. In December 2004, a tsunami, with its epicentre off the west coast of Sumatra, Indonesia, triggered a series of devastating tsunamis on the Indian Ocean coasts killing thousands of people and causing extensive damage in Indonesia, Sri Lanka, India, and Thailand. In August 2006, Hurricane Katrina, one of the deadliest hurricanes in the history of the United States, devastated the city of New Orleans, caused extensive damage along the entire Mississippi coast, and led to the loss of over 1,500 lives. In May 2008, Cyclone Nargis flattened buildings, claimed over 100,000 lives, and rendered over 1 million people homeless in Myanmar. The recent earthquakes in Turkey, New Zealand, and Haiti; hurricanes and tornadoes in the Americas and the Caribbean, and severe flood, famine and drought in parts of Africa, overwhelmed the capacity of local communities to mitigate their impact.

Disasters raise complex policy questions for international cooperation and assistance. As observed by the World Health Organization (WHO) Collaborating Centre for Research on the Epidemiology of Disasters (CRED), a disaster is "...a situation or event, which *overwhelms local capacity*, necessitating a request to national or international level for *external assistance*." As unforeseen and often sudden events, disasters cause "great damage, destruction and human suffering." The key questions remain: is there an obligation on the affected country to accept external 'humanitarian' assistance without delay where a significant percentage of its population is vulnerable to starvation, suffering, and imminent death? Do other

States have an obligation to offer humanitarian assistance to a state hit by a disaster? Most importantly, how best could disaster diplomacy coordinate the various actors (local, national, international) and multiple stakeholders in disaster risk management framework? This book addresses some of the gaps in disaster diplomacy, especially the need to look beyond national governments to involve all stakeholders from all the relevant sectors: civil society and non-governmental organizations, business and the corporate sector, inter-governmental and humanitarian organizations, foundations and charities, and many others.

As natural and man-made disasters are bound to continue to emerge and re-emerge in various regions of the world, the question of how best to mitigate their impact on vulnerable populations within the affected local communities will continue to pre-occupy the academic and policy communities. As a basic first step, the local, national and international communities must re-focus on the best ways to improve the effectiveness of humanitarian assistance and how to better coordinate response to disasters. This book is therefore a welcome contribution to the academic and policy debate on disaster risk management. The contributors open up new frontiers that will enhance the understanding and effectiveness of disaster diplomacy.

Obijiofor Aginam
Senior Academic Officer
Chief of Section, International Cooperation and Development
Institute for Sustainability and Peace
United Nations University Headquarters
Tokyo, Japan

Adjunct Research Professor
Carleton University
Ottawa, Canada

Visiting Professor
Integrated Research Systems for Sustainable Science (IR3S)
University of Tokyo, Japan

Foreword

Natural disasters have been becoming more regular, deadly and destructive. This situation is expected to worsen as a result of climate change, as noted in the findings of the most recent report by the Intergovernmental Panel on Climate Change. Such an outcome is particularly worrying if one considers figures from some of the most significant recent natural disasters: the 2004 Indian Ocean tsunami resulted in more than 226,400 deaths and Cyclone Nargis in Myanmar in 2008 caused more than 138,300 deaths. If one widens the scope to consider displaced persons, the numbers are truly staggering: the 2008 Sichuan earthquake displaced over 15 million people, and in 2010 over 42 million people were displaced by natural disasters. And even if compared to the last decade 2011 was a below average year in terms of the number of natural disasters that occurred, it proved to be the most expensive on record. This was owing to a number of major disasters in developed countries, notably in Australia, Japan and New Zealand. What these facts all point towards is that natural disasters represent a very grave threat to our lives and wellbeing. While we can never fully prevent from occurring, there are many things that we can do – individually and collectively – to limit and minimise the death and destruction caused by these events. In THIS REGARD, *Disaster Risk Management – Conflict and Cooperation* is a valuable book that makes a sustained contribution to our knowledge about this pressing set of issues.

When considering natural disasters, there is a common tendency to juxtapose them against manmade disasters, such as interstate conflict or civil war. Seeing natural disasters as 'acts of god' is thoroughly misleading, however. Doing so ignores the significant role human choices and behaviours play in turning natural hazards into disasters. In the 2010 Haiti suffered a magnitude 7 earthquake resulting in more than 316,000 deaths; the following year a magnitude 9 earthquake off the coast of Japan triggered a tsunami that collectively resulted in more than 15,800 deaths. Of course there were significant natural factors that influenced the loss of life and damage caused: notably the epicentre of the Haiti earthquake was very close to Port-au-Prince, whereas the Japan quake occurred approximately 70 kilometres off the coast. Yet human factors were just as significant – if not more so – in explaining the massive difference in terms of death and damage these two disasters caused. Haiti is one of the world's poorest countries, and has a long history of internal conflict and poor government. In contrast, Japan is one of the most industrialised, wealthy countries in the world. It is also a leader in disaster preparation and prevention. There is nothing 'natural' about these aspects that helped shape the disasters. These are due to human decisions, behaviour and human-made structures that have influenced the respective fates of these two countries. In particular, the vulnerability of Haiti and Japan to natural hazards is a result of significant structural factors. This issue is something dealt with here, in chapters such as the one by J.C. Gaillard, who correctly observes that 'vulnerability is actually rooted in a deep tangle of structural constraints that are social, historical and cultural as well as politico-economic in nature.' Acknowledging this entails serious consequences, however. The most effective route to long-term disaster mitigation is through addressing the inequalities and underdevelopment that leaves many countries and people dangerously exposed to natural hazards. This kind of longer-term perspective stands in contrast to the strong focus that is usually placed on the immediate relief phase *after* a disaster has occurred. Yet it is much less costly to prepare for such events *before* they happen. Taking this longer view suggests that responding to, and preparing for, disasters should be part of a much more basic focus on socio-economic development. In this regard, the *2005 Hyogo Framework for Action* notes that 'sustainable development, poverty reduction, good governance and disaster risk reduction are mutually supportive objectives.' Aligning these goals into a cohesive approach to development, thereby reducing the vulnerability of people to natural hazards, is a major challenge, but something that must be done.

Building more resilient communities cannot simply be a top-down process, however. An important theme of this book is the value of bottom-up initiatives, and the importance of building local capacity to deal with natural hazards. Immediately after a disaster there are many things that affected people cannot do, and they do need help from other actors: the central government, as well as the international community. Yet it is a mistake to view them as passive victims. This is an important point that Patralekha Chatterjee considers in her chapter: 'sometimes, unwittingly, we impose permanent victimhood on the disaster-affected. Disasters, like other crises, also throw up opportunities for empowerment.' Indeed, this point can be extended to a more systemic observation: natural disasters are certainly crises, but they need not be complete catastrophes if they are also taken as opportunities: a chance to respond, to build back better, to address societal problems that leave certain people more vulnerable and marginalised.

One of the priorities for action identified in the *Hyogo Framework* was to 'use knowledge, innovation and education to build a culture of safety and resilience at all levels'. *Disaster Risk Management – Conflict and Cooperation* directly contributes to this important goal. Suman Ranjan Sensarma and Atanu Sarkar have compiled a valuable collection that successfully highlights a range of significant issues that arise in the context of responding to, and preparing for, natural disasters. By incorporating a diverse range of perspectives and case studies, this volume provides the kind of knowledge that is needed for building a world that is better able to handle the massive challenge that natural disasters pose.

Dr. Christopher Hobson
Research Associate
Institute for Sustainability and Peace,
United Nations University
Tokyo, Japan

Preface

Within the existing disaster risk management policies and practices, there is an urgent need for multi-stakeholder participation in order to avoid potential or ongoing conflicts. By and large, the traditional approaches are mostly top down, which essentially disregard the local community in decision-making process. Hence, there is a need felt for constructing a local–regional–international policy framework articulating disaster risk management and development at different levels. As disaster does not follow any geographic boundary, the cooperation evolving from different sectors is needed. In fact, the Total Disaster Risk Management (TDRM) conference in Hyogo (Japan) in 2003 have emphasized on importance of corporate sector participation in disaster risk management. This was probably the first time that a corporate participation on a global platform has been invited. At the regional level, example can be cited from different agreements among the central Asian countries. Disaster diplomacy is another area of international cooperation among the confronting countries (such as Greek-Turkish conflict and cooperation). Hyogo framework of action has strongly recommended that though national governments are the most important stakeholder in the implementation of the framework, stakeholders from all the sectors must participate in disaster risk management policy and operation.

The disaster risk management process has a great impact on people's survival and the country's development. So far, not much attention has been paid to really articulate the conflict resolution process in disaster risk management practice. There is an urgent need to find out the cooperative solution in order to bolster ongoing effort of sustainable development. In the book, we have aimed to analyze the conflict and cooperation aspect with regard to disaster risk management and to look at the process and impact of disaster mitigation at different levels. The major significance of the book is to open up discussion on conflict and cooperation, cutting across the disciplinary boundaries. In the first chapter, Jean-Christophe Gaillard has discussed the policies set up by western government to address disaster risk in the south. It was argued that despite massive transfer of knowledge, experience and funding, disasters are occurring on an increasing frequency. The author identified the gap between the objectives of the policies and the actual root causes of the disasters and suggested an increasing cooperation between a larger array of stakeholders, especially at the local level and including local communities. Muneta Yokomatsu, Wei-Bin Yu and Norio Okada in the second chapter, have looked at the increasing effect of disaster on agricultural communities in China and inadequacy in the corresponding disaster risk management. The authors partly blamed the insurance industry's limited knowledge about local natural disaster, farmers' weak consciousness for insurance and monetary factor. However, microcredit had become more and more popular in rural China and this chapter discussed how to enrich microcredit's role in disaster risk management in agricultural communities. Chapter third is by Haley Rich and Ilan Kelman, showing how building and maintaining local capability for preventing and dealing with disasters requires support and action from individuals through global organizations. The chapter reported a school emergency response training, which started in Colorado, USA and importance of the programme in wider context. Chapter fourth is by Bijayanand Misra and Ruma Chakrabarty who have analyzed the emerging issue of City disaster management plan which needs, to be fine tuned, it will be cutting edge knowledge and technology for developing holistic and comprehensive risk management policies for better risk governance and conflict resolution. The fifth chapter is by Arindam Dasgupta, who has offered his experience on disaster risk management and need for local level cooperation and coordination among the different stakeholders in an Indian State of West Bengal. Dasgupta has identified delink and lack of coordination among non-government organizations, community based organizations and eventually affecting disaster preparedness and crisis management at the community level. Chapter sixth is by Suman Ranjan Sensarma dealing with the analyses of conflict and cooperation process between governmental organization and opposition group over water and flood risk management. He has utilized the game theoretic approach in the Graph Model for Conflict Resolution (GMCR) to analyze the conflict.

In the seventh chapter by Ravi Sannabhadti, the experiential learning, emerging out of the set-up and management of information centres that were set-up in post Gujarat earthquake (2001), has been discussed. The information centres were instrumental in streamlining the process of reconstruction by collaborating between civil society players, local government functionaries and affected communities.

Chapter eighth is by Tao Ye, Muneta Yokomatsu, Peijun Shi, and Norio Okada and they have talked about the disaster insurance and its role to cope with disaster risk. The authors have argued that international insurance market and the connection between insurance market and capital market are not efficient enough to back-up insurance industry. Participation of government has been believed to be very important to cope with market failure in transferring disaster risk through intervention. Chapter ninth is by Ilan Kelman and Bob Conrich, looking at the para-diplomacy, refers to non-sovereign islands dealing with state governments other than their governing state and international agencies for disaster-related activities, covering pre-disaster and post-disaster actions. The study is based on the case studies of the Caribbean, the South Atlantic, and the Pacific islands. It has highlighted the issues, such as sovereignty, transportation access, natural resources, population size, ability to engage in para-diplomacy, and loyalty to the governing state. In the tenth chapter, Maiko Sakamoto has discussed a hierarchy decision system which has been modelled with non-cooperative game theory in extensive form, and the way the coalition evolved as equilibrium was analyzed on the case of regulation over the river Ganges where Nepal, India and Bangladesh have been the stakeholders. It has been argued that more efficient to conclude any agreement among all concerned stakeholders in a region dependent on the equity of the stakeholders. Maaike Warnaar, in the eleventh chapter, has looked at the aftermath of the earthquake that took place in Bam (Iran) in December 2003. It has described how the international community showed tremendous compassion towards the survivors by sending huge amounts of relief aid. The study has shown the influence of cold US-Iran diplomatic relation on disaster aid by the US aid delegation and the role of disaster diplomacy. In the twelfth chapter, Atanu Sarkar has analysed the impact of the global climate change on disaster and role of cooperation on disaster preparedness as pre-emptive measures. He has analyzed the extent of vulnerability due to possible climate change related disasters in different parts of the world and nature of cooperation needed at various levels. Chapter thirteen is by Soumitra Roy, showing how floods left differential impacts on human lives, which could be attributed to various geographical, socio-economic and political factors. His study has shown that the economic status of the households primarily determined the vulnerability or resilience levels of the community as well as individual to the flood hazard. The magnitude of flood losses has been the highest among the economically deprived sections and suffered from multiple impacts. The fourteenth chapter is by Ana Maria Cruz who has presented an overview of Natech hazards (natural hazard/disaster-triggered chemical accidents), their characteristics, complexities, and the problems associated with Natech risk management. The chapter has represented the results of a Natech workshop, which was participated by several countries and professional backgrounds with the objective to apply and test a Natech risk assessment methodology of a case study community. In the fifteenth chapter, Patralekha Chatterjee has analyzed the differences of the scale of media attention to cover disasters or why is mediaselective? She has argued that the level and intensity of coverage of the disaster depends on proximity, levels of interest of readers/viewers and the economic stakes involved, rather than the scale of the actual suffering. As media had a role to reduce the vulnerability of communities to disasters, it was important challenge before the disaster managers on how to harness the influence of media.

Contents

Profile of the Contributors

Arindam Dasgupta is an Assistant Professor in Geography at Krishnagar Govt. College, India. At present he is working on social and economic impacts of Kolaghat Thermal Power Plant, Purba Medinipur and Quantification, monitoring of Urban Srawl and its effect on the surrounding villages in Burddhaman Block-I & II. He was selected as an associate in Indian Institute of Advanced Studies, Shimla from 2003-2005 sponsored by U.G.C. The author has also completed some research projects funded by U.G.C.

Ana Maria Cruz is an international consultant in the area of risk management and emergency response practices for conjoint natural and technological (Natech) disasters in Europe, the United States, Turkey, Japan and China. Dr. Cruz's research interests include modelling and assessment of flood, storm, earthquake, tsunami and climate change – induced Natech disasters; investigation of Natech accidents and consequence analysis; and disaster prevention/ preparedness and implementation. Dr. Cruz holds an interdisciplinary Ph.D. in Environmental Engineering and Applied Development from Tulane University, and she is an experienced chemical engineer. Dr. Cruz is an Adjunct Professor of Kyoto University and does international consulting. Prior to moving to France, Dr. Cruz was a Senior Scientist at the Joint Research Centre of the European Commission in Italy. She was also a faculty member at University of North Texas, and a research fellow at the Disaster Prevention Research Institute at Kyoto University.

Atanu Sarkar is an Assistant Professor of the Division of Community Health and Humanities, Faculty of Medicine, Memorial University, St. John's, Newfoundland and Labrador, Canada. He teaches environmental and occupational health. Dr. Sarkar studied Medicine at Burdwan Medical College, West Bengal (India) and did his Ph.D. from Jawaharlal Nehru University, New Delhi (India). He completed Masters in Environmental Studies at Queen's University (Canada) before taking the current position at Memorial University. He was involved in various national and international research projects focusing on health, environment, disaster, food security. He was directly engaged in various disaster management and research project, such as relief operation of super cyclone in Orissa (India), medical rehabilitation of internally displaced persons in Jammu & Kashmir (India), industrial disaster in Bhopal (India), polio/measles outbreaks (India) and famine in Ethiopia. He was involved in several projects on climate change, food security and health. He was one of the core team members of the employment condition and health dimension (EMCONET), Commissions of Social Determinants of Health, the World Health Organization (WHO) and global mercury project of the United Nations Environmental Programme (UNEP). He presented numerous research papers in international conferences in Asia, Africa, Europe, North and South America. He has also published several papers in international peer reviewed journals and books.

Ilan Kelman is a Senior Research Fellow at the Center for International Climate and Environmental Research-Oslo (CICERO). His Ph.D. dissertation was on houses collapsing during floods in England. Ilan's main research and advocacy work relates to two areas: island sustainability (creating and maintaining safer and healthier communities on islands and in other isolated areas) and disaster diplomacy (how and why disaster-related activities do and do not reduce conflict and create peace). His research, writings, and photographs have appeared in international, national, and local media around the world.

Bob Conrich is a retired Arbitrator with a background in law, business, construction, public works, government, history, journalism and politics. A resident of Anguilla, British West Indies for over twenty years, he is an active member of the Biodiplomacy network, specializing in environmental, social, political, economic and cultural developments in the UK's Overseas Territories. He has a special interest in underwater archaeology and the protection of historic shipwrecks from treasure hunters.

Maiko Sakamoto is an Associate Professor in Department of Civil Engineering, Faculty of Engineering, Nagasaki University. Before joining Nagasaki University, she worked as a researcher in Disaster Prevention Research Institute, Kyoto University and as an Assistant

Professor in Centre for Northeast Asian Studies, Tohoku University. Her major expertise in conflict management on water resources development using game theoretic approach.

Tao Ye has completed his Ph.D. from Graduate School of Engineering, Kyoto University and received his Bachelor and Master Degrees in Beijing Normal University, China. Mr. Tao Ye's current research field is financial management of disaster risk. His most recent study topic is inter-sectoral and inter-temporal diversification of agricultural disaster risk, addressing why agriculture risk cannot be efficiently transferred to other sectors of an economy, whether government subsidy to agriculture producers can create right incentives for better allocation of resources and risk-bearing and the impact of grain reserve policy on the allocation of risk-bearing between agriculture and manufactory sectors.

Muneta Yokomatsu is an Associate Professor in Disaster Prevention Research Institute, Kyoto University. He received his Doctorate Degree at Kyoto University in 2003, majored in civil engineering. He worked for Tottori University for 2001-2005, and moved to Kyoto University in 2005. Dr. Yokomatsu also worked in many institutions and universities in different countries as a visiting scholar, e.g. IIASA (2001), University of Minnesota (2008). His research field is cost-benefit analysis of disaster risk management and infrastructure provision. His current interests are macroeconomic dynamics under catastrophic risks and fiscal policy.

Norio Okada is the Director of Disaster Prevention Research Institute (DPRI), Kyoto University, Japan. Prof. Okada majored in Civil Engineering and received his Doctor's Degree in Engineering from Kyoto University in 1977. He has been leading the disaster and environmental risk management research group at DPRI, Kyoto University. He has long been taking initiatives to explore a new cross-disciplinary area by promoting several important international conferences/workshops, including IIASA-DPRI Annual Forums on Integrated Disaster Risk Management, Japan-UK Disaster Reduction Research Seminars, and Japan-China Joint Seminars on Sustainable Development of Cities and Regions under Disaster and Environmental Risk. Prof. Okada contributed his scholarly inputs in the cooperative game theory applied to regional water resources management. He is well known for his work on a new core-based notion, named 'Proportional Nucleolus'.

J.C. Gaillard is a senior lecturer at the School of Environment of the University of Auckland in New Zealand. He has been working for 15 years on disaster-related issues in insular Southeast Asia (Philippines and Indonesia) and more recently in African (Comoros and Cape Verde) and Caribbean (Guadeloupe) Islands, Nepal and the Pacific. His research interests include Disaster Risk Reduction (D.R.R.), participatory tools for D.R.R., the cultural and ethnic dimension of disasters, gender and disasters, post-disasters reconstruction, and the interplay between armed conflicts and disasters.

Maaike Warnaar received her Ph.D. from University of St. Andrews. She is specialized in Middle East politics and her Ph.D. thesis is on the political implications of the Bam earthquake for the foreign policy behaviour of the leadership of the Islamic Republic of Iran towards the West. She is currently teaching several courses in International Relations and Foreign Policy at the University of Amsterdam, Department of Political Science.

Wei Bin Yu has done masters of Management from Chinese Academy of Sciences with Master of Management and received Ph.D. Degree from Kyoto University. His research areas are risk management, modelling, analyzing and designing systems related with disaster risk reduction, such as public-private systems for disaster risk communication systems.

Patralekha Chatterjee is an independent journalist-photographer, author, and consultant working with mass media, specialist publications, NGOs and international agencies in UK including the United Nations. She has been educated in Oxford, Paris, Delhi, Pune and Kolkata. She has travelled extensively across the world, and reported from dozens of countries in Asia and Europe on a range of development issues. Currently, she has a fornightly column "Dev 360" in *The Asian Age* and *Deccan Chronicle*, two multi-edition English language Indian newspapers with a combined circulation of 1.4 million. A partial list of publications and websites worldwide which have carried her reports and photographs include *Liberation* (Paris), *Panos* (UK), *The New Internationalist* (UK), *The Guardian* (UK), *Chicago Tribune* (USA), *The Christian Science Monitor* (USA), *MSNBC.com* (USA), *The Urban Age* (a quarterly magazine brought out by The World Bank Group), *Habitat Debate* (Publication of the UN-HABITAT), *Khaleej Times* (Dubai), *The Economic Times* (India),

Sunday (India), *Hindustan Times* (India), *Indo-Asian News Service* (India), *Inter Press Service* (International) and IRIN—the humanitarian news and analysis service supported by the UN Office for the Coordination of Humanitarian Affairs. Her reports about public health challenges in Haiti, Sub-Saharan Africa, Cambodia, Hong Kong, Maldives and India have been published in *The Lancet*, one of the most prestigious and influential journals dealing with global health issues. These reports are cited worldwide in academic and other publications. She has reported several natural disasters in Asia. Her work on natural disasters includes two documents commissioned by UN-HABITAT (text, photographs, editing) on rehabilitation work in tsunami-ravaged Sri Lanka and Maldives.

Suman Ranjan Sensarma has received his Ph.D. in Urban Management from Kyoto University, Japan. He has contributed his expertise on a wide range of various projects in the development fields. He has work experiences with International Organizations, Consulting Agencies, Central/State Governments and Research Institutes. Currently, he is associated with the GHK INTERNATIONAL on a DFID-Ministry of Housing and Urban Poverty Alleviation (Government of India) joint initiative project—"Support to National Policies for Urban Poverty Reduction". He is also a Co-Principal Investigator for "Comparing Climate Change Policy Networks (COMPON): Effect of Advocacy Networks and Participation on Climate Change Policy Formation" project, University of Minnesota, USA. His work published in various international journals and paper presented on reputed international conferences.

Ravi Sannahadti is an Assistant Professor at the Faculty of Planning & Public Policy, CEPT (Centre for Environmental Planning & Technology) University, Ahmedabad (India). A social worker and planner by education, he has experience of more than a decade working in the areas of community development, participatory governance, institutional design and capacity development.

He has worked in assignments focusing on disaster preparedness, integrated water resource management, sustainable livelihoods and urban poverty alleviation for multilateral donor agencies (like UNDP, DFID & US-AID), international networks (like Cap-Net), government ministries (like Ministry of Housing & Urban Poverty Alleviation), research/academic institutions (like IRMA, Anand), corporate consultancies and non-governmental organizations. These engagements, have involved the development of 'knowledge tools and products' to aid decision-making and improve governance and service delivery.

His experiences of working with grassroots-level disasters affected communities of Kutch after the Gujarat Earthquake 2001; in development of local institutional mechanisms and community based information systems for governance are reflected in the current publication.

Bijayanand Misra has over 35 years of experience in human settlement development, rural and urban. Special expertise in areas, namely equity and efficiency issues in urban management, urban strategic vision planning, integrated risk management and urban land management. He has been involved with the UNDP & UNDESDA projects (1997-2001) focused on urban governance, municipal capacity building, social development, and poverty eradication. During 1999-2000 worked in China with UNDESA, Government of China, China Society for Gwangcai Programme on Eradication of Poverty through social development, social integration, and public-private partnership. His experience includes national and international consultancy work, independent research work and teaching/research at the university graduate level. Currently he is the Coordinator & Senior Adviser of Global Centre of Excellence Human Security Engineering for Asian Mega cities, Mumbai Project, Kyoto University, and Kyoto, Japan.

Haley Rich attended college at Brenau University in Georgia and, in 1998, graduated from the University of Southern Colorado, achieving her MBA with honours. Her work and business focused on projects and activities that encouraged youth and community betterment. She founded Teen SERT/CERT, as described in the chapter in this book, along with the Alliance for Empowerment which aims to create, implement, and evaluate youth and community betterment projects. Haley was working for the Transportation Technology Center Inc. in Colorado but continued her numerous, energetic volunteer activities around her home community of Pueblo, Colorado. These included Keep Pueblo Beautiful, Pueblo Emergency Response Team, Mesa Pride, and Pueblo West Fire Department. Sadly, Haley passed away on 18 February 2010 as this book was going to press. She will be missed by her family, her friends and all those whom she touched, or saved the lives of, due to Teen SERT.

Ruma Chakrabarty is a Ph.D. from Nagpur University in Geography. She began her career as a Senior College Lecturer in Vasant Rao Naik Government Institute of Arts and Social Sciences. Since last 10 years she has been actively working in Spatial Planning & GIS. Currently she is working as an Associate Vice President in Vayam Technologies Limited, where she heads the GIS, e-Governance and Transport sector. She had worked on several research projects, which includes Disaster Management, Agriculture Geography, Sustainable Regional Planning etc.

Peijun Shi is Executive Vice-President of Beijing Normal University. He is a member of the Expert Committee under the National Disaster Reduction Committee, housed in Ministry of Civil Affairs of China and also a member of OECD's High Level Advisory Board on Financial Management of Large-Scale Catastrophes. His research focuses on natural disaster theories and risk management. He has been charged with many national and international programmes and has numerous publications. Now he is co-chairing Integrated Risk Governance Core Science Project of International Human Dimensions Programme (IHDP-IRG) on Global Environmental Change, focusing on how multi-level governance of risks could be improved.

Soumitra Roy is a Post Graduate in Sociology from Kanpur University and completed his Doctoral Thesis titled "Disaster Management and Health: A Case Study of Murshidabad District in West Bengal" from Centre of Social Medicine and Community Health, Jawaharlal Nehru University, New Delhi. He started his career as National Relief Coordinator with in Indian Red Cross Society during the critical days of devastating Tsunami on Indian Ocean Rim. Later on he moved to manage a childhood blindness control programme run by an International NGO named ORBIS International in India for a short stint. He taught Sociology and Development Psychology in the University of Guyana, Cooperative Republic of Guyana, West Indies. He was also actively associated with Oxfam GB to implement community-based disaster preparedness programme in coastal regions of Guyana. Currently he is associated with UNICEF in a Health and Social Awareness Generation Programme being implemented in one of most backward districts in India where he made significant contribution in innovating techniques of community mobilization and development of IEC. He also had exposure to work with several renowned organizations like World Bank Institute, Pan-American Health Organization etc.

1

Missing the Target : Western Disaster Management Policies versus Root Causes of Calamities in the Developing World

J.C. GAILLARD

This chapter challenges the policies set up by Western Government to address disaster risk in the South. It argues that despite massive transfer of knowledge, experience and funding, disasters are occurring on an increasing frequency. The failure of the West to reduce disaster risk in the South is rooted in the gap which exists between the objectives of the policies and the actual root causes of the disasters. Disasters should indeed be seen as the extension of hardship in the everyday life of the victims rather than the consequence of extreme and rare natural hazards. Disasters are, therefore, the outcome of development failure rather than nature's guilt. To fully address the root causes of disasters, the article suggests an increasing cooperation between a larger array of stakeholders, especially at the local level and including local communities. The study is based on a case study from the delta of the Pampanga River in Northern Philippines.

Disasters in the Developing World

The scope of damage brought by the 26th December, 2004 Indian Ocean Tsunami and the 8th October, 2005 Pakistan earthquake served as a powerful reminder that the so-called "developing countries" bear the brunt of disasters identified with natural hazards. According to the EMDAT database compiled by the Centre for Research on Epidemiology of Disasters–CRED (2008), 75 per cent of the events recorded in 2005 occurred in countries which Human Development

Index is below the 0.8 mark or the threshold set by the United Nations between high and medium human development. Each of these events killed at least more than ten people, hindered the life of more than 100 individuals, or required international aid. Asia and the Pacific countries are the most frequently struck by disasters (40% of the events in 2005), followed by African countries (20%), Latin America and the Caribbean (15%). Over the last three decades, 70 per cent of the events recorded by CRED occurred in countries with HDI below 0.8.

The recurrence of disasters in developing countries is accentuated by the large scope of human casualties and economic damage brought by each event. In 2005, almost 97 per cent of the people killed due to natural phenomena were Asians, Oceanians, Latin Americans, Caribbeans and Africans. The ratio between the number of people affected and killed and the whole population of given countries is very significant. In most of African and Asian countries, between 1974 and 2003, almost 5,000 individuals were affected or killed for every 100,000 inhabitants (Centre for Research on Epidemiology of Disasters, 2008). Compared to local resources, the economic damage wrought by disasters are much greater in developing countries than in industrialized nations. Abramovitz (2001) notes that, between 1999 and 2001, the overall economic losses of developing countries reach 13 per cent of the given countries' GNP. On the other hand, it limits to 2 per cent in industrialized countries.

These large-scale disasters should not hide the importance and burden of small-scale disasters which prove to be more damaging on the long run (Lewis, 1984; Lavell, 2000). For example, the DesInventar database of the Corporacion Osso and La Red de Estudios Sociales en Prevencion de Desastres en America Latina (2008) lists 19,000 disasters in Colombia between 1971 and 2002 whilst the EMDAT records only display 97 events for the same period. Overall the impact of these thousands of small disasters turned out to be more damaging in terms of both people's life and livelihoods.

Since 1970s, the increasing occurrence of disasters identified with natural hazards has been drawing a growing attention within the international community. Yet, the support and aid provided by the Western world and its allies failed to mitigate the impact of disasters in the developing world. The West's incapacity to prevent the occurrence of disasters largely lies in its inability to address the root causes of calamities in developing countries. This chapter is an attempt to expose the reasons for such a failure. It will particularly focus on the Philippines which is known as one of the most disaster-prone countries in the world. Between January 1900 and December 2007, the EMDAT database listed 419 disasters which struck the country (Centre for Research on Epidemiology of Disasters, 2008). These events caused economic damages worth US$ 7 billion and killed more than 48,000 people. Millions of other Filipinos were directly or indirectly affected.

The first section of this chapter will be reviewing Western disaster management policies and their scientific background. The second section will be focusing on the increasing number of disasters in developing countries. The third section will be addressing the root causes of calamities. The fourth section will be exposing the gap between root causes and Western responses. The final section will be advocating for an increasing collaboration between the different stakeholders of the disaster management realm.

The West in the Face of Increasing Disasters...

In the 1970s, Western countries and allied international organizations spurred support to the developing world where disasters identified with natural hazards wrought increasing damage. Western aid and disaster management policies followed the usual command-and-control, top-down schemes and patterns of economic development and poverty alleviation programmes fostered at that time. Disaster policies further found legitimacy in the science realm. Disasters were commonly viewed in the academe as the consequence of extreme, in magnitude and rare, in time, natural hazards (Burton *et al.*, 1978). The increasing occurrence of disasters was thus explicitly or implicitly attributed to natural events. Commenting on the 1970s Sahelian famines, French anthropologist J. Copans (1975) ironically refers to a "climatic terrorism" thesis. Along this dominant scientific paradigm, earth sciences have focused on a better knowledge and prevision of these exceptional phenomena while social sciences assess the perception of rare hazards in order to better understand population behavioural failures (*e.g.* Kates, 1971; Burton *et al.*, 1978).

Looking at disasters as the result of extreme natural hazards leads to disaster management policies geared towards dealing with the "extraordinary" (Gaillard, 2007a). These policies have often relied on specific and technical measures: the building of dikes to control exceptional floods, installment of state-of-the-art monitoring systems, the preparation of warning and contingency plans, etc. At best, structural and technocratic policies have been complemented by hazard awareness campaigns to raise people's perception of risk. These measures have of course drawn on the finest Western technologies and massive financial support. Western intervention thus appeared as an imperative necessity. Yet, international disaster management policies have been rooted in powerful and globalizing forces which are political (transfer of knowledge), economic (transfer of technology) and scientific (fundings of research programmes) in nature (Hewitt, 1983, 1995). Throughout history, Western control on disaster policies have followed the West's struggle *versus* infectious diseases and poverty in face of which developing countries were allegedly unable to cope alone (Bankoff, 2001).

Western control on international disaster management policies was formalized at the dawn of the 1990s and the launching of the International Decade for Natural Disaster Reduction (IDNDR) by the United Nations. According to M. Benblidia (1990), a member of the group of experts in charge of setting the direction for the IDNDR, disasters in the developing world were caused by people's lack of knowledge on natural hazards, the absence of monitoring systems, the failure of warning systems, the weakness of emergency planning, the disorganization of post-disaster management and finally, by the lack of security measures. Priorities for the IDNDR, therefore, included improved awareness campaigns, modern technologies for all, training of local scientists and researchers and increased funding capacities. To justify these measures, Benblidia (1990: 16) stated that "*(...) developing countries do not have enough capacities to do it by their own. They have to call for expertise and assistance from the most advanced countries to develop their national capacities*".

The Philippines has been one of the favourite playgrounds for the transfer of Western disaster management policies. The measures set up to respond to increasing flooding in the delta of the Pampanga River are a significant example. In this region, the Philippine Government has exerted much effort "*to augment the reduced carrying capacities of the silted waterways*" (Mount Pinatubo Emergency Project Management Office, 1998). Preventive measures have focused on dredging activities and protective structures such as dikes and river walls. During the late 1990s, the Pampanga River bed has been enlarged and huge dikes and sluice gates have been built to control and channel floodwaters towards the sea as part of the Pampanga Delta Development Project. This project was funded by the Japanese Government which disbursed around 66 million US$ between 1990 and 2001. The construction of the dikes has been undertaken by Korean and Philippine contractors (Tsubugo, 2005). The former villages which were located on the original riverbanks were inundated and vast tracts of agricultural lands were condemned to accommodate the river in the event of major discharge. The government had to eventually facilitate the resettlement of hundreds of families beyond the dikes. Japanese funds further enabled to construct public buildings but no project pertained to the livelihoods of the relocatees.

In the Pampanga Delta as elsewhere in the world, the structural and technocratic measures to prevent natural hazards largely failed to preclude disasters to occur.

... or the Rout of a Strategy

Despite fantastic scientific progress, huge financial investments and the mobilization of thousands of researchers, the occurrence of disasters has been increasing. The CRED-EMDAT database shows that, worldwide, the number of disasters increased from 667 events during the first half of the 20th century to 6,466 during the second half. The last twenty years have been the most significant with 4,620 events. Since then, the first eight years of the 21st century already recorded 3,687 disasters (Centre for Research on Epidemiology of Disasters, 2008). Even if this list may underestimate disastrous events in the first half of the century, it still underlines that disaster management policies as considered for more than fifty years failed to revert the trend. Western policies may have contributed to slightly inflect the impact of natural hazards but they obviously missed their target which was to prevent the occurrence of disasters. Conversely, in many cases, technological adjustments fostered by the West have deeply eroded traditional systems of coping with natural hazards and the intrinsic capacities of traditional societies to overcome the impact of disasters (Torry, 1978a; Waddell, 1983; Cijffers, 1987).

It is noteworthy that disasters hit predominately societies in transition between traditional subsistence agriculture on the one hand and industry and service-oriented economy on the other. Traditional societies prove to be well armed to face natural hazards and overcome disasters when they occur. Their livelihoods and everyday course of life often consider the threat of natural hazards. In the event of a disaster, they are able to temporarily or permanently adjust to the damage brought by the occurrence of natural phenomena (Torry, 1978b; Gaillard, 2007b). Conversely, industrial and service-oriented Western societies usually possess enough resources to face natural hazards and reduce people's vulnerability. When disasters strike these societies, it chiefly reflects a political failure in the fair allotment of these resources towards people who are vulnerable (e.g., Wisner and Walker, 2005). In between, the so-called developing societies lose traditional means of coping with natural hazards and disasters and often become food and economically dependent on the rest of the world. Moreover, they do not have enough resources to engage in efficient and sustainable mitigation measures. Transition between traditional and Western modelled societies thus results in extreme vulnerability in facing natural hazards.

In the Philippines, the number of disasters rose from fifteen between 1900 and 1949 to 404 between 1950 and 2007 (Centre for Research on Epidemiology of Disasters, 2008). In the Pampanga Delta, flooding is still increasing and more people are affected every year (Gaillard *et al.*, 2008). This area has always been severely hit by floods. However, the nature of flooding has dramatically changed during the last two decades. Until the 1980s, flooding was largely associated with heavy rainfall and river overflow. There eventually was a critical shift with the fast subsidence of the delta of the Pampanga River. In some places of the Delta, land is sinking by three to four cm per year. The most significant consequence of this phenomenon is the inland progression of seawater during high tide resulting to almost permanent flooding in the lower areas. In time of heavy rainfall, it further blocks the rapid evacuation of floodwater towards the sea and thus lengthens flooding. Rodolfo and Siringan (2006; Siringan and Rodolfo, 2003) suggest that the first and foremost factor in explaining land subsidence and the shift in the nature of flooding in the Delta of the Pampanga River is the important extraction of groundwater to sustain agricultural and domestic needs. The almost permanent dredging of the Pampanga River below sea level also favours the penetration of seawater inland. Despite these evidences, anthropogenic subsidence is largely ignored by the authorities (Rodolfo and Siringan, 2006) which still associate flooding with heavy rainfall and increasing riverbed siltation.

The critical shift in the nature of flooding had a deep impact on the daily life of the locals. The most significant change has been the shift from subsistence farming to cash aquaculture. Until the 1980s, the people of the Pampanga Delta used to till rice on a bi-annual scheme. This was enough to sustain one-year needs. At that time, farmers also planted vegetables and fruits on the paddies dikes and caught fishes in the surrounding rivers and creeks. They were food secured. Eventually, the progressive incursion of seawater compelled farmers to abandon rice, vegetable and fruit farming and to shift to fish ponds. Nowadays, the locals thus depend on the sale of fishes, crabs and prawns to buy rice and other foodstuffs. Along with livelihoods, rituals and traditions associated with rice farming progressively vanished. Increasing floods also brings growing health problems. During flooding episodes, children are further affected by the suspension of classes at the local high school and neighbouring elementary schools (Gaillard *et al.*, 2008).

In the Pampanga Delta and among all developing countries, the failure of Western measures largely lies in the gap between policies focusing on the "extreme" dimension of natural hazards and the real causes of disasters that are rooted in daily constraints materialized by the vulnerability of hazard-prone regions and countries.

Disaster and Development : Looking for the Root Causes of Calamities

Disasters first affect those who are situated in daily life emergency and forgotten by development (e.g., Wisner *et al.*, 2004). Victims of disasters are vulnerable through marginalization. Disaster victims are marginalized geographically because they live in hazardous places, socially because they are members of minority groups, economically because they are poor and marginalized politically because their voice is disregarded on the political scene.

A set of indicators reflects the vulnerability of disaster victims (Cannon, 1994). They frequently comprise women, children, elderly, disabled individuals, refugees, prisoners. Disasters also hit individuals with limited and fragile incomes (low wages, informal jobs, lack of savings) that reduce the capability to protect one's self in the face of natural hazards (location of home, type of housing, knowledge of protection measures). Vulnerability also results from inadequate social protection (health insurance, health services, construction rules, prevention measures, etc.) and limited social capital (solidarity networks).

Vulnerability is actually rooted in a deep tangle of structural constraints that are social, historical and cultural as well as politico-economic in nature. Social factors include the difficulty to access land and resources for a quickly growing population. Access to resources determines the capacity and capability to live in a secure place and build safe housing. In search of food security, thousands of Latin American and Asian landless farmers prefer to settle on informal and dangerous sites in flood-prone areas or on steep mountain slopes. Indeed, it looks better to face seasonal typhoons or decennial volcanic eruptions rather than give up 75 per cent of one's harvest to powerful landlords. Similarly, armed conflict pushed hundreds of families to face natural hazards to escape decades-long fights. The threat of centennial tsunami does not weigh heavy in the face of everyday violence and torture when choosing a place to settle. The fact that the two countries (Indonesia and Sri Lanka) which were most affected by the 26th December, 2004 tsunami were both stricken by multi-decennial armed conflicts is significant.

Disaster vulnerability is constructed through historical processes. In the developing world, unfair distribution of resources and land is a colonial heritage. Colonial powers have concentrated economic and political powers into the hands of the elite and enclosed disaster victims in chronic poverty. The increasing orientation of developing countries' economy towards cash crops has also increased people's vulnerability by limiting the access to resources and threatening food security. Food security has long been considered as a critical issue in the disaster literature in Africa, South Asia and elsewhere in the world (e.g., Comité d'Information Sahel, 1975; Sen, 1983; Watts and Bohle, 1993). Religion and traditional beliefs further play a role in defining people's vulnerability in the face of natural hazards by facilitating the acceptance of disastrous events or by leading to gender discrimination.

Social, historical and cultural constraints are accentuated by the politico-economy context. The cash crop economy set up by colonial governments resulted in a high level of vulnerability and dependency on the world economic context through a classic core–periphery relationship. When the prices of cash crops collapsed on international markets in the 1970s and 1980s, developing countries had no other alternatives but to rely on massive loans to fund their economic development and purchase oil products. The burden of debt crisis is also of significant influence on disaster vulnerability by constraining investments in basic social services such as education and health. Moreover, the prevalence of private elitist interests and widespread corruption keep a large fraction of national financial resources away from the larger part of the population and orient hazard prevention projects which benefit a few.

The vulnerability of the Philippine society in the face of natural hazards well reflects this situation (Bankoff, 2003; Gaillard *et al.*, 2005). In the Pampanga Delta, subsidence-enhancing extraction of groundwater is possible because of the non-respect of national laws which prevent the drilling of deep wells within given distances. It further reflects the prevalence of client-patron relationships between local politicians and rural poor. Deep wells are often drilled in time of election campaigns at the initiative of political candidates who look for allegiance among the masses. In return, the poor are those who suffer the most from flooding. Indeed, the vulnerability of the locals in the face of increasing flooding largely depends on the strength of people's livelihoods. Rich fish ponds owners or businessmen do not much suffer from flooding. They usually own two or three-storey houses which are often raised on embankments. They have savings on bank accounts and food security is usually not a problem. Small fish pond owners have significant incomes but limited savings. They further possess resistant houses and small capital which they can rely on in time of emergency. Fish pond tenants depend on small monthly wage and sometimes benefit from one 50-kilo sack of rice per month. They are allowed to catch as many fishes as they need for their personal consumption. However, during flooding episodes, they suffer from the lack of fish and can only rely on their small wage and sack of rice to sustain their daily needs. The hardest hit in time of flooding are daily wage and other informal workers. After the initial demand for raising ponds dikes, daily-wage workers quickly suffer from the lack of job in the village and starvation. People engaged in local transportations and small retailing businesses are also affected as floods hinder them to continue their livelihood activities (Gaillard *et al.*, 2008).

Reshaping Disaster Management Policies : Extreme Hazards versus Everyday Life

The root causes of disasters thus rather lie in daily constraints that trap victims in permanent vulnerability rather than in the "extraordinary" dimension of natural hazards. Disasters should be considered as the extension of permanent emergency situations and should not be considered as accidents in society (Hewitt, 1983; Maskrey, 1989; Wisner, 1993). Disasters ultimately reflect development rather than behavioural failure. In that context, attributing the responsibility of disasters to nature is just resorting to scapegoat. In line with this, the contemporary climate change constitutes a perfect and easy alibi for political leaders to escape their own responsibility in the developing world's increasing vulnerability (Kelman and Gaillard, 2008).

Surprisingly, the still-dominant Western view on disaster management underscores the "exceptional" dimension of hazards and not the "daily life" conditions of vulnerability. Talking about "risk and disaster management policies", therefore, means enclosing prevention and mitigation measures around hazards and considering disasters as phenomena out of the regular social fabric. Following this approach leads to dissociate risk and disaster from daily life and thus to overlook underlying structural constraints. Talking about risk and disaster management policies means treating symptoms while debunking the root sources of harm. As early as 1983, K. Hewitt (1983) referred to the dominant paradigm as the "archipelago of disasters" and argued for a total rethinking of the contemporary approach of disasters.

Fostering increasing Cooperation in Disaster Management and Reduction

The so-called "Yokohama Message, Strategy and Plan of Action" published at the end of the World Conference on Natural Disaster Reduction convened by the United Nations in Yokohama in 1994 marked a significant step towards the revision of Western disaster management policies and their application to the developing world as promulgated at the dawn of the IDNDR. The revisited principles of the IDNDR (Nations Unies, 1995: 6) stipulate that "*vulnerable developing countries should be enabled to revive, apply and share traditional methods to reduce the impact of natural disasters, supplemented and reinforced by access to modern scientific and technical knowledge.*" This requires "*the application of traditional knowledge, practices and values of local communities for disaster reduction, thereby, recognizing these traditional coping mechanisms as a valuable contribution to the empowerment of local communities and the enabling of their spontaneous cooperation in all disaster reduction programmes.*" More recently, the "Hyogo Framework for Action (HFA) 2005-2015" agreed upon by the representatives of 168 countries which participated to the World Conference on Disaster Reduction, held in Kobe, Hyogo, Japan, in January 2005, further stresses the importance of:

- making disaster risk reduction a priority;
- knowing the risks (in its whole dimension not only its hazard-related dimension) and enhancing early warning system;
- building understanding and awareness using local and scientific knowledge;
- reducing the underlying, hazard-independent, factors of risk; and
- strengthening disaster preparedness for effective response at all levels.

This 10-year agenda for disaster risk reduction involves blending both hazard-related and non-hazard-related measures. It sets the threat from disasters beyond the sole dimension of natural hazards and locates it clearly within people's vulnerability in the face of nature's threat. It recommends culturally sensitive mitigation measures, which consider the cultural, social, economic and political context. The HFA further emphasizes the importance of people's livelihoods and asserts that "*natural hazards cannot be prevented, but it is possible to reduce their impacts by reducing the vulnerability of people and their livelihoods*" (United Nations International Strategy for Disaster Reduction, 2005: 4).

Disaster management and reduction should, therefore, be embedded into the specific context of each vulnerable region of the developing world and enhance local capacities to face natural hazards. In the Philippines, the populations of the Pampanga Delta resort to a large array of coping strategies in the face of increasing flooding (Gaillard *et al.*, 2008). These measures are technical (evacuation, embankments), social (adjustments in daily diet, traditional solidarity networks) and economic (livelihoods adjustments, pawning and selling of assets). Yet, local capacities have been overlooked by the Philippine Government in its struggle *versus* recurrent flooding.

It is today acknowledged that one of the most sustainable ways to reduce people's vulnerability in the face of natural hazards is through Community Based Disaster Risk Reduction (CBDRR) programmes coupled with development objectives (e.g. Anderson and Woodrow, 1989; Maskrey, 1989; Delica-Willison, 2004). CBDRR emphasizes the participation of affected communities in both the evaluation of their needs and in the ways to sustain them. CBDRR empowers communities with self-developed and culturally acceptable ways of coping with crises brought by the occurrence of natural hazards. It further stresses the importance of sustainable livelihoods in enabling people to live with risks (Cannon *et al.*, 2003; Twigg, 2004; United Nations International Strategy for Disaster Reduction, 2004). In the Philippines, a number of Non-Governmental Organizations (NGOs) have achieved great success by adopting such a community-based bottom-up approach (e.g., Anderson and Woodrow, 1989; Delica, 1999; Heijmans, 2004; Luna, 2001), notably in flood-prone areas (Heijmans and Victoria, 2001; Luna, 2003; Allen, 2003, 2004).

Local level cooperation is crucial to reduce disaster risk. Disasters are first and foremost local issues. Disastrous events involve local communities as both victims and initial sources of relief. As they are within the affected area, local communities are always the first to respond to emergency situations. Quarantelli (1989) underlines that 90 per cent of disaster victims are actually rescued by neighbours and other people nearby. Furthermore, as emphasized by Abarquez and Murshed (2004: 12), "*nobody can understand local opportunities and constraints better than the local communities themselves*" and "*nobody is more interested in understanding local affairs than the community whose survival and well-being is at stake*". Beyond communities, local authorities are the closest from the disaster scene and are the promptest to respond to victims' need should they have not been themselves impacted. Local agencies moreover have the best command and knowledge regarding affected communities. For all these reasons, it is of overarching importance to strengthen local capacities to face natural hazards and reduce disaster risk. This requires a close cooperation between a large array of stakeholders.

Scientists from the social and earth sciences realms now join NGOs and local authorities in cooperating with threatened communities to reduce disaster risk. Such a collaboration between different stakeholders seem to be the most appropriate manner for reducing disaster risk. It seems that scientists are well able to convene participatory activities to assess hazard-prone areas, people's vulnerability and community capacities. Yet, their ability to fully organize the target community and implement the previously designed risk mitigation strategies for effective and long-lasting CBDRM is doubtful. There is a need to involve NGOs in the organization of the community and the monitoring of the project in the longer term. Local authorities should overview these activities and foster their development within their jurisdiction. This emphasizes the need for a cooperation and coordination between local authorities, the scientific realm, the NGO sector and beneficiary communities (Maceda *et al.*, 2009). It further stresses the importance of integrating bottom-up and top-down disaster mitigation measures. Despite their great capacity of action and reaction in the face of disaster threat (Quarantelli and Dynes, 1972; Davis, 1978), victims are not capable of all tasks. Quick and large evacuations require transportation means which may not be available locally. Similarly, medical teams may be needed to cope up with serious injuries and damaged structures necessitate external intervention to be cleaned or repaired. In the Pampanga Delta, flood victims are well able to detect and anticipate flooding from high tides, storm surges or typhoons. Yet, they deplore the lack of official warning when dams are brutally open to control upstream waters.

Sustainable disaster risk reduction finally requires more sensitive international cooperation for reducing the weight of daily structural constraints which entrapped disaster victims in chronic vulnerability. In the Philippines, there has been a recent and welcome evolution in the official discourse on disaster management which involves both international and national organizations (Delfin and Gaillard, 2008). The World Bank and the National Disaster Coordinating Council (2004) recently acknowledged the importance of poverty alleviation in reducing disaster risk at the national level. While still largely focusing on hazard-related measures, the latest four-point action plan of the National Disaster Coordinating Council (2004) emphasizes the importance of capacity building for local authorities in identifying vulnerable areas. A 2007 circular further underlines the need for government agencies to collaborate with NGOs and other local and international organizations to address priority cross-cutting issues (e.g., population age, diversity, environment, gender, human rights) for needs assessment, analysis, planning, monitoring and response (National Disaster Coordinating Council, 2007). In conclusion, disaster risk reduction goes far beyond the sole, still essential, prevention of "rare" and "extreme" hazards and requires poverty alleviation, fair access to resources and adapted social and societal protection. Those are part of the larger development policies and do not refer to disaster management programmes disconnected from their social and politico-economic context.

References

Abarquez, I., Z. Murshed, (2004): *Community-based Disaster Risk Management: Field Practitioners' Handbook*. Asian Disaster Preparedness Centre, Pathumthani.

Abramovitz, J. (2001): *Unnatural Disasters*. Paper No. 158, Worldwatch Institute, Washington D.C.

Allen, K. (2003): Vulnerability reduction and the community-based approach. In Pelling M. (Ed.), *Natural Disasters and Development in a Globalizing World*. Routledge, London, pp. 170-184.

Allen. K. (2004): *Building Community Resilience to Disaster in the Philippines*. In International Federation of Red Cross and Red Crescent Societies, 2004 World disaster report: Focus on community resilience. International Federation of Red Cross and Red Crescent Societies, Geneva, pp. 100-119.

Anderson, M., P. Woodrow (1989): *Rising from the Ashes: Development Strategies in Times of Disasters*. Westview Press, Boulder.

Bankoff, G. (2001): Rendering the world unsafe: 'vulnerability' as western discourse, *Disasters,* 25(1): 19-35.

Bankoff, G. (2003): *Cultures of Disaster: Society and Natural Hazard in the Philippines*. Routledge, London.

Benblidia, M. (1990): Les priorités de la décennie pour les pays en voie de développement. *UNDRO News* Jan./Feb.: 14-17, 21.

Burton, I., R.W., Kates, G.F. White (1978): *The Environment as Hazard*. 1st Ed., Oxford University Press, New York.

Cannon, T. (1994): Vulnerability analysis and the explanation of 'natural' disasters. In A. Varley (Ed.), *Disasters, Development and Environment*. John Wiley & Sons, Chichester, pp. 13-30.

Cannon, T., J. Twigg, J. Rowell, (2003): *Social Vulnerability, Sustainable Livelihoods and Disasters*. Conflict and Humanitarian Assistance, Department and Sustainable Livelihoods Support Office, Department for International Development, London.

Centre for Research on Epidemiology of Disasters (2008): *EM-DAT: the OFDA/CRED International Disaster Database*. Université Catholique de Louvain, Brussels, http://www.cred.be/emdat, accessed 1st March, 2008.

Cijffers, K.M. (1987): Disaster relief: Doing things badly. *Pacific Viewpoint* 28(2): 95-117.

Comité d'Information Sahel (1975): *Qui se nourrit de la famine en Afrique?* F. Maspero, Paris.

Copans, J. (1975): Images, problématiques et thèmes. In J. Copans (1), (Ed.), *Sécheresses et famines du Sahel I: Ecologie/ Dénutrition/Assistance*. F. Maspero, Paris, pp. 9-39.

Corporacion Osso, La Red de Estudios Sociales en Prevencion de Desastres en America Latina (2008) *DesInventar online 8.1.9-2: sistema de inventario de efectos de desastres*. OSSO/La Red de Estudios Sociales en Prevención de Desastres en América Latina, Cali. http://online.desinventar.org/, accessed 31 October, 2008.

Davis, I. (1978): *Shelter after Disaster*. Oxford, Oxford Polytechnic Press.

Delfin, F.G. Jr., J.-C. Gaillard (2008): Extreme *vs.* quotidian: addressing temporal dichotomies in Philippine disaster management. *Public Administration and Development,* 28(3): 190-199.

Delica, Z.G. (1999): Community mobilization for early warning. *Philippine Planning Journal,* 30(2): 30-40.

Delica-Willison, Z. (2004): Vulnerability reduction: A task for the vulnerable people themselves. In G. Bankoff, G. Frerks, D. Hilhorst (Eds.), Mapping Vulnerability: Disasters, Development and People. *Earthscan*, London, pp. 145-158.

Gaillard, J.-C. (2007a): De l'origine des catastrophes: phénomènes extrêmes ou âpreté du quotidien? *Natures, Sciences et Sociétés,* 15(1): 44-47.

Gaillard, J.-C. (2007b): Resilience of traditional societies in facing natural hazards. *Disaster Prevention and Management*, 16(4): 522-544.

Gaillard, J.-C., C.C. Liamzon, E.A. Maceda, (2005): Act of nature or act of man? Tracking the root causes of increasing disasters in the Philippines. *Philippine Geographical Journal*, 49(1-4): 46-68.

Gaillard, J.-C., M.R.M. Pangilinan, J.R. Cadag, V. Le Masson, (2008): Living with increasing floods: insights from a rural Philippine community. *Disaster Prevention and Management,* 17(3): 383-395.

Heijmans, A. (2004): From vulnerability to empowerment. In G. Bankoff, G. Frerks, D. Hilhorst (Eds.), Mapping Vulnerability: Disasters, Development and People. *Earthscan,* London, pp. 115-127.

Heijmans, A., L.P. Victoria, (2001): *Citizenry-based and Development Oriented Disaster Response: Experiences and Practices in Disaster Management of the Citizens' Disaster Response Network in the Philippines.* Centre for Disaster Preparedness, Quezon City.

Hewitt, K. (1983): The idea of calamity in a technocratic age. In K. Hewitt Ed., *Interpretation of Calamities.* The risks and hazards series No.1, Allen & Unwin Inc., Boston, pp. 3-32.

Hewitt, K. (1995): Sustainable disasters? Perspectives and powers in the discourse of calamity. In J. Crush (Ed.), *Power of Development,* Routledge, London, pp. 115-128.

Kates, R.W. (1971): Natural hazard in human ecological perspective: hypotheses and models. *Economic Geography,* 47(3): 438-451.

Kelman, I., J.-C. Gaillard, (2008): Placing climate change within disaster risk reduction. *Disaster Advances,* 1(3): 3-5.

Lavell, A. (2000): Desastres durante una década: lecciones y avances conceptuales y prácticos en América Latina (1990-1999). *Anuario política y social de América latina* 3: 1-34.

Lewis, J. (1984): Environmental interpretations of natural disaster mitigation: The crucial need. *The Environmentalist,* 4(3): 177-180.

Luna, E.M. (2001): Disaster mitigation and preparedness: The case of NGOs in the Philippines. *Disasters,* 25(3): 216-226.

Luna, E.M. (2003): Endogenous system of responses to river flooding as a disaster subculture: A case study of Bula, Camarines Sur. *Philippine Sociological Review* 51: 135-153.

Maceda, E.A., J.-C., Gaillard, E., Stasiak, V., Le Masson, I. Le Berre, (2009): Experimental use of Participatory 3-Dimensional Models in island community-based disaster risk management. *Shima: The International Journal of Research into Island Culture,* in press.

Maskrey, A. (1989): *Disaster Mitigation: A Community-based approach.* Development Guidelines No. 3, Oxfam, Oxford.

Mount Pinatubo Emergency-Project Management Office (1998), *Pinatubo-Related Flood Mitigation Activities–Pampanga Delta*

Area (Pinatubo Side), Mount Pinatubo Emergency–Project Management Office, San Fernando.

National Disaster Coordinating Council (2004): *Four Point Action Plan for Disaster Preparedness*. National Disaster Coordinating Council, Quezon City.

National Disaster Coordinating Council (2007): *Institutionalizing of the Cluster Approach in the Philippine Disaster Management System, Designation of Cluster Leads and their Terms of Reference at the National, Regional and Provincial Level.* National Disaster Coordinating Council, Quezon City.

Nations *Unies* (1995): *Stratégie et plan d'action de Yokohama pour un monde plus sûr: directives pour la prévention des catastrophes naturelles, la préparation aux catastrophes et l'atténuation de leurs effets—Conférence mondiale sur la prévention des catastrophes naturelles—Yokohama, Japon, 23-27 mai 1994.* United Nations, New York/Geneva.

Quarantelli, E.L. (1989): *How Individuals and Groups React during Disasters: Planning and Managing Implications for EMS Delivery*. Preliminary Paper No. 138, Disaster Research Centre, University of Delaware.

Quarantelli, E.L., R.R. Dynes, (1972): When disaster strikes: it isn't much like what you've heard and read about. *Psychology Today,* 5(9): 66-70.

Rodolfo, K.S.; F.P. Siringan, (2006): Global sea-level rise is recognised, but flooding from anthropogenic land subsidence is ignored around Northern Manila Bay, Philippines. *Disasters*, 30(1): 118-139.

Sen, A.K. (1983): *Poverty and Famines: An Essay on Entitlement and Deprivation.* Oxford University Press, Oxford.

Siringan, F.P., K.S. Rodolfo, (2003): Relative sealevel changes and worsening floods in the Western Pampanga Delta: Causes and some possible mitigation measures. *Science Diliman* 15(2): 1-12.

Torry, W.I. (1978a): Bureaucracy, community, and natural disasters. *Human Organization,* 37(3): 302-308.

Torry, W.I. (1978b): Natural disasters, social structure and change in traditional societies. *Journal of Asian and African Studies,* 13(3-4): 167-183.

Tsubugo, T. (2005): *Pampanga Delta Development Project-Flood Control Component*. Project Evaluation Report, Japan Bank for International Cooperation, Tokyo.

Twigg, J. (2004): *Disaster Risk Reduction: Mitigation and Preparedness in Development and Emergency Programming. Good Practice Review,* Number 9, Humanitarian Practice Network, London.

United Nations International Strategy for Disaster Reduction (2004): *Living with risk: A Global Review of Disaster Reduction Initiatives*. United Nations International Strategy for Disaster Reduction, Geneva.

United Nations International Strategy for Disaster Reduction (2005): *Building the Resilience of Nations and Communities to Disaster: An Introduction to the Hyogo Framework for Action.* United Nations International Strategy for Disaster Reduction, Geneva.

Waddell, E. (1983): Coping with frosts, governments and disaster experts: Some reflections based on a New Guinean experience and a perusal of the relevant literature. In K. Hewitt (Ed.), *Interpretation of Calamities.* The risks and hazards series No.1, Allen & Unwin Inc., Boston, pp. 33-43.

Watts, M.J., H.G. Bolhe, (1993): The space of vulnerability: The causal structure of hunger and famine. *Progress in Human Geography,* 17(1): 43-67.

Wisner, B. (1993): Disaster vulnerability: Scale, power, and daily life. *Geojournal,* 30(2): 127-140.

Wisner, B., P. Walker, (2005): Katrina and Goliath: Why the greatest military and economic power in the world didn't protect New Orleans. *Humanitarian Exchange* 32: 46-47.

Wisner, B., P. Blaikie, T. Cannon, I. Davis, (2004): *At Risk: Natural Hazards, People's Vulnerability and Disasters.* 2nd Ed., Routledge, London.

World Bank, National Disaster Coordinating Council (2004): *Natural disaster Risk Management in the Philippines: Enhancing Poverty Alleviation Through Disaster Reduction.* World Bank/National Disaster Coordinating Council, Pasig City/Quezon City.

2

Institutional Innovation and Disaster Risk Management in Agricultural Communities in China

MUNETA YOKOMATSU, WEI-BIN YU AND NORIO OKADA

Disaster has a great and increasing effect on agricultural communities while corresponding disaster risk management is not adequate. This problem can be more serious in developing countries such as China. The disaster risk management in Chinese agricultural communities is far from enough because of insurance industry's limited knowledge about local natural disaster, farmers' weak consciousness for insurance and monetary factor. Owing to its poor-focus intention and local level cooperation, microcredit becomes more and more popular in the global undeveloped areas including rural China. In this article, we would like to discuss how to enrich microcredit's role in disaster risk management in agricultural communities in China through some institutional innovation based on local realities. By combining microcredit (from cooperative sectors and private sectors) and transaction of farmland management right, we find that disaster risk can be diversified and farmers' incentive for disaster mitigation will be improved. Through promoting farmers' efficient participation in cooperative sectors' management and operation, agricultural communities' financial ability against disaster risk and farmers' long-term welfare will be improved. We further try to prove that the application of micro group loans in the development of disaster-mitigation infrastructures will improve agricultural communities' sustainability and farmers' welfare. According to the above study and discussion, as an ending, some policy and mechanism suggestion and advice will be proposed.

Introduction

Communities worldwide have been facing an increasing frequency and variety of disasters, which have had a number of direct and indirect causes as well as effects. Worldwide the number of people affected by disasters, whether hydro-meteorological, geological or biological, and the economic loss resulting from the disasters have increased correspondingly (Srinivas and Nakagawa, 2007). At the same time, the corresponding disaster risk management is far from enough. The main reasons are absence of updated disaster risk management consciousness and lack of necessary disaster risk management fund. The adequate disaster risk management ideas are necessary for leading local people to pay attention to disaster risk management while the indispensable fund is necessary for applying corresponding disaster risk management ideas.

The conflict between increasing disaster risk and inadequate disaster risk management can be more serious in undeveloped countries or areas. In general, developing countries or areas are very poor in above two important aspects for disaster risk management: idea and fund. Generally, the main objective of the people in undeveloped areas is economic development. That means they have no extra or enough effort and money for practicing necessary disaster risk management. That is why, popularly, undeveloped areas have big problem with disaster risk management and no motivation to solve it. In the past quarter century over 95 per cent of disaster deaths occurred in developing countries and direct economic losses as a share of national income were more than double in low income *versus* high income countries (Arnold and Kreimer, 2004).

For improving disaster risk management, we should supply local people with combination of suited idea and necessary capital. The latter includes direct appropriation or some mechanism design for disaster risk financing. Furthermore, we should focus on the disaster risk management in the undeveloped countries or areas. The Hyogo Framework of 2005 concludes that natural hazard risk reduction should be a core component of economic development assistance, and that attention should be directed to financial strategies that hold promise for reducing the burdens on the poor (UNISDR, 2005).

Issues of Disaster Risk Management in Agricultural Communities

The General Problems in Agricultural Communities

In general, especially in developing countries, agricultural communities are among undeveloped areas. And according to above introduction, there are many problems about disaster risk management in undeveloped areas because of many detailed reasons. According to current related study, generally, problems regarding disaster risk finance in agricultural communities are categorized as follows:

(1) *Vulnerability Assessment*—In general, agricultural communities lack consciousness, fund, expertise, data, laws and institutions to ensure the effective implementation of risk and vulnerability assessment and keep it sustainable (Linnerooth-Bayer *et al.*, 2007; Cochard, *et al.,* 2007).

(2) *Disaster Risk Financing*—In developing countries, for preventing and reducing disaster losses happened in agricultural communities, governments always use money from finance income. But the national finance is not equal to the disaster risk that becomes greater and frequent. Therefore, how can highly exposed governments take advantage of novel risk transfer instruments to reduce their financial vulnerability to disasters becomes more and more popular among the study on disaster risk management in agricultural communities.

(3) *Catastrophe Insurance*—Catastrophe insurance in agricultural communities, sometimes named by crop insurance, is relatively mature disaster risk financing system in agricultural communities. But it still has some inherent problems such as how to pre-measure catastrophe risk before farmers buying crop insurance and how to post-measure the crop losses after the catastrophe happens. Furthermore, how to integrate the power from government and private factor has been becoming more and more important during recent years.

Traditional Methods and Innovation

According to current study (Warner, 2007), for disaster risk management at the community level, the financial services (products) refers broadly to any financial arrangement involving a party outside of the household or community unit, regardless whether it is being provided by the (formal) private financial services sector, or semi- or non-market institutions, such as other financial institutions, government, Non-Governmental Organizations (NGOs), local civil organizations. Financial services can help absorb and redistribute the cost of hazard-related losses. They may also shape incentives which encourage disaster risk reduction. They may consist of investments in risk reduction through accessible credit, and of risk spreading through insurance mechanisms. In recent years, various international institutions have investigated the role financial services could play in managing disaster risk. Some limited disaster finance schemes have become available, such as partnerships with NGOs, insurance companies, or local savings and credit institutions.

In many developing countries, most financial and other resources for disaster risk reduction and adaptation activities come from households—mainly through consumption of available resources or savings. But the ex-post household disaster finance was considered the most costly and least efficient means of paying for disaster losses (Warner, 2005).

Definitely, above common disaster risk financing approach requires augmentation from other financial services to effectively address the risk of losses from natural hazards (Honohan, 2004). Synchronously, there is a need to overcome obstacles to provide affordable and appropriate financial services at the local level—and from actors which are best suited to manage and finance disaster risk and risk reduction. In general, there are several available schemes as follows:

(1) National Government-initiated Scheme;
(2) Local Government-initiated Scheme;
(3) NGO-initiated Scheme; and
(4) Micro-finance initiated Scheme.

MFIs (Micro-finance Institutions) provide a variety of financial services to communities in developing countries. Microcredits have become a mainstream product throughout the world, which has been underscored by the award of the Nobel Peace Prize to Mr. Mohamed Yunus and the Grameen Bank in 2006. Micro-insurance products offered by Opportunity International (www.opportunity.org) help such groups better manage their risks and also benefit microcredit operations by preventing loan default in the case of an unexpected event (Mapfumo, 2005). Like NGOs, MFIs have strong links to local clients and are able to efficiently administer group policies. Partnerships with private sector companies help MFIs overcome specific challenges.

Diffusion of Microcredit and Challenges for the Future

According to above statement, micro-finance can play an active role in disaster risk financing, especially in developing countries. In general, micro-finance includes micro-saving, microcredit and micro-insurance (Zeller and Sharma, 2000). Compared with micro-saving and micro-insurance, microcredit got most attention and extension. For example, many MFIs such as BRAC, ASA and Grameen Bank focus on microcredit (Zeller and Sharma, 2000).

There are many kinds of definitions for microcredit from governmental organizations, NGOs (such as the World Bank and OECD) and MFIs (such as Grameen Bank and ASA). Here, we would like to show the definition from OECD as follows:

Microcredit programmes offer loans and/or technical assistance in business development to poor people. Generally, programmes have one or more of three goals: (1) improvement of self-sufficiency and welfare of poor entrepreneurs, (2) development of stable sources of income and full-time employment, and (3) expansion of micro-enterprises to larger firms (OECD, 1996).

The first appearance of microcredit, according to our knowledge, happened in Europe. The birth of microcredit in Europe dates back to tremendous increases in poverty since the sixteenth century. In Ireland, loan funds emerged in the 1720s, using peer monitoring to enforce the repayment in weekly instalments of initially interest-free loans from donated resources (Seibel, 2003). A special law in 1823, which turned the charities into financial intermediaries by allowing them to charge interest on loans, enabled them at the same time to collect interest-bearing deposits. The government established a Loan Fund Board in 1836 for their regulation and supervision. In Germany, the community-owned financial institutions started during the latter part of the 18th century. Having learnt from the early Irish charities that charity is not sustainable, the first thrift society was established in Hamburg in 1778 and the first communal savings fund (Sparkasse) in 1801. As the movement spread, the rural and urban saving and credit cooperatives occurred. The turnaround came in 1989, when both the rural and the urban networks of credit associations were brought under the law: the Cooperative Act of the German Reich, the first cooperative law in the world. At the same time, joint liability, which had kept back the growth of the system, was replaced by limited liability. Until 1914, the number of rural cooperatives in Germany increased to more than 15,000 and spread to many other countries.

Starting in the mid-1980s, microenterprise finance organizations began shifting their focus from experimentation in programmer development to more highly cost-effective and professional operations (OECD, 1996). Out of the investments in microcredit organizations, a handful of permanent financial institutions serve millions of poor entrepreneurs while covering their annual operating costs with interest income and service fees paid by their customers. These programmes recognised that microentrepreneurs want and need liquidity—not just credit—and developed the capacity to mobilize large amounts of savings from their customers, as well as provide them with loans. In addition, their successes have spawned a large number of small, village-based microcredit programmes in developing countries around the world.

Paralleling with the extension and popularization of microcredit, the role of it in disaster risk management becomes more and more active and outstanding. For example, in Bangladesh, where NGO microcredit operations are particularly significant, NGOs are experimenting with various mechanisms both to support clients in reducing their hazard vulnerability and recovering from disaster and to safeguard their own portfolios (Benson *et al.*, 2001). Microcredit interventions have been able to reduce the idiosyncratic risks faced by the poor households and could also be applied to reduce the impact of natural disasters (Kumar and Newport, 2005).

Compared with traditional banks or other financial institutions, MFIs or microcredit programmes have the following advantages (Parker and Nagarajan, 2000):

(1) MFIs serve difficult-to-reach clients, with whom they maintain regular contact, a relationship which is essential for interacting with vulnerable populations both before and after disaster strikes;

(2) High-quality MFIs develop a trust-based relationship with clients, which increases the MFI's ability to discuss difficult topics or to interact during crises; and

(3) Because MFIs often work with organized groups of clients, information and services can be delivered on a leveraged basis, either for disaster preparedness or for disaster response.

Another important role of microcredit in disaster risk management is smaller MFIs, even the smallest MFI can play a constructive role in disaster preparedness (Parker and Nagarajan, 2000). MFIs are unique in the regular contact their staff has with even the most remote clients. In the event of an emergency, MFI loan officers are often the first to reach affected communities. Client preparedness is another area where any MFI can play a constructive role. Because MFIs serve the poor, their clients often live in highly vulnerable physical locations. MFIs can help vulnerable client groups to mentally prepare for disasters and have plans on how to respond.

Because of above innovative assigns and visible advantages, microcredit programmes have been playing an active role in the global disaster risk management, especially in agricultural communities.

The Self-Employed Women's Association started in 1972 as a trade union and today it is the largest MFI in India with 688,743 members. Over the years, SEWA has developed a variety of financial products for the poor. While historically it provided microcredit to start/grow small enterprises, it now also offers the following catastrophe-related services: (1) Preventative loans for monsoon-proofing one's home; (2) Loans to replace or repair a roof, wall or door (SEWA, 2008).

In Bangladesh, when the calamitous floods of 1998 spread over two-thirds of the country and impacted more than 30 million people The Grameen bank quickly developed disaster response mechanisms such as releasing client savings, rescheduling people's loans, and issuing new housing rehabilitation and other emergency loans (Hasan, 1998).

Trickle-Up in Philippines began offering loan products as safety nets after the volcanic eruption of Mount Pinatubo in 1992, as well as the earthquake of 1990, and various typhoons that have struck the 7,000 islands of the nation. Microcredit clients could qualify for cash grants of $50-$100 that did not need to be repaid if they had a solid credit listing with the MFI (Woodworth, 2006).

Proshika is an NGO in Bangladesh that was founded as a humanitarian aid non-profit in the 1970s. During its inception it was motivated to give cash subsidies to victims of disaster. Then it shifted into becoming an MFI in the 1990s. Over time, Proshika has installed a series of disaster insurance products that consist of a Participatory Livestock Cooperation Fund that reimburses clients for the sudden death of farm animals such as goats, cattle and chickens (Proshika, 2008).

Besides its obvious positive function in disaster risk financing, microcredit also faces some challenges or limitations in the future. Two underlying assumptions shape the long-term challenges that microcredit organizations, including those in transition economies, must face and overcome (OECD, 1996). First, programme services should be delivered in a manner that matches the realities of the economic, social, and institutional context in which the potential customers work and live. Second, programmes that provide credit and related business services to the micro-sector should be cost-effective and sustainable over time. In other words, it is assumed that these programmes are interested in developing institutions not demonstration projects. Like hospitals, schools, and financial institutions, there is a symbiotic and accountable relationship that must exist between the customers or clients and the microcredit programmes so that client needs are met in ways that insure the survival of the institution. Accordingly, microcredit programmes face the following specific challenges (OECD, 1996):

(1) Maintaining vision and commitment in the face of obstacles;
(2) Balancing development impact with financial sustainability;
(3) Identifying clear outcome goals and relevant performance measures;
(4) Defining the role and cost of technical assistance; and
(5) Developing efficient programme operations.

As for disaster risk management, most microcredit programmes or MFIs face the following problems (Parker and Nagarajan, 2000):

(1) Most MFIs do not have the liquidity position (or access to a Disaster Loan Fund) to respond quickly or fully in a disaster context.

(2) Most MFIs—from management, to field staff, to reserves, to information and communication systems—are not currently prepared to either weather or respond to a natural disaster situation.

(3) Most MFIs have not considered client needs from an emergency perspective; rather products and services are primarily geared to day-to-day business or household concerns.

(4) Demand for special services may be small, yet may require significant institutional investment. Therefore, individual MFIs are unlikely to invest in developing or maintaining these services.

(5) Regulatory restrictions and limits to institutional capacity will keep most MFIs from mobilizing voluntary savings for the foreseeable future.

Among above detailed problems, the sustainability is definitely very pivotal. Sustainability is the ability of the microcredit programme to maintain its operations and continue to provide service to its customers or clients. The sustainability is the key point that makes microcredit different from subsidy or donation. And only with adequate sustainability, microcredit programme can extend its impact and achieve active outreach. Unfortunately, the situation of most microcredit programmes' financial sustainability is not so good. Research shows that no microcredit programme has yet to achieve sustainability (OECD, 1996). Some programmes have come close to achieving sustainability—Grameen Bank and BRI Unit Desa System of Indonesia (Boomgard and Angell, 1990), for example, most others have a considerable way to go (OECD, 1996). Research further shows that no microcredit programme can be sustainable at its inauguration. Programmes near to achieving sustainability have only been able to do so by becoming more efficient, usually over a period of years. No programme is self-sufficient.

A programme is sustainable when a combination of external grants, loans, and internally generated revenues are sufficient to cover all programme expenses over the long term. Furthermore, self-sufficiency—one of sustainability—occurs when the microcredit programme can cover all of its operating expenses (including loan losses and the cost of capital) entirely with internally-generated sources of income (OECD, 1996). In general, only the microcredit programmes with long-term sustainability or self-sufficiency can make themselves be real independent MFIs and supply customers with durative microcredit service.

In general, the sustainability is affected by the following factors (OECD, 1996):

(1) Interest rates and the cost of capital;
(2) Availability of funding sources;
(3) Types of services provided—training and technical assistance and other non-revenue generating services can be more costly to provide;
(4) Administrative structure, especially staffing structure;
(5) Service delivery methodology and partnership maintenance;
(6) Demand for services and the scale that can be achieved; and
(7) Loan fund repayment performance that related with moral hazard and credit programmes monitoring.

Generally, the most important factors are interest rates and the cost of capital and loan fund repayment performance. These two factors decide the liquidity of microcredit programmes that may be more challenged during the post-disaster time (Kumar and Newport, 2005). Providing services in post-disaster settings entails both direct and indirect costs. The high direct costs are occurred because of poor logistics and indirect costs due to reduced savings levels and lower repayment rates. During the post-disaster, there will be a heavy withdrawai of savings and also no fresh savings, non-repayment of the existing loans, huge demand for housing reconstruction loan and other personal loans. Moreover, the MFIs loan repayment to their external borrowings will also be affected. This leads to a huge liquidity crisis.

Chinese Disaster Insurance Market

The General Characteristics of Chinese Insurance Market

After entering WTO, Chinese insurance industry has been developing very quickly. Premium income has increased from 211 billion RMB (2001) to 432 billion RMB (2004). And the number of insurance companies has increased from 35 to 61 (Yang, 2005). Total asset has reached 1.36 trillion RMB till June of 2005 with an increase of 15 per cent compared with the end of 2004. In the invested insurance capital, the rate of bond has exceeded that of bank deposit for the first time. Insurance company has become the second largest organization investor in the bond market. The consciousness of insurance organizations to serve the development of economics and society has been improved. In 2005, the insurance payment has achieved 54 billion RMB with 12.9 per cent increase compared with 2004 (Zheng, 2005).

Along with opening of Chinese insurance market and relaxing of admittance limitation, the number of insurance companies is increasing quickly while the market shares of relative large companies are decreasing step by step. It is seen from Table 2.1 and Table 2.2 that the monopoly in insurance industry is being broken gradually with more and more market competition (Yang, 2005).

Table 2.1 : The Change in Numbers of Insurers

	Life Insurer	*Property Insurer*	*Foreign Property Insurer*
2001	16	17	7
2003	30	24	14
Per cent Up (from 2001 to 2003)	87.5%	41.2%	100%

Note: Please Refer to (Yang, 2005).

Table 2.2 : The Change in Market Shares (Property Insurance)

	PICC	Other Insurers (Except Top 3)
2000	77.3%	3.65%
2003	66.88%	11.75%

Note: Please refer to (Yang, 2005). Here, PICC is the People's Insurance Company (Group) of China.

In 2003, China Insurance Regulatory Commission (CIRC) allowed property insurers to operate suddenness insurance and health insurance. Since that time, Chinese insurance industry became more and more integrated and competitive. At the same time, for improving Chinese insurance industry's international competition ability, CIRC allowed establishing several professional insurance companies such as Endowment Insurance Company, Healthy Insurance Company and Agriculture Insurance Company (Yang, 2005).

Corresponding with above development and challenges, Chinese insurance market has the following insufficiencies (Zhao, 2004; Fan, 2005; Zhang, 2004):

(1) Deficient capital abundance level;
(2) The core challenge: the lack of solvency;
(3) Congenitally inadequate original capital;
(4) Low profit rate;
(5) Weak consciousness for insurance in China;
(6) Faith in changing potential demands to real ones;
(7) Inter-local, inter-insurant and inter-market imbalance; and
(8) The limited insurance function.

The Deficiency of Chinese Disaster Insurance

Because of the inadequate development in the research on huge disaster insurance, the property insurance companies only involve flood risk as especial additive insurance. And considering about the operation steadiness, insurers exclude the insurance related with earthquake and tsunami that also concerned by people very much.

Chinese are less of insurance consciousness or some kinds of huge disaster risk are not insured. So the sufferers can only depend on the national alms-giving, social contribution and self-rescuer. In the blowout accident happened in Chongqing City in 2003, insurance claim is only 20 million RMB. And the disaster losses caused by the super flood in 1998 were more than 248 billion RMB while the related insurance claim was only 3 billion RMB. Insurance's function in disaster reduction is far from enough.

China has long been using national finance to prevent and reduce disaster losses. The huge disaster risk is totally burdened on national finance. That disaster prevention and reduction system based on national free alms-giving are becoming more and more unsuitable for the development of society and economics along with the development of the economical system and reforming-and-opening. The basal principles for national finance budget is that it should be decided according to the future spending while huge disaster risk is random and unknowable. One side, it is very difficult for finance to get enough capital for huge disaster losses in very short time. On the other hand, the sudden and huge spending of finance will cause finance deficit. In recent years, Chinese natural disasters have become more and more frequent. National almsgiving ability is not enough for post-disaster almsgiving and rebuilding. And furthermore, under this kind of disaster prevention and reduction system, the potential sufferers will not get insurance before disaster and just depend on national almsgiving after disaster. That is conflict with market economics system. According to experts' opinions, Chinese Government should gradually establish Chinese own huge disaster defending system through the method that consists of government and market behaviours based on international experience and Chinese realities (Xiong, 2005).

The Measures for Developing Disaster Insurance

(1) *Making the law of disaster insurance*: Disaster insurance law should focus on establishing huge disaster ensuring system through legislative methods.

(2) *Pre-disaster governmental intervention*: The governmental intervention in huge disaster insurance can strengthen huge disaster capital, encourage commercial operation in huge disaster risk and lighten the burden on national finance.

(3) *Establishing huge disaster insurance fund*: The role of huge disaster insurance fund in separating and dealing huge disaster risk will become more and more important along with its investment, value increasing and development.

(4) *Founding public-private partnership for risk mitigation*: All the related persons and organizations should do their best to help or promote the poor to do some positive actions for risk mitigation and recovery.

(5) *Floating huge disaster risk securities*: Floating huge disaster insurance securities is to raise huge disaster risk reserve from advanced capital market, transfer huge disaster risk from insurance market to capital market and strengthen insurance industry's ability to resist huge disaster risk.

The Combination of Microcredit and Transaction of Farmland Management Right

Background

Microcredit is the extension of small loans to enterprises that are too poor to qualify for traditional bank loans. It has proven an effective and popular measure in the ongoing struggle against poverty, enabling those without access to lending institutions to borrow at bank rates, and start small business.

In 1996, the reform of rural financial system made Chinese Rural Credit Cooperatives (RCCs), a main function of which is to supply farmers with necessary loan for agricultural production and more independent of supervision by the Agricultural Bank of China. Namely RCCs became the cooperatives that make their own management decisions (Kawahara, 2005a). They put into practice the individual and group-lending microcredit loan in 1996, which have gradually been popularized since 2000s. The amount of the loan varies from 8,000 to 10,000 RMB in developed areas and from 3,000 to 5,000 RMB in underdeveloped areas, while the interest rates are decided by each RCC considering they should be close to the basic interest rate given by People's Bank of China. The contract time not needed is one year in most of the cases. In the case where bigger amount of loan is demanded, group-lending is available with the loan group consisting of 3-5 rural households, who mutually help and monitor each other to repay the loan (Kawahara, 2005a). Diffusion of the microcredit has changed the composition of the financial market in the agricultural area. For example, it is pointed out (Yan, 2002) that, in 1998, only 21 per cent of farmers' loan came from the agricultural banks and RCCs, who did not seem in favour of providing credit, while 74 per cent of farmers' loan was from the private financing sectors. However, according to a survey in certain areas of rural China by (Kawahara, 2005a), the amount of the loan from the agricultural banks and RCCs is almost equal to that from the private sectors during 2001-02. Availability of the formal loan operated by the agricultural banks and RCCs are increasing, while the private loan including informal lending by the business partners like traders still play an important role in the financial supply of rural China.

Before 1980, the main land utilization system in rural China was agricultural cooperation and land communization. Since 1978, the state has been encouraging and popularizing the contractual management system in respect of land in the rural areas. Under the contractual management system, farmers get the farmland management right while the collective still owns the farmland. Farmers can make their own decisions on agricultural production and marketing. And since 1990, the state has been encouraging the circulation of the right to the farmland contractual management, which is effected according to the law, on a voluntary basis and with the compensation (Kawahara, 2005b; National People's Congress of the People's Republic of China, 2002; Baidu, 2007).

Concern

Considering the recent institutional movement above, it must be true that the RCCs' microcredit loan has improved the farmers' ability of risk financing, although the following questions still remain unsettled:

(1) Why have RCCs supplied not enough credit to farmers but "micro" credit?
(2) How are the coexistence of RCCs and private financing sectors in current rural financial market characterized? Why do not RCCs completely dominate the market in spite of their devastating advantage in risk pooling over the private sectors?
(3) What kind of effect does the liquidation of the farmland management right have on the disaster risk management in the agricultural areas?

As the viewpoint of the study, we focus on RCCs' limited ability to control farmers' moral hazard in the disaster risk management, which is caused by the following factors:

(1) There is information asymmetry between farmers and RCCs because RCCs are connected to the member farmers only through the financial transaction, saving and borrowing, that is, for example, different from the agricultural cooperative system in Japan that has integrated cooperative relationship with the member farmers.
(2) Farmlands cannot serve as collateral for the loan because they belong to the collective. Farmers are also limited to use their houses as a guarantee.
(3) Guarantor system is not very effective. It is also costly for RCCs to monitor debtor and his guarantor's economic condition.

This study develops the risk management models in the agricultural villages of China to describe the following structures:

(1) The circulation of the right to farmland contractual management will make the risk exposure more homogeneous among the farmers.
(2) For that reason, the ability of the RCCs and the private financing sectors to manage the risk is increased, resulting a decrease in the risk premium included in the interest of the loan.
(3) Moreover, by involving the private financing sectors as the stakeholder, who can monitor the farmers' condition with low cost due to long-term relationship, the farmers are less motivated to go into moral hazard in risk mitigation.

Analyses

Here we only introduce the essence of our analyses. For the detail, please refer to Yokomatsu *et al.* (2007). The essential assumptions are as follows: Firstly, for studying the effect of the liquidation of the farmland management right on diversification of disaster risk, we do not consider the RCCs and the microcredit, and assume that all the loan is provided by the private sectors through interlinked transactions, in which two parties trade in at least two markets on the condition that the terms of all such trades are jointly determined (Bell, 1988). The market interlinkage generally provides a way of partially circumventing incomplete or non-existent markets in the developing societies (Bardhan and Udry, 1999). Now, we suppose the local traders as private financing sectors in the model, who respectively have long-term relationship with a farmer as each client, and therefore, know the farmer's condition and behaviour well. We further assume that traders are homogeneous, competing with one another in the market, and moreover, each trader has one farmer as his partner, respectively. Hence the local traders not only buy agricultural products from the farmers but, before production, supply them with private financing service such as loan. Farmers are heterogeneous only with respect to the initial endowment of wealth. The farmer gets the loan from the trader with a contract that he will pay back the loan with interest after the successful crop. Then, if the successful crop comes as wish, the farmer will get income without any difficulty, from which he repays the loan to the trader with the interest payment that includes the risk premium. If the crop fails, the farmer and the businessman will get nothing back. Assuming that the trader is risk averse, the market competition implies that the trader's expected utility equals to zero.

Based on above assumptions, we respectively studied Case I in which the farmland is allocated averagely and Case II in which there are transactions of farmland management. Through Case I, we found that the reduction of the aggregated risk premium can improve the social welfare. And based on Case II, it turns out that the liquidation of the farmland management right can diversify disaster risk among farmers and make social utility increase.

Secondly, for solving the problem of moral hazard and improving farmers' incentive for disaster mitigation, we integrated the roles of rural credit cooperatives and private financing sectors in supplying microcredit loan to farmers. In the preceding discussion, we investigated the effect of liquidation of the farmland management right on redistribution of risks in the society. In this section we are concerned with how the functions of the private financing sectors and RCCs can be effectively coordinated in the disaster risk management scheme in rural China. We expand the discussion in two ways; the RCC that provides the microcredit to the farmers and the practice of risk mitigation by the farmers are introduced, while for simplification we assume that there are only two farmers in the society, who are the members of the same RCC and whose initial endowments are different (wealth is distributed).

In Case III, we assume that the RCC provides the loan to farmers 1 and 2 respectively. We further assume that the farmers' disaster risks are identical and independent. Each farmer demands the loan from the trader by the amount which covers the shortfall of monetary resource. And if the cropping is successful, RCC and the trader will ask farmers for interest payment that includes risk premium. On the other hand the farmers can mitigate the losses in the state of disaster by the mitigation behaviour before the event. We find that the RCC would like to supply individual farmer with the same loan and ask for the same risk premium, besides the private loan is also identical between the farmers. Finally, the level of the farmers' effort for disaster mitigation is equalized in the social optimal situation.

In Case III, we considered the problem where the social planner determined all the variables in the society so as to maximize the sum of expected utilities as the objective function. Accordingly, there was no problem caused by information asymmetry. In Case IV, we consider the individual optimization by individual farmer who can induce the moral hazard that he may devote less effort than the social optimal effort. We suppose that the farmers are given disaster education with some instruction manual at the beginning, and they are required to devote optimal level of effort. On the other hand, the RCC has limited information on the farmers' situations, and provides the social optimal size of the microcredit and does not behave strategically. On the contrary, each farmer behaves in the market so as to maximize his expected utility with respect to the size of the farmland management right and the mitigation effort. Accordingly there may be some difference between individual effort and that optimal one required in Case III. Now we suppose that the trader monitors each farmer's behaviour without any cost and discovers this difference. He seeks the farmer a penalty for deviation from the optimal mitigation effort by the amount of which is proportional to the level of the moral hazard. The unit of the penalty is given by labour or time. The following is the event-sequence in Case IV:

(1) The farmers are instructed by the public sector to devote optimal effort for the mitigation.
(2) The RCC gives the farmers the microcredit by the amount of optimal one stated in Case III.
(3) The trader announces the risk premium function.
(4) The farmers transact the farmland management right in the market, make private loan contract, and determine the level of effort.
(5) The market of the farmland management right reaches the equilibrium.
(6) The trader discovers the moral hazard and seeks the penalty.
(7) Disaster occurs or not.
(8) The farmers get crop and make repayment to the RCC and the trader.

Based on above analysis, we find we can reach social optimal condition if traders choose adequate penalty function. Moreover, by transacting the farmland management right in the market, the size of the private loan is equalized between the farmers and, furthermore, identical to the social optimal level. Hence, with the optimal risk management scheme, the social optimal welfare is achieved in the decentralized market.

Summary

We have developed the risk management models in the agricultural villages of China to investigate the effective coordination between the RCC and the private financial sectors in the liquid market on the farmland management right. The circulation of the farmland management right makes the farmers' loan and disaster mitigation effort more homogeneous in equilibrium, that increases the ability of the RCCs and the private financial sectors to pool the risks, resulting in decrease in the risk premium included in the interest of the loan. Moreover, by making use of the private financing sectors' monitoring ability, farmers are less motivated to go into the moral hazard in disaster risk mitigation. In that sense, the microcredit system that leaves some roles for private financial sectors and the liquidation of the farmland management right complementarily work in the risk financing.

As for the future work, we should investigate more circumstantially practical conditions of the inter-linkage market. Moreover we should take into account RCCs' operational strategy and interaction with the farmers; the cooperative characteristics of RCCs, the farmers' motivation for contributing in RCCs' sustainability, for example. We are also concerned about the township and village enterprises' ability to absorb the capital and surplus workforce and try to involve the township and village enterprises into the risk financing model in rural China.

Improvement of Microcredit's Sustainability and Farmers' Welfare

The Study on the Institutional Reformation of Rural Credit Cooperatives

Background

The micro-credit loan in China has the history of more than ten years. During the past ten years, the microcredit loan from RCCs has been doing much effective effort on the development of agricultural communities in China (Chen and Qiu, 2006):

(1) Microcredit loan from RCCs supplies farmers with necessary production capital;
(2) Microcredit loan from RCCs improves farmers' employment opportunities;
(3) Microcredit loan from RCCs increases farmers' income; and
(4) Microcredit loan from RCCs completes rural financial system.

Because of above positive roles, the development of microcredit loan from RCCs will do more and more productive job in developing new agricultural communities in China in 21st century. But at the same time, the microcredit loan from RCCs still face the challenge of sustainability because of the following insufficiencies :

(1) Shareholders (RCCs' members) do not participate in the management of RCCs efficiently (Wang, 2006; Shangguan, 2006).
(2) There are too many political interventions that affect RCCs' operation and management seriously (Zhang, 2006; Tao, 2006; Ji and Zhang, 2006).
(3) The loan from RCCs is mainly allocated to traditional agricultural production that suffers very much from disasters. If the disaster happens, RCCs' repayment rate and profit rate will be affected seriously (Wang, 2006).
(4) In general, farmers do not care about RCCs' sustainability because they are not aware of the possibility of RCCs' bankruptcy after the reformation because of their deficient participation in RCCs' management and operation (Zhang, 2006; Shangguan, 2006).
(5) RCCs' staff does not have enough motivation to focus on RCCs' daily operation and business extension (Wang, 2006; Shangguan, 2006; Ji and Zhang, 2006).

Correspondingly, according to the present related research, the following counter measures should be considered :

(1) Give members corresponding discounts on loan interest rates according to their individual investment in RCCs. Furthermore, RCCs should allocate the profit to the members

according to their individual contribution (Wang, 2006; Shangguan, 2006).

(2) Make RCCs more independent through the legislation for rural credit cooperation (Zhang, 2006; Wang, 2006; Shangguan, 2006).

(3) Support rural enterprises and make relatively higher profit income from them (Zhang, 2006; Wang, 2006; Tao, 2006; Ji and Zhang, 2006).

(4) Carry out new management mode and property right system reformation according to local realities (Zhang, 2006; Wang, 2006; Shangguan, 2006; Ji and Zhang, 2006; Liang, 2006).

(5) With adequate financial risk management and proper operation, RCCs should mainly support agriculture, rural economy and farmers (Zhang, 2006; Shangguan, 2006; Tao, 2006; Liang, 2006).

Concern

According to the above statement, it is true that the participation of shareholders (RCCs' members) in RCCs' management is very important for RCCs' efficiency and sustainability improvement. Only with the efficient management from members, can RCCs really work for their real owners' benefit and the development of rural China. This section will focus on the farmers' participation in the management of RCCs.

Analyses

Here we only show the essence of our analyses. Please see Yu *et al.* (2008a) for the details. As mentioned above, there are assumed to be only two parties, RCCs and farmers. The latter is the only investor to RCCs. That means farmers are the only members and owners of RCCs. After the investment, the managers of RCCs will make the decision about daily operation and loan allocation. During the decision process, by assumption, there is no intervention from the government after some successful institutional reformation. And farmers can voluntarily choose whether or not they want to participate in RCCs' management. As mentioned before, the main loan of RCCs is allocated to traditional agricultural production that depends too much on natural disaster.

Correspondingly, that will greatly affect the repayment and profit rate of RCCs. It is natural for us to think about lending the main loan to other kinds of production with a relatively stable return. But one important job of RCCs' is to support agriculture. That means some kind of balance should be made among several loan allocations. As an innovative way, it is assumed that RCCs' loan will be separated into three parts: agricultural loan, credit to other financial institutions (such as saving in commercial banks) and some risky investment (such as lending to rural enterprises). The main job of RCCs' management process is to decide the exact ratio among the three loan allocations. After the ratio decision, farmers will receive the loan from RCCs and do the cultivation. In general, the crop will be affected if the disaster happens. By assumption, farmers' disaster mitigation investment will decide on the remaining ratio of post-disaster crop. Finally, RCCs will receive the repayment from the farmers' crop, interest income from other banks and profit return from risky investment. Later it will be examined whether the RCCs' asset is less than before. If the answer is negative, the similar process of loan allocating, loan lending, cultivating, disaster mitigating, loan repaying and RCCs' asset checking will happen continuously. And if the answer is positive, that means RCCs cannot afford the loan to farmers anymore. In other words, at least as for farmers, RCCs fall in the bankruptcy. That will disable farmers' continuous agricultural production.

For simplification, the event-sequence is arranged as follows :

(1) Farmers make investment to RCCs.
(2) RCCs' managers make loan allocation among agricultural loan, safe investment and risky investment.
(3) Farmers get the loan from RCCs.
(4) Farmers cultivate land and mitigate disaster.
(5) Disaster happens with the certain probability.
(6) RCCs' get the repayment from farmers, other banks and risky investment.
(7) RCCs will continue to supply farmers with a loan in the next period if their asset is more than the initial one.

According to the above arrangement, it is shown that loan allocation ratio and farmers' mitigation investment will affect RCCs' sustainability. And RCCs' sustainability decides farmers' long-term benefit. That means that there is the farmers' potential motivation to participate in RCCs' management and optimal disaster mitigation effort for optimizing their own long-run benefit. In other words, the job is to find out how to encourage farmers to participate in RCCs' management and what is the optimal disaster mitigation investment through the coming model.

For simplification, the number of farmers and that of RCCs are respectively standardized to be 1. The initial asset of RCC consists of common reserve fund and farmers' investment (necessary for becoming RCC's member). And it is assumed that the loan amount for the agricultural loan is fixed. The management process of RCC is to decide the ratio between the safe investment and the risky investment.

For comparative analysis, we will study the following four cases:

(1) Case I : Farmers' utility before institutional reformation—Before institutional reformation of RCC, let us suppose that farmers do not know and neither care about RCC's decision on the ratio between the safe investment and the risky investment. They only care about their income from cultivating. And RCC will not fall in bankruptcy even if farmers fail to pay a loan and interest back to RCC in the case of huge disasters; because the government will support RCC anyway. In other words, farmers know that the disaster will not affect the probability of getting the loan in next time.

(2) Case II : Farmers' utility without perfect information about RCC's management after institutional reformation—In this case, farmers are supposed to behave again according to their original knowledge about RCC's management and operation before institutional reformation. But actually, the probability for farmers to get loans in the next period will be affected if RCC's sustainability is destroyed by the unsuccessful repayment induced by the huge disaster. At the end of each period, after getting the repayment from farmers, the return from safe investment and that from risky investment, RCC's asset will be compared with that of initial one. If the former is bigger than the latter, RCC will survive and farmers will get RCC's net income at the end of this period and the agricultural loan in the next period. If RCC's asset is smaller than that of initial one, RCC will fall in bankruptcy and farmers will not get the

agricultural loan in the next period. That means the farmers' cultivation will be stopped.

(3) Case III : Farmers' utility with perfect information about RCC's decision—In this case, farmers are assumed to have perfect information about RCC's decision about the loan allocation ratio between safe investment and risky investment. Although farmers can get all the profit from the above investment, they cannot affect the investment ratio. Farmers can only maximize their expected utility by choosing adequate disaster mitigation effort.

(4) Case IV : Farmers' utility with efficient participation in RCC's management—In this case, farmers are supposed to efficiently participate in RCC's management by deciding loan allocation ratio between a safe investment and a risky one. Here, farmers can maximize their expected utility by choosing adequate disaster mitigation effort and loan allocation ratio.

After mathematical analysis, we got the following results :

(1) $\sigma^{IV} = \sigma^{III} > \sigma^{II} = \sigma^{I}$ where $\sigma^{i}(i = I, II, III, IV)$ is farmers' disaster mitigation effort in Case I, II, III and IV.

(2) $W^{IV} > W^{I} > W^{III} > W^{II}$ where $W^{i}(i = I, II, III, IV)$ is farmers' expected utility in Case I, II, III and IV.

(3) $P^{II} < P^{III} < P^{IV} = 1$ where $P^{i}(i = II, III, IV)$ is the probability of RCCs' post-disaster surviving in Case II, III and IV.

(4) With the rise of the variety of capital market, the optimal ratio of the loan allocated to risky investment decreases. That means, with the full ability to affect RCC's decision, the more risky the capital market, the more carefully farmers manage investment.

Summary

Farmers' long-run benefit depends on RCCs' sustainability which is determined by the repayment rate and profit rate. Without enough knowledge about RCCs' management, farmers will not make adequate disaster mitigation effort and without the supervision from RCCs' members (farmers), RCCs' staff will not have enough motivation to do efficient loan allocation to maximize profit rate. After the institutional reformation, with the efficient participation in RCCs' management, farmers' disaster mitigation effort, RCCs' sustainability and farmers' long-run utility will be increased at the same time. Furthermore, with full ability to decide loan allocation ratio, farmers can and actually do practice adequate investment strategy to maximize RCCs' profit rate and their own long-term utility.

As for the future work, we should investigate more circumstantially practical conditions of the inter-linkage market. To make the combination of microcredit system and inter-linkage market more practical and efficient, we should make it clear how inter-linkage market works in Chinese agricultural communities concretely. Then, based on local realities, we can formulate feasible principles and policies to monitor and promote the development of inter-linkage market with considering its potential and positive role in disaster risk financing in rural China.

Contribution of Group Loan to Sustainability of Agricultural Communities

Collaborative Development of Community Disaster-mitigation Infrastructure

Background

In China, more and more farmers move to urbanized areas because of the subsistence problem induced by natural disasters and an increase in income in urban areas. That makes the urbanization in China occur excessively fast. At the same time, too much farmland is occupied and the sustainability of agricultural communities is under a direct threat (Zhou, 2006). To mitigate the above problems, besides improving rural disaster risk transfer, the Central Government requires governments at all levels to develop the community-based disaster-mitigation infrastructure, such as early warning systems, shelters, emergency pre-plans, disaster mitigation facilities, and residents' awareness of disaster mitigation (the General Office of the State Council, 2007).

Unfortunately, farmers do not have enough motivation to develop the community-based disaster-mitigation infrastructure primarily for the following reasons (Chen, 2008).

(1) Farmers are too poor to be involved in developing the infrastructure. Although the disaster-mitigation infrastructure will make the post-disaster harvest enough for farmers' subsistence, its development takes time. Before the infrastructure is finished, the farmers' post-disaster harvest is still very low and cannot afford the infrastructure development and their own subsistence at the same time. So, farmers will face the subsistence problem if they spend money for infrastructure developing.

(2) Even if some farmers have enough money to develop the disaster-mitigation infrastructure, it will not be economical and efficient because their production scale is always very small.

On the other hand, there are potential incentives for farmers (including the former farmers working in cities) to develop community-based disaster-mitigation infrastructures. Firstly, infrastructure development will help increase their post-disaster harvest. Secondly, after collaborative work on the infrastructure, farmers' interpersonal relationships will become strengthened and active community knowledge and awareness on disaster mitigation will come out. This will improve the community's ability to conduct disaster mitigation and relief, such as mutual aid, special care for disadvantaged groups, and mutual enlightenment or comfort. All these things compose some kind of community culture (social capital at the community level) that will also increase farmers' post-disaster utility in rural areas. Obviously, the former farmers working in cities cannot benefit from the similar community culture existing among urban residents. It is impossible for them to be involved in urban community disaster-mitigation because they just work and live in urban areas provisionally (Zhao *et al.*, 2004; Li *et al.*, 2006; Liu, 2007; San, 2005). This means the development of the community disaster-mitigation infrastructure can increase farmers' post-disaster welfare and encourage former farmers working in cities to come back to their original agricultural communities and be involved in infrastructure developing. Then, the sustainability of agricultural communities will increase.

The group microcredit loan from RCCs has been supplying farmers with necessary funds for post-disaster reconstruction and restoring of production (Chen, 2008; Anhui Rural Credit Cooperative Union, 2007;

Zhuang and Wu, 2008). For example, after the earthquake in Sichuan, China on May 12, 2008, Jiulong Rural Credit Cooperative (in Wangcang County, Guangyuan City, Sichuan Province) supplied the affected farmers (who do not have a guarantee) with group loans for after-earthquake reconstruction (Chen, 2008). In order to mitigate the problem with shortage of funds necessary for developing disaster-mitigation infrastructures, some agricultural sectors of rural China started to apply the group loan supplied by RCCs to promote the development of the community-based disaster-mitigation infrastructure (Haiyan Rural Credit Cooperative Union, 2007; Haining Rural Credit Cooperative Union, 2007; Song, 2008; Wang, 2008). For example, in Cangxi County, Sichuan Province, China, RCCs supply farmers with group microcredit loans to support the collaborative development of small farmland water systems (Song, 2008). In general, the collaborative work is operated and managed by a union of households which consist of farmers from the same village or several adjacent villages. Farmers can invest in the collaborative development by way of money or labour. In the whole Cangxi County, based on this kind of mechanism, more than 1,700 small farmland water systems have been developed in 2007. And the mechanism, called "Cangxi Mode" is being extended in the whole Sichuan Province, especially the agricultural sectors where the local governments face financial difficulties.

Concern

To sum up, the key problem is stated as follows: Although the infrastructure can improve every farmer's welfare by increasing the post-disaster harvest and developing community culture, it is not economical and efficient for partial farmers to develop the infrastructure without the help of others. In other words, this requires collaborative work that also requires the participation and contribution of former farmers working in cities. On the other hand, although the welfare-improvement induced by the infrastructure is attractive to former farmers working in cities, they cannot come back to agricultural communities and take part in the development of the infrastructure because they cannot survive during the process of infrastructure development. So the major question is to figure out how to achieve the collaborative work by making former farmers survive during the process of infrastructure development, if some mechanism is designed based on community.

From the above statement, it follows that the group loan from RCCs can help rural disaster victims with disaster risk financing for subsistence and post-disaster reconstruction. This means farmers can refer themselves to group loans when they face the post-disaster subsistence problem under the situation where they are developing a disaster-mitigation infrastructure. So, with a view to relax the subsistence constraint and motivating collaborative development of infrastructure, let us consider how to make use of group loans in developing the disaster-mitigation infrastructure to improve community-based disaster mitigation and agricultural communities' sustainability in rural China.

Analyses

Here we only introduce the essence of our analyses. For the detail, please refer to Yu *et al.* (2008b). For simplification, a two-period model is constructed in this study. There are two farmers: *R* (skilled) and *P* (unskilled). Formal loan from RCCs is applicable only if the household can repay it after one-period time. With a disaster, *R* can survive through two periods, while *P* has to move to an urbanized area for subsistence. For developing the community-based disaster-mitigation infrastructure, *R* and *P* should work together. To help *P* to survive, *R* supplies *P* with internal subsidy. Correspondingly, *R* will require *P* to provide some labour for developing the infrastructure. So the internal subsidy here is one kind of inter-linked transaction between consumption and labour in informal financial market. At the same time, as an option, *R* can choose to obtain a group loan with *P* or just get an individual loan from RCCs. With involvement in the collaborative work for developing the community-based disaster-mitigation infrastructure, *R* and *P* will benefit from increased post-disaster harvest and the utility-rise induced by the community culture (the social capital at the community level). That will make the Pareto improvement possible and former farmers working in cities will have incentives to return their original community.

For comparative analysis, we have studied the following four cases :

(1) Case I : There is no disaster-mitigation infrastructure—If there is no community disaster-mitigation infrastructure, *R* consumes his production, while *P* leaves the community at

the beginning of period I and lives in an urban area because he knows that he would not be able to survive after a disaster in rural area.

(2) Case II : There is the disaster-mitigation infrastructure based on the individual loan from RCCs to *R*—If farmer *R* and *P* decide to develop a community disaster-mitigation infrastructure, *R* gets 1 unit loan from RCCs at the beginning of period I (it should be repaid at the end of period I) and invests it for the infrastructure. At the same time, *R* requests *P* to provide 1 unit labour for the infrastructure by promising to supply *P* with internal subsidy in the future. After a disaster, *R* supplies consumption goods to *P* to let *P* consume subsistence-level commodity at the end of period I. For his own subsistence in period 1, *R* borrows an individual loan from formal lender (RCCs) and repays it in period II.

(3) Case III : There is the disaster-mitigation infrastructure based on the group loan from RCCs to *R*—In this case, *R* borrows 1 unit loan (it should be repaid at the end of period I) from RCCs and invests it for the infrastructure at the beginning of period 1. At the same time, *R* requests *P* to provide 1 unit of labour for infrastructure by promising to supply *P* with internal subsidy in the future. As for subsistence in period I, *R* and *P* borrow the group loan from RCCs, that is just enough to make sure *R* and *P* can consume subsistence-level commodity in period I. And in period II, after repaying the group loan to RCCs, *R* supplies *P* with internal subsidy to let *P* consume subsistence-level commodity in period II.

(4) Case IV : Periodic wage in cities is high enough to make *R* has the incentive to migrate to urban areas.

After mathematical analysis, we got the following results :

(1) The application of the group loan can decrease *P's* dependence on *R*.
(2) The application of the group loan will not change community's loan demand.
(3) High periodical wage in cities will decrease the possibility for a sustainable community.

Summary

In this study, with a view to relax the subsistence constraint and promoting collaborative action among farmers, how to introduce the group loan in the community-based disaster-mitigation infrastructure development in rural China has been discussed. Besides making the comparative analysis between non-group-loan and group-loan cases, we have also studied the situation where the periodical wage in the urbanized area is high enough to motivate skilled farmers to migrate.

With the community-based disaster-mitigation infrastructure, the farmers' welfare will increase because of the increased post-disaster harvest and utility-rise induced by the community culture which is derived from collaborative work and involvement in the infrastructure development. Under the situation where *R* and *P* decide to develop the community-based disaster-mitigation infrastructure, the application of group loans can decrease *P's* dependence on *R*. This positive effect can make the collaborative development of the disaster-mitigation infrastructure also work in the rural areas where the community's ability to supply internal subsidy is relatively low. Furthermore, the application of the group loan will not increase the community's loan demand. The design of group loans just changes the way to allocate loans among the community. This is good news for rural development because the present loan supply in rural China is far from enough. If this idea of developing infrastructure by applying group loans induces an extra loan demand in rural China, it will become less practical. When the local agricultural production level is relatively low, the application of the group loan can expand the possibility for the development of the disaster-mitigation infrastructure, and for Pareto improvement and the sustainable community. Definitely, this positive effect induced by the group loan can make the idea of the collaborative infrastructure development suitable for more rural areas, especially the relatively undeveloped agricultural communities located in middle and western China. The high wage level in the cities will decrease the possibility for the development of the disaster-mitigation infrastructure, and for Pareto improvement and the sustainable community. Adequate attention should be given to improving and extending local conventional culture or functions when applying some innovative ideas to improve the community disaster-mitigation infrastructure. In other words, the complement between revised institutions and traditional functions is important and meaningful for disaster risk management in agricultural sectors of China.

Conclusion

In recent years, natural disaster has been becoming more and more frequent and tremendous. This unfortunate trend affects the whole world includes undeveloped countries such as India and China. The latter's economic losses induced by disaster has become the third biggest in the world, just after America and Japan. That drives a global focus and study on disaster risk management in rural areas, especially agricultural communities. Many new and innovative theories and ideas have been brought out such as the interaction between environmental change and disaster effect. Beyond that, scholars and research agree with that disaster risk management consists of two basic factors: updated ideas and adequate fund. As for agricultural communities, the main problems are vulnerability assessment, disaster risk financing and catastrophe insurance. For innovative methods for disaster risk financing, there are several available schemes such as national government-initiated scheme, local government-initiated scheme, NGO-initiated scheme and microfinance-initiated scheme. Because of its poor focus and continuous innovation, microcredit has been doing much positive effort on poverty mitigation and disaster prevention in the whole world, especially in agricultural communities. Besides its great diffusion, microcredit programmes face the following challenges in its future development and practice including its application and role in disaster risk management.

(1) Maintaining vision and commitment in the face of obstacles;
(2) Balancing development impact with financial sustainability;
(3) Identifying clear outcome goals and relevant performance measures;
(4) Defining the role and cost of technical assistance; and
(5) Developing efficient programmes operations.

Based on this thinking, in this chapter, we discussed the following topics through studying the cases of agricultural communities in China by theoretical models and mathematical analysis:

(1) How to apply microcredit loan in disaster risk management in rural China with integrated formal sectors, private sectors and the liquid farmland management right;

(2) How to improve the sustainability of microcredit loan and farmers' long-term welfare in agricultural communities of China; and

(3) How to improve rural disaster-mitigation infrastructure development and agricultural communities' sustainability with applying micro group loans from RCCs.

Firstly, by developing the risk management models in the agricultural villages of China, we investigated the effective coordination between the RCCs and the private financial sectors in the liquid market on the farmland management right. The circulation of the farmland management right makes the farmers' loan and disaster mitigation effort more homogeneous in equilibrium, that increases the ability of the RCCs and the private financial sectors to pool the risks, resulting in decrease in the risk premium included in the interest of the loan. Moreover, by making use of the private financing sectors' monitoring ability, farmers are less motivated to go into the moral hazard in disaster risk mitigation. In that sense, the microcredit system that leaves some roles for private financial sectors and the liquidation of the farmland management right complementarily work in the risk financing.

As for the future work, we should investigate more circumstantially practical conditions of the inter-linkage market. Moreover, we should take into account RCCs' operational strategy and interaction with the farmers.

Secondly, it has been studied how to improve Chinese agricultural communities' financial ability against disaster risk by increasing RCCs' sustainability and farmers' welfare through promoting farmers' efficient participation in RCCs' management and operation. Here efficient participation has two aspects :

(1) Comprehensive understanding of RCCs' new operation mechanism.

(2) Full ability to decide RCCs' loan allocation between different investments.

Farmers' long-run benefit depends on RCCs' sustainability, which is decided by the following factors :

(1) Repayment rate, which is determined by farmers' disaster mitigation effort.
(2) Profit rate which depends on RCCs' loan allocation among agricultural loan, safe investment and risky investment.

With farmers' efficient participation in RCCs' management and operation, RCCs' commercial sustainability and farmers' long-term welfare can be improved from the following aspects :

(1) With comprehensive understanding of RCCs' new operation mechanism, farmers will increase their disaster mitigation effort because farmers become aware that their disaster mitigation effort will affect RCCs' post-disaster commercial sustainability and their own long-run benefit.
(2) With full ability to decide loan allocation ratio, farmers can and actually do practice an adequate investment strategy to use capital market in order to maximize RCCs' profit rate, increase RCCs' financial ability against disaster (financing disaster losses by the return from capital market) and also improve their own long-term welfare.
(3) With efficient participation and supervision from farmers on RCCs' financial risk management, maintaining RCCs' main job of supporting agriculture, RCCs can make use of capital market to improve the sustainability while making farmers' long-run benefit free from the financial risk.

As for the future work related with this topic, we should figure out how to make farmers' efficient participation in RCCs' management and operation more realistic, practical and obtainable.

Finally, it has been studied how to improve disaster-mitigation infrastructure development and agricultural communities' sustainability in rural China by applying the group loan supplied by RCCs. With community-based disaster-mitigation infrastructure, farmers' welfare will increase because of increased post-disaster harvest, and utility-rise induced by the community culture (social capital at the community level) which is derived from collaborative work and involvement in developing infrastructure. That will encourage former farmers working in cities to come back to their original rural sectors; this makes agricultural communities more sustainable. But here arise two major obstacles for community-based disaster-mitigation infrastructure development in rural China : (i) subsistence constraint; (ii) welfare difference between rural and urban areas. The former makes agricultural communities unable to develop infrastructure. And the latter makes farmers (at least partial) not motivated to be involved in the collaborative development of infrastructures. Collaborative development of community-based disaster-mitigation infrastructure based on group loan can expand the possibility for the development of disaster-mitigation infrastructure, and for Pareto improvement and the sustainable community from the following aspects:

(1) The application of group loan can make collaborative development of disaster-mitigation infrastructure also work in the rural areas where community's ability to supply internal subsidy is relatively low.
(2) There will not be extra pressure on RCCs to supply much more loans to farmers when RCCs carry out group loans among agricultural communities to promote collaborative development of infrastructure.
(3) The application of group loan can make the idea of collaborative infrastructure development suitable for more rural areas, especially the relatively undeveloped agricultural communities located in middle and western China. First, the application of group loan will decrease the requirement on the community's ability to implement collaborative development of infrastructure. Second, the application of group loan can reduce the minimum amount of utility-rise for farmers to obtain enough incentives tc achieve collaborative development of infrastructure.
(4) Collaborative development of community-based disaster-mitigation infrastructure based on group loan also works in those agricultural communities located in relatively undeveloped provinces where industry cannot support agriculture and agricultural communities in terms of development.

Furthermore, the utility-rise induced by the community culture (social capital at the community level) which is derived from collaborative work and enjoyed by farmers together, is very important to reduce the welfare difference between rural and urban areas and give farmers enough motivation to be involved in the collaborative development of the disaster-mitigation infrastructure. In general, this kind of community culture is based on local interpersonal relationships or traditional functions. This means that adequate attention should be given to improving and extending local culture or conventional functions when applying some innovative ideas to improve the community-based disaster-mitigation infrastructure. In other words, the complement between revised institutions and traditional functions is important and meaningful for disaster risk management in agricultural sectors of China.

References

Anhui Rural Credit Cooperative Union: Opinion on Developing Microcredit to Support the Industry of Raising Living Pig, 2007. Available: http://www.china-ah.com/news/2007/11/20/136339.html

Arnold, M. and A. Kreimer: The socio-economic costs of disasters. In: Mathur, A., Burton, I., van Aalst, M. (Eds.), *An Adaptation Mosaic: An Example of Emerging Bank Work in Climate Change Adaptation*, Final Draft, Washington DC, World Bank Global Climate Change Team, The World Bank, pp. 5–14, 2004.

Baidu: *Household Contractual Management*, 2007, Available: http://baike.baidu.com/view/811095.htm.

Bardhan, P. and C. Udry: *Development Microeconomics*, Oxford University Press, 1999.

Bell, C.: Credit markets and interlinked transactions, in *Handbook of Development Economics*, Volume I, Edited by H. Chenery and T. N. Srinivasan. Netherlands: Elsevier Science B. V. 1988.

Benson, C., J. Twigg, and M. Myers,: NGO Initiatives in Risk Reduction: An Overview, *Disasters*, Vol. 25, No. 3, pp. 199-215, 2001.

Chen, L.Y.: Research on Disaster Prevention System in the Rural Area of Minbei, *Minbei Daily*, 2008 (the time refer to). Available: http://www.66163.com/Fujian_w/news/mbrb/041213/3_1.html

Chen, Y.Y. and X.G. Qiu: On Sustainability of Rural Microcredit in

China, *Journal of Southwest Agricultural University* (Social Science Edition), Vol. 4, No. 2, pp. 38-42, 2006.

Cochard, R., *et al.*: The 2004 tsunami in Aceh and Southern Thailand: A review on coastal ecosystems, wave hazards and vulnerability, Perspectives in Plant Ecology, Evolution and Systematics, Article in Press, Available online in 2007.

Fan, J.X.: Insurance Fund & Capital Market, *Journal of Henan Institute of Financial Management*, Vol. 2, pp. 59-62, 2005.

Haining Rural Credit Cooperative Union, 2007 (the time we did the survey to it).

Haiyan Rural Credit Cooperative Union, 2007 (the time we did the survey to it).

Hasan, M. Emrul. *SANMFI.* Dhaka, 1998.

Honohan, P.: Financial Sector Policy and the Poor: Selected Issues and Evidence, *World Bank Working Paper 43*, World Bank, Washington *DC, 2004.*

Ji, Y.R. and Zhang, C.C.: Property Right Analysis for the Reformation of Rural Credit Cooperatives, *Finance and Economy*, 2006(9), pp. 76-78, 2006.

Kawahara, S.: The Progress of the Rural Finance and the Character of Organization of Rural Credit Cooperatives in China—*Journal of Agricultural Policy Research*, No.9, pp.1-32, 2005a.

Kawahara, S.: *Legal Contents and Applied Legal Principles of Rights to Undertake to Manage Farmlands in China*, No.10, pp.1-32, 2005b.

Kumar, T.S.A. and J.K. Newport: Role of microfinance in disaster mitigation, *Disaster Prevention and Management*, Vol. 14, No. 2, pp. 176-182, 2005.

Li, M.S., D.L., Wang, F. Yan: An Exploratory Discussion on Preventing Agriculture Calamities in the Construction of New Rural Areas, *Chinese Journal of Agricultural Resources and Regional Planning*, No. 4, pp. 6-9, 2006.

Liang, Y.: Study on the Property Right System of Rural Credit Cooperatives, *Group Economy*, No. 215, pp. 213-214, 2006.

Linnerooth-Bayer, J., Amendola, A. N. Okada, and P.J. Shi: Disaster risk management: Pro-active financing to reduce vulnerability, *Environmental Hazards*, Vol. 7, No. 1, pp. 1-6, 2007.

Liu, Z.X.: Construction of public safety in community, *City and Disaster Mitigation*, No. 4, pp. 16-18, 2007.

Mapfumo, S.: *What are the Opportunities to Help Communities*

Reduce Disaster Risk and Adapt to Climate Change using microfinance? Presentation at the Red Cross Work Conference on Climate Change and Disaster Risk Reduction, The Hague, 22 June 2005.

National People's Congress of the People's Republic of China: *Law of the People's Republic of China on Land Contract in Rural Areas*, in 29th Meeting of the Standing Committee of the Ninth National People's Congress, 2002, Available: http://english.gov.cn/laws/2005-10/09 content_ 75300.htm.

OECD/GD: Microcredit in Transitional Economies. Paris: Territorial Development Service, Organization for Economic Co-operation and Development, OCDE/GD (96)40, 1996.

Parker, J. and Nagarajan, G.: Can Microfinance Meet the Poor's Financial Needs in Times of Natural Disaster?, *Microenterprise Best Practices (MBP)*, 2000, Available: http://www.gdrc.org/icm/disasters/Can_Microfinance_Meet_the_Poors_Financial_Needs.pdf.

Proshika: Accessed on February 14, 2008. Available: www.proshika.org

San, S.: Construction of Safe Community: Fundamental Engineering for Society's Disaster Reduction, *City and Disaster Mitigation*, No. 4, pp. 9-14, 2005.

Seibel, H.D.: History Matters in Microfinance, *International Journal of Microfinance and Business Development*, Vol. 14, No. 2, pp. 10-12, 2003.

SEWA: Accessed on February 14, 2008,
Available: www.sewahousing.org/eq-reconstruction4.htm

Shangguan, X.F.: *The Problems in the Property Right System and Operation Mechanism of Rural Credit Cooperatives and Corresponding Reformation Advice*, Jia Ge Yue Kan, 2006(11), pp. 15-17, 2006.

Song, S.X.: Cangxi Mode for the Development of Farmland Water Systems, *Farmer Daily*, 2008.
Available:http://www.agri.gov.cn/xxlb/t20080704_ 1076740.htm

Srinivas, H. and Y. Nakagawa: Environmental implications for disaster preparedness: Lessons Learnt from the Indian Ocean Tsunami, *Journal of Environmental Management*, Article in Press, 2007.

Tao, L.Q.: The Reformation of Rural Credit Cooperatives and the

Development of Agriculture Industrialization, *Productivity Research*, 2006(10), pp. 42-43, 67, 2006.

The General Office of the State Council: The Outline of China's Eleventh Five-Year Plan for National Integrated Disaster Mitigation, 2007.
Available: http://www.xjhm.gov.cn/shownews.asp?news_id=2805

UNISDR (United Nations International Strategy for Disaster Reduction): *Final report from the World Conference on Disaster Reduction*, Kobe, Hyogo, Japan, 18–22 January 2005.

Wang, Y.: The Problems in the Reformation and Development of Rural Credit Cooperatives and Corresponding Advice, *Xinan Finance*, 2006(12), pp. 35-36, 2006.

Wang, J.: Chongqing Rural Credit Cooperative's Loan Policy for Drought Resisting, *Chongqing Daily*, 2008.

Warner, K., L. Bouwer, M. and W. Ammann,: Financial services and disaster risk finance: Examples from the community level, *Environmental Hazards*, Vol. 7, No. 1, pp. 32-39, 2007.

Warner, K., S. Dannenmann, W. Ammann: Risk reduction (dis) incentives: Findings of a survey in Latin America. In: Jeggle, T. (Ed.), *Know Risk*. Tudor Rose, London, pp. 50-51, 2005.

Woodworth, W.: Microcredit in Post-Conflict, Conflict, Natural Disaster, and Other Difficult Settings. Canada: The Microcredit Summit Campaign in 2006.
Available: http://www.microcreditsummit.org/papers/Workshops/32_Woodworth.pdf.

Xiong, Y.: The requirement from South-Asian shipwreck on Chinese disaster insurance, *China Insurance*, Vol. 2, pp. 12-15, 2005.

Yan, S.-P.: Institution and Performance of China's Rural Finance in the Reform Period, St. Andrew's University, *Economic and Business Review*, Vol. 44-2, pp. 107-126, 2002.

Yang, L.: The characteristics and trend of the competitive pattern in Chinese insurance market, *China Insurance*, Vol. 4, pp. 14-17, 2005.

Ye, T., M. Yokomatsu, and N. Okada: Combined International and Intergenerational Disaster Risk Diversification: An Innovative Instrument for Government Intervention into the Private Disaster Insurance Programme, 2007 IEEE International Conference on Systems, *Man and Cybernetics*, 2008.

Yokomatsu, M., W.B. Yu, and N. Okada,: Micro Credit, Transaction of Farmland Management Right and Diversification of Disaster

Risk in Agricultural Villages in China, 2007 IEEE International Conference on Systems, *Man and Cybernetics*, 1776-1781, 2007.

Yu, W.B., M. Yokomatsu, and N. Okada,: Improvement of Micro-credit's Sustainability and Farmers' Welfare: The Study on the Institutional Reformation of Rural Credit Cooperatives in China, *Annuals of Disas*. Prev. Res. Inst., Kyoto Univ., 2008a.

Yu, W.B., M. Yokomatsu, and N. Okada,: Contribution of Group Loan to Sustainability of Chinese Agricultural Communities: Collaborative Development of Community Disaster-prevention Infrastructure, *The 21st EAROPH World Congress and Mayors'* Caucus, 2008b.

Zeller, M. and M. Sharma: Many borrow, more save, and all insure: implications for food and micro-finance policy, *Food Policy*, No. 25, pp. 143-167, 2000.

Zhang, L.Z.: Reform Achievements and Systematical Reflection on Present Rural Credit Cooperatives, *Reform*, 2006(12), pp. 43-48, 2006.

Zhang, P.Y.: The saturation in Chinese insurance market, *Market Forum*, Vol. 3, pp. 51-52, 2004.

Zhao, B.: The segmentation model for Chinese insurance market, *Economical Sciences*, Vol. 4, pp. 46-54, 2004.

Zhao, S.Q.,Y. Zhou, and S.L. Zhao: Study on Mechanism of Earthquake Prevention and Disaster Reduction in Urban Community in China, City and Disaster Mitigation, No. 6, pp. 10-12, 2004.

Zheng, L.L.: Five main characteristics of Chinese insurance market, *China Insurance*, Vol. 8, pp. 6, 2005.

Zhou, M.J.: What Kind of Urbanization We Need, *China Development Observation*, 2006.

Zhuang, Y. and X.Y. Wu: Zhouning Rural Credit Cooperative Supports Restoring Spring Ploughing, *Fujian Dongnan News Net*, 2008. Available: http://www.fjsen.com/fujian/2008-03/06/content_440211.htm.

3

School Emergency Response Training in Pueblo, Colorado (USA)

HALEY RICH AND ILAN KELMAN

Building and maintaining local capability for preventing and dealing with disasters requires support and action from individuals through global organizations and many examples exist around the world of local teams for disaster risk reduction. This chapter reports on one programme for local disaster teams which is directed at secondary school students: School Emergency Response Training which started in 2003 at Pueblo West High School in Pueblo, Colorado, USA. The basis and history of the programme are discussed along with the curriculum and the programme's demonstrated success in saving lives. This material provides templates which can be used to develop and run other similar programmes, as long as the material and teaching approach is localised for each specific location.

Local Teams for Disasters

Building and maintaining local capability for preventing and dealing with disasters requires support and action at all space scales, from individuals and families through national governments and global organisations. However, while top-down guidance and support are useful for many aspects, such as providing resources and standardising legal and policy frameworks, the most successful outcomes tend to be seen with initiative and involvement at the local level (e.g., Lewis, 1999; Twigg, 1999-2000; Wisner *et al.*, 2004a). Community-based work is not a panacea (Cooke and Kothari, 2001; Kennedy *et al.*, 2008) but is an essential part of the processes of disaster risk reduction, community development and sustainability—and of linking all these processes.

Many examples exist of community-based teams and programmes for implementing disaster risk reduction at the local level (Table 3.1). The rationale for such teams is that, following a major event, external help is unlikely to arrive for at least 72 hours (EMA, 2003; FEMA, 2004), including for immediate emergency response tasks such as rescuing people from buildings and giving emergency medical assistance. Recently, many emergency managers have been suggesting that households and communities should be self-sufficient for one or two weeks at minimum after a major event. For instance, a pandemic or a terrorist attack releasing biological, chemical, or nuclear contaminants might make it unsafe to travel for that length of time.

Table 3.1: Examples of Community-Based Disaster Risk Reduction Teams and Programmes

Location	*Programme Name*
Asia	Townwatching (Ogawa *et al.*, 2005)
Australia	Community Fireguard (Boura, 1998)
General	Disaster-resistant and quality-of-life community (Geis, 2000)
General	Shanghai Principles (https://training.fema.gov/EMIWeb/downloads/Theshanghai-principles.doc)
Japan	Jishu-bosai-soshiki (Bajek *et al.*, 2008)
Taiwan	Integrated Community-Based Disaster Management Programme (Chen *et al.*, 2006)
Turkey	Community Disaster Volunteer Training Programme (Petal *et al.*, 2008)
USA	Community Emergency Response Teams (CERTs; Flint and Brennan, 2006; Simpson, 2001)
USA	Relocalisation (Kelman and Karnes, 2007; Kelman, 2008)
USA	Wingspread Principles (http://www.smartcommunities.ncat.org/wingspread2/wingprin.shtml)

Other events suggest that people might need to be ready to evacuate at short notice at any time and be prepared to be away from their community for weeks. A hurricane often provides hours of lead-time for evacuation, but in the case of chemical spills or tsunamis, there might only be minutes of warning that large areas must be evacuated without knowing when return will be feasible. For volcanoes, many case studies document citizens receiving hours of notice that their entire community was being moved and would stay away for months, without knowing if return might be feasible (e.g. Chester, 1993).

This chapter reports on a programme for local disaster training and teams that is directed at secondary school students, especially youth between the ages of 15 and 18. It is called School Emergency Response Training (SERT) and the programme started in 2003 at Pueblo West High School in Pueblo, Colorado, USA, a city of 100,000 people. Because the programme is aimed at teenagers in secondary school, the name used is Teen SERT. The text in this chapter focuses on the experience of Pueblo West High School.

Schools, being centres of learning amongst other community activities, are considered to be important places for disaster-related education (Gordon *et al.*, 1999; Ronan and Johnston, 2005; Wisner, 2006). In recent years, immense effort has been put into making schools safe, not just keeping the structure sound during a disaster event, but also embracing the wider definition of "safety" to make schools feel secure and to encourage learning about safety, security, and disasters (Kelman, 2007; OECD, 2004; Wisner *et al.*, 2004b). As such, the Teen SERT programme ensures the intersection between disaster-related education, school safety, and community disaster response while training the next generation to be responsible citizens who care about and contribute to their community.

CERT and Teen SERT

The USA's CERT programme (Table 3.1) is run by the Federal Emergency Management Agency (FEMA), which is the USA's national disaster risk reduction agency, using the model created in 1985 by the Los Angeles City Fire Department (for more background to CERT, see Flint and Brennan, 2006; Simpson, 2001). Since 1994, FEMA has promoted nationwide use of the CERT programme leading to its establishment in hundreds of communities. The programme is most often implemented by community-based groups or municipal authorities and is designed to target the general population.

Yet pre-teens and young adults, generally the age of secondary school students, tend to be more receptive to basic citizenship-building initiatives. Creating a Teen SERT curriculum-based programme offers opportunities to extend such education by mentoring others through the school's clubs and organisations, as well as through offering opportunities to include the parents and relatives of the Teen SERT students in the training and exercises. The Teen SERT programme is thus targeted at youth, but is based on the more general CERT curriculum.

An additional benefit of Teen SERT is the opportunity to track graduates beyond high school. These data could be used to determine if the early introduction to Teen SERT through a mandatory school curriculum has an effect on choosing a career or volunteer work in the field of first response, other disaster-related endeavours, or wider community work. That can also help in planting the seed for establishing or joining CERT programmes in the Teen SERT school's community or in communities where the students migrate, such as for university or jobs. Where CERT programmes already exist, Teen SERT has provided a cadre of trained and interested volunteers rather than having to start at the beginning with early career professionals who are often struggling to balance starting a family with establishing a career.

The core Teen SERT programme has three main goals. First, to provide students with a knowledge base on the causes and effects of disasters. Second, to build decision-making and problem-solving skills and strategies to help students make informed decisions regarding disaster risk reduction for themselves and their communities. Third, to provide students with hands-on training using reality-driven drills and exercises.

Forming Teen SERT

Starting a major community programme from the beginning is not easy. To ensure that this chapter records the lessons from Teen SERT for others to use, the rest of this section is a personal perspective from this chapter's first author (Haley Rich from Pueblo, Colorado) regarding her experience in founding Teen SERT and seeing the idea through to its successful implementation at Pueblo West High School. As such, this section provides a first-hand account of the long process and how to continue with that process, despite common frustrations and obstacles. The events in this section were in 1998 unless otherwise noted.

My first presentation opportunity came in early spring, when North Mesa Elementary School's Principal, John Musso, requested develop an emergency preparedness programme for his primary school pupils. I recognized this request as an opportunity and I evaluated the best approach to take in order to effectively communicate emergency preparedness skills to such a young audience, in addition to reaching the students' parents with the information.

The first step in emergency preparedness is to determine the potential disaster risks to which a community is exposed. Steve Douglas, Director of the Pueblo County Department of Emergency Management (PCDEM), described those to me as being an incident at the Pueblo Chemical Depot, transportation of nuclear waste and chemicals on a nearby highway (Interstate 25), corporations in Pueblo who produce and/or transport hazardous materials, tornadoes, floods, thunderstorms (lightning), moderate earthquakes, winter weather (especially blizzards and ice), and wildfire.

I then researched information about emergency preparedness for Pueblo's risks. Karen Ashcraft, Coordinator of the PCDEM, provided information from FEMA, Civil Defense Agency, and the Colorado Office of Emergency Management. Numerous interviews provided additional information and then began the next step: evaluating my potential audience.

Coincidentally during this phase, Pueblo experienced a disastrous flood, Oklahoma was hit by a devastating tornado, and a massacre occurred at Columbine High School in Jefferson County, Colorado, near Denver. I noticed the effect that these events had on my own young children. They asked many questions regarding why and how the disasters occurred, in addition to making insecure statements about their own safety in their schools. I approached their teachers requesting how they are responding to the children's questions at school. The need for developing emergency preparedness education became a priority for me, as their response was, "How can we explain something to the children that we can't understand ourselves?"

After some planning and further interviews of teachers and students at North Mesa Elementary School, I developed two programmes for different ages with the same messages :

- Emergency preparedness for floods and tornadoes.
- The difference between a watch and a warning.
- How to evaluate a situation, including determining the safest place to go and the best physical positions to take for protection.

- Mentioning the recent disasters and the power of knowing what to do in an emergency which helps to ensure their safety.

Each class was given printed material to share with their parents and instructed to return and tell me what their parents determined was the safest place in their home to go in case of a tornado. From kindergarten until grade 3, the students received a colourful PCDEM calendar. Students from grades 3-5 received the "Are You Prepared?" booklet issued by FEMA (the current edition is FEMA, 2004) with detailed instructions on how to prepare for many different types of emergencies (so grade 3 students received both).

The delivery of my presentation was structured differently to ensure complete understanding by the younger students. This presentation involved visual prompts in addition to verbal instruction. A volunteer from the audience put on a large dark-coloured poncho to represent a tornado. Four other volunteers became "responders" as they put on my FEMA and Pueblo Emergency Response Teams (PERT) T-shirts. The "tornado" twirled and made noise and as it approached the children, they enacted the tornado-safe position of lying facedown on the floor with their hands cupped on the back of their heads. The "responders" were the leaders of the tornado drill and led the children to safe positions in the school.

Also, during the tornado portion of the presentation, we pretended that we were on Grandpa's farm, in the middle of the pasture, with no shelter available, as much of the area around the school is farmland. In every field, there is a drainage ditch. Drainage ditches have slopes, therefore, the children were instructed to lie down in the tornado position on the downward sloping area of the ditch, on the opposite side of the approaching tornado.

With the recent flooding in Pueblo, many of the children were animated in their participation. They shared experiences of being evacuated and identified my PERT T-shirt as the people who evacuated them in the flood. This unexpected participation added enormous interest of the children to the programme and credibility to my presence as I was also wearing my PERT T-shirt.

Evaluating the presentations was simple. I made myself available for three days at the school during lunches and breaks. Groups of children surrounded me, eager to share their parents' comments and they also asked questions. Teachers approached me expressing appreciation for the education that they had received. Many children stopped me in public and introduced me to their parents, grandparents, and other family members. Often the family members asked me questions and shared experiences of their own.

Deciding to develop a standard presentation for use of all ages was difficult. Using local and national information sources, and checking with emergency managers and teachers, helped me immensely. Following some further presentations, Pueblo County Commissioner John Klomp phoned me. He had been a judge during the recent "Community Pride Week" event also held at North Mesa Elementary School. During the event, he was informed of the activities regarding emergency preparedness that were held, in addition to the guidebook. He requested, we meet for lunch that same day.

I reviewed with Commissioner, Klomp all the information I had compiled over the previous months and the activities I had participated in, coordinated, and implemented in my determination to promote individual emergency preparedness. He explained to me his vision of expanding the information into a series of television programmes that would be shown on the local governmental television channel. We brainstormed the vast opportunities for education that this avenue of exposure could offer. He requested that I become a member of a task force he has appointed that would continue to develop emergency preparedness programmes for Pueblo County.

Shortly, after meeting with Commissioner, Klomp, I was deployed by FEMA to respond to floods elsewhere in Colorado, during which I met FEMA employees Venice Hollis and Heather Leigh. Venice revealed her interest in developing emergency preparedness in her local community in Washington, D.C., so I shared my recent experiences and gave her copies of every paper I had written on the subjects as well as a copy of the guidebook.

On 2nd July, 1999, Commissioners, John Klomp and Loretta Kennedy informed me of their plans to implement emergency preparedness education as part of the school curriculum for the Pueblo County School Districts. My guidebook would be used as a resource in the development of the emergency preparedness programmes. From these initiatives, it was a small step towards formulating Teen SERT, as discussed in this chapter.

Teen SERT Curriculum

The Teen SERT programme is instinctive in its approach in that specially trained, primary responders participate in the classroom lessons. The responders cover emergency medical, search and rescue, law enforcement, firefighting and emergency management services. Teen SERT students hear about firsthand accounts of experiences with a wide variety of situations. This aspect of the programme not only intrigues the students but also helps them to foster a positive relationship between the students and public safety agencies and organizations, thereby building community spirit in the long-term.

The standardized curriculum offered by FEMA is thus adjusted to include the local hazards and vulnerabilities that exist in each specific location. For example, despite the threat of volcanic ash from the northwest USA, volcanic eruptions tend to less important for Colorado than snowstorms; however, it is important not to entirely eliminate the possibility of certain events because people travel and move, so they must be aware of and prepared for any hazard.

This curriculum is not meant to replace those of previously established initiatives. Rather, it incorporates them in their entirety and focuses on increasing knowledge and skills in seven disaster-related areas: (1) cognitive information, (2) recognizing hazards, (3) planning skills, (4) consequential thinking and risk taking, (5) team-building and communication skills, (6) decision making, and (7) individual responsibilities within the community. Some of these lessons focus on raising awareness in skill areas, while others emphasize their practical application. The lessons provide factual information about disasters, with an emphasis on recognising and mitigating hazards and vulnerabilities, as well as teaching basic response and recovery skills through role playing and other techniques.

Samples from the Teen SERT course from Pueblo West High School in Colorado are given in Appendix I. This model requires approximately 45 hours to complete and teaches students to:

1. Describe the types of hazards most likely to affect their homes and communities.
2. Describe the functions of CERTs and their roles in immediate personal response.
3. Take steps to prepare themselves for a disaster.

4. Identify and reduce potential fire hazards in their homes and workplaces.
5. Apply basic fire suppression strategies, resources, and safety measures.
6. Apply basic first aid techniques for opening breathing airways, controlling bleeding, and treating shock.
7. Conduct triage under simulated conditions.
8. Perform head-to-toe assessments for first aid's casualty assessment.
9. Employ basic treatments for various wounds, including bandaging and splinting.
10. Identify planning and assess requirements for potential search and rescue situations.
11. Describe the most common techniques for searching a structure.
12. Use safe techniques for debris removal and victim extrication.

In addition to the training time and materials development, programme support is required for equipment and supplies. Sponsorship or donations might need to be found for medical and first aid supplies, hard hats, vests, safety goggles, fire extinguishers, gloves, backboards or scoops and neck guards for suspected spinal injuries, bindings and straps, blood pressure equipment including stethoscopes, CPR dolls for training, dust masks, alcohol swabs for hygiene and disinfection, and other items as per the needs of the specific school and programme.

For teaching the curriculum, students are grouped into teams and complete the course as a unit. Homework assignments often include the parents or guardians of the students, such as creating an emergency family communication plan and preparing household emergency kits or evacuation bags (see also Risk RED, 2007). Lectures are always balanced with practical table-top and team-building exercises to ensure that practical skills are not taught by sitting at one's desk.

As the final test of the course, a disaster simulation is staged at the school to allow students to apply their newly acquired skills in a realistic environment with multiple casualties. The trained students choose their Incident Commander while the Drama Club plans the scenario and provides the "victims" that are "moulaged" to add realism.

Moulage refers to the art of using make-up for fake injuries, from burns to impalements, and the results look shockingly realistic, supported by the theatrics of the "victims" screaming in pain and calling for help.

In one year, one student responder could not complete the exercise due to the intensity and realism of the situation. The possibility of students being disturbed and upset by the exercise must be carefully monitored. During the exercise, adults and teachers monitor the situation for safety and to evaluate the students, but the entire disaster response and first aid treatment is carried out by the students. As well, the adults and teachers play an important role in documenting the exercise, through photos and videos, which significantly assists in future promotion of the programme, accountability for funds and time spent, and reviews for improving the programme.

Key skills learned and practiced throughout the curriculum, particularly emphasised by the final exercise, are :

- Recognizing the potential hazards associated with a particular type of event in order to take appropriate action.
- Taking steps to get to safety and to help others to do so in a more organized fashion.
- Assuming a leadership role with those who are not trained to deal with the event.
- Triaging casualties and administering first aid.
- Identifying, organising, and using available resources.
- Performing needs assessments and then documenting and communicating needs to local authorities.
- Allowing better allocation of emergency resources by assessing and monitoring a situation and properly advising emergency responders.
- Deferring to and assisting emergency response authorities upon their arrival.

To maintain the level of training and the students' interest, the students must realise that they are an integral part of the school's support base in a real situation in addition to participating in other outreach and leadership opportunities. Therefore, students and graduates will be asked to periodically attend activities and public gatherings, to staff exhibits, to hand out literature, and to help in the outreach efforts for Teen SERT. Independent study courses and continuing education will be encouraged and supported.

To further evaluate the effectiveness of the programme, a quiz of emergency response questions (Appendix II) is given to each class at the beginning of the programme to determine each student's level of understanding of emergency planning and response. At the end of the programme, the same quiz is given in order to provide comparative measures. The result is usually a significant increase in the number of students who get correct answers.

An open-ended survey is also given to the students to find out whether or not they enjoyed the course and to identify the good and bad parts of it, in order to improve. Appendix III gives the results from the answers of one class in Pueblo, Colorado.

To promote the "Train-the-Trainer" concept of CERT and to keep the teenagers' interest in the programme and the community, opportunities are given for students involved in leadership organizations, such as their school's Student Council, to develop and implement emergency preparedness educational outreach programmes for the area's younger students, through middle and elementary schools. Through this mentoring approach, these programmes provide leadership experience to the students and help to share the knowledge with all ages in the community.

Partnerships can also be developed with local businesses to allow access to creative efforts employed throughout the commercial sector while seeking sponsors for Teen SERT. Businesses benefit from the public relations visibility and from being better connected to their own community, as is often identified regarding corporate social responsibility for disaster risk reduction (Twigg, 2001).

Successes of Teen SERT and Beyond

Demonstrating the successes of Teen SERT, Table 3.2 provides examples of Pueblo West High School Teen SERT graduates using their skills. The programme started in 2003 and is now mandatory for all ninth graders. One student commented "I would go home and share the information with my parents. It was almost as if my entire family completed the programme with me." A teacher remarked "With Teen SERT, teens are no longer feeling helpless. They now feel like they can help and save lives."

Table 3.2: Examples of Teen SERT Graduates using their Skills

Year	*Teen SERT Individual*	*Incident*
2004	16-year old	Recognized heart attack symptoms and took family member to the hospital.
2004	16-year old with Down's Syndrome	Used stomach thrusts to stop her 7-month old nephew from choking.
2005	16-year old	Recognized heart attack symptoms and took family member to the hospital.
2006	15-year old	Used stomach thrusts to stop her little sister from choking on a small toy.
2006	15-year old	While the student was skiing, a snowboarder fell, resulting in a compound fracture to his arm. The student splinted his arm, stabilized him, and helped him to the bottom of the slope.
2007	15-year old	Awoke to the smell of gas, covered her and her younger sister's mouths and noses and went outside. While her mother was on the phone calling for help, her mother fainted from breathing the fumes. The student covered her mother's mouth and nose and carried her from the house using a blanket for transport.
2007	15-year old	Pulled an unresponsive 4-year old boy from a swimming pool and revived the child by clearing the airway.

The skills learned and spirit generated by Teen SERT have also permeated other aspects of community life, leading to assistance beyond emergency response and disasters. In Pueblo, Colorado, as part of the community approach to Teen SERT, students at Skyview Middle School were encouraged to support the *Make A Difference Day* project in order to learn the value of community service. Over 140 seventh grade students participated for three weeks in *Make a Difference Day* by performing activities that not only supported the community, but also had a positive impact in their own homes with their own families.

Examples of activities were picking up trash around homes and schools and in parks, gathering needed items for an emergency shelter, volunteering at an animal shelter, visiting a local senior care centre, raising funds for a family in need, and holding doors open for and helping the elderly with their shopping bags. Activities were done daily in order to report them in class the following day. Students were organized in teams that planned activities as a group, either to do them together or to conduct the same activity in separate locations. The school administration requested information about the planned team activities to be able to help with parents' questions and to provide overall support.

Outstanding activities were chosen by staff and students to be recognized by a small reward such as plastic toys (spiders, snakes, or insects) or collectable coins. Acts of good behaviour in the classroom were rewarded with star stickers. Daily conversations took place with parents to determine if the students' behaviour influenced their households. Parents reported positive reactions and support for the project.

A long-term impact was also witnessed because many students continued their activities after *Make A Difference Day* ended, including forming a community-based group to pick up litter, to visit seniors, and to volunteer at the animal shelter. A major part involved mentoring younger students in positive behaviour, academics, and overall community and social development, therefore, also providing a template for the younger students' higher education and future community service.

Conclusions

The successes from Teen SERT provide important templates which are now available to be applied to other Teen SERT programmes around the world—as long as the material and teaching approach is localised for each specific location. Other, independent endeavours already emulate the approach and success of Teen SERT.

In Fiji, *Tadra Kahani* is a national show developed by 6-19 years old and their teachers by selecting one United Nations Millennium Development Goal (UN, 2000) in order to dramatize or choreograph its meaning. This approach reaches, in order, educators, youth, the youth's families, their wider community, the national level, and—by making it an annual tourist event and by advertising it through the national airline Air Pacific—visitors to the country. This idea could be emulated for disaster risk reduction themes.

In Nepal, the National Society for Earthquake Technology (http://www.nset.org.np) uses a simple shake table to demonstrate in public that a scale-model standard house collapses in the same earthquake in which a scale-model earthquake-resistant house survives (see also

Petal *et al.*, 2008). This powerful visual display captures interest for explaining the principles of earthquake-resistant buildings and the low cost and relative simplicity of retrofitting. Witnesses then gossip to their neighbours and communities about what they saw, generating a collective will for action. As with *Tadra Kahani*, an awareness chain, formal and informal, is created to disseminate the information throughout the community. The distant form of disaster is made relevant to day-to-day activities, as is the basis of Teen SERT.

The principles and practices of these disaster-and-development-related endeavours apply directly to community-based work for other development, environment, and sustainability endeavours. The "community teams" concept, as drawn directly from the disaster risk reduction work shown in Table 3.1, applies to communities tackling longer-term trends such as desertification and climate change; communities tackling day-to-day concerns such as water, food, energy, and health; and communities tackling deeper causes of these challenges manifesting such as poverty, injustice, and inequity.

Preparing for and dealing with crisis often develops a sense of camaraderie and trust amongst those involved. Specific disaster-related skills in first aid, building rescue, and water rescue help to save lives in the immediate aftermath of a specific event, but also foster the ability to address other challenges, to create a community which works together irrespective of the threat, and to apply collaborative, grassroots values and attitudes to any challenge.

Interest is often generated for developing community skills and community spirit by highlighting high profile events, such as hurricanes and earthquakes, or by placing the work within the context of contemporary paradigms, however, artificial and unhelpful they might be, such as the USA's focus on terrorism and "homeland security". Maintaining that disaster-related interest can be harder without specific events or when paradigms change. In contrast, ever-present day-to-day concerns maintain the needed momentum by using the community teams' talents and energy for other activities, whether that be picking up litter or conducting vulnerability assessments to inspire action for vulnerability reduction.

Such teams could then be called "Community Sustainability Teams" (CSTs) developed through Community Sustainability Training. The teams would be available to undertake flexible and varying projects by learning and expanding their skill set and expertise. By starting with School Sustainability Training for teenagers

(Teen SST), the advantages from Teen SERT are apparent: teenagers bring these ideas home to their families and learn leadership and community participation by teaching the skills, values, and behaviour to even younger students. The result is a true community basis for building and maintaining local capability for preventing and dealing with disasters.

Abbreviations

CERT	Community Emergency Response Teams
CST	Community Sustainability Teams
FEMA	Federal Emergency Management Agency
PCDEM	Pueblo County Department of Emergency Management
PERT	Pueblo Emergency Response Team
Teen SERT	Teen School Emergency Response Training

References

Bajek, R., Y. Matsuda, and N. Okada. (2008) Japan's *Jishu-bosai-soshiki* community activities: Analysis of its role in participatory community disaster risk management. *Natural Hazards*, 44(2): 281-292.

Boura, J. (1998): Community Fireguard: Creating Partnerships with the Community to Minimise the Impact of Bushfire. *Australian Journal of Emergency Management*, 13(3): 59-64.

Chen, L.-C., Y.-C. Liu, and K.-C. Chan.(2006) Integrated Community-Based Disaster Management Programme in Taiwan: A Case Study of Shang—A Village. *Natural Hazards*, 37: 209-223.

Chester, D.K. (1993). *Volcanoes and Society*. Edward Arnold, London.

Cooke B. and U. Kothari. (2001). *Participation: The New Tyranny?* Zed Books, London.

EMA. (2003). *Preparing for the Unexpected*. EMA (Emergency Management Australia), Canberra.

FEMA (2004). *Are You Ready? An In-depth Guide to Citizen Preparedness*. FEMA (Federal Emergency Management Agency), Washington, DC.

Flint, C. and Brennan. M. (2006): Community Emergency Response Teams: From Disaster Responders to Community Builders. *Rural Realities*, 1(3): 1-9.

Geis, D. (2000): By design: The disaster-resistant and quality-of-life community. *Natural Hazards Review*, 1(3): 151-160.

Gordon, N.S., Farberow, N.L. and Maida, C.A. (1999). *Children and Disasters*. Taylor and Francis, Philadelphia.

Kelman, I. (ed.) (2007): Earthquake Safety of Schoolchildren. Special issue of *Regional Development Dialogue*, 28(2).

Kelman, I. (2008): Relocalising Disaster Risk Reduction for Urban Resilience. *Urban Design and Planning*, in press.

Kelman, I. and E. Karnes (2007). Relocalising Disaster Risk Reduction in Boulder, Colorado. *Australian Journal of Emergency Management*, 22(1): 18-25.

Kennedy, J., J. Ashmore, E. Babister, and I. Kelman (2008). The Meaning of 'Build Back Better': Evidence from Post-tsunami Aceh and Sri Lanka. *Journal of Contingencies and Crisis Management*, 16(1): 24-36.

Lewis, J. (1999): *Development in Disaster-prone Places: Studies of Vulnerability*. Intermediate Technology Publications, London.

OECD. (2004): *Keeping Schools Safe in Earthquakes*. OECD (Organisation for Economic Cooperation and Development), Paris.

Ogawa, Y., A.L. Fernandez, and T. Yoshimura. (2005): Town watching as a Tool for Citizen Participation in Developing Countries: Applications in Disaster Training. *International Journal of Mass Emergencies and Disasters*, 23(2): 5-36.

Petal, M., R. Green, I. Kelman, R. Shaw and A. Dixit (2008): Community-based construction for disaster risk reduction. Chapter 10, pp. 191-217 in Bosher L. (ed.), *Hazards and the Built Environment: Attaining Built-in Resilience*, Taylor and Francis, London.

Risk, RED (2007): Community-based Disaster Preparedness Worldwide. Poster at the *Annual Hazards Research and Applications Workshop*, Boulder, Colorado, 11-12 July 2007, http://www.riskred.org

Ronan, K. and D. Johnston. (2005) *Promoting Community Resilience in Disasters: The Role for Schools, Youth, and Families*. Springer, New York.

Simpson, D. (2001). Community Emergency Response Training (CERTs): A Recent History and Review. *Natural Hazards Review*, 2(2): 54-63.

Twigg, J. (1999-2000). The Age of Accountability?: Future Community Involvement in Disaster Reduction. *Australian Journal of Emergency Management*, 14(4): 51-58.

Twigg, J. (2001). *Corporate Social Responsibility and Disaster Reduction: A Global Overview*. Benfield UCL Hazard Research Centre, London.

UN (2000): *Millennium Development Goals*. United Nations, New York http://www.un.org/millenniumgoals

Wisner, B. (2006): *Let Our Children Teach Us! A Review of the Role of Education and Knowledge in Disaster Risk Reduction*. Books for Change, India.

Wisner, B., P. Blaikie, T. Cannon, and I. Davis (2004a): *At Risk: Natural Hazards, People's Vulnerability and Disasters*, 2nd edition. Routledge, London.

Wisner, B., I. Kelman, T. Monk, J.K. Bothara, D. Alexander, A.M. Dixit, D. Benouar, O.D. Cardona, R.C. Kandel, and M. Petal. (2004b): *School Seismic Safety: Falling Between the Cracks?* Radix, August 2004, http://www.radixonline.org/resources/school-seismic-safety-august2004.doc.

Appendix I

Teen SERT Course Samples

Based on the course at Pueblo West High School in Pueblo, Colorado, the Teen SERT training curriculum is designed to cover the following:

- Disaster Preparedness.
- Fire and firefighting safety.
- Disaster medical operations.
- Triage.
- Treating life threatening injuries.
- Light search and rescue.
- Disaster psychology.
- Terrorism.
- Moulage.
- Federal disaster declaration process (USA specific).
- Communication using the local emergency number service (e.g. 911 in the USA and Canada, 999 in the UK, 112 across Europe, 111 in New Zealand, and 000 in Australia).
- Hazardous materials.
- Responder roles and opportunities for youth involvement.
- Final exercise of a full-scale disaster simulation.

The specifics of any curriculum should be designed to match the local situation.

On the first day of the course, give the first quiz (Appendix II) and an overview of the programme:

- Citizen Corps programme explanation.
- CERT module explanation.
- The USA's Federal Declaration Process and the need for 72 hours or more of self-sufficiency.

- Activity: Identifying fears. Write, in order of priority, your top five fears. Then, collect and discuss the top common fears.
- Movie: *Youth Engaged in Homeland Security.*
- Share experiences, why Teen SERT and CERT were started.
- Homework: *Are You Ready?* manual (FEMA, 2004) introduced along with the manual's list of items to be found around the house and placed in an emergency kit. Parents should participate in the homework and sign the appropriate page in the manual. Parents and students should establish a communications plan with a local number and an out-of-state number identified in case they are separated during an emergency. The people at these numbers are contacted and asked if they mind being contacts, if parents and students are ever separated during an emergency. Both parents and students write down these numbers and put them in a place that will always be close by (e.g. purse, wallet). Note that cell phones might not work in an emergency.
- Later, periodically call out in class, "Communications Plan" and when students produce the numbers, they receive extra credit.

Disaster Preparedness Module

- *Activity*: Have the students break into groups of six and tell them that they are at their leader's house having a pizza and movie party. Your parents are in another location, but they know about the party and its location. The forecast is blizzard conditions, but we live in Colorado and that always means the weather is always changing, so why worry? You start your movies and are having so much fun, that you don't notice how heavy the snow is falling. You begin to hear the wind increasing, but you're having so much fun that you ignore it. Six hours later, you are in trouble. The power goes out, there is no running water, no heat, no cell phone service, no telephone service, and no sanitation (toilet). You are on your own for at least minimum six days. Plus, you can't open doors or windows due to snow and there is no chance for any outside contact, including responders. As a team, decide the following and assign a speaker to deliver your decisions :

- What do you need to survive? Where are you going to get it? They just did the disaster supplies identification homework, so all should know the answers.
- What are you going to eat? What should you eat first? Drink? Where are you going to get water? Should you use water for sanitation?
- How will you stay warm? Where are you going to go to the bathroom? What are you going to do for entertainment?

Let them talk for a few minutes, then say, "One of your members is diabetic. How do you plan for that?" A few minutes, then say, "Uh-oh! One of your members has never used a manual (non-electric) can opener and they just slit their wrist. What are you going to do?" Have them present their decisions from each group.

- Homework: During this module, they need to read the *Are You Ready?* manual (FEMA, 2004).
- Movie: *Shelter in Place* by Agrium.

Fire Safety Module :

- Homework: With parents participating, design a fire evacuation plan which means including the layout of their home with a route drawn for evacuating. Require the parent's signature on plan.
- Optional movie: *Backdraft*.

Other options :

- Weather spotting.
- What to expect when dialling the local emergency number (a dispatcher overview).
- More speciality situations for safety and rescues (e.g., water, ice, cliffs, caves).

Family lessons, for schools, homes, and in the community:

- Family disaster plan.
- Emergency kits.
- Emergency evacuation bag.
- Lockdown procedures and practices.
- Safety scan: Fire extinguisher status evaluation and hazards such as electricity, gas, and chemicals.

Appendix II

Quiz Given Before and After the Course

Name: ______________________ Date: ______________________
Organization/School/Neighbourhood: ____________________

1. In the family/home preparedness kit, there should be _______ gallon(s) of water per day, per person.
   a. One b. Two c. Three d. Four
2. How many days should the average family prepare for to be self-sufficient?
   a. One b. Three c. Seven d. Fourteen
3. Fire requires what three elements to exist?
   a. Oxygen, Heat, Fuel b. Oxygen, Carbon, Fuel
   c. Oxygen, Heat, Carbon
4. Triage includes three categories. What are they?
   a. Current, Later, Dead b. Now, Then, Dead
   c. Immediate, Delayed, Dead
5. During triage, one looks for "the killers"—what are they?
   a. Delirious behaviour, swelling, bleeding
   b. Airway obstruction, excessive bleeding, signs of shock
   c. Loss of consciousness, pupil dilation, rapid breathing
6. To purify water, bring it to a rolling boil for ____ minute(s).
   a. One b. Two c. Three d. Ten
7. Moulage is :
   a. French for dead b. Fake injuries
   c. French for bleeding
8. What is the primary concern of a rescuer?
   a. Victim assistance b. Self safety
   c. Escape
9. Circle the categories of terrorists' chemical weapons :
   a. Blister agents b. Blood agents

c. Choking agents d. Nerve agents
e. Riot-control agents

10. The weapon of choice for terrorist is :
    a. Conventional explosives b. Airplanes
    c. Large, box trucks
11. Name three things you can do right now for your personal preparedness is.
12. Three factors that significantly affect safety at a terrorist incident are :
    a. Time exposed to the incident area
    b. Distance between the incident and you
    c. Shielding from the incident
    d. Moving to the incident
13. In taking self-decontamination action :
    a. Seconds count b. Blot dry
    c. Leave your clothing on d. Use cool water

Answers

1. a
2. b
3. a
4. c
5. b
6. a
7. b
8. b
9. all
10. a or b
11. make disaster kit, CPR training, plan escape routes/evacuation plan, communication plan, emergency contacts list
12. a, b, c
13. a, b, d

Appendix III

Some Survey Results

The results provided here are from one course at Pueblo West High School, Colorado in 2003 with students aged 14-18. The number of respondents for each answer is in brackets.

1. What have you learned in Teen SERT that will help you in your life?
   - CPR (21)
   - To act in a situation, both responsively and professionally (20)
   - Basic treatment and triage (19)
   - Helping people/save lives (7)
   - Head to toe assessment (3)
   - Leadership (1)
   - "Surprised at what I learned and how I can use it through my life." (1)
   - Many other things (3)
   - "More things than I could write, that will help me and other people in crisis situations." (3)
2. What participation did your parents/guardians have in your homework assignments/discussions. What were some of their thoughts/comments?
   - Supportive (20)
   - Great/cool (9)
   - Didn't (i.e. didn't know about it) (9)
   - Surprised at course's focus on family plans, etc. (5)
   - "Mom's now getting a kit for her car." (1)
   - "(My parents think) it should be a high school requirement." (1)
   - "Proud that I can save a life." (2)

3. Do you feel better prepared to respond to an emergency, as a result of your participation in Teen SERT?
   - Yes, know what to do in an emergency situation/less scared (40)
   - Yes, more comfortable (2)
   - "Really proud that (I) can make a difference." (2)
   - "Yes, and with new and more effective training techniques." (1)
   - "I feel 110% better with simple lessons to help me in everyday life." (1)
   - "Would have to be there to know." (2)
   - "... controlled chaos, not just plain chaos." (1)
   - "Before I took this class, I would have no clue in the world on what to do." (1)
4. As a result of your taking this class, do you know more about first responders? Explain.
   - Now I know what they do and go through (30)
   - "Bravest people" "Super Heroes" "compassionate" (many variations)
   - Hard workers, but after responding, they have a great sense of accomplishment. (3)
   - "Didn't realize how much patience, time, and separation from your personal feeling is ·involved?" (2)
   - "What they mean to our community." (1)
   - "Yes, before this, I never knew about first responders." (1)
   - "You can do so much before the paramedics get there to save someone's life." (1)
5. What did you like the most about Teen SERT?
   - Moulage (13)
   - Treatments (4)
   - Real life scenarios/final (11)
   - CPR (9)
   - Teamwork (9)
   - Hands-on (10)
   - Triage (3)
   - Search & rescue (2)
   - Fire safety (2)

- Everything (5)
- Talking to speakers (1)
- Car kits (1)
- Course knowledge (1)
- Meeting new people (1)
- Making new friends (1)
- Natural hazards (2)
- Ambulance tour (1)
- Simple and effective techniques (1)
- Psychological separation (1)
- Teaches something that is not well known (2)
- "I liked all (of) the hands-on participation and learning the things that everyone should know." (1)
- "I'm glad we were offered this course. Thank you." (1)

6. What do you think should be changed to make the class better?
   - Great as is (15)
   - Longer (9)
   - More classes (3)
   - More hands-on (3)
   - More stories/pictures/experts (4)
   - Pairing of teams balanced in stature (1)
   - More mass casualty situations (2)
   - Would be better with Health Class (1)
   - More moulage training (3)
   - "Teach more!" (1)
7. Would you encourage other students to take the class? Why?
   - Yes (42)
   - Everyone needs this, it can save lives (33)
   - "Fun" (8)
   - Learned a lot (7)
   - Increase in responder base (1)
   - Great experience (1)
   - New career options introduced (1)
   - Depends on the school (1)
   - No, only unless serious about the training (1)
   - "Will need to know it someday, it's better to start early." (1)

- "All students should know how to handle these situations." (1)

8. Do you think this training is important enough for it to become a regular class in school? Why?
   - Everybody needs this training (should be a requirement) (36)
   - "Absolutely. It's part of being a responsible citizen." (1)
   - "I think so, but I don't know how interested other students would be." (1)
   - "I think it is important enough, but maybe offered as a different class-separate from Life Skills." (1)
   - "More important..., it's a real life situation." (1)
   - "Yes, but (the course) needs more time." (1)
   - "Makes me want to come to school-we need it." (1)

4

Disaster Risk Management : Challenges and Conflicts in Twenty-first Century Governance, Mega City Mumbai

BIJAYANAND MISRA AND RUMA CHAKRABARTY

The life and livelihood of 100 million people in coastal regions are threatened if the sea level rises by one metre due to climate change globally. IPCC identified 21 large coastal cities of the world, including Kolkata and Mumbai, two Indian megacities, which are vulnerable and exposed to serious coastal flooding due to climate. This chapter makes a general review of disaster vulnerability and potential risk for Mumbai and attempts to highlight the main conflict areas in sustainable development of the city. The major observation of this chapter is strategic orientation towards long-range and proactive urban planning using cutting age scientific and technological knowledge and more efficient mechanisms of governance and conflict resolution for Disaster Management.

Here we try to identify the risk and vulnerability of building, infrastructure, port, availability of fresh water, coastal ecology, environment informal settlements in the city of Mumbai, due to the possible rise in sea level owing to global warming. A critical evaluation of the existing disaster management plan of the Mumbai has been carried out, specially taking into account the threat posed by the 2005 floods in Mumbai and the impending risk that may arise due to climate change and sea level rise.

Here we discuss the emerging issue of City Disaster Management Plan which need to be fine tuned with cutting edge knowledge and technology for developing holistic and comprehensive risk management policies for better risk governance and conflict resolution.

Introduction

Sustainable development and good governance have become the *mantra* for the twenty-first century. Sustainability makes good business and social sense and it is closely tied to how prepared we are to mitigate risks to life, property and built environment, financial systems and the development process. Recently we see that sustainability is threatened by increasing risks, natural and man-made, in all communities around the world. New uncertainties are emerging and it is important how we respond to the uncertainties and risks and adapt to the changing times. Our development paths, therefore, are challenged seeking for new methods of governance and resolution of conflicts.

Low-lying coastal regions around the world which contain large gateway port cities are of vital economic and social importance and are too valuable in a global sense to allow their resource depletion to continue and threats to their sustainability to rise. These regions are host to a huge and growing percentage of the world's population, they contain critical centres of international economic and industrial activity such as ports and harbours, as well as provide essential ecological and economic resources. Because these are focal areas of intensive and high value added development, there are many conflicts among the stakeholders in the paths of development they follow. Good governance of these regions, therefore, requires resolution of conflicts; conflicts in interest, land use, intensity of development, environmental protection, etc.

The low-lying coastal regions are also exposed to direct impact of climate change. Increasing concern about the long term effects of global climate change on sea level rise and storm frequency and intensity has begun to focus more attention on these critical parts of the world. These coastal regions, fragile as they are, already face serious risks from numerous natural hazards like cyclones, storm surges, tsunamis, earthquakes, etc. It is estimated that nearly 10 per cent, 700 million, of the global population live on vulnerable coastal low-lying regions. In India, it is estimated, life and livelihood of 100 million people in coastal regions are threatened if the sea level rises by one metre due to climate change and in the three coastal mega cities five million such people are highly vulnerable.

The emerging risks demand better and more responsive governance and better resolution of inherent conflicts in the development process.

The need is most pronounced in the governance of mega cities such as Mumbai, a low lying coastal mega city, financial capital of India and a 'hot spot' in risk management.

Mumbai as a gateway port city for Asia and a national financial hub aims to enhance its global competitiveness while ensuring that the city is safe from risks and its growth is sustainable. In the context the city's and its region's governance is challenged and the policy-makers face the complex task of conflict resolution among various stakeholders, namely, the city municipal government, the State development agencies, the airport authority, the port authority, the developers and the different communities.

As a response to this need, the city municipal government prepared and put into operation a plan for disaster management in 1999 for the area under its jurisdiction. The rest of the Greater Mumbai urban area is much larger than the municipal area and the area has different authorities, namely, Maharashtra Area and Housing Development Authority (MAHADA), Mumbai Metropolitan Regional Development Authority (MMRDA), Airport Authority of India (AAIA), Port Trust of India (PTI), Mithi River Development Authority (MRDA), Dharavi Redevelopment Authority (DRA) and the Government District Administration Agencies. Besides, there is a number of related agencies operating within the Greater Mumbai area, such as, Pollution Control Board, Sewage & Drainage Board, Coastal Guard, etc. Added are a large number of slums and low income people areas that are located on highly vulnerable, especially low lying parts of the city who fight for their legitimacy of existence.

Disasters are the result of a series of preceding events and conditions. Despite the City Disaster Management Plan coming in force in 1999, the city experienced the greatest disaster of urban flood in 26th July, 2005. Though the city systems of management were suddenly confronted with an unprecedented rainfall of 999 mm in a day followed by another 1300 mm in the next two days, the impact of the flood disaster was highly exacerbated by human interventions. Faulty land use especially on fragile areas, construction of fragile slope areas, filling of natural depressions which previously worked as rain water collectors and rechargers, cutting of natural vegetation and high density development have been the main reasons for heightened disaster impact. Hundreds of people dead, thousands of buildings damaged, widespread water borne diseases occurred and on the whole the city transportation and function was paralyzed for almost a week.

The unpreparedness of the city even to be resilient to a third of the rainfall that fell on July 26th, 2005 was the indicator of the poor governance and poor conflict resolution between development impulses and safety.

It is realized now that the city disaster management plan needs to be fine tuned with cutting-edge knowledge and technology for developing holistic and comprehensive risk management policies and projects and for adoption of better and more productive methods of inter-agency conflict resolution. It seems also imperative for the city to enhance partnership between the local government, the civic society, the NGOs and national and international think tank institutions for synergetic inputs to mitigate risks. These are important tasks for better risk governance and conflict resolution.

Natural and Human-induced Environmental Hazards and Disasters

The impact of natural disasters and hazards continue to increase all over the world, over the twentieth century the recorded frequency of such disasters almost increased three times reaching 2,800 by the 1990s. Over the last forty years of the century amount of property damage has been almost doubled in each seven-year period. By the end of the twentieth century it is estimated that about 4 billion people are affected by the natural and man-made disasters.

The recen' revelations about the impact of climate change in the IPCC reports of the UN clearly show the impending increase of vulnerability to disasters in many parts of the world. The increase in vulnerability is mainly seen in the coastal low-lying areas through sea level rise and inundation, increased incidence of storm and wave surge, subsidence of lands, floods and landslides besides draught, flash floods and other crazy weather conditions inland. IPCC identifies 21 large size coastal cities over the world which would be most vulnerable to the impact of climate change. Among these the three most vulnerable coastal large cities are Rio in Brazil, Shanghai in China and Mumbai in India. Besides Mumbai, Kolkata is the other mega city in India on the IPCC list of 21.

Being low lying and coastal, as mentioned above, Mumbai is doubly vulnerable to the impact of climate change especially to sea level rise, wave surge, saline ingression, storms, etc. Mumbai's vulnerability is exacerbated significantly due to heavy concentration of population and activities, large number of non-engineered buildings, persistence of extensive poverty and the habitats of the poor invariably located on fragile environmental and inundation prone areas. Over and above, a rather weak governance and management capability on the part of the authorities adds further to vulnerability.

Mumbai—The Gateway Port and Mega City

Mumbai, the island mega port city, is the financial core of India and the sixth most populous urban agglomerations in the world. The estimated population in 2007 of the city proper is 11.9 million whereas for the urban agglomeration 18.34 million. The city proper is on an island of 68 sq. km area. The suburbs of the city extend far beyond over 370 sq. km of area. Thus the total agglomeration area is 437 sq. km. The Greater Mumbai, defined for planning and management purposes by the government spreads over 45,989 sq. km.

Mumbai is a "gateway" port of India and the financial capital accounting for 17 per cent of national income tax, 37 per cent of national corporate tax and 30 per cent of India's GDP. It is the gateway port of India as it handles bulk of the international shipment and it is the nodal point for a significant part of the shipping in whole of South Asia and also East Asia.

Because of the national and international gateway character Mumbai is a strategic port mega city for the whole of South Asia and South-East Asia regions. Therefore, it is important that Mumbai's future development is made free from disaster and hazard risks and there is no repetition of the 2005 flood disaster which paralyzed the city for more than a week and the cost was in billions of rupees.

Mumbai is increasingly prone to a variety of risks, from cyclones, storm surges, inundation due to sea level rise and other impacts of climate change. Protection of critical and life-line infrastructure and the lives and livelihood of more than a million people who live in the highly vulnerable low-lying areas are the priority tasks.

Urban Planning and Urban Risk Governance

Urban risk governance is a new evolving discipline. The city governments world over are becoming more concerned about safety and sustainable development and make effort to mainstream risk governance and emphasize it as a thrust area in policies. However, a lot of efforts to be made to make disaster risk management a multi-hazard, multilateral and multi-disciplinary based on an integrated approach. In recent years, towards this objective, the concept of Integrated Disaster Risk Management (IDRM) has evolved and is widely accepted now as a purposive viewpoint.

In contemporary urban planning in India, which is almost a half century old, the aspect of disaster management has always been as peripheral, at best, if at all, focusing on disaster ex-facto response. Never there has been any comprehensive approach to disaster management and never any serious attempt to understand the inherent vulnerability and risk factors. Therefore, disaster has always been taken as a contingency, non-frequent in occurrence and to be responded to as and when they occur. It is only since the turn of the century that urban disaster risk governance is being introduced to Indian urban planning. Due to the magnitude of the problem of disaster risk, as mentioned in the case of Mumbai, the challenge is huge. It is not only to plan and implement disaster risk management plans as separate interventions, but more importantly, there is the pressing need to integrate risk management and conventional urban planning.

Conventional urban planning is undertaken within a fixed planning time period and the plan targets for each sector are based on the projection of trends. In the case of natural disasters, however, projection of trends and forecasting is extremely complex task and often accurately not possible. Therefore, in the context of occurrence natural disasters setting of targets in planning has to be based on probability assessment and simulation exercises. Risks caused due to human interventions, such as unplanned land use, informal settlements that have high vulnerability, industrial and fire hazards, however, can relatively be accurately assessed and predicted.

Urban risk governance in the context of natural disasters essentially should be conceived within dynamic cycles of occurrence with varying degree of probability. Planning for mitigation of risks of natural disasters for a dynamic cycle requires a different type of approach than usually followed for other types of risks such as institutional risks, financial risks, etc., in conventional urban planning. Understanding the rhythm in the dynamic cycle of risk due to natural disasters is important. Scientific simulation exercises on natural disasters, at best, can only provide some idea about future scenarios.

Nonetheless, in view of the growing risk threats to sustainable urban growth, both urban planning and risk management need to be integrated for sustainable urban growth in cities. Particularly, the integration is most needed in terms of land use planning and planning for the critical life-line infrastructures. For sustainable urban growth it is essential to scientifically understand the factors and forces that cause vulnerability to disasters analyze their inter-relationships. For example, poverty is a known factor exposing the poor to vulnerability. Poverty, we know, also directly impact housing condition, incidence of disease and health, sanitation, etc., poor quality or absence of which, in turn, exacerbate vulnerability of the poor to disasters. Potential risks are also due to ineffective or faulty urban land use and spatial planning. Potential risks are caused by very high concentration of population, inadequate road surface for movement, location of hazardous industries, building on fragile slopes, water and air pollution, etc. The factors and forces that cause vulnerability and the conditions of urban development that generate potential risks are related, therefore, those need to be understood in an integrated way (Fig. 4.1).

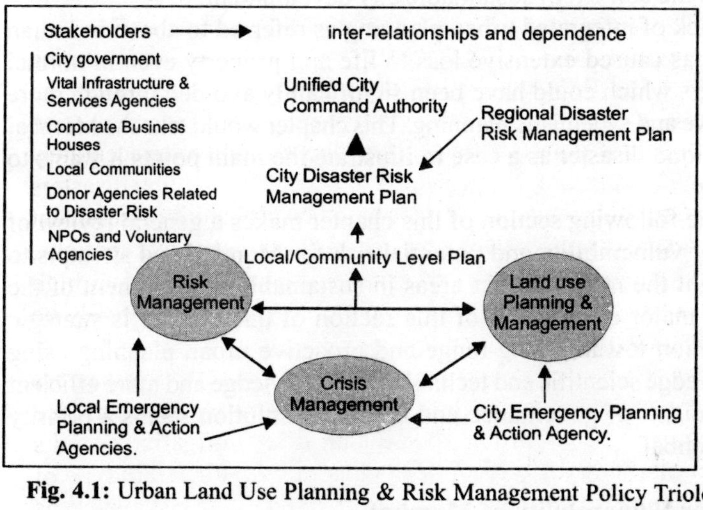

Fig. 4.1: Urban Land Use Planning & Risk Management Policy Triology

In traditional urban planning in India, designation of a planning reference area and preparation of a city master plan for the same is common and the plan is mandatory to be followed by various agencies operating within the planning area. At the plan preparation stage itself, generally speaking, the city development authorities traditionally do not consider disaster risk management as a part of the mainstream development process. At best, as in the Master Plan for Delhi 2021, disaster management for the first time takes a minor place, but the approach to this important sector of planning is weak and not based on rigours of analysis and comprehension. As a result, disaster risk management remains in backline of development, at best, perfunctorily addressed. In fact, it is not uncommon to observe that the city plan making authorities do not have the expertise and capability to adequately address to the aspect of disaster risk management.

Further, various government agencies responsible for various aspects of development often function without necessary coordination much less in terms of disaster risk management. Therefore, factors that enhance vulnerability and potential risks are not addressed adequately, let alone comprehensively. The result is, there remain serious conflicts in planning and execution of the various development projects enhancing disaster risks. Conflict resolution of this nature is vital in the context of sustainable city development.

Lack of integrated urban planning as referred to above in Indian cities has caused extensive loss to life and property even in normal disasters which could have been significantly avoided through more sensitive and synergistic planning. This chapter would take the Mumbai 2005 flood disaster as a case to illustrate the main points it wants to convey.

The following section of this chapter makes a general review of disaster vulnerability and potential risk for Mumbai and attempts to highlight the main conflict areas in sustainable development of the city. A major observation of this section of this chapter is strategic orientation towards long-range and proactive urban planning using cutting edge scientific and technological knowledge and more efficient mechanisms of governance and conflict resolution seems a priority for Mumbai.

Disaster Vulnerability of Mumbai

Mumbai city and its immediate suburban areas have been subject to a variety of natural disasters in history such as, moderate to severe earthquakes, flash floods, cyclones, landslides, coastal erosion, strong wind, land subsidence and ingression of salinity. There have also been also major human-induced disasters and the biggest one was the SS Fort Stikine explosion at Victoria dock in 1944 which killed 6,000 and brought extensive damage to 1.2 sq. km area near the heart of the city. Mumbai has about 1,000 old industrial units which are hazardous and their neighbouring communities are highly vulnerable to risks. Such industrial units have no capability to address to the impact of a disaster outside their sites.

Further, Mumbai also has in its vicinity large and vital nuclear research installations, BARC and AERB, whose protection from all types of risks is imperative.

The cyclone-based flash flood that occurred on 24th July, 2005, paralyzed the mega city and brought wide ranging damage to property and business. Later in this section impact of the 2005 flash flood disaster on Mumbai and its suburbs is reviewed.

Seismic Risks for Mumbai

According to the Bureau of Indian Standards (BIS) Mumbai lies in seismic zone III and it had experienced seismic activity in history at less than 5 in magnitude in 1618 and 1933. The most recent big seismic event was in 1951 when the magnitude was little less than 6.8. The seismic research team at IIT, Powai has designated Mumbai to have a moderate to severe earthquake risk. Some recent earthquake scenarios estimate that in a severe quake event, similar or higher than that in 1951, as high as 40,000 people may die and 118,000 may be injured in Mumbai.

The Latur earthquake (magnitude 6.3 on Richter scale) in 1993 which occurred in the hilly areas in the Mumbai region not very far from the Mumbai city was a warning signal for similar types of earthquakes in which the city may be directly affected. The 1993 Latur earthquake and the devastation it caused to the small town Latur and its surrounding areas jolted the State Government's sensitivity towards natural disasters.

Disaster Management Plans

An ambitious programme has evolved over a period of three years, from 1996 to 1999 for effective disaster management for the State of Maharashtra, which included State and district disaster management plans, a communications network, control rooms, and development of a geographic information system, as part of the overall governance framework. Maharashtra State thus became the first State in the country to have a disaster management plan. The disaster management plan was conceived as a multi-dimensional plan covering multi-hazard scenarios. The Maharashtra Disaster Management Plan had become operational in March 2000.

"The Mumbai Municipal Commissioner *vide* order No. ENV/1093/DEA/CR/36/TK dated 16th February, 1994 was appointed as the District Disaster Officer for Greater Mumbai. It is anticipated that the MMC will manage disaster situations without intervention from State authorities in most circumstances.

A Mumbai Disaster Management Committee (MDMC) was constituted in January 1996 and made responsible for establishing priorities, supervision and monitoring of disaster management and relief activities, coordinate the activities of control rooms, coordinate with NGOs, and aid agencies and enlist services of GOI/GOM laboratories and expert institutions for specialized services through the office of ACS (Additional Chief Secretary) as and when required.

The chief of MDMC is the top bureaucrat official in-charge of Home Affairs of the State and it comprises following 20 permanent members including Municipal Commissioner, Deputy Municipal Commissioner, Chief Executives (Collectors) of Greater Mumbai District, Mumbai Suburban district and Thane, Transport Commissioner, Joint Commissioner of Police, Additional Commissioner of Police Traffic, Chief Fire Officer, General Managers of Central and Western Railways, Director of Medical Services, Executive Health Director BMC, Director Civil Defence and Home Guards, General Managers of BEST and BSES, Technical Director of MSEB, Executive Engineer Water and Sanitation BMC, Controller of Rationing, Director, Industrial Safety and Health, Chief Engineer, PWD and Director General, Information and Public Relations.

MDMC is to ensure effective inter-departmental co-ordination between all State departments, provide policy decisions when required, keep the government informed about disaster situation, review disaster related activity reports, coordinate the activities of lateral, and Central Government agencies like Defense Services, SRP, CRPF, Coast Guards, CISF, MTNL, AAI, Port Trust, FCI, DD, AIR, Meteorology Department, MPCB, BARC.

This crucial regulating and coordinating body comprises a large number of public officials but does not have any effective representation from private sector. Further, a large membership would create difficulties in resolution of the conflicts of interest that would arise among various stakeholders in context of disaster risk reduction.

The response to disaster was two-fold: first, establishment of a Special Disaster Management Cell within the administration which is made directly responsible for planning and coordination at all levels, and second, preparation of a comprehensive Disaster Management Plan (DM Plan) for the city and its suburban areas called Greater Mumbai. The plan was intended to :

(a) Identify levels of vulnerability to different disasters and hazards particularly flood risks within the reference area and analyze their possible pattern.
(b) Put in place technical solutions to mitigate such risks and also set up mechanisms required for emergency and crisis management situations.

A Review of the 2005 Flood Disaster and the Impending Risks due to Climate Change

A brief review of the Mumbai, 2005 flood disaster is made here in order to highlight the severity of disasters the city is prone to and the related city's response.

On 24th July, 2005, Mumbai, India's financial capital, experienced torrential rainfall, the heaviest in the recorded history in one day. The heavy rainfall day was also followed by a week of heavy to intermittent rainfall and another week of scattered and intermittent rainfall. Described as the most severe downpour experienced in a day in the western part of India, it left the urban infrastructure systems of Mumbai into shambles.

The breakdown of city's 150 years old governance institutions were clear and serious weakness in the city emergency management system became bare.

Maximum recorded rainfall in Mumbai in a day in history is :

10/09/1930–548 mm
05/07/1974–575 mm
05/08/1976–265 mm
10/09/1991–475 mm
26/07/2005–944 mm

According to the city government the city drainage system is capable to manage 250-300 mm rainfall and the system is designed to carry 25 mm of rainfall an hour. Further, the time of rainfall if coincides with high tide, the city government says, even 75 mm rainfall would cause serious flooding. The 26th July, 2005 rainfall was more than three times the city's capacity to handle and the disaster was obvious.

The extent of damage caused by this unprecedented rainfall was extensive. In Mumbai city 72 were dead and in the region 300.

Within the first two days the estimated loss was rupees 2,400 crore later total loss was put at rupees 6,000 crores

The city was totally paralyzed for a week.

For the city's slum-dwellers who make up 60 per cent of the population, the devastation was the worst. The water swept away many shanty dwellings and subsequent heavy landslides destroyed large number of houses. Livelihood of hundreds and thousands of families in these low-lying areas was devastated and was subsequently threatened by health hazards.

Almost all the lifeline infrastructure, particularly transportation, road, rail and air, facilities were out of gear and became dysfunctional. Communication systems were down and for most areas the power supply had to be snapped for safety reasons. The city was simply paralyzed for days with severe damage. The entire country was affected because of the Stock market slump and damage to the telecommunication hubs snapped operation of mobile phones and ATMs in many parts.

As regards to flood disaster, the 1999 plan had identified vulnerable points and areas in each locality of the city, including designation of slums and informal settlements that are vulnerable to flooding. The plan also identified 10 and 12 sections along the vital central and western railways, respectively along with other 235 locations within the city which are vulnerable to flooding.

But in spite of this, the 2005 cyclonic flood became a great disaster paralyzing the city. A clear lesson was that proper action on the ground was not taken up during 1999, the start of operation of the plan and 2005, the disaster event, to mitigate the risk of flood disaster. This clearly pointed to the gaps in the city governance methods and great failure in emergency management. Mumbai's stark exposure to future disaster risks became vivid.

The above would show how ineffective the city authority was to respond to the flood disaster. The government was totally unprepared and had neither plans nor the means to respond effectively such a disaster. Mumbai's vulnerability to flooding is closely tied up with the timing of high tide. If tide and flooding times coincide the result often is extensive flooding. There was no weather and rainfall monitoring system for early warning for such disaster.

The flood was the cause of unprecedented rainfall never experienced by the city in history and the crazy rainfall is likely to be a recent trend influenced by the impact of climate change. The city government had not been sensitive towards the trendy impact of climate change until the disaster struck in 2005.

Obviously, the city systems to mitigate flood disaster were totally inadequate and ill managed. For example, the city drainage system not only over a century old but it normally operates at a general efficiency level of only about 60 to 65 per cent and it is designed to manage only one-third of the total rainfall at 100 per cent efficiency that fell on the disaster day, 26th July, 2005. At many micro hot spots the efficiency of the drainage system is even much lower.

Decentralization of Disaster Risk Governance in Mumbai

Consequent to the 2005 flood disaster, the Mumbai Municipal Corporation (MMC) made a review of the 1999 disaster management plan in order to make it directly action oriented and also to integrate the plan with governance structure at all levels.

The city plan was disaggregated into ward level and community level plans within a decentralized frame in order to make the plan implementation effective at lower levels. The decentralized framework of the plan was intended to relate disaster management to the local needs and governance. The city disaster management plan was disaggregated into disaster management plans at the urban district level and at the local community levels.

Focus was brought on the protection of the communication and infrastructure systems and the informal settlements within the city which are highly vulnerable to disasters and hazards.

The Mumbai Plan provides a vulnerability profile for the city, identifies possible hazards that may impact the city and also lays down procedures to respond to different hazards and disasters.

However, the vulnerability assessment is incomplete and

inadequate. Scientific assessment of physical vulnerability has not done as required data on the terrain and slope conditions is not yet available with the city authority. As a result a scientific contour mapping critical for analysis of floods is not yet done.

The plan now provides setting up of special committees responsible for specific type of disasters and the placement of special governance control rooms to coordinate activities during emergency situations. However, the plan does not provide for scientific approach to resolve possible conflicts between the different stakeholders in undertaking their development projects and also adhere to the city disaster management plan.

The test of the efficiency of the new plan would depend on the following four factors :

(a) How effective is the perception of vulnerability to risks and use of cutting-edge technologies to realistically estimate and simulate risks.

(b) How effective the plan is in ensuring emergency response at all levels particularly at the community level.

(c) How effective the plan is in blending the mitigation efforts with efforts for long term coping and preparedness against disasters and hazards at all levels.

(d) How effective the plan is to resolve possible conflicts that commonly arise among the various stakeholders between their own interests in development and the interest of the city in disaster management. Among many conflict of interest two examples are cited here to illustrate the point. First, the conflict of interest between the powerful private sector which drives the market driven developments and the city authority advocating disaster risk management needs. The upmarket Bandra-Kurla commercial complex development located along the highly vulnerable Mithi river is an example. Second, is the conflict between the right to live and livelihood interests of the poor who live in slums which are highly vulnerable to disaster risks and the interest of the city authority which wants to redevelop the areas. These conflicts can be resolved in a win-win manner provided scientific and innovative approach is taken in the City Disaster Management Plan and the stakeholders are taken into confidence to a common purpose oriented development.

Conflicts in Decision Making in the Context of Potential Risks Due to Natural and Man-made Disasters and Climate Change

The meaning of climate change is given subsequently. However, normally it is accepted that climate change is caused by human activity. The UN Framework Convention on Climate Change defines climate change as "a change of climate which is attributed directly or indirectly to human activity that alters the composition of the global atmosphere and which is in addition to natural calamite variably observed over comparable time periods". In this sense Climate change can perhaps be defined as man-made. However, man-made disasters also refer to different types of human intervention in the natural and built environment, for example, destruction of natural vegetation and hydrological systems, unplanned development and pushing development onto undesirable slopes and terrain.

The Inter-governmental Panel on Climate Change (IPCC) of the UN estimates that about 643 million one-tenth of the world's population, who live in low lying coastal areas are at great risk of oceans-related impacts of climate change. 15 out of the 20 projected mega cities of the world are coastal cities. IPCC identified 21 large coastal cities of the world, including Kolkata and Mumbai, two Indian mega cities, which are vulnerable and exposed to serious coastal flooding due to climate change.

IPCC estimates the sea level could rise to l8 to 58 cm by the end of twenty-first century if there is the 'tipping point' with the melting of Greenland and Antarctica glaciers. For the western coast of India a general sea level rise of 33 cm is likely by 2050. In this event significant areas of the city will be inundated and critical infrastructure seriously affected. More important question is the sea level rise will very adversely affect about a million people who live in the low-lying coastal areas of the city and what could be the city government response to this risk.

The sea level rise would inundate low lying areas, drown coastal marshes and wetlands, erode beaches, exacerbate flooding and increase the salinity of rivers, bays and groundwater. Old and totally inadequate drainage systems, possibility of subsitence of land especially in the valuable reclaimes lands, and protection of critical transportation and other facilities in flood-prone parts of the city are some of the special concerns for Mumbai.

The city is particularly vulnerable to storm surge and other events that could produce high water levels. Simulations with climate models and observations indicate that rainfall extremes such as the Mumbai deluge of July 2005 could become more frequent in India under the impact of climate change. Both 2005 and 2006 had spells of excessive rainfall that normally would have occurred once in about 100 years. It has been observed that till 1989 the average rainfall of Mumbai was 2129 mm. However, during 2005-06 the average annual rainfall was 3214 mm, an increase of 50 per cent.

Increase in rainfall and rise in the Mean Sea Level (MSL), coupled with the poor drainage of the city will significantly increase the frequency and severity of floods in Mumbai.

The study by TERI on a district-level ranking of vulnerability to one-metre rise of sea level using a weighted index method states that Mumbai is among the very highly vulnerable spots. The estimated economic costs of this sea level rise could range from Rs. 2.3 billion to Rs. 3.6 billion in the case of Mumbai.

Vulnerability to Risks in Mumbai due to Climate Change and Sea Level Rise

Analysis of risk vulnerability of the city has been carried out focusing on the low-lying areas, critical infrastructure that is vulnerable, informal settlements, fragile coastlines, vital water resources, etc.

Impact on Critical Infrastructure

Critical infrastructure of Mumbai which are likely to get affected due to the impact of sea level rise are first the ports namely the old Mumbai port and the new Jawahar Lal Nehru port.

Mumbai Port is the busiest port in India. Being the biggest and most important port in India, Mumbai harbour is the nerve centre of sea transportation of the country. It is a natural harbour with three enclosed wet dock. They are named as Indira Docks, Prince's Docks (built in the year 1885) and Victoria Docks (built in the year 1891) The Mumbai harbour is a major harbour in the country. In 2006-07 it handled 52.36 million tonnes of cargo traffic comprising 31.09 million tonnes of imports and 21.27 million tonnes of exports. Mumbai Port handled 1.38 lakh TEUs in 2006-07, in the same year the Port handled 17,164 ICD containers (TEUs).

The port will suffer more due to storm surges causing flood inside the port complex, rather than direct inundation due to the sea level rise as such.

Impact on Other Infrastructure

The storms and torrential rainfall due to climate change, similar to that in 2005, are going to affect the following important infrastructure in Mumbai. The analysis is based on the experience of 2005 cyclonic flash flood.

- Disruption of the city local trains due to submergence of lines at various points dislocating the flow of passengers by the system which is the life line for the city. The city disaster management plan identifies 10 sections on the Central Railway and 12 sections on the Western Railway as vulnerable to inundation.
- A large number of buildings which have basements and are on relatively low-lying areas will be flooded blocking access and endangering the electricity lines and the building structures.
- The nerve and control centres of mobile telephone networks are vulnerable and so are such centres for the landline telephones too. 2005 flood showed that because many of these centres were directly affected by flood the Internet services which could provide the backbone in case of disruption of landline telephones went out of operation for days.
- Vulnerability of the telecommunication network also makes the ATM network for banks countrywide vulnerable. During 2005 flood several national level banks, namely Citibank, ICICI, HSBC and the Reserve Bank of India were all reported to have experienced serious problems with the ATM networks.
- The Mumbai International Airport, Sahara, is also partly vulnerable to floods. During 2005 disaster it was only partially operational.

Impact on the Informal Settlements

Almost one-fourth of Mumbai comprises low-lying areas (below or at

MSL). And ironically these low-lying areas despite highly vulnerable to surface floods and also ingression of salinity are the habitat for most of the low-income and poor people of the city which account for nearly 50 per cent of Mumbai's population, 6.5 million. These millions of people are highly vulnerable to floods, storm surges and ingression of salinity

Frequent floods and salt-water intrusion would make the structural stability of many high-rise buildings which are mushrooming at an increasing rate in the low-lying areas vulnerable. Floods, especially in the low-lying areas of the city, bring in a large chain of related hazards even disasters leading to loss of lives. The experience of 2005 flood disaster shows that flash floods which stay for more than 3-4 days will result in serious problems of sanitation and health. In these vulnerable habitats, invariably, drinking water pipes are laid along with the sewage pipes and along or within the drainage channels which enhances drinking water pollution manifold. Such pollution normally leads to serious health problems due to contagious diseases even deaths. All age groups of people are subject to this type of vulnerability. A simulated exercise on economic loss in a cumulative manner over the period 2005-2050 due to extreme events of flooding in the low-lying areas of the city puts the figure at 82 million dollars *(Rakesh Kumar, Parag Jawale, and Shalini Tandon in* Economic Impact of Climate change on Mumbai).

Impact on the Availability of Fresh Water

The average annual temperature is estimated to increase by 1.25 to 1.75 degree C by 2050, this will result in decrease in rainfall during the first part of the year (January–August), endangering the city's complete dependence on locally stored rainfall sources for its water supply. Further the drought situations in the hinterland, a common occurrence during recent years and the reason ascribed to climate change impact, could trigger migrations from surrounding agricultural areas which could further tax the city's resources.

Impact on Fragile Coastal Areas and Beaches

The most significant impact of the impending rise of the sea level, together with storm surges, would render uninhabitable the coastal and the adjacent low-lying areas, already mentioned earlier, where large squatter communities are located. This potential risk raises a chain of conflicts in the decision of the authorities. Relocation of these hundreds and thousands of families to higher grounds is not only a tough and costly task the very scarcity of land available for the purpose would make it almost impossible. Remote relocation in far off places outside the city would destroy the livelihood of these people. Therefore, upgrading the vulnerable habitats to withstand, partially or fully, the potential risks could be a possible solution. This requires innovative planning and design and use of indigenous knowledge and also a change in the conventional mind set of the city authorities which seldom even try to promote innovative *in situ* disaster reduction solutions as called for in this context. A well-planned and holistic approach is required for resolution of this sort of conflict in decision making.

Moreover, the landfill and reclaimed areas from sea constitute nearly two-thirds of the total land area of the Mumbai city proper. Ironically, despite that these areas are vulnerable to a number of potential risks such as sea level rise and rise in the ground water table and intrusion of salinity that would affect the structural stability of the buildings these areas contain development of most of the high value properties. Mumbai's landfill and reclaimed areas contain a mixture of high value commercial properties, such as the stock exchange, important public facilities, train stations, major transportation lines and several high value residential high-rise developments. Besides, some such vulnerable landfill and reclaimed sites are occupied by squatter colonies too. Sustainability of the development in these vulnerable areas pose a serious challenge for the authorities and also a serious conflict in decision making as to who would dictate the correct solution, the owners of the high value properties or the city authority.

Impact on Coastal Ecology

The rich biodiversity of the wetlands on the western coast of India is threatened by loss of wetlands due to sea level rise it will change the salinity distribution and hence the productivity. The effect of sea level rise will depend on the type of mangrove forest, these may either keep pace with the rising sea level rise or these may be submerged. Such vulnerability is a reality in the coastal strips in the suburbs of Mumbai on the mainland. Damage to or submergence of these coastal vegetation will make the entire ecosystem of the coastal sections of the Mumbai region highly vulnerable. Such ecological changes add to the vulnerability of the city of Mumbai.

Vulnerability of Buildings

As per the 1991 census, Greater Mumbai has 2,768,910 dwellings, including residential, commercial and industrial establishments. Of these, only 9.08 per cent of the dwellings were made of reinforced concrete while 31.35 per cent were engineered masonry constructions. Thus, 59.57 per cent of all constructions were non-engineered.

There are 19,642 buildings in Mumbai city district the owners of which did not take up any maintenance of buildings for several years (due to the Rent Control Act restrictions against raising the monthly rent) and this has resulted in the deterioration of the buildings making them highly vulnerable to collapse with changes in the ground conditions due to flood or seismic activity. Out of the total 19,642 buildings, some of the buildings have been reconstructed and some have collapsed. The number of such highly vulnerable buildings today is around 18,580. The Engineers of the Housing Board are responsible for the upkeep of these buildings but maintenance is slack due to paucity of funds increasing the vulnerability of the buildings.

Assessment of Disaster Management Plan, Mumbai city

Ward Level Disaster Management Plans

Micro-level plans at ward level have been prepared for all the 23 wards incorporating specific responsibilities of ward officer who will act as Ward Disaster Manager. The ward-wise disaster management plan identifies the type of risk, the type of vulnerability in terms of impact on settlements and impact on infrastructure. It provides the list of the city level agencies which will be approached for assistance through the BMC Control Room, in event of any disaster. It also delineates the responsibility of different departments during emergency. The ward officer will provide all informations as given in the ward plan to the field officers of the line departments. The ward officer will be directly responsible for the execution of the relief and rehabilitation tasks through BMC staff.

However, in cases of disasters of exceptionally large magnitude which require coordination with a wide range of lateral agencies including Central Government agencies, the Additional Chief Secretary (Home) within the State Government will assume the responsibility of Disaster Manager for Mumbai.

Disaster Mitigation at the Community Level and Provision for Capability Building

The city government identified selected private sector business units, NGOs and other voluntary organizations as resource groups for involvement in community preparedness measures. Capability of these agencies is planned to be augmented through training by several private expert training providing agencies, namely, Apnalaya, AVEHI, Bombay Environmental Action Group (BEAG), Foundation for Research in Community Health, Jagruti Kendra, Mohalla Committee Movement Trust, Nirmala Niketan School of Social Work, Parisar Asha, Save Bombay Committee, SIDDHI, Slum Rehabilitation Society, SPARC, Tata Institute of Social Sciences, YUVA, and YWCA.

Department of Disaster Management called Disaster Management Cell

The Department of Disaster Management was formed in December 2000 within the Mumbai Municipal Corporation. The Department is also named as the Disaster Management Cell and it is headed by the Municipal Commissioner of Greater Mumbai. The officer in-charge is the Additional Commissioner MMC. It has 12 full-time employees and, in emergency, has additional support from adequate number of engineers, medical officers, firefighters and other employees of MCGM and other line departments.

The Disaster Management Department is a single-point source for all tasks regarding disaster management, namely, rescue, relief, recovery, mitigation and preparedness. It is the command and control agency between central administration of the city government and the field units.

Disaster management component is now incorporated into specific planning and development projects in the city, namely, the priority rail projects proposed under the MUTP II, road over bridges and flyovers, road widening and additional roads, special corridors for BEST run buses and no-parking roads, etc.

Major Risk Management Concerns in the Physical Structure and Planning for Mumbai

1. Risk management is a multilateral complex task. A close coordination among the stakeholders and acceptance by all a common goal of risk reduction are crucial requirements. It is only with these conditions in place that a proper enabling environment can be created to resolve conflicts in decision-making keeping disaster risk reduction at the core. However, at all stages human values and ordinary peoples', especially the low income and the poor, interest should be in focus in all conflict resolution efforts. In resolution of this sort of development related conflict of interest it is essential that the authorities adopt time tested scientific methods and procedures of conflict resolution.
2. Very high intensity of building and extensive coverage of ground space by buildings in Mumbai, particularly in its old parts, increase vulnerability to all sorts of risks. In the older parts the roads are narrow and lined with 4 to 6 storey buildings very densely packed in space which not only multiplies vulnerability in case of disaster also makes any kind of rescue and relief operation in emergency extremely difficult, often impossible. While this is so, new building construction approvals are being given in the same areas exacerbating the vulnerability situation. As said earlier, 59.57 per cent of all building constructions were non-engineered and large percentage of population is living in the slums with very dense development. The Mumbai plan has identified the problem in the context but concrete action to reduce vulnerability is not in hand. Retrofitting or reconstruction of the vulnerable buildings, opening of minimum access into very densely developed old areas, planning evacuation routes in case of emergency, identification and marked route guidance to shelters, etc., are some of the important actions that are required.
3. Realistic land use planning, including appropriate counter-measures in anticipation of flood effects is lacking. Using information on the environmentally fragile areas including the low-lying areas permission for land use changes or building

construction should be expressly controlled. The vulnerability caused by the hazardous industries, 1000 in number, must be reduced to protect the nearby communities in case of disaster. A special coastal management sub-plan should be prepared to protect and preserve the coastal sections of the city.

4. Mumbai also has several vital touristic resources which should be protected and their vulnerability to risks reduced under a special sub-plan under the disaster management strategy.
5. Scientific simulation of sea level rise would reveal the extent and type of critical infrastructure of the city in danger. Pro-active plans should be prepared without losing time as what can be done to protect such critical infrastructures and, if necessary, realignment and alternatives should be planned to sustain city activities.
6. Realistic assessment of gaps through systematic analysis of what is planned, what is currently being done and what modifications are necessary in the implementation of the vital projects should be of great help in fine tuning the existing disaster management plan. The proper gap analysis should help fix realistic timeframes, vital plan refinement requirements and better coordination between agencies.
7. Land tenure clarity and its proper documentation is also another important area where action is called for in order to make the disaster management efforts effective. Though nearly half of the total land area of the city is owned and controlled by the city government, the mechanisms available to control and coordinate the use and development on the rest 50 per cent of the city land are rather weak.
8. A major factor that contributes to high vulnerability to risks is the land value in the city. Mumbai is the eighth most expensive city in the world in terms of land value. (Richard Ellis, Global Rent Review, 2000, and Aromar Revi, Lessons from the Deluge, 2005, *The Economic and Political Weekly*, September 3, 2005. The primary outcome of this is that more than 55 per cent of its residents cannot afford to live in anything other than squatter settlements, slums and 'chawls', even though their per capita incomes are significantly higher than many other regions in India. This needs a new strategy in

urban organization and land management to enhance access of the low-income even the lower-middle income groups to land market and housing on the one hand and on the other to plan for more effective dispersal of these groups of population to smaller urban centres without disruption in their livelihood opportunities.

Strategic and innovative planning should be done to gradually reduce the current concentration of population in the low-lying ecologically fragile areas particularly from those areas which are likely to come under water due to sea level rise in few decades. Relocation of families from the most vulnerable areas, though a very difficult task, should be a priority task. In other vulnerable areas micro-zoning should be done to clearly distinguish lands from where relocating families is not necessary but local risk mitigation measures are possible through retrofitting the existing structures, growing coastal plantation, constructing bunds etc. These tasks should be effectively done in a coordinated way between land use planning measures and disaster mitigation measures.

Other Aspects of City Governance related to Disaster Risk Management and Conflict Resolution

A standard governance operating procedure details the various departments to be activated during an emergency. Considering the pressing need for information flow during a disaster emergency a disaster communications network has been planned as an integral component of the city disaster management plan. The network is based on the VSAT and VHF networks in each of the 30 districts of the State including that for Mumbai. This network can also be used for general government administration including management of the rural development programmes.

The Maharashtra Disaster Management Plan became operational in March 2000 and it incorporate the planning, coordination and awareness issues. The plan is a multi-hazard disaster plan provides for district level and micro-level resource charting. The plan incorporates a response strategy to counter subversive activities that would aggravate vulnerability. The plan provides for institution of an experts group to advice the government action. Under the plan effective coordination among all the involved agencies for effective disaster mitigation response has been one of the major concerns. It is not only coordination between the various agencies within the government important, it is equally important to take up disaster awareness and risk communication tasks seriously at all levels. Therefore, the State plan underlines the need to enhance awareness and risk communication and provides for training campaigns to sensitize and inculcate concepts about disasters, safety measures etc. among the school and college students, teachers, governmental organizations and NGOs.

The Hyogo Framework for Action 2005-2015 'Words into Action: A Guide for Implementing the Hyogo Framework', ISDR, UN emphasizes strengthening of disaster preparedness for effective response at all levels. Achieving this depends on good governance. Good governance, as we know, is based on trust and vision between the civil society and the government.

Constant interaction with all the stakeholders and taking the leadership to bring them to a common platform of communication and action to enhance personal and collective security is the important task in governance. It is in this precise sense that risk communication becomes a critical input. The government, therefore, has to show the leadership to ensure effective risk communication at all levels. This firstly requires the government to be abreast with the scientific information, technology and knowledge required for the purpose. Integrating scientific information, technology, action plans, law enforcement and trust with the civil society together through active participatory process should be the governance responsibility for the government.

Generally speaking, the civil society of Mumbai reckons well the long city governance experience of the MMC over the century and its capabilities to guide the city development in the past. However, the city growth in recent years has become complex and it demands new directions and innovations in governance and in guiding the city for the future. The recent revelations on the impact of climate change and the 2005 flood disaster have brought in greater pressure on city governance seeking new and more scientific ways to face the growing risks and growth challenges.

Radical institutional and arrangements seem necessary to seriously promote 'bottom-up' planning and responses to match up with the long standing 'top-down' planning system. Land use planning is an important area of intervention in the context. There should be explicit emphasis on the preparation of 'local area plans' with focus on disaster risk management and the mechanisms and procedures for the purpose should be promoted. Experience in the preparation of 'local area plans' from other cities, especially, Delhi, may be used for guidance.

City governance must hold a mirror up to it with indicators of achievement inscribed on it to reflect on the actual capabilities in the context of the changing scenarios. Events that challenge the government capabilities like the 2005 flood disaster emergency should be evaluated to learn lessons, pinpoint areas of weakness in governance and improve response for the future.

In good governance more than quick fixes are needed. Use knowledge, information and innovation to build a culture of safety and resilience at all levels especially at the community level are vital. To achieve this, as mentioned earlier, building of trust with the civil society through demonstration that the government can actually deliver during emergencies is important and building trust is closely tied with transparency and accountability in the style of governance.

Training—A Vital Input in Risk Communication and Action at All Levels

Training for strengthening disaster preparedness capability is a critical input. Use of advanced training systems and e-training methods are essential and for this the government needs to take the leadership in organization and facilitation of training with the help of expert agencies. Of course, media can play a critical role especially among communities.

The city government of Mumbai promotes media coverage oriented to preparedness, opinion programmes and NGOs and private sector participation in diffusion activities. The Indian Institute of Technology in Powai (IIT-Powai), and different NGOs have organized several programmes and workshops for administrators, teachers, students, and citizens of Mumbai. In order to enhance the quality and reach of awareness campaigns, partnerships with different national and international organizations such as UNICEF, UNDP, EMI, All India Institute of Local Self-Government (AILSG), and others has been looked upon.

Risk Communication at Local Level

Community participation in mitigation and emergency preparedness is promoted through media coverage oriented to preparedness, opinion programmes and NGOs and private sector participation in diffusion activities. The IIT at Powai and different NGOs have organized several programmes and workshops for administrators, teachers, students, and citizens of Mumbai. In order to enhance the quality and reach of awareness campaigns, partnerships with different national and international organizations such as UNICEF, UNDP, EMI (Phillippines) and All India Institute of Local Self-Government (AIILSG) are in place.

Decentralization of planning process and organization of community are important necessities and for promotion of participatory practices including specific opportunities for women to be involved in decision-making. It involves empowerment and ownership, at community level. The three-level planning process, regional, city and local needs to be integrated into a common strategy for disaster management.

Conclusion

Development cannot be sustained without integrating disaster management with the development process through effective governance mechanisms. In case of Mumbai, management of the coastal zone particularly the vulnerable low-lying areas and integration between land use planning policies and disaster risk management are critical necessities. Governance mechanism should clearly identify the roles and responsibilities assigned to different heads and bodies and the related reporting evaluation mechanisms need to be clearly defined with emphasis on quick response to emergency and resource management. Good governance also should incorporate mechanisms for ensuring effective links for information flow and training on risk communication. Emphasis has to be on transparency and accountability in governance to build trust of the civil society.

References

Aggarwal Diksha and Murari Lal Centre for Atmospheric Sciences, Indian Institute of Technology, Delhi, *Vulnerability of Indian Coastline to Sea Level Rise.*

Bhandari1, R.K, D.I.C (Lon), Ph.D. (Lon), F.I.E (India), C. Eng, F.I.C.E (Lon), F.N.A.E (India); *Disaster Management in India—a New Awakening.*

Dwivedi, Dwijendra Nath, Sharma (Dr.) Vinod Kumar, Proceedings of the 14th Biennial Coastal Zone Conference, New Orleans, Louisiana, July 17 to 21, 2005; *Analysis of Sea Level Rise and its Impact on Coastal Wetlands of India,*

Mathur Shveta and Sharma Anshu, Coordinates; Mumbai Floods: Another wake-up call.

Mumbai Disaster Management Plan, Department of Relief and Rehabilitation, Government. of Maharashtra.

Sherbinin Alex de, Schiller Andrew and Pulsipher Alex; *The Vulnerability of Global Cities to Climate Hazards.*

"Words into Action: A Guide for Implementing the Hyogo Framework", Hyogo Framework for Action 2005-2015, ISDR, United Nations.

"Lessons from the Deluge", *Economic & Political Weekly, September 3, 2005.*

www.unisdr.org/.../African-regional-consultation-2-3-jun-04/ Disaster-Risk-Reduction-and-Governance.ppt

3CD City Profiles Series—Current Working Document—http:// emi.pdc.org/cities/CP-Mumbai-09-05.pdf.

5

Disaster Risk Management in West Bengal : Need for Local Level Cooperation and Coordination among Different Stakeholders

ARINDAM DASGUPTA

The incidence of various types of disaster are gradually growing worldwide due to increasing anthropogenic effects on the environment and the scale of impact of these disasters are rising day-by-day. The reasons are lack of preparedness on the part of administration and poor coordination between local administrative bodies and the community concerned. In India around seventy per cent (70%) of the total population live in rural areas and they suffer most in disasters. Coming to West Bengal, most of the districts are flood prone and especially coastal districts such as Purba Medinipur, Pachim Medinipur and South 24 Parganas. These districts also suffer huge amount of losses of human life, property, agricultural crop and livestock due to cyclonic storm. The people of northern district, i.e., Darjeeling are affected badly every year by landslides during monsoon months. In these cases local level government and non-governmental organizations are supposed to be the first set of agencies which will take up relief and rescue operation and as well as take measures for prevention from the adverse effects of disasters. However, these organizations often find themselves under-resourced and powerless. Political differences sometime make things difficult in their functioning. There is also lack of coordination and communication between these organizations and the affected communities. Government and Non-Governmental Organizations try to work independently and this has restricted their areas of functioning. As a result certain aspects of preparedness become incomplete which may reduce the risk of affecting from disasters. In fact the Panchyati Raj Institution members have a key role to play in the community preparedness. They are the coordinators between administration and the community. They will inspire the community to be more active and create space for their participation implementing various action plans, related with disaster management. The members are also key facilitators to regularly update the contingency plan. They have the great responsibility to identify the safe shelters, safe storage facilities and can also guide the community in pre-positioning of food, cattle feed, medicine and water before any disaster strikes. The Panchayat representatives and the volunteers of non-governmental organizations may carry on awareness campaign, Small motivation camps in order to make aware the community about possible problems which they may face after the disaster. The representatives can provide legal and legislative support to the victims. The role of NGOs by virtue of their proximity to the people and their comparative flexibility in operations can be very useful. The main problem is NGOs are sometimes compelled to represent views of powerful people. This distorts the truth and reduces the acceptability of these organizations to the masses. There is also a lack of coordination and conflict between these private organizations and the administration regarding way of functioning. But they should be complementary to each other in every level of disaster risk management. Under the circumstances, this chapter is a modest attempt to outline the responsibilities, potential and limitation of different stakeholders activities regarding disaster risk management and to suggest the ways through which a common platform can be evolved for their cooperation and coordination in formulating the plan for mitigating disaster risk effectively in West Bengal.

Introduction

Hazards, in fact, are the natural or human induced processes or events with the potential to inflict heavy loss to human lives and affect their welfare. Flood, earthquake, cyclone, landslide and other hazards have been occurring all over the world prior to the history of mankind. When a large number of population exposed to a hazard are killed, injured, the event is termed as the disaster. Disaster risk represents the vulnerability of different strata of population where the natural hazard strikes. Vulnerability has been defined as the degree to which a system, or part of a system may react adversely during the occurrence of hazardous event and for vulnerable people, access to resources either at a household, or at an individual level is the most critical factor in achieving a secure livelihood or recovering effectively from a disaster (Kumar, S., 2001). About twenty-five per cent of the world's population lives in areas at risk from natural disasters. Hazards are mainly controlled by the environmental setting and the risk is primarily influenced by socio-economic and demographic variables, i.e., characteristics of population. Similarly, the supporting institutional and administrative machineries are always guided by socio-cultural elements as well as economic and political principles. So there is need to understand the socio-cultural milieu of the disaster-prone region for which disaster risk management plan has to be formulated. Disaster Risk Management is a combination of a number of steps, i.e., collection of data regarding various natural hazards by setting up monitoring centres in vulnerable zones, modern warning system, good coordination among local administration, i.e., Panchayats in villages and Municipalities or Nagar Palikas in urban areas, community and non-governmental organizations (NGOs) which helps in carrying on Awareness campaign among local people and encourage them in capacity building process which is essential in reducing disaster risk.

West Bengal : A Vulnerable State to Various Disasters

The people of West Bengal suffer from mainly flood cyclonic storms and landslides. Most of the districts in West Bengal are affected by flood during monsoon months (June to October). The coastal districts such as Purba Medinipur, Paschim Medinipur, South 24-Parganas often lose considerable number of human and livestock population, property, agricultural land due to severe cyclonic storms either before the onset of the monsoon (March-May) or during the time of withdrawal of the monsoon (October-December). Besides these districts, Nadia, Murshidabad, Burdwan, Maldah are very much flood prone. At present around 42.3 per cent of the total area of the State is susceptible to flood spread over 110 blocks in eighteen districts. The highest affected area of flood in 1978 is about 30,607 sq. km. About 23,970 sq. km. of area were devastated by flood in 2000 (Ray, 2006). The landslide hazards in West Bengal has been observed mostly in the hilly terrain of Darjeeling district. In 1968, floods in Darjeeling area destroyed vast areas of West Bengal and neighbouring state of Sikkim by unleashing about 20,000 landslides and killing thousands of people. These landslides occurred over a three-day-period with precipitation ranging from 500 to 1000 mm in an event of 100 years return period (*Source*: *Landslide Hazard Zonation Atlas of India,* New Delhi, 2004). The western portion of West Bengal, i.e., Purulia, Bankura, and Birbhum suffers from droughts in almost every year due to inadequate or deficient rainfall and adverse soil condition. These districts are hit hardly by agricultural drought which is resulted from lack of sufficient soil moisture. This is a long duration disaster and its impact is severe especially on the regional economy.

West Bengal experiences earthquakes at a relatively lower frequency. The Bureau of Indian Standards places the region in the seismic Zones II-IV, corresponding to peak ground acceleration (PGA) of 0.1, 0.2 and 0.25 (1 g = 980 gal) respectively (Source: BIS: IS 1893-2002; Part-I, 2002). The lowest perceived hazard Zone-II, is in the south-western part of West Bengal (Purulia), while Zone-IV covers the north and south-east of Kolkata and as well as Darjeeling, remaining part of Jalpaiguri, Cooch Behar, North and South 24-Parganas and Malda. Zone-V is delineated on the eastern parts of Jalpaiguri and Cooch Behar. The districts of Kolkata, Murshidabad, Birbhum, Barddhaman, Hoogly, Howrah, Nadia, Bankura, Purba Medinipur and Paschim Medinipur come under Zone-III (Nath, Roy and Singh Thingbijan, 2008). This zonation enables decision-making process towards planning and organization of land use, response and mitigation.

Moreover, West Bengal is highly vulnerable to any kind of natural hazard because of high population density and concentration of industrial and agricultural activities across the State. As developmental activities have increased in high-hazard zones, i.e., mushrooming of hotels for tourism purpose on the restricted coastal zone (Digha, Sankarpur), the risk or vulnerability scenario appears to be worsening with time.

As over seventy per cent of the population live in rural Bengal and most of the sufferers are rural people, therefore, Panchayats have assumed an important role to play in disaster risk management.

Panchayati Raj System in West Bengal

The experience of West Bengal with respect to Panchayati Raj has been unusual in many respects relative to many other Indian States.

With the advent of the Left Front dominated government at the State level since 1977, a functioning three-level panchayat system with a mandated election every five years was instituted since 1978. Significant responsibilities previously in the domain of the State bureaucracies were devolved *de facto* to these panchayats. These include responsibility in implementing land reforms, identifying beneficiaries for land transfers, IRDP loans, agricultural extension programmes, employment programmes (such as NREP, RLEGP, JRY), housing and other welfare programmes, raising local revenues from taxes and non-tax sources, and administering local infrastructure projects. West Bengal thus has experienced a functioning panchayat system for over a quarter century, well in advance of the 73rd and 74th Constitutional Amendments passed in 1993. The Panchayati Raj has a three-tier structure in the State. The atomic unit is called a Gram Panchayat, which is the Panchayat organization for a collection of villages. The block-level organizations are called Panchayat Samiti, and the district-level organizations are named Zilla Parishad.

As per the West Bengal Panchayat Act, 1973, each Block has a Panchayat Samiti, whose members include the Pradhans of the constituent Gram Panchayats, and the MLAs from the block. A Panchayat Samiti is headed by a Sabhadhipati. The third tier of the Panchayati Raj is Zilla Parishad, a district level organization with the Sabhapatis of the constituent Panchayat Samitis and the MLAs from the district as its members. A Zilla Parishad is headed by a Sabhadhipati. For the Darjeeling district, the Zilla Parishad has ceased to exist, but a similar organization for the Siliguri subdivision exists, which is designated as a Mahakuma Parishad.

Responsibility and Participation of Panchayat in Disaster Risk Management in West Bengal

One of the objectives of Panchayati Raj is to ensure people participation through an institutional framework. Article 243(G) of the Constitution visualizes Panchayats as institutions of self-government. A comprehensive list covering 29 subjects which are mostly related to development has also been provided in the Eleventh Schedule of the Constitution. To perform these activities, the system needs adequate devolution of powers, functions, personnel and finances of these local administrative bodies which have not been taken place so far. Disaster management as a subject has not been listed under eleventh schedule which gives 29 subjects to Panchayati Raj System. Nevertheless, in West Bengal Panchayat Rules, 2004 the Upa-Samiti of Gram Panchayat on Finance and Planning has been assigned to deal with the subject of Disaster Control Management. This is a practical approach and integration of disaster with development and planning.

In West Bengal Panchayat System there are standing committees at Zilla Parishad and Panchayat Samiti level, i.e., "Cottage and Small Industries, relief and social welfare" (Standing Committee No. 7). But the role and duties of these committees regarding disaster management has not clearly mentioned. Besides, there are no such committee at Gram Panchayat level which is the true representative of the concerned village. So it is clear that neither the responsibilities of the Panchayats regarding disaster risk management have been well delineated nor the public-private-community framework has been outlined in the act. Naturally this inadequacy in imparting the responsibilities to the local government has affected its participation in various disaster related programmes. For example, in case of West Bengal, the flood in 2000, all over the State destroyed more than 1,00,000 rural dwellings, more than 3,500 Gram Panchayats were affected and property of approximately 200 crore of rupees was destroyed (*Source:* Department of Relief, Govt. of West Bengal, 2003). As Panchayats were not integrated properly in relief and rescue operation, inefficient co-ordination among concerned district administration, local administrative bodies and non-governmental organizations, charitable institutions, i.e., Bharat Sevashram Sangha, Ramakrishna Mission has made the entire effort unsuccessful where thousands of poor people did not receive any relief or a. sistance during the need of hour. In contrast, the Panchayati Raj Institutions (PRIs) will provide a base for integration of various concerns of the community which can be incorporated in disaster risk management. Besides Panchayats, NGOs and Voluntary Organizations (VOs) may also play crucial role in risk management but there is a necessity to define the role and responsibility of Panchayat representatives and the Non-Governmental Organizations and so that they can work together without opposing to each other. Besides this, people participatory approaches in disaster risk management have proved to be quite fruitful where the people will be involved directly in decision-making processes.

The objective of involving Panchayat into this risk management is to sensitise the local community and through them there will be an effort to develop coping mechanism in preparedness to minimise its destructive effect on life and property at local level. There is a view that activities like distributing immediate relief in the form of money, foodgrains, medicare, medicines, cloths, tents, vessels, drinking water and other necessities, activities of restoration, rehabilitation of villages or towns can be implemented better with the involvement of local bodies. It is also found that in certain cases, particularly in West Bengal, Panchayati Raj Institutions have played crucial role in crises situation. For example, the lead taken by the PRIs in the wake of calamities like the 1993 flash floods in Jalpaiguri district of West Bengal is a positive step towards counter-disaster preparedness operation (Hussain, A., 1999). There are a number of good examples in North Bengal where panchayats along with local voluntary organizations and NGOs are doing good work in disaster management during the time of landslides, flash floods and river bank erosion especially in selected blocks of Maldah. In spite of these, in majority of the cases the Panchayats in West Bengal has not actively and intensively participated in disaster risk management programmes such as the participation of Panchayats in Purba Medinipur district regarding flood related risk management or developing proper arrangements to save human life during cyclone storm has not been satisfactory.

Stakeholders in Disaster Management along with Panchayat in West Bengal—Potential and Problems

It is true that disaster risk management is a multi-phase programme and it needs the participation and cooperation of private agencies i.e., NGOs, Voluntary Organizations, and local community in order to ensure effective operationalisation of disaster mitigation strategies at local level and provide a broad-based framework for disaster risk reduction and mitigation.

The role of NGOs in disaster management has evolved from relief and emergency response to disaster mitigation and preparedness. Increasingly, disaster preparedness programmes have been added to the agenda of NGOs. These organizations have adopted community-based approaches that assist communities in mitigation and preparedness through organising, capacity building, training, small-scale structural measures and preparation of counter-disaster plan. Development NGOs are traditionally engaged in relief and rehabilitation and have also incorporated the measures related to the building of capacity building of local governments in disaster preparedness. NGOs which are engaged in environmental conservation have reoriented their environmental programmes to integrate disaster prevention in their advocacy, environmental education and mobilisation activities. If disaster risk management is considered to be a multi-stakeholder cooperation of which NGO is one of the parties (Fig.5.1).

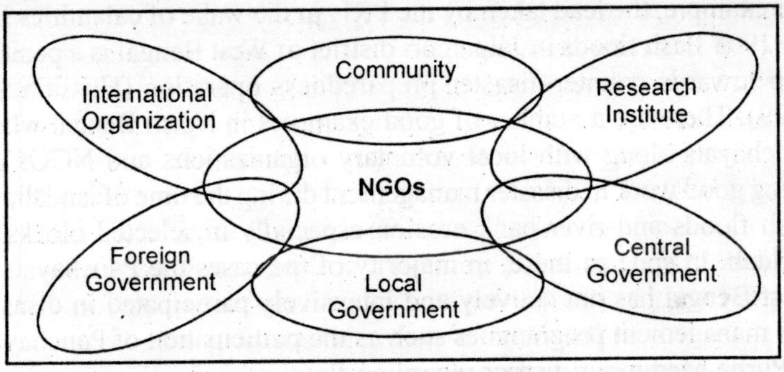

Fig. 5.1: Schematic Diagramme showing the Role of NGOs in Multi-Stakeholder Cooperation (after Rajib Shaw, 2003)

Coming to NGOs in West Bengal, there are total 141 enlisted NGOs in Kolkata and in total there are 362 NGOs in different districts. But a few NGOs are actively participating in disaster management. So far, there are only nine or ten NGOs who are specialized for disaster management. Some of them are: All India Council for Mass Education and Development, Ramakrishna Mission Loksluksha Parishad, Oxfarm GB (India), Gana Unnayan Parishad, etc.

In West Bengal there is a need to increase Government especially local government-NGO cooperation so that various informations regarding disasters can be exchanged. Government infrastructure in all the disaster affected places or disaster prone places will not be adequate always. NGOs can also help the government to develop required arrangement regarding mapping different available resources of the area, formation of Community Based Organization (CBO), launch awareness programme among people in order to make them aware about the possible impact of the disaster, do's and don'ts in pre- and post-disaster situation, regional training of trainers and ensuring the concepts, principles and skills are transferred, disseminated in the local language, covering local hazard issues. In Maldah an NGO is working on building up of the temporary shelter at Panchanandapur with local Panchayat for those people who have lost their houses and other properties due to deadly river bank erosion at Ganga. The NGOs role in various phases of disaster cycle can be illustrated wherein preparedness, rescue, relief and rehabilitation stages NGO plays role of coordinator between government, people and local administration. (Fig. 5.2).

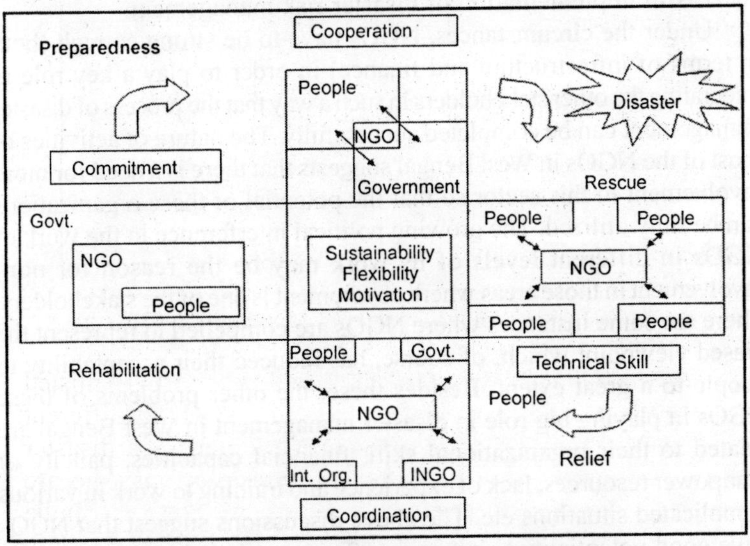

Fig. 5.2: Model showing Roles of NGOs in different Stages of Disaster Cycle (After Rajib Shaw, 2003)

They can also assist the government in comprehensive vulnerability analysis of disaster prone areas, i.e., Maldah, Purba Medinipur, South 24-Parganas incorporating past disasters, socio-economic conditions of the population living in the area and inventories of major structures of public concern. Risk assessment and hazard mapping would delineate areas vulnerable to natural hazards and the frequency, intensity, impact and return period of each hazard. Community based approaches to disaster management have contributed to the empowerment of communities. It has also enhanced coordination and strengthened working relationship between Government Organizations and NGOs as it advocates partnership between Government Organizations, Non-Government Organizations and the community.

In West Bengal, although a number of NGOs are at present working on child health, environment, disabled persons, sanitation, drinking water facilities, etc., very few NGOs are found to be active in the arena of disaster management. Actually disaster management is a vast area where a number of stakeholders, i.e., Government, Community, Donor Agencies, Non-Governmental Organizations or Voluntary Organizations (VO) will be present. Cooperation and efficient networking among these stakeholders is the key for successful implementation of disaster risk management.

Under the circumstances, NGOs have to be strong enough (both in terms of infrastructure and finance) in order to play a key role in integrating the other stakeholders in such a way that the process of disaster management can be completed successfully. The nature of activities of most of the NGOs in West Bengal suggests that there is a need for more involvement in this sector so that the potential of these organizations can be fully utilized. The growing political interference in the work of NGOs in different levels of its work may be the reason for non-involvement in those areas where government is one of the stakeholders. There are some instances where NGOs are compelled to represent the biased viewpoint which, of course, has reduced their acceptability to people to a great extent. Besides these, the other problems of these NGOs in playing big role in disaster management in West Bengal are related to their organizational skill, financial capacities, paucity of manpower resources, lack of experience and training to work in various complicated situations etc. The above discussions suggest that NGOs have good potentiality to act as an efficient stakeholder in the whole processes of disaster risk management in coordination with the local administration especially the panchayats in rural areas and simultaneously the district administration has to boost the local NGOs and voluntary organization sector by assimilating them in the different phases of disaster risk management.

Community Based Organizations

Nowadays, Community Based Disaster Management (CBDM) has gained prominence world over. In India, the high power committees has realized the need for CBDM and emphasized the role of local government, i.e., Municipalities and Panchayati Raj Institutions. In the context of CBDM, a community is referred to as the whole population of a village or habitat since the objective of CBDM is to make every member of the village community to be aware of various types of hazards leading to vulnerability and risks, which affect their lives and livelihood.

The role of Community Based Organizations (CBOs) in the context of CBDM has assumed significance. The CBOs can be defined as formal and informal which emerge either from the initiative of the whole community around some common interests or organized by government and non-governmental organizations to meet certain specific objectives of development affecting the whole or part of a community or a specific target group.

The informal community-based organizations are those which emerge from the community itself, e.g., formation of a Forest Protection Committee, Pani Panchayat, Mahila Mandal, Youth Club. In such cases, the community itself selects the members of the committee and decides the tasks to be performed by them. Generally, the resources by those organizations are mobilized by those organizations from the community itself and are rarely dependent on outside sources (Hussain, A.,1999).

The formal community-based organizations are: Self Help Group, Water Users Association, Joint First Management Committee formed by the Forest Department, etc. The CBOs have specific rules and regulations for its members and ensures greater representation of the community (Hussain, A., 1999). In West Bengal there are thousands of self-help group formed by the rural women in order to be economically self-reliant and play an important role in giving tremendous support to the rural economy. In the forest areas of Paschim Medinipur district there are Joint Forest Management Committees to look after the forest resources and sustainable development of the resources. These Self-Help groups or the joint forest committees can be very much useful in disaster risk management. The members of these organizations can be trained in order to participate in different stages of disaster management.

Coordination and Cooperation among different Stakeholders in Disaster Risk Management

There is a need to have good coordination between Gram Panchayat (GP), NGOs and CBOs for capacity building among the people, institutions which are important factor in disaster risk management. In reality it is found in almost all the villages of West Bengal especially in disaster prone districts that there is absolutely no link or coordination among NGOs, CBOs and the Gram Panchayat as they have separate client groups that have been engaged in specific tasks. GP is the only organization in West Bengal at the village level which represents the whole village community and is able to take a holistic view of the disaster management at the village level. The GP, being a local government unit has also the capacity to coordinate the activities of NGOs and CBOs to strengthen its effort for disaster preparedness and crisis management at the community level.

The Panchayat and Rural Development Department of Government of West Bengal has prepared a vision document for the role of three tiers of Panchayati Raj system in different aspects where disaster management was also taken care of. There it has been suggested that there will be a standing committee at Gram Panchayat, Panchayat Samiti and Zilla Parishad level which will have executive powers and the committee shall draw up disaster/calamity management plans and carry out a programme or action plan in respect of their territorial jurisdiction for prevention, preparedness, mitigation, response, warning, emergency operations, rescue and evacuation, relief, recovery and rehabilitation. This committee will also arrange training programmes on search, rescue and first aid for the disaster management team at different levels. The Committee shall take up mock drills twice in every year before disaster seasons with Village Disaster Management Committees and Teams. The Committee shall issue timely warning within their territorial jurisdiction to the people likely to be affected by any natural calamity regarding risks and hazards. The Committee shall utilize services or facilities from Government Department or Agency and seek support/assistance from any institution, organization, authority, both Government and Non-Government to manage disasters. In this vision document it has been accepted that the role of Non-Governmental Organizations in disaster management has assumed significance as these institutions can sensitize the local community about disaster risk in a wholistic manner and help the local administration to carry out different training and awareness programme through which community capacity building can be possible.

In this context it can be said that the coordination among PRIs (Panchayati Raj Institutions), NGOs and CBOs need to be more so that the positive, constructive and functional relationship will facilitate, activate and accelerate the process of development. The field of coordination between these three key factors have to be extended in different levels of disaster management replacing the elements of conflict. People or community have potential and capacity which is needed for transformation but they also need a support system and mechanism. Gram Sabha should become a driving force and main focal point for people's involvement in development process. The meeting of Gram Sabha should be regular, organized and create an environment where freedom of expression should prevail. This will inspire the people of different ideologies to think together and make a cohesive effort in order to combat the disasters. Apart from this, the initiative must be taken regarding the formation of disaster risk management cell and sub-cell at least in all the Zilla Parishad and at block office of the disaster prone district. These cells will collect data regarding the past occurrence of types of disaster in that district, identify the most vulnerable section of the population there, maintain active connection with the disaster management sub-cell at different block office, play the role of coordinator between State Government and rural or urban administration, estimate the amount of relief material needed during the time of disaster based on the data furnished by the different blocks, efficiently distribute the material through the block. Similarly the coordination between the block office and Panchayat office should be strengthened in respect of disaster risk management so that administratively the crises situation can be tackled. On the other hand, Gram Panchayat should take up the awareness programme among the village people in connection with the prevention, preparedness, response, rescue and relief operation needed at the time of disaster with local NGOs. Moreover the Panchayat must encourage the NGOs to help the villagers for forming community-based organisation which will be independent and with the help of local peoples wisdom and experience combat the disaster effectively.

References

Aich, B.N. (1999). *Natural Calamities: Mitigation and Management*, in Mukhopadhyay, A.D., Dutta, K.K. & Sanyal, P. (ed.) Disaster Management, Jadavpur University, Kolkata.

An Outline on Disaster Management Plan 2003-04, Department of Relief, West Bengal, Kolkata, 2003.

Baluchamy, S (2004): *Panchayati Raj Institutions*, Mittal Publication, New Delhi.

Banerjee, S. Chakraborti (2002): *Social Background of Panchayat Leaders in West Bengal,* Dasgupta & Co., Kolkata.

Bhattacharya, M. (2002): *Panchayati Raj in West Bengal: Democratic Decentralization or Democratic Centralism*, Manak Publication, New Delhi, 2002.

BIS: IS 1893-2002 (Part-1), Indian Standard Criteria for earthquake-resistant design of structures, Part-1-General provisions and buildings, Bureau of Indian Standards, New Delhi, 2002.

Chaturvedi, T.N (1981): *Panchayati Raj*, Indian Institute of Public Administration, New Delhi.

Dharamraj, J. (1996): *Mobilizing Community Participation in Disaster Management*, PREPARE, Madras.

Ghosh, Buddhadev & Kumar, G. (2003): *State Politics and Panchayats in India*, Manohar Publishers, New Delhi.

Harichandan, H. (2003): Community Participation in Disaster Mitigation and Risk Reduction (with Special Reference to Cyclone) in Sahni, P. and Ariyabandhu (ed.), *Disaster Risk Reduction in South Asia*, Prentice Hall of India Private Limited, New Delhi, pp. 210-216.

Hussain, A (ed.) (2006): *Empowering Panchayats and Community Disaster Preparedness*, Sumit Enterprises, New Delhi, pp. 156-183.

Kapur, A. (2005): *Disasters in India, Studies in Grim Reality*, Rawat Publications, New Delhi, pp. 24-56.

Kumar, S. (2001): *Disaster Management: Analyzing Vulnerability in Disaster Mitigation—Experiences and Reflections*, Prentice Hall of India Private Limited, pp. 92-99.

Landslide Hazard Zonation Atlas of India (2004): Building Materials and Technology Promotion Council, New Delhi, 2004.

Maltias, E. (2000): *Panchayati Raj Institutions and Role of NGO*, New Delhi, Indian Social Institute.

Medury, U. (2001): Coping with Disasters: A Community-Based Approach in Sahni, P.; Dhameja, A & Medury, *U. Disaster Mitigation—Experiences and Reflection*, Prentice Hall of India Private Limited, New Delhi, pp.155-170.

Mohapatra, P.K. & Singh, R.D (2003): Flood Management in India, *Natural Hazard*, Vol. 28, No. 6, 131-143.

Murshed, Z. (2003): Community Capacity Building for Risk Reduction in South Asia in Sahni, P. and Ariyabandhu (ed.), *Disaster Risk Reduction in South Asia*, Prentice Hall of India Private Limited, New Delhi, pp. 145-161.

Nath, S. Kumar, Roy, Debasis, Thing Baijan and Singh, K.K (2008): Disaster Mitigation and Management for West Bengal, India—An Appraisal, *Current Science*, Vol. 94, No. 7, 10th April, pp. 858-864.

Okazaki, Keniji & Shaw, R. (2003): Empowerment of Local People for Sustainable Disaster Mitigation: Experience of Developing Countries, *Regional Development Dialogue*, Vol. 24, No.1, Spring, pp.1-24.

Panchayat & Rural Development Department, Government of West Bengal (2009): *Road Map for the Panchyats in West Bengal: A Vsion Document*, pp. 37 & 61.

Panigrahi, N. (2000): *Super Cyclone in Orissa: Response of Welfare Agencies for Relief, Rehabilitation and Reconstruction*, Occasional Paper No. 51, NCDS, Bhubaneswar.

Ray, C. (2006): *Floods and Role of The People–Perspective of West Bengal*, Department of Irrigation and Water Department, Government of West Bengal, India.

Reddy, A.V.S., Thapliyal, B.K. & Sastry, R.R (2000): *Disaster Mitigation Through Peoples Participation: Role of Local Self Government Institution*, Paper presented in the National Conference on Funding Disaster Prevention and Mitigation, NIRD, Hyderabad, December 19-20.

Reddy, G. N. (2002): *Empowering Communities through Participatory Methods*, Manak Publication, New Delhi.

Sahni, P. and Dhameja, A. (2003): Disaster Risk Reduction through Capacity Building of the Community and Panchayati Raj Institution in Sahni, P. and Ariyabandhu (ed.), *Disaster Risk Reduction in South Asia*, Prentice Hall of India Private Limited, New Delhi, pp. 162-184.

Samal, C.K. *et. al.* (2005): *State, NGOs and Disaster Management*, Rawat Publications, pp. 60-80, pp.209 and 230.

Sharma, Vinod K. (2006): Disaster Management Strategies in India in Valdiya, K.S. (ed.): *Coping with Natural Hazards: Indian Context*, Orient Longman, Hyderabad, pp. 250-257.

Shaw, R. (2003): Role of Non-Governmental Organizations in Earthquake Disaster Management: An Asian Perspective, Regional Development Dialogue, Vol. 24, Number 1, pp. 117-129.

Singh, A. and Singh, R.B. (2003): *Community Participation in Disaster Mitigation in India* in R.B. Singh (ed.) Natural Hazard and Disaster Management, Rawat Publication, New Delhi, pp. 313-320.

Srivastava, A.K. (2003): *Community based Disaster Management: Indian Experience* in R.B. Singh (ed.), Natural Hazard and Disaster Management, Rawat Publications, New Delhi, pp. 321-334.

Sudhakar, V. (2002): *New Panchayati Raj System: Local Self Government Community Development,* Mangal Deep Publications, Jaipur.

Taori, Kamal (2002): *Disaster Management through Panchayati Raj*, New Delhi, Concept Publishing, New Delhi, pp.4-9, 23-31.

Vulnerability Atlas of India (1997): Building Materials and Technology Promotion Council, Ministry of Urban Development, Government of India.

6

Game Theoretic Analysis on Conflict and Cooperation : An Illustration from Flood Risk Management

SUMAN RANJAN SENSARMA

This chaper analyses conflict and cooperation process between governmental organization and opposition group over water and flood risk management. To model and analyze this conflict the GMCR as an ordinal preference based game theoretic approach is used to understand the strategic interaction and possible equilibrium of the game under different circumstances. GMCR defines outcome (states) first and strategies are determined as move between states. Thus it helps to model the real world conflict more on to practical perspective.

Conflicts over Yoshino River Weir

About 250 years ago during the Edo period (1603-1867), the existing Daijuzeki dam on the Yoshino River—14 kilometres upstream from the Kii-sudio, a channel between Shikoku and the mainland—was built of stone masonry by the local farmers. According to the Ministry of Construction (MOC) officials, to prevent future flooding, the present fixed dam (Koteizeki) made of piles of stones must be removed and replaced by a movable modern dam (Kodazeki) to prevent the future flooding. Since the weir has become old, it has become an obstacle to river flow in case of flood. That increases the risk of inundation upstream. The total estimated cost for constructing the movable dam on the Yoshino is over 100 billion yen (US $1 billion), with an annual maintenance cost of 700 million yen (US $7 million). In 1993, the local people came to officially learn about the proposal they established a study group (benkyokai) to gather information and raise the question of validity of replacement of the old weir. The opposition group with the support of local leaders began to start anti-dam movement in Tokushima. Their main arguments were as follows:

i. The new weir may not be as effective as compared to the cost of constructing the new renewal project.
ii. Inferior of water quality and ecosystem.

But despite of the people's protest, in 1997 the prefectural government and the assemblies of two cities and seven towns in Tokushima prefecture voted in favour of the new dam which triggered the opposition group to demand a referendum on the project. By the Japanese law, the result of a referendum in a municipality does not have any formal binding on the decision of the national government. At first, the Tokushima municipal assembly rejected to legislate a local ordinance for introducing a referendum. However, the political groups supporting the referendum successfully obtained a majority in the election in April, 1999. The new assembly approved the institution of referendum, and this was carried out finally on January 23, 2000. In the referendum, 90 per cent turnouts (almost a half of voters) voted for "opposition for the project" (http://www.topics.or.jp/daijyuzeki/). After the referendum, the mayor of Tokushima expressed his position to oppose the project. In August 2000, the government declared suspension of the project, and called for establishing dialogues with the opposition group. However, communication did not work well because the opposition group complained that the Ministry of Land, Infrastructure and Transport (re-established in 2001 from the former Ministry of Construction and the Ministry of Transport) would still not exclude the originally proposed project from the prospective alternatives.

In 2002, the Governor of the Tokushima prefecture who had constantly been supporting the project was arrested for bribery and forced to leave office. Thereafter a new governor elected declared his position in support of complete abortion of the project. But this conflict is yet not fully resolved till date. Both of those supporting and opposing have been trying to stay in dialogue, thus it has been undergoing successive stages of conflict and cooperation respectively. The information is synthesized from different sources like official reports (The Yoshino River—Its Outline and Conservation, 1990), newspaper clippings (http://www.topics.or.jp/daijyuzeki/), etc.

Graph Model for Conflict Resolution

GMCRII provides a simple strategic representation of conflict, with minimal information requirements that can be analyzed for a range of stability patterns that represent different styles of decision-making in a real-world conflict. This is founded upon a mathematical framework utilizing concepts from graph theory, set theory and logical reasoning. It represents a conflict as moving from one state to another state (the vertices of a graph) via transmissions (the arcs of the graph) controlled by the decision-makers. Mathematically, Let $N = \{1, 2, \ldots, n\}$ be the set of players and $K = \{K_1, K_2, \ldots, K_u\}$ be the set of states of the conflict, and n-tuple $\{D_i\}$ (i=1, 2..., n) be the set of directed graphs where $D_i = (K, V_i)$. Set of arcs V_i means player i's possible move between states. Let $k_l k_m$ be the arc from state k_l to state k_m. If, $k_l k_m \in V_i$ it implies that player i can move from state k_l to state k_m unilaterally. Payoff function P_i specifies player i's preference order for states. If $P_i(k_l) > P_i(k_m)$, player i prefers state k_l to state k_m. The Graph Model for Conflict Resolution (GMCR) is presented by 4-tuple $\{N, K, V, P\}$, where $N = \{1, 2, \ldots, n\}$, $K = \{1, 2, \ldots, k\}$, $V = \{V_1, V_2, \ldots, V_n\}$ and $P = P_i / i \in N\}$.

One advantage of the graph model over a more traditional game theoretical approaches is that it can represent irreversible moves. In such cases, a decision-maker can unilaterally move from state k to state q but not from q to k. Preferences in graph model are expressed in terms of pair of binary relations $\{\succ i, \sim i\}$ on S, where $s_1 \succ s_2$ indicates that player i prefers s_1 to s_2, and $s_1 \sim s_2$ means that player i is indifferent between s_1 and s_2 (or equally prefers s_1 and s_2). Three subsets of the state S are defined as:

$\Phi_i^+(s) = \{s_m : s_m \succ_i s\}$; all states that player i prefers to s.

$\Phi_i^-(s) = \{s_m : s \succ_i s_m\}$; all states that player i prefers less than state s.

$\Phi_i^=(s) = \{s_m : s_m \sim_i s\}$; all states are indifferent to s for player i.

$R_i^=(s) = R_i(s) \cap \Phi_i^=(s)$; all equally preferred states reachable from state s by player i.

When a player does not have an incentive to move from a particular state, the state is called stable for the player, and the state is called equilibrium if it is stable for all the players.

$G = (S, (A_i: i \in N))$......... (1)

The main stability definitions currently used in graph model analysis include Nash Stability (Nash), General Metarationality (GMR), Symmetric Metarationality (SMR), Sequential Stability (SEQ), Limited Move Stability (L_h), and Non-Myopic Stability (NM) (Kilgour *et al.*, 2005).

Modelling

The whole process of the conflict is modelled into three phases to analyze how parties gradually find their cooperation ground over a series of interactions. The game theoretic modelling gives players different possible strategic moves to resolve the conflict.

Phase I (1982-1999)

This conflict is modelled by use of GMCR II, a game theoretic model to find out the possible move of different players within a fixed set of options and preferences, and within which equilibrium of the cooperation can be reached.

Based on the analysis of the background of the conflict, two players are identified. One is governmental agency (player *G*), and the other is the opposition group (player *O*). Player *G* consists of the Ministry of Construction, prefectural government, and some municipalities located upstream. At that time, players, their relative options, and the *status quo* are inferred as listed below in Table 6.3. Mathematically, there are a total of 32 (2^5=32) possible states, but after removing all infeasible states, there are 16 feasible states in total as shown in Table 6.4. Some states are infeasible because they are mutually exclusive. In Tables 6.1 and 6.2, '*Y*' means 'Yes' and indicates that the option is taken for a corresponding state, and '*N*' means 'No', where the option is not taken. In the first phase of this conflict, the state is 7 is an equilibrium under Nash and sequential stability concepts. In this equilibrium, player *G*, proceeds the project and calls for dialogue. On the other hand, player *O* pushes the referendum and does not accept the call for dialogue. This was also the *status quo* state during this time. This equilibrium can be interpreted as an initial situation of this conflict. But historically the state 16 occurred at the end of this game where the governmental agency has suspended the project. An aspect of decision-making that is poorly captured by game theory involves the cost of searching the solution space for an optimal result (Picard *et al.*, 1999), and within the fixed frame of game, players find their best outcome. This cannot allow the game to change, which means we cannot break the rules as fixed in the beginning of the conflict. As we know, due to the strong people movement, the government agency has already started to communicate with the opposition group. They decide to alter the preference structure to adapt to the public opinion which pushed the game to move on to the second phase of the conflict.

Table 6.1: Players and their Options (Phase I)

Players and their options	*Status Quo State*
Governmental agency	
1. Proceed the project	Y
2. Suspend the project	N
3. Dialogue with opposition group	Y
Opposition group	
4. Push Referendum	Y
5. Dialogue with governmental agency	Y

Table 6.2 Feasible states of the Conflict (Phase I)

Options \ *States*		*1*	*2*	*3*	*4*	*5*	*6*	*7*	*8*	*9*	*10*	*11*	*12*	*13*	*14*	*15*	*16*
Governmental agency	1	Y	N	Y	N	Y	N	Y	N	Y	N	Y	N	N	N	Y	N
	2	N	Y	N	Y	N	Y	N	Y	N	Y	N	Y	N	Y	N	Y
	3	N	N	Y	Y	N	N	Y	Y	N	N	Y	Y	N	N	Y	Y
Opposition group	4	N	N	N	N	Y	Y	Y	Y	N	Y	N	N	Y	Y	Y	Y
	5	N	N	N	N	N	N	N	N	Y	Y	Y	Y	N	Y	Y	Y

A distinct shift in the nature of the conflict began as a result of public referendum. But it was not a random event. In Tokushima, local environmentalists, including Masayoshi Himeno who later became the leader of the movement for a public referendum took a strong role to stop the dam project. During this period, the proposed constructions of Nagara River Barrage in Gifu prefecture became a national debate issue. Awareness of anti-dam movement has further enhanced by wide range of media coverage. Yoshino river project faced this trend against dam. This contextual external event forced the conflict to move on to the second phase of the conflict where the focus shifts towards whether the project is completely aborted or not.

Phase II (2000-2002)

Thereafter, as the players continued to bring up various issues of pros and cons in public debates a new orientation of player interactions and counter-interactions become more important. After the referendum the project has already been suspended, the opposition group tries to pressurize the government to abort the project. The governmental agency tries to revitalize the project proposing the partial change of the plan. Thus players' new options and preferences are identified as shown in Table 6.3. There are a total of 32 (2^5=32) possible states, but after removing all infeasible states, there are 16 feasible states in this second phase of the conflict (Table 6.4). This game has 3 equilibria, i.e., state 4, 8, 11 and 15. Equilibrium 4 and 8 are stable under both Nash sequential stability solution concepts. In equilibrium 4 and 8, governmental agency does not abort the project and propose their own alternative. The basic difference from equilibrium 4 to 8 is that, in equilibrium 8, and governmental agency also accepts the opposition group's alternative proposal. The equilibrium 11, and 15 are not stable under Nash solution, they are sequentially stable. In the equilibrium 11, player G aborts the project but does not accept the alternative proposal and in equilibrium 15, player G aborts the project and accepts the alternative proposal. But in fact, after the results of the referendum were announced, the then new Construction Minister (Mr. Masaki Nakayama) advised that he would not insist on going ahead with the plan if a better alternative could be found. Prior to the vote, Nakayama had maintained that construction work should be in process regardless of the local residents' opinion. Actually the equilibrium 8 (where governmental agency can aborts the project) can be interpreted as the actual outcome at the beginning of this phase. We may interpret that some political climate changes again forced the game to move on to phase III of this conflict.

Table 6.3: Layers and their Options (Phase II)

Players and their options	*Status Quo State*
Governmental agency	
1. Abort the project	Y
2. Propose the partial change of the plan	Y
3. Dialogue with Opposition group	Y
Opposition group	
4. Propose its own alternative	Y
5. Dialogue governmental agency	Y

Table 6.4: Feasible states of the Conflict (Phase II)

Options \ *States*		*1*	*2*	*3*	*4*	*5*	*6*	*7*	*8*	*9*	*10*	*11*	*12*	*13*	*14*	*15*	*16*
Governmental agency	1	Y	N	Y	N	Y	N	Y	N	Y	N	Y	N	N	N	Y	N
	2	N	Y	N	Y	N	Y	N	Y	N	Y	N	Y	N	Y	N	Y
	3	N	N	Y	Y	N	N	Y	Y	N	N	Y	Y	N	N	Y	Y
Opposition group	4	N	N	N	N	Y	Y	Y	Y	N	Y	N	N	Y	Y	Y	Y
	5	N	N	N	N	N	N	N	N	Y	Y	Y	Y	N	Y	Y	Y

Phase III (2003-2007)

The shift to phase III began with new governor appointment and his further initiative to control the flood measure. In effect of this, the major focus shifts towards the flood management. In this phase both parties interaction become dominant. Although the players continued to disagree over the river weir issues, they increasingly became engaged in close communications and negotiations to find out some meeting point and to explicitly consider each other's views. Thus players' new options and preferences are specified in Table 6.5. There are a total of 32 (2^6=64) possible states, but after removing all infeasible states, there are 32 feasible states in this second phase of the conflict (Table 6.6). In the case of equilibrium 32, the governmental agency compromises with the opposition group. In this phase the governmental agency preferences shifted towards the opposition group and a new option to repair the old weir and flood control measures took place. The governmental agency now gives emphasis on dialogue with the opposition group. Still there remains a voice in favour of construction of the new weir, which might turn it to another conflict phase. The old weir may not have enough functions to control the floods, so the other measures should be considered to control the floods.

Table 6.5: Players and their Options (Phase III)

Players and their options	*Status quo state*
Governmental agency	
1. Construction of new weir	N
2 Repair the old weir	Y
3. Flood control measure	Y
4. Dialogue with opposition group	Y
Opposition group	
5. Propose its own alternative	Y
6. Dialogue governmental agency	Y

Table 6.6: Feasible states of the Conflict, Phase III

Options \ *States*		*1*	*2*	*3*	*4*	*5*	*6*	*7*	*8*	*9*	*10*	*11*	*12*	*13*	*14*	*15*	*16*
Governmental agency	1	Y	N	Y	N	Y	N	Y	N	Y	N	Y	N	N	N	Y	N
	2	N	Y	N	Y	N	Y	N	Y	N	Y	N	Y	N	Y	N	Y
	3	N	N	Y	Y	N	N	Y	Y	N	N	Y	Y	N	N	Y	Y
Opposition group	4	N	N	N	N	Y	Y	Y	Y	N	Y	N	N	Y	Y	Y	Y
	5	N	N	N	N	N	N	N	N	Y	Y	Y	Y	N	Y	Y	Y
	6	N	N	N	N	N	N	N	N	N	N	N	N	N	N	N	N

		17	18	19	20	21	22	23	24	25	26	27	28	29	30	31	32
Governmental agency	1	Y	N	Y	N	Y	N	Y	N	Y	N	Y	N	Y	N	Y	N
	2	N	Y	N	Y	N	Y	N	Y	N	Y	N	Y	N	Y	N	Y
	3	N	N	Y	Y	N	N	Y	Y	N	N	Y	Y	N	N	Y	Y
Opposition group	4	N	N	N	N	Y	Y	Y	Y	N	N	N	N	Y	Y	Y	Y
	5	N	N	N	N	N	N	N	N	Y	Y	Y	Y	Y	Y	Y	Y
	6	Y	Y	Y	Y	Y	Y	Y	Y	Y	Y	Y	Y	Y	Y	Y	Y

Conclusion

The argument of this case study is to manifest a methodology of conflict resolution which has an emphasis on collaboration. In this Yoshino river weir conflict now both players' preferences gradually appear to be shifting towards more integrated flood management issue. But within the same group some of the members still prefer the construction of a new weir. In order to resolve the further conflict referendum can be taken as a direct democracy.

Acknowledgements

I thank Professor Norio Okada, Director, DPRI, Kyoto University for his valuable suggestions and guidance.

References

Fang, L.; Hipel, K.W.; and Kilgour, D.M. (1993): *Interactive Decision Making–The Graph Model for Conflict Resolution*, Wiley, New York.

Fang, L.; Hipel, K.W.; and Kilgour, D.M. (1988): "The Graph Model Approach to Environmental Conflict Resolution", *Journal of Environmental Management,* Vol. 27, pp.195–212.

Hipel, K.W.; Kilgour, D.M.; Fang, L.; and Peng, X (1997): "The Decision Support System GMCR in Environmental Conflict Management", *Applied Mathematics and Computation*, Vol. 83, No.2 and 3, pp. 117–152.

Hipel, K.W.; Fraser, N. (1991): "Cooperation in conflict analysis", *Applied Mathematics and Computation*, Volume 43, Issue 2.

Kilgour, D.M. and Hipel, K.W. (2005): "The Graph Model for conflict resolution: Past, Present, and future", *Group Decision and negotiation,* Volume 14, Number 6, 439–440.

Kilgour, D.M.; Hipel, K.W.; and Fang, L. (1987): "The Graph Model for Conflicts," *Automatica,* Vol. 23, 41-55.

Fraser, N.M.; and Hipel, K.W. (1984): *Conflict Analysis Models and Resolutions*, New York : North Holland.

Okada, N. and Sakakibare, H. (2002): "Game Theory-derived policy Implications for the Yoshino River Weir Conflict in Tokushima, Japan, *Systems, Man and Cybernetics*, 2002, IEEE International Conference on, Vol.6, Issue. 6-9.

Okada, N. and Sakakibara, H. (2004): "Conflict Management as a part of integrated disaster risk management–issues, socio-cultural contexts, and methodological leverages", *IEEE Transition on Systems, Man, and Cybernetics.*

Pruitt, D.G. and Rubin, J.Z. (1986): *Social Conflict: Escalation, Stalemate, and Settlement*, New York, Random House Inc.

Sakakibara, H. and Kidear, K. (2004): "The study on the process of constructing a game from a conflict in participatory planning," *IEEE Transition on Systems, Man, and Cybernetics.*

Sakakibara, H.; Okada, N.; and Hipel, K.W (2000): "Modelling public conflicts over infrastructure renewal using a Japanese case study," *IEEE Transition on Systems, Man, and Cybernetics.*

Tokushima Work Office (Ministry of Construction) (1990): *The Yoshino River—Its Outline and Conservation.*

Von Neumann, J. and Morgenstern, O. (1944, 1953): *Theory of Games and Economic Behaviour,* 1st edn, 1944; 3rd edn. 1953. Princeton University Press, Princeton, New Jersey.

Web Page of Tokushima Shinbun (In Japanese) http://www.topics.or.jp/daijyuzeki/.

7

Facilitating Cooperation through Cluster Level Information Centres for Community Rehabilitation : Case of *Setus*, Post Gujarat Earthquake 2001

RAVI SANNABHADTI

This chapter synthesizes the experiential learning emerging out of the set-up and management of Information Centres that were set-up post Gujarat Earthquake 2001. The information centres were instrumental in streamlining the process of reconstruction by collaborating between civil society players, local government functionaries and affected communities. These catalysts actively facilitated the rehabilitation efforts by customizing the rehabilitation efforts to suit community needs while making optimum use of information to coordinate available resources with the government agencies or departments and NGOs (both local and international). The evolution of these information centres and their changing roles in response to emerging needs has been attempted to be captured by this chapter.

About Kachchh

Kachchh (sometimes also spelled as 'Kutch') district in the State of Gujarat which is the largest district in the country, having a total land area of 45,652 sq. kms (Census of India, 2001 area figures). It is subdivided into 11 talukas (administrative sub-district units) and has a population of 1,583,225 (Census of India, 2001). Kachchh is sparsely populated with a population density of around 33 persons per sq. km (Census of India, 2001) which was 65 persons/km^2 in 1991excluding the desert and *banni* areas (Gujarat Ecology Commission, 1996). The density of population in the district is quite low as compared to the rest of the State which is 258 per sq. km (Census of India, 2001), with village settlements which are situated far from each other. Compared to the human population, the animal population in Kachchh is higher at 73 animals/km^2 (Gujaart Ecology Commission, 1996). This is also due to the existence of a large population engaged in pastoral way of life.

Kachchh is geologically, geographically and culturally unique. Geologically speaking Kachchh—as the name suggests—is shaped like the 'back of a tortoise' and has risen out of the sea, on account of the Indian plate pushing against the Eurasian plate. It lies on the major tectonic fault lines (Karanth, 2001) and is prone to earthquakes falling in seismic zone V. It is historically documented, (as well as noted by Bilham, 1998) that in 1819 a major earthquake struck the region which changed the course of the tributary of river Indus by creating a natural bund termed as the 'Allah bund'. Drought is a natural phenomenon in this region as only once in three years it does receive a normal monsoon rain. The region falls in the arid part of the country and is prone to cyclones.

The district is encircled by the Gulf of Kachchh in the south and west, while the Great Rann (desert) and Small Rann of Kachchh effectively delineate it in the north and east. It borders Pakistan and before independence, had trade links with Sindh province, which presently forms a part of that country. Kachchh stands at the confluence of two cultures, i.e. Gujarati and Sindhi. A mix and match of these two cultural influences is seen as one moves across the district.

Gujarat Earthquake 2001

The Gujarat Earthquake occurred on the 26 January, 2001 morning whose epicentre was about 17 km away from Bhachau town in Kachchh district. The earthquake measured 6.9 on the Richter scale (Indian Meterological Department) and estimated to be 7.7 MW by the US Geological Survey (GSDMA, 2001). The earthquake caused destruction to property and life across 21 of the 25 districts in the State. The total destruction in terms of changes to life and property of the population may never be known but official documents state that 13805 people were dead and about 1,67,000 number of people were injured during the earthquake (Thiruppugazh, 2007). The earthquake caused widespread destruction to property, the extent of which might never be fully known but it is estimated that around 2,15,000 houses collapsed and 9,28,000 houses were partially damaged (Mishra, 2004). The majority of this damage was caused in Kachchh district as the epi-centre was based in the region.

About Kachchh Nav Nirman Abhiyan

Kachchh Nav Nirman Abhiyan (KNNA commonly known as Abhiyan) is a federation/network consisting of 30 NGOs (numbering 22 prior to the earthquake) working for the development of the region on various different aspects. The network was started in June 1998 as a collaborative effort to effectively respond to the cyclone called Kandla cyclone, affecting Kachchh in that year. The objectives of the network are "to synergize human, knowledge, physical, and financial resources and collaborate towards Kutch, which is governed by community initiatives, encourages self-help development especially with the marginalized sections, integrates tradition wisdom with new technologies and innovation and balances issues of human rights with human responsibilities"(Kutch Nav Nirman Abhiyan, 2004).

Conditions during the Early Days of Relief Phase

The relief phase began immediately after the earthquake as teams from local civil society groups and local communities started removing the trapped, dead and wounded from the damaged and collapsed structures. Help in this regard, from the army and paramilitary units based in the region also started immediately. Teams of volunteers from within and outside the State (including those mobilized by government efforts) started arriving, the day after the earthquake. A massive effort to garner relief material for purposes of distribution in affected areas began a day after the earthquake, with the start of voluntary efforts to collect materials like clothes and food from the unaffected regions within and outside the State.

But the situation on the ground just after the disaster was chaotic. Hardly any feedback was available from the government machinery as the local government set-up and infrastructure were widely ravaged by the disaster. Infrastructural damage was spread across the district on account of heavy damage to electric substations and lines, water supply pump houses and pipelines, telecom equipment, fibre optic cables and other phone lines (Vatsa, 2001). There was minor damage to roads, though the Surajbari bridge which was the major connection between Kachchh district and rest of Gujarat State was damaged substantially and remained open to light vehicles only for a period of 15 days after the earthquake.

Due to these reasons, local government functioning had almost come to a standstill and was unable to take stock of the extent of damage. There was lack of machinery and trained manpower to clear the debris and rescue the trapped from the debris. Lack of coordination and non-availability of information was the greatest hindrance to the furtherance of rescue and relief efforts. Ravaged government machinery was of little help to the arriving teams of volunteers coming to the district for relief work, spurred by media reports. Simultaneously, large chunks of the population were left without minimal or no access to basic needs like food, water and clothing (particularly in the cold windy dry desert climate in the month of January, which is peak winter season).

For facilitating relief work, teams had to be sent out everyday to 'take stock' of the situation and to gauge the need for relief in different areas affected by the earthquake. This delayed the relief work. The presence of relief teams (trained and untrained) arriving and proceeding on their own without any coordination was leading to duplication and lacunae in the relief efforts. An example of lack of coordination mechanism was seen in the fact that initially relief material was distributed only along the main roads while the interior regions were left out. This was primarily due to the media reflections, which concentrated mainly on the urban areas of Bhuj, Anjar and Bhachau in the initial days after the earthquake. All these circumstances necessitated the setting up of a coordination and information sharing mechanism which took the form of sub-centres prior to the formal set-up of the *Setus*, to coordinate and direct relief in the interior rural areas of Kachchh.

Precursor to the *Setus*: Sub-centres during the Relief Phase

Immediately within the first two days post-earthquake, Abhiyan Group undertook a preliminary village level survey at the behest of the district administration to access the damage across the district, which formed the baseline for the start of relief operations. Based on the preliminary assessment a fair idea about the extent of damage across the district emerged which helped the district administration to gauge the relative need for relief efforts in different parts of the district. Analysing these needs, the district administration and the Abhiyan group realized that large tracts of interior rural areas of the district (particularly in Rapar and Bhachau) had a more urgent need for relief efforts than previously estimated. The lack of information sharing mechanism was leading to misplaced and misguided relief efforts by teams of volunteers and disaster workers arriving from outside the district who relied chiefly upon media reports to undertake their relief efforts. Thus the Abhiyan group of NGOs with the support of the district administration, set up 33 sub-centres three days after the earthquake–initially as depots where relief material could be stored and from where relief work could be coordinated. These sub-centres were supposed to coordinate the relief by catering to the information related needs arising from the different stakeholders. In order to reach out to the interior rural areas, these sub-centres were set up at the cluster level covering around 15-20 villages each. These sub-centres were set up strategically at nodal places (transport centres or cluster level market centres) which were well-connected to the cluster of villages that each represented. Cumulatively, all these sub-centres together covered 468 villages that were most affected by the earthquake at that point of time.

These sub-centres were a brain child of Abhiyan group and the district administration. Initially most of the sub-centres were run by staff of volunteers from the Abhiyan group of NGOs. As most of the buildings were in a damaged condition, the sub-centres' operations were run from tents in the premises of public or government institutions like PHC, primary schools, etc. The sub-centres were provided with a four-wheeler and some rations of food and medicines. Most of the sub-centres had no access to electricity and/or phone lines.

Even so the staff of the sub-centres had conducted a preliminary survey of the villages and supplied credible data regarding the extent of damage caused in each of these villages within 48 hours of the government demanding such a data. The sub-centres went to each village and community for the collection of this data. They collected this "critical data" on the basis of which the government's relief work was facilitated in the initial stages of relief.

The sub-centres were initially involved in the distribution of relief supplies. The sub-centres acted as depots where relief material was pooled and stored before distribution. The staff of the sub-centres would undertake a stock taking exercise on a day-to-day basis while undertaking relief work. The different teams of relief workers would converge at the sub-centres in the evening to formulate their strategy for the next day's relief efforts based on the information collected during the day's relief efforts. Many of the villages and *vandhs* (hamlets or a sub-village level settlements) in the cluster of villages under the coverage of the sub-centres were not connected with metalled roads and very difficult to access, but even these were supplied with relief material. During this relief phase, the sub-centre staff established rapport with the community leaders in the villages. The community leaders would approach the sub-centre staff with their problems and issues connected to the relief efforts. Gradually this mechanism evolved into a formal set-up in each village of Gram Navrachana *samitis* (Village Rehabilitation/Redevelopment Committees) or Information Samitis. These samitis (committees) comprising of community representatives in each village facilitated the interaction between the sub-centres and village communities by representing the problems of communities in each village during the relief phase.

Due to their regular interaction and unbiased conduct, sub-centre staff managed to acquire an image as 'objective and neutral facilitators of relief efforts' with the affected village communities. Thus the sub-centres gradually began to function as coordination platforms for supplying information and directing the different disaster teams arriving from outside the district. But it must be noted here that even though the sub-centres tried to make the relief available to all the villages by directing the relief teams arriving from outside, they were only partially successful as there was no official mandate regarding the sub-centres' role to act as mediators. Thus many of the relief agencies went about the relief work on their own without approaching the sub-centres. The sub-centres continued their relief efforts in the manner mentioned above for almost three months till the formal set-up of *Setus* (in Kodki and Dhamadka clusters) in May 2001.

Formalization of the *Setus* from the Sub-Centres

The change and formalization of Sub-centres into '*Setus*' happened between April–June 2001, when the relief activities in the district, were also transiting from relief to interim rehabilitation measures.

During this time with the approaching monsoon season in July, the primary objective of the NGOs/voluntary organizations was to provide the houseless with temporary shelter for protecting them against the rains (though a normal rainfall is seen in the region only once in three years). As the relief phase was ending and when the rehabilitation process was starting, various problems surfaced such as :

1. Lack of credible feedback to the government from the grassroots level.
2. Lack of information to the community on available resources and rehabilitation policies of government and NGOs.
3. Concentration of NGOs in areas that were easily accessible and not necessarily those which had been badly affected. Many of the affected areas were being left out of the rehabilitation efforts, particularly in provision of temporary shelters. For example in the villages covered by Kodki *Setu*, most of the initial rehabilitation activities were concentrated in five villages that were the easiest to approach and which had community leaders with better political connections.

The *Setus*, in this period transited out of a predominantly relief coordination role, and facilitated the interim rehabilitation activities to overcome the above stated problems. The interim measures supported by the *Setus* chiefly consisted of:

- Support the provision of semi-permanent shelter to the affected communities by facilitating their access to the construction material/goods for temporary shelter;
- Aid in the repairs of water resource structures before the monsoon season started to prevent them from being inundated or further damaged;
- Facilitating the debris removal from village settlement areas by coordinating with the village communities and the government functionaries;
- Detailed damage assessments and taking note of associated grievance redressal issues for providing inputs to district and local authorities;
- Discussion with communities to aid the development of plans

for housing relocation or *in situ* housing development plans; and

- Training of masons for the huge reconstruction that was to follow, and setting up demonstrations of seismic safe features in construction.

Concept of the *Setus*

The concept of the *Setus* emerged from the initial role played by the sub-centres and the work undertaken by them during the interim relief phase. *Setus* as the name suggests was envisaged to serve as a bridge between the communities, various NGOs working in the field of rehabilitation and the government machinery. This was done with the view to fill the gaps between the government machinery and the communities, particularly because of the unusual circumstances arising out of a natural disaster situation (earthquake), which were furthermore compounded by the prevailing drought conditions.

The concept of the *Setu* was based on that of e-governance through the use of information. This means that the communities were promoted and facilitated to have a direct say (not through the political setup or the long chain of bureaucrats) in the way they wanted rehabilitation efforts to progress. It was an experiment at providing an opportunity to the individuals and the communities for deciding the course of the rehabilitation process by making use of information. So it was an experiment in 'empowerment through information' wherein *Setus* acted as unbiased facilitators for the flow of information.

The following assumptions led to the creation of *Setus* as information centres :

1. Community needs information but it is not easily accessible or not accessible at all.
2. Community will come to a local centre for information if it is made available in a manner useful to them.
3. Community understands and is able to reflect the kind and amount of information it wants.
4. Community will use the given information for the intended purpose, that is, for its growth and self-renewal.

The concept of the *Setu* was not functionally clear (i.e. how to put it into practice) when it was put into operation in Kodki and Dhamadka clusters because there was no precedent for such a project in a disaster situation and the model had to be developed by trial and error. So the development of the *Setu* evolved gradually over a period of time responding to the upcoming circumstances and challenges while trying to fultil the following objectives for which the *Setu* had been set up :

- To be a source of valid information to the community.
- To empower the local community by enhancing their access to information.
- To make *setu* a part of the community whereby daily decision-making process is enhanced and transparency increases in the governance process.
- To facilitate accurate and regular flow of information back and forth between the community, individual, government agencies and NGOs.
- To assess the community's need for the type of information and suggest the ways by which the information can be presented.
- To clarify community apprehensions regarding earthquake and related issues.

Gradually by July 2001, the rural areas in the district, began to move towards long term rehabilitation measures, with the Government freezing most of its rehabilitation packages for the rural area. NGOs and villages began to finalize their partnerships in various reconstruction activities and self-supported reconstructions by affected households also started. Around 20 *setus* were set up by July 2001 each with a newly recruited team headed by a trained social worker. These were later expanded to 33 *setus*. The coverage area of the *setu* network at that time extended across the talukas (sub-district administrative units) of Bhuj (Pachcham and Pavar belt), Bhachau, Anjar, Rapar, Abdasa and Mundra.

The Gujarat Government looking to the experiences of sub-centres and the emerging *setus* mandated them *setus* as Earthquake Rehabilitation Support Centres (ERSC). Such a mandate was to enable effective and speedy rehabilitation by supporting and coordinating the very many rehabilitation efforts through a flow of information. Post July 2001 the *setus* undertook efforts to :

- Coordinate information needs of the different stakeholders,
- Identify, forward and follow up grievances to facilitate the redressal mechanisms, particularly with respect to entitlements for compensation.
- Support advocacy in terms of influencing Government decision-making through quantitative and qualitative feedback on the rehabilitation process. This was particularly seen when information collected by the *setus* was used to advocate '*in situ*' rehabilitation measures with the Gujarat government.(UNDP, 2001).
- Facilitate partnerships between NGOs and villages for different rehabilitative aspects (particularly in rebuilding permanent shelter).
- Facilitate retrofitting efforts to partially damaged and undamaged houses by awareness generation and programme support.
- Undertake proactive rehabilitation and implementation with the most vulnerable—especially paraplegics, injured, widows, orphans, and economically poor.
- Support the extensive door-to-door physiotherapy in four blocks of the district by the health agencies.

Till then *Setus* had essentially coordinated with the Abhiyan headquarters in Bhuj to link up the needs emerging from village communities and the resources available to meet them for rehabilitating the affected people. *Setus* till June 2001 had responded to the need based requirements that came from the stakeholders by using Abhiyan as a medium for advocacy and coordination. But when the *Setus* were being formalized, a Central Coordination Unit (CCU) for all the *Setus* was established in Bhuj which formed the link between the district level agencies, NGOs and the different *Setus* established all across the district. The CCU formed the nodal unit representing all the *Setus* collectively.

Another aspect of coordination tried out was related to the Gram Nav Rachana Samitis set up during the relief phase. These committees consisted of community representatives and were set up at the village level in the villages under the coverage of the *setu* network. These had become non-functional after the initial rehabilitation phase as more number of people started approaching the *setus* directly. This had come about primarily because the *samitis* were not given an issue, taking which they could continue functioning. So the initiative of Gram Nav Rachana Samiti (village level coordination committee) died down once the relief work was complete. The efforts were once again initiated to refashion these committees so that these could start functioning and take up the various issues affecting them during the rehabilitation phase.

Use of Information by the *setus* During the Rehabilitation Phase

In the aspect of information collection, the major activities undertaken during this phase were collection of data on :

- Status of construction of permanent shelter (started/not started/levels of construction);
- Status of seismic safety of the houses constructed;
- Status of the distribution of financial compensation for reconstruction (given for construction of houses);
- Status of the distribution of financial compensation for repair of damaged houses;
- Status of construction and of seismic safety of health and education infrastructure like schools;
- Other need based information collection like Participatory Rural Appraisals for identified thematic areas based on external NGO requirements; and
- Apart from those mentioned above, *setus* had collected information based on the requirements of different stakeholders and to support their own initiatives (e.g., information on panchayats, health services, schools, etc.).

The collected information was supplied in raw form or after a preliminary analysis to the government and to the NGOs who asked for it. The information collected was also used by the *Setus* for advocacy purposes and to raise public awareness. *Setus* had also taken information from the government, wherever and whenever possible, about the status of surveys and resurveys done by the government technical teams, and disseminated it to the villagers who needed it. Thus information was used as a tool to seek cooperation of the different stakeholders in the rehabilitation process. Such information supply in a non-biased manner was intended to reduce the confusion and decrease chances of manipulation by vested interests in the rehabilitation efforts. The information dissemination in different forms was intended to reduce information asymmetry among the different stakeholders and bring all of them on an equal footing, whereby informed dialogue could take place for achieving cooperation among the different players.

Wide dessimination about entitlements based on government survey results were done, because initially when the surveyors came to the villages for the first time for damage assessment survey at the end of relief phase, nobody in the village knew about its purpose and how it was going to affect them. It was conducted in a haphazard manner because even the government did not have a clear idea and criteria, about the way in which it was to be conducted. The engineers who conducted the survey were not professionally equipped and there were no clear administrative and technical guidelines for them to go by (procedure to be followed). The government just wanted to finish the survey so it could start paying compensation because of the hue and cry in the media over non-payment of compensation.

Moreover due to lack of uniform and clear cut policy with respect to the construction of permanent shelters by the NGOs, Government and community partnerships the whole situation was chaotic and nobody could assess whether a person had received what was his due. As the MOUs signed between the various NGOs and the government were not made public so the people did not know what they were entitled to get. So they could be misled, which had happened with a number of communities. These communities were promised something and given something else.

Development of Software

There were a number of users for the data generated by the *setus*, so even on a single theme there were different people or organizations which wanted different kinds of data from different levels and at different frequencies. So the need for a software, to satisfy the complex user requirements of all the users was felt necessary. In order to systematize the process of data collection and develop a database on the district, a software known as the "*setu* information management system" was developed. Information of 12 sectors was envisaged to be collected and fed into this system that would be able to generate reports based on the queries. Information to shelter to disability, handicrafts and vulnerable sections of the society were to be collected from household or person-wise in the villages and this was intended to be updated annually. This software was developed with an intention to develop a database on the region which would help disaster mitigation and development efforts. TCS was involved by Abhiyan to develop this software. An information coordinator had been recruited for each *Setu* who was basically a data entry operator whose role was to manage soft data and the filing systems of the *Setus*.

Other Uses of Information as a Tool for Empowerment

Apart from the above information related activities which formed the core of *Setu* work, some of the other activities undertaken by the *setus* using information as a tool for empowerment are mentioned below:

Distribution of "Mahiti Booklets" in the Village

During December–March 2002 Khari *Setu* initiated an important process of taking villagers' views on the rehabilitation work done over the past year, documenting it, and then giving the same information back to the villagers in the form of booklets. *Setu* received an encouraging response from the villagers and as a result, it strengthened its own faith in the process of sharing information with the community.

The mahiti booklets were booklets containing all the information of a particular village. All the information collected by the *Setu* in relation to that particular village was present in the mahiti booklet. Khari *Setu* took the initiative in giving the village information back to the villagers in compiled and collated form. Thus all the information whether collected from the government sources, NGOs or from the villagers themselves was disseminated back to them. It was an attempt to bring about transparency between the *Setu* and the village communities in addition to making available to all the communities, the information which actually belonged to them.

The mode of distribution of these booklets was by conducting Gram Sabhas (village level gatherings) where the whole village was invited and the booklets were distributed to all the key persons, the community representatives and the village leaders. A copy of this booklet was presented to the panchayat (village level elected body). The booklet could act as a brochure for the village in case some agency from outside came to the village and asked for basic information of the village. During the Gram Sabha a process of "evaluating the rehabilitation process" by the village communities was also taken up. What do the village communities feel about the different aspects of relief phase, rehabilitation phase and the present *status*. A year after the earth quake—In this process it was expected that the communities express and evaluate not just the performance of NGOs or Government but also their own role in the process of rehabilitation. Such a dialogue also strengthened the community awareness about their own roles and capacities in the disaster mitigation process.

Based on this precedent set by Khari *Setu*, six other *Setus* undertook this same process in the villages under their coverage.

Anti Corruption Campaign

Three *Setus* had taken up awareness activities as a part of their anti–corruption campaign. Dhamadka, Kharoi and Kabrau had initiated the anti-corruption campaign. A systematic and long running campaign was launched by Kharoi *Setu*. The campaign consisted of school competitions, street plays, programmes by folk singers and campaigning through billboards. The anti corruption campaign focused upon the irregularities that had occurred during the distribution of compensation for the earthquake affected. It was equally critical of both the government officials and the community which had hand in glove indulged in this corruption process. This campaign was launched in all the villages under Kharoi *Setu*. Kharoi setu had faced a lot of flak from the community and the local government officials on account of this anti-corruption campaign being conducted by it. A lot of opposition and threats were also received by Dhamadka and Kabrau *Setu* who played a major role in exposing the corrupt practices of select local government officials and community leaders in their areas.

Identification of the Most Needy and Vulnerable

Seven *setus* had identified the neediest and the vulnerable in their respective clusters based on which coordination with organizations like Care-Today and Janvikas was done to provide the most vulnerable individual households with monetary and non-monetary support to help them to sustain themselves. Thus a data bank of such persons under each *setu* was initiated and when required it could be immediately forwarded along with all the details to the agency requesting such information.

Grievance Redressal

Seven *setus* had conducted legal clinics for the redressal of grievances with respect to compensation in the rehabilitation process. Another objective of these clinics was to reduce the number of misconceptions regarding the entitlement that the people thought they were supposed to receive. Those cases which were genuine and had certain substance in them were provided with proper legal advice by the lawyers from the Centre for Social Justice, so that these cases could get registered at the proper forum in the right manner.

Putting up Information Boards

Information boards giving the basic information about the village and damage suffered were developed and put up in all the villages covered by the *Setus*. This was done with the purpose of creating public information platforms for sharing of information. This also helped voluntary agencies visiting the village to get authentic information about the village and damage suffered. In some cases the village communities became accustomed to make use of the information boards for their own information sharing purposes.

Promoting Ownership of Information

In some of the villages, systems had started to develop whereby the village youths and community elders had started gathering their own information on a voluntary basis and passing them on to the *Setus* when encouraged to do so. This was a system, where the village collected its own data, got a sense of ownership out of this process by making use of the information to fulfil their needs (e.g. data of blood group, animal husbandry). This was the particular case of Chhadura *Setu* and Dhamadka *Setu*. Encouraged by Chhadura *Setu* the yuvak mandal in Chhadura village organized a blood group testing camp. Cards informing the people about their blood groups were disseminated in the village. Thus an initiation was done in creating a data bank related to the blood group in the village, which could be used in any disaster or emergincy situation. In Dhamadaka *Setu*—A group of people representing the people involved in animal husbandry, prepared the list (related to people involved in animal husbandry, milch animals in the village and the number/type of animals owned by each person). Based on this a cattle camp was conducted in the village. Such initiatives by the communities were promoted to create local institutional mechanisms owned by the communities which helped them to create and maintain their own data banks for their needs.

Thus *Setus* used information as a communication and advocacy tool in various forms. This was similar to the important role of communication that was proposed later in the Gujarat State disaster management policy which stated, "Communication activities are necessary to convey to the larger community the scope and nature of the proposed reconstruction and rehabilitation effort so as to increase the stakeholder awareness and buy-in for the ongoing activities." This policy advocates the use of communication for purposes of public relations, community management and seeking feedback on rehabilitation measures. Thus it advocates what the *Setus* followed in action prior to the policy coming into effect.

Setus in the Post Rehabilitation Phase : Gradual Shift to Developmental Activities

The various efforts which aimed at relief and rehabilitation after the earthquake, tried to restore the communities to their prior status. As the focus was on relief and rehabilitation, the developnmental issues were given less attention. *Setu* was to some extent successful in creating a common platform for all to come together and played a role in resolving the misunderstanding by sharing of information. The *Setus* over a period of time had developed not exactly as envisaged, i.e. as purely information centres but also played a part in smooth implementation process of permanent shelter reconstruction by becoming mediators between the communities, government and

NGOs. *Setu* as an institution again underwent changes as the rehabilitation phase was nearing an end. Earlier the primary work of the *setu* used to be related to information and coordination with the various agencies involved in the different aspects of rehabilitation. At the end of the rehabilitation phase the volume of work in terms of rehabilitation had decreased and the attention was slowly being diverted towards developmental aspects like education, health, water, etc. Thus many of the *setus* put forth various proposals to facilitate issues related to development related work emerging from the village communities where they were active. The information related work undertaken by the *setus* during rehabilitation phase helped the *setus* to transit their efforts to developmental activities with the intention of using information as a catalyst in the development process.

Support to Set up "Community Maintained Institutions"

A total of 18 *setus* had put forth their proposals on aspects related to which they proposed to set up small community models. The purpose of institution building within the communities had been taken up so that these could at a later stage develop into community based institutions which could independently handle developmental issues. The vision was "community is the major stakeholder and the major contribution should come from them" in order to ensure the sustainability of the proposed models. These developmental models were sought to be undertaken basically in four sectors namely health, education, water and governance.

Health Sector

Two *setus* had started work on the identification of personnel who could be trained as village level health workers (VHWs). The idea was to get people in the village trained so that in case of emergencies or small ailments these trained personnel could handle it at the village level. This would both help in saving the cost, time and in case of emergencies first aid would be immediately available.

Such a step was important for getting a community prepared to handle disasters. Moreover, in an area like Kachchh where the population is sparse and scattered away from the urban centres and where the modes of transportation are not immediately available, this step of training village level health workers was sorely needed. The idea was to get these village level workers trained, by coordinating with the organizations working in the health sector. Once trained these VHWs would cater to the rural communities who would in turn bear the cost of the services available to them. This would be comparatively cost effective to the communities as the communities would not need to travel to urban centres for simple ailments. Moreover, the idea was that in the long run these trained personnel could act as life savers during emergencies.

Education Sector

Four *setus* had started work in the sector of education, either in adult education, non-formal education and/or improving the quality of formal education. Each village had a village education committee but in most cases these were non-functional. The idea was to make the communities in the villages to take responsibility of getting themselves and their children educated.

In two *setus* after a dialogue with the communities they had recognized the importance of education. They started supporting an educated unemployed youth from the community as a teacher for their children by paying half of the salary in return for teaching their children. In two other *setus* the process was underway whereby the community took up the responsibility of maintaining the quality of education in the formal schools by directing the village education committee or monitoring the attendance/performance of the staff in government run schools.

Water Sector

Nine *setus* had started a dialogue with the communities in their area so that the communities realized the importance of non-dependence on centralized mechanisms of water supply. The idea was that the communities need not have to depend solely on the government water supply but their basic needs of water could be met by reviving the traditional and present sources of water in the village. The *setus* had started a dialogue so that the communities realized that they were the main stakeholders and the primary responsibility of revitalizing and maintaining the common water sources rested with them. In three of the *setus* this was supposed to be done through the mechanism of the panchayats while in other cases the community groups had taken up this responsibility.

Governance-Revitalization of Panchayats

Four *setus* had evinced an interest in strengthening the working of the panchayat system in their areas. It had been felt that panchayat being the basic unit of governance at the grassroots level, strengthening these would help in making local self-governance more responsive towards meeting local aspirations. The local problems and its solutions could be handled effectively if the panchayat members knew their responsibility and roles. This opportunity presented itself when elections to the new panchayat bodies took place in December 2001. With this purpose in mind one of the *setus* conducted a meeting of all the panchayat body members in its area. The problems that the new panchayat members faced in their day-to-day functioning were discussed. Most of the newly elected members as well as some older members had no idea as to their roles, responsibilities and the powers vested in them. Thus the need to design activities and programmes for strengthening the panchayat system and motivate the elected representatives to maintain transparency in their everyday activities was initiated.

Some Key Lessons Learnt for Information use during Relief and Rehabilitation

- The experience of *setus* seems to indicate that it was critical for communities and villages to have one neutral (neither Government, nor NGO) coordinating mechanism that is accessible at the local level which would consider local needs and accordingly facilitate others—the numerous actors, and ensure there was no duplication of disaster mitigation initiatives.
- The key to the spread of information was envisaged through formal and informal networks between different villages through multiple channels and key individuals. To ensure percolation and spread of information in the community multiple channels like information boards, written and verbal communication, booklets, visual media, etc., should be used as per local needs and theme to be communicated. Communication through different key persons like village elders, community leaders, panchayat members, youth groups, women groups, other key government officials like

teachers, postmasters, health officials, bus drivers, conductors, etc., must be explored. These same sources should be used to crosscheck data and use of information by the community. Moreover, all information should not be given periodically as a matter of routine to all these people but should be placed into the community strategically so that it finds easy acceptance and faces the least resistance.

- Transparency can be possible only if information percolates down to each faliya (sub-village settlement pattern) and each person. *Setu's* job was to make information more accessible but it was sometimes hindered by the lengthy bureaucratic procedure involved in seeking information from the government sources. The existence of *setu* cannot be justified if the information sought is not easily accessible to the individuals and communities.
- Need for information of each village/hamlet, *faliya*/caste, class, etc., is different, so information should be personalized as per their need and taking into consideration its usability by the stakeholder seeking the information.
- Information must be made available to the community before it becomes redundant (in a time bound manner). The people should have sufficient time to take advantage of the information and pass it around to others before the information becomes redundant.
- With the constant change in circumstances, government policy, seasons, progress in the stage of rehabilitation and so on, the information needed by the people also changes and these have to be anticipated beforehand so that they could be met in a timely fashion, e.g., the knowledge of different methods of reconstruction had to be provided accurately to the villagers before the construction began.
- It is difficult to spread information in the low population density villages. The low rate of literacy is also an impediment to the spread of information. Putting up boards do not serve much of a purpose if people could not read and decipher boards were a challenge to them. So information must be provided in a manner needed by them, only then interest can be sustained and interaction can be established. Information flow can be

facilitated by the formation of Youth groups or Yuvak Mandals. They can be utilized to bring new information to the villages particularly so because the village youth regularly travel and are open to new ideas.

- The information provided should be accurate and non-biased as the information provided is often crosschecked by the communities before using them. In case found ineffective or inaccurate the faith in the information sharing system is lost.
- Kachchh being a low population density area, the villages are connected to one another through roads, which serve as information pathways as all the villages did not have many other means of communication like telephone, radio, TV, etc. So if the roads are cut off, the information flow is also cut off. Buses plying along these routes could act as messengers. But with the advent of cost effective mobile telephony such means of communication use is also becoming more relevant.
- Despite the *setus* being mandated by the Government, and despite the *setus* being a body which had been perhaps more accepted, and interfaced with, by the district administration and support from GSDMA, the Government was not able to leverage the strength of the *setus*. Rather than proactively using the *setus*, the district government in the post-rehabilitation phase did not enthusiastically respond to the issues that were brought up through the *setus*.
- Since it was a disaster situation, the *setus* performed under tremendous pressure, with little time for extensive trainings. There was no role model, no precedence, which they could follow. Although some training and capacity building was undertaken, this was not adequate in comparison to the magnitude or the scale of work. Thus, trainings and capacity building of the *setu* team in developmental issues, and methodologies had not been undertaken to the extent that it should have been.

Conclusion

The *setus* had been 'used' quite extensively in the first year and had been able to respond as a support agency, to more than 60 NGOs for provision of critical interventions in the rehabilitation process. The *Setus* had been able to sustain and develop their ability to be reliable, neutral and extensive sources of information for the village, and for the Government, as well as NGOs. Their ability to reach out all at once, to scale, and not compromise on quality had worked during the rehabilitation phase. At that time, their understanding of the villages, communities, attitudes, resources, dynamics in their cluster was a critical resource, and helped the smooth transition of communities to overcome the disaster by facilitating different players to come together on a more equitable and informed basis. Setu was a mechanism which could help the affected people to access necessary information, in a need based manner making information meaningful within a local context for disaster rehabilitation.

Acknowledgments

I am thankful for the guidance received while working for the development of setus from Mr. Srinivas Chokkakula, and Mr. Bhaskar Niranjani who were at that time with Environmental Planning collaborative, Ahmedabad and Kutch Nav Nirman Abhiya, Bhuj.

References

Bilham, Roger (1998). Slip parameters for the Rann of Kachchh, India, 16 June 1819, earthquake, quantified from contemporary accounts, *Geological Society, London, Special Publications*; 1998; v. 146; p. 295-319

Census of India, (2001). Data on area of India available http://www.censusindia.gov.in/ Census_Data_2001/India_at_glance/area.aspx

Census of India (2001). Available at http://www.censusindia.gov.in/Dist_File/datasheet-2401.pdf

Gujarat Ecology Commission, (1996), *Process of Desertification in Kachchh and Banaskantha Districts of Gujarat*, India.

GSDMA (Gujarat State Disaster Management Authority) (2001). Unpublished report titled "Gujarat Earthquake reconstruction and rehabilitation policy 2001" available at www.gsdma.org/pdf/Earthquake%20Rehabilitation%20Policy.pdf

GSDMA (Gujarat State Disaster Management Authority), (2001). *Gujarat State Disaster Management Policy.*

Indian Meteorological Department, (2001), Figures available at http://www.gsdma.org/rehab_package1.htm

Karanth, R.V. (2001). Unpublished report titled "Structure and tectonics of Kachchh region of western India: An appraisal", available at http://www.gisdevelopment.net/application/natural_hazards/earthquakes/nheq0004c.htm

Kutch Nav Nirman Abhiyan, (2004), Unpublished report titled Abhiyan's Journey Post 2001 Earthquake.

Kutch Nav Nirman Abhiyan (2004), Unpublished Report titled Abhiyan-AIF partnership: An Initiative to rebuild Kutch

Mishra, P.K. (2004). *The Kutch Earthquake 2001; Recollections, Lessons and Insights*, New Delhi: National Institute of Disaster Management.

Thiruppugazh, V. (2007). *Post-disaster Reconstruction: A Case Study of Gujarat Earthquake Reconstruction*, Australian National University.

UNDP (United Nations Development Programme) (2001). *From relief to Recovery: The Gujarat Experience*, October 2001

UNDP(United Nations Development Programme) (2002), *Gujarat Transition Recovery Team—A Synopsis*, January 2002.

Vatsa, Krishna S. (2001), pp. 7-8, The Bhuj Earthquake District of Kutch, State of Gujarat (India), January 26, 2001: A Reconnaissance Report—Identification of Priority Issues, Prepared for DRM—World Institute for Disaster Risk Management, March 16, 2001.

8

Government Intervention into the Disaster Insurance Market : Issues and Alternatives in Japan and China

TAO YE, MUNETA YOKOMATSU, PEIJUN SHI, AND NORIO OKADA

The major catastrophic experience since the 1990s has resulted in wide concern that disaster insurance is not so competent as it was supposed to be in coping with disaster risk. Inherently, the spatial dependence of disaster risk units lowers the effect that insurance could have achieved in transferring disaster risk. Meanwhile, insurers are not motivated to keep liquid reserves with sufficient size which enable them to diversify the risk inter-temporally. Moreover, the international insurance market and the connection between insurance market and capital market are not efficient enough to back up insurance industry. All the factors above restrain the markets for disaster risk from working efficiently.

To cope with market failure in transferring disaster risk, governments are suggested playing a more important role to cope with market failure in transferring disaster risk through intervention. The principle of intervention is proposed to have as many households insured as the sustainability constraint of disaster insurance industry is held. As an illustrative model, an inter-temporal (intergenerational) approach for financing disaster risk is formulated and highlighted as an extension of the Malinvaud-Arrow disaster insurance in the temporal dimension. It is an inherent and robust tool that a government can apply to raise funding resources and diversify disaster risk among generations in the long run. The article further investigates current practices in Japan and China as examples in developed and developing countries, showing how a government can use fiscal resources to cap the unexpected peak losses and motivate potential policyholders to purchase coverage, respectively.

Introduction

The human society has entered a new era of frequent and intensive disasters. Statistics show that from 1987 to 2006, the number of natural disasters occurred around the world increased dramatically (Hoyois *et al.*, 2007). Over the period 1984-2003, more than 4 billion people were affected and the costs of disaster were more than 15 times higher than that during the period of 1950-1959 (World Bank, 2006). In contrast to the devastating consequences of disaster, proactive financing measures are far from mature. The global insured losses have been increasing but the insured proportion shows no significant growth (Munich Re, 2007). Since the 1990s, insurers in developed countries faced serious challenge from catastrophic events where disaster insurance lines are widely provided to households. The disasters of Hurricane Andrew (1992) and the Northridge Earthquake (1994) alone totalled over $45 billion in 1997, with the insured component running to almost $28 million, causing the failure of nine insurance companies (Froot, 1999a). In developing and economy-emerging countries, small scale disasters are frequently hitting our rural and poor areas, doing a lot of damages (Guha-Sapir *et al.*, 2004). The extremely low insurance penetration makes *ex post* survival issues of victims rely only on very limited government relief and humanitarian donation.

With the major failure experience of the catastrophic insurance market, researchers started the discussion on the roles of private and public sectors in financing disaster risk. It reached to the conclusion that neither the government nor the market could manage disaster risk independently, and the only approach is to integrate their advantages (Kleindorfer and Kunreuther, 1999; Kunreuther, 2001), and well designed national or regional financing systems will help to integrate both sectors (Scawthorn, 2006). Due to the difference of political scheme and culture, strategies among countries should be different where either public or private sector would enact as the leading role (Kunreuther, 2000). With the innovations in the financial instruments for disaster risk management, the government-insurer partnership was developed further into the so-called "Safety Nets" in which NGOs and international institutions and donors get involved in (Linnerooth-Bayer and Mechler, 2007).

Economic literature has put considerable discussion on the organization of private-public partnership in disaster risk management, e.g., public investment in mitigation plus private efforts in financing, the optimum investment sharing mechanism of private and public sectors in mitigation infrastructure, and roles of them in financing disaster risk. This article exclusively discusses the role of government in supporting the private sector in financing disaster risk.

Issues and Challenges in Disaster Insurance

Difficulty in Identification of Risk Curve

Disasters are dentified as large-scale and high-severity events with hundreds of thousands of people affected in one single event. The idiosyncrasy of the disaster risk violates the presumption of independence between risk units and consequently makes it difficult to price disaster insurance lines. It is quite tough to obtain cumulative density function (*c.d.f.*) and Exceedance-Probability (*EP*) curve meeting actuarial accuracy when comes to disaster risk, which are indispensable in designating stop-loss premium rates for insurance lines. On the one hand, limited historical records are not sufficient to extract valid probability density functions and the unique feature (low frequency with bulky arrivals) of disaster risk makes statistical (generally Bayesian) approach that is widely adopted in pricing other insurance lines much less effective. On the other hand, no credible correlation coefficients among risk units are available for constructing copulas to describe the multivariate distribution when Monte Carlo method is employed to determine the stop-loss premium rate. As a result, insurers have to add risk premium on the actuarial premium rate to reflect the cost of ambiguity (Kunreuther *et al.*, 1995; Schade *et al.*, 2002), which could be 1.8 times higher than when insuring events with well specified probability and loss estimation (Kunreuther *et al.*, 1993). Nowadays, academic institutions, insurance brokers, and government agencies are trying to develop catastrophic models to estimate the probability and consequences of future events so that insurance companies could have solid foundation to price their products. However, various approaches of modelling and considerable variation in quality and sophistication make insurance and reinsurance companies hesitated to make decisions (Jones, 2007).

Insufficient Liquid Capital allocated for Peak Losses

The problem of insufficient funds allocated to fulfil underwritten policies by insurers was realized since the major catastrophic experience in the 1990s (Mürmann, 2001). It is known that modern insurance industry diversifies risk by creating large portfolios of identically and independently distributed risks, so that the variance of risk in the portfolio becomes small. Although the spatial correlation of disaster risk units largely reduces the effect of interspatial diversification and increases the risk of insolvency, insurers are still believed to be able to survive as risks can be diversified not only among units from different geographical regions but also time periods. What an insurer needs is a large pool of liquid capital through premium accumulation and business surplus which can cushion the large random shocks. Insurance companies, however, have strong incentives for not keeping such reserves in liquid cash (Jaffee and Russel 1996). (1) Accounting practice in property/casualty insurance preclude an insurance corporation from setting up a reserve fund against a loss which has not yet occurred, even though the occurrence of that loss at sometime is highly likely. (2) Even if insurers are allowed to set up reserve funds, they have no incentive to do so because cash in this reserve as well as interest incomes are taxed in many countries. (3) Companies who hold large stocks of cash are likely to be taken over in the stock market. As a matter of fact, insurers are either not capable or not prepared to handle the unexpected peak claims and generally face serious liquidity crisis when catastrophic disaster hits. The crisis could then probably develop into a bankruptcy.

High Costs for Ceding and Risk Capital Sources

With innovations in the financial management of disaster risk, insurers now have plenty of choices to cede and cap their exposure, using reinsurance and Alternative Risk Transfer (ART) approaches. These approaches, however, are highly capital-dependent and investors' concern on the rate of return has significant impact on the cost of ceding and adopting ART approaches. The cost of ceding to international property-casualty reinsurer follows underwriting cycles with the arrival of mega-catastrophes and the market goes through alternating phases of "hard" and "soft" markets, which can be vividly depicted by the World Rate on Line Index developed by Guy Carpenter & Company (2007). The existence of cycles implies that the response of insurance markets to large events losses is not necessarily fully efficient in the sense that prices are not predictable and supply shortages may develop periodically (Cummins, 2007). It is believed that the cycles are driven by capital market and insurance market imperfections with high friction preventing the free flow of capital (Cummins and Danzon, 1997; Cummins and Doherty, 2002). Insurance-Linked Securities (ILSs), particularly Catastrophic Bond (CAT Bond), are designed to connect disaster insurance market to international capital market by securitizing disaster risk. The connection, however, suffers from significant transaction costs which add up to a large proportion of the premium. The "deadweight" loss of creating a pool can be large relative to the premium that the pool can generate (Froot, 1999b). In early years, ART approaches as young instruments for financing disaster risk were not widely accepted and adopted by investors. The low demand in CAT Bonds also levelled up the costs of issuing. Fortunately the situation is changing. The latest literature from Cummins (2008) claims that CAT bonds have been attracting much more interest from institutional investors with a booming market since 2005 and they are more competitive with conventional reinsurance than earlier analyses may have suggested. Coupled with the new funding approaches for reinsurance such as sidecar, a more efficient disaster risk financing system is likely to emerge in the coming years and the efficiency of the market for financing the high-layer losses is expected to improve.

Government Intervention Into the Insurance Market

Principles for Government Intervention

In order to finance the losses claimed by natural disasters in a proactive and market-oriented way, a government is suggested intervening into the market to help handle inherent and external flaws. The problem faced by a government is to have as many disaster-prone households insured as possible and to keep the risk transfer business solvent, given the fact that disaster risk is not completely washed away and a large proportion of population is not or partially covered by insurance. The two are the so-called "affordability" and "sustainability" principles, respectively (Gurenko, 2007).

The principle of affordability touches upon the question that why rational households purchase only partial coverage or even no coverage. The structure of premium rate would help give the key to this question. As known to all, the true cost of transferring risk equals the probability of the event, given that the risk is *i.i.d.* In such sense, the premium rate is equivalent the probability of the event and households shall purchase full coverage. When the risk is dependent across risk units, however, there would be extra costs attached to the pure premium rate, reflecting the cost of diversifying collective risk among contemporary households, the so-called "risk premium" of the Malinvaud-Arrow insurance. If so, households will optimally purchase partial coverage but note that economic efficiency is still achieved through the exchange even if some households are not fully covered by insurance (Cass, *et al.*, 1996; Yokomatsu and Kobayashi, 2000). Beyond the risk premium, premium rate is further levelled up by various kinds of costs, e.g. costs for the ambiguity of the risk itself, costs for adverse selection, transaction costs in policy underwriting and loss inspection, etc. Given individual expected utility maximization problem, households can insure only a small part of his risk when risk premium and loading factors are significantly large. Moreover, in reality, insurance coverage is not sold as continuous goods written in text-books but in packages which are generally not dividable. When come to such kind of discrete goods, households would face the problem of "take-it-or-leave-it" and it consequently leads to the situation that considerable households are uncovered by any disaster insurance.

If households are risk averse and rational, to increase affordability means to reduce the loading factors and risk premium attached to premium rates. Various policy and fiscal tools have been proposed, e.g., decreased administrative cost through tax exemption or reimbursement, legislation against insurance fraud, compulsory insurance against adverse selection, discriminated premium rate for both adverse selection and *ex ante* moral hazard based on risk mapping, etc. Meanwhile, government investment in catastrophic modelling could help diminish ambiguity on disaster risk. Furthermore, although Pareto efficiency could be achieved by Malinvaud-Arrow disaster insurance, there is still space for improving social welfare if inter-temporal disaster risk diversification is available, which would be put in details in the next section. Last but not the least, direct fiscal intervention into the pricing of insurance lines, e.g., government operated or sponsored disaster insurance programmes with low premium rates, would be very popular with households.

The principle of sustainability implies that all intervention must be controlled so that the business of disaster insurance will not be forced to break down. This is particularly important as now various types of government intervention programmes are being carried out and the market is distorted more or less. A government should enact the last resort of disaster insurance, either to cap the unexpected peak losses which cause private insurers insolvent, or take the place of private sector to take care of the policyholders. Obviously, neither alternative would be cheap. There are several funding approaches for governments to raise liquid capital, e.g., disaster reserve fund, contingent capital, government debt or catastrophic bonds. Among those fiscal instruments, *ex ante* approaches are strongly recommended.

Intergenerational Disaster Risk Diversification

As mentioned in the previous section, in a given time instant, social optimum allocation of disaster risk could be achieved through the exchange of Malinvaud-Arrow insurance, which is a bundled security with mutual insurance contracts plus pure Arrow security. When it reaches equilibria, households purchase partial coverage and risks are not completely washed away. This allocation is Pareto efficient as in the given environment no Pareto improvement can be made. There is a room, however, for better allocation of disaster risk and welfare improvement if the assumption of contemporary (intra-temporal) is removed. This is the so-called "intergenerational (intertemporal) disaster risk diversification" to propose in the following texts.

Intertemporal or intergenerational risk diversification has solid theoretical basis. Yaari (1976) proved that a household would diversify his risks intertemporally by an efficient borrowing-lending strategy that perfectly smoothens his consumption along the time. In the face of random shocks on their future revenues, consumers could reduce the volatility of their consumption by reducing or increasing their reserves, so called the buffer stock strategy (Gollier, 2002). The idea of intertemporal risk diversification is creative in the way that although the probability of disaster risk is not *i.i.d.* across households living in different regions, it is not necessarily the same case along the time. Insurers may have tried to do so but they failed for reasons regarding the liquid reserve mentioned in previous sections. In practice, this kind of inter-temporal diversification pool can only be operated by governments, as they are of little credit risk, sufficient liability and long survival period. They also have power in a centralized economy to redistribute the wealth in the society and balance citizens' welfare. Moreover, governments have easier to access to low interest loans to smooth the shocks along the time.

In order to diversify disaster risk among generations, the government will have to firstly set up a disaster reserve which collects tax revenues from citizens. The tax revenue is then kept either in national bank or trust fund provided by international financial service. When disaster hits the liquid capital would be used to subsidize victims. If the capital in the reserve is contingently not enough, the government will have to make loans from international financial institutions and foreign countries, or get post disaster donors' grant to fill the resources gap. After the disaster, tax revenues would be used to repay the loan on the one hand and accumulate fund in the disaster reserve on the other (Fig. 8.1). The reserve would perfectly smooth the consumption among generations if the ratio of tax to subsidy is appropriately given, and if the government does not face constraint in making international loan.

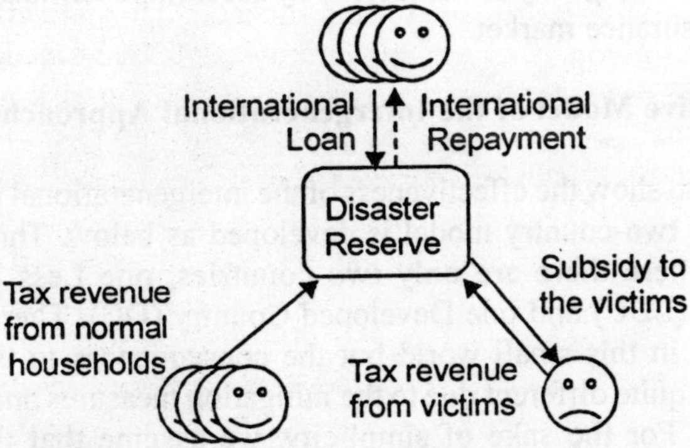

Fig. 8.1: Funding Process of the Disaster Reserve

Once a government sets up the intergenerational disaster risk diversification system, there are several options to conduct intervention. The capital could be used to deal with affordability issues, by either launching public insurance programme or subsidizing households in private insurance programme. In public insurance programmes, the risk premium would be less as the intergenerational diversification mechanism works. Meanwhile, loading factors induced by transaction costs on the premium rate would be less and thus households could get coverage at a more favourable premium rate. In government-sponsored private insurance programmes, a government could use the capital to subsidize policy holders. It could be a lump-sum subsidy or proportional subsidy, while the latter one is widely adopted in practice. When households purchase private insurance coverage, the government would be obligated to pay a certain proportion of the premium. This measure is very effective in most developing and economy-emerging countries, as it will create incentives for households to join in disaster insurance programme. It is because on the one hand the premium rate is much lower (e.g. 50% of the premium is paid by the government) and the participation of government demonstrates the importance and validity of insurance contract.

Alternatively, the liquid capital kept in the reserve would be very compatible to cap the unexpected peak losses for private insurance industry. It can be provided either in the form of state reinsurance programme (Lewis and Murdock, 1996) or emergency capital with predefined terms. Moreover, a government can further expand the risk transfer capacity of the reserve by accessing international capital and reinsurance market.

Illustrative Model of the Intergenerational Approach

In order to show the effectiveness of the intergenerational instrument, a simple two-country model is developed as below. Think about a world where there are only two countries, one Less Developed Country (LDC) and one Developed Country (DC). There are some disasters in this small world but the consequences to the DC and LDC are quite different due to the mitigation measures and financing systems. For the sake of simplicity, we assume that the LDC is damage-prone and its capital assets would be damaged at a certain ratio, $(1-e)$. In contrast, the DC is damage-free. The population is described as a two-period overlapping generations setting, which is a highly abstracted model of individuals' lifetime investment-consumption problem (Fig. 8.2). In such a setting, individuals live for only two periods, young and old. At each period, both young and the generations live contemporarily. One of the most important implications of this setting is that in the later period of individual's lifetime, he must not be in debt and thus loan is not accessible. This matches our previous argument that inter-temporal smooth of consumption purely by individual saving and borrowing behaviour is too ideal to carry out due to the lifetime constraint of households.

Period	1	2	3	4	5	...
Generation	o					
1	y	o				
2		y	o			
3			y	o		
4				y	o	
5					y	o
...						...

Fig. 8.2: Structure of the Two-Period Overlapping Generations Model

Households are rational expected utility maximizers with strictly concave preference. They face a simple two period portfolio management problem: at the first period they get endowment and invest while at the latter one they consume. The disaster strikes at the end of period one with a fixed probability of *m*. The international investment is unilateral and it is only possible for the DC households to invest in LDC, namely the LDC households cannot invest in production in DC. There are several approaches for the LDC households to transfer their risks: (1) purchase international private insurance coverage provided by the DC households; (2) participate in the intergenerational diversification programme operated by the government (Fig. 8.3).

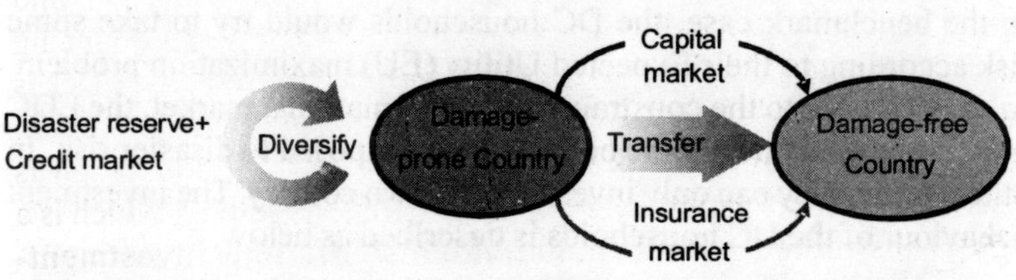

Fig. 8.3: Viable Approaches of Disaster Risk Transfer and Diversification

In this model, an important assumption is since the LDC is less developed and sometimes struck by disasters, the total amount of capital for production would be always less than that in the DC. As the production function is strictly defined as concave, the rate of return of investing in the LDC would be higher than in the DC. Thus, the DC households would always be willing to make their portfolios to take some disaster risk for higher rate of return. Given the list of symbols as below (Table 8.1), we turn to the mathematical part of the model.

Table 8.1: List of Symbols.

Description	*LDC households*	*DC households*	*Description*	*the LDC*	*the DC*
Initial endowment	w_t	w_t^0	Interest rate when disaster does not occur (net, gross)	r_{t+1}^n, R_{t+1}^n	r_{t+1}^0, R_{t+1}^0
Investment in LDC	s_t	s_t^0	Interest rate when disaster occurs (net, gross)	r_{t+1}^d, R_{t+1}^d	r_{t+1}^0, R_{t+1}^0
Investment in DC	—	s_{0t}^0	Total capital investment for production	k_{t+1}	k_{t+1}^0
Consumption when disaster does not occur	c_{t+1}^n	c_{t+1}^{0n}	Damage ratio	$1-\varepsilon$	0
Consumption when disaster occurs	c_{t+1}^d	c_{t+1}^{0d}	Probability of disaster	m	m^o
Insurance premium rate	ν				
Insurance coverage	m	m^0			

(1) Benchmark Equilibrium

In the benchmark case, the DC households would try to take some risk according to their Expected Utility (EU) maximization problem. In contrast, due to the constraint of the international market, the LDC households have no choice but to be fully exposed to disaster risk. In other words, they can only invest in their own country. The investment behaviour of the DC households is described as below:

$$\max_{s_t^0, s_{0t}^0} \mathrm{E}\left[t^0\right] = (1-\mu)u\left(c_{t+1}^{0n}\right) + \mu u\left(c_{t+1}^{0d}\right)$$

$$\text{s.t.} \quad w_t^0 = s_t^0 + s_{0t}^0 \qquad \text{...(1)}$$

$$c_{t+1}^{0n} = R_{t+1}^n s_t^0 + R_{t+1}^0 s_{0t}^0$$

$$c_{t+1}^{0d} = R_{t+1}^d \in s_t^0 + R_{t+1}^0 s_{0t}^0$$

Asset pricing condition is derived as one of the first order conditions as follows:

$$(1-\in) R_{t+1}^n u'\left(c_{t+1}^{0n}\right) + m\mu R_{t+1}^d u'\left(c_{t+1}^{0d}\right) = R_{t+1}^0$$

$$\left[(1-\mu)u^{-}\left(c_{t+1}^{0n}\right) + mu'\left(c_{t+1}^{0d}\right)\right] \qquad \text{...(2)}$$

The optimum choice for the DC households could be denoted as $s_t^{0^*} = s_t^0(w_0)$, $s_{0t}^{0^*} = s_{0t}^0(w_0)$.

Meanwhile, as a general equilibrium, the equilibrium conditions in the capital market and labour market are given in eq. (3) and eq. (4).

$$r_{t+1}^n = f'\left(s_t + s_t^0\right)$$

$$r_{t+1}^0 = f\left(s_{0t}^0\right) \qquad \text{...(3)}$$

$$r_{t+1}^d = f'(e\left(s_t + s_t^0\right)$$

$$w_{t+1}^n = f\left(s_t + s_t^0\right) - r_{t+1}^n \cdot \left(s_t + s_t^0\right)$$

$$w_{t+1}^d = f\left(\in \cdot \left(s_t + s_t^0\right)\right) - r_{t+1}^d \cdot e \cdot \left(s_t + s_t^0\right) \qquad \text{...(4)}$$

$$w_{t+1}^0 = f\left(s_{0t}^0\right) - r_{t+1}^0 \cdot s_{0t}^0$$

All following risk transfer or diversification programmes are discussed in the context of the benchmark equilibrium.

(2) Disaster Risk Transfer through the International Insurance Market

The existence of insurance market depends on whether mutual advantages could be achieved through the contract exchange. The

LDC households would like to buy insurance coverage to diversify their portfolio if affordable on the one hand, and the DC households will be glad to offer insurance coverage if the expected rate of return is too good to refuse on the other. Suppose one needs to pay the premium of νm to cover a physical capital of m. Households would like to maximize their expected utility subject to their lifetime budget constraint. The optimization problem for the individual in the LDC is:

$$\max_{s_t, m} \mathrm{E}[u] = (1-\mu)u(c_{t+1}^{n}) + m\mu(c_{t+1}^{d})$$

$$\text{s.t.} \quad w_t = s_t + vm$$

$$c_{t+1}^{n} = R_{t+1}^{n} s_t \qquad \text{...(5)}$$

$$c_{t+1}^{d} = R_{t+1}^{d} \in s_t + m$$

Assuming interior solutions, the first-order condition for maximization is

$$\frac{u^{-}(c_{t+1}^{n})}{u^{-}(c_{t+1}^{d})} = \frac{\mu m}{1-\mu} = \frac{1-VR_{t+1}^{d}}{vR_{t+1}^{n}} \qquad \text{...(6)}$$

The optimization problem for the individual in the DC is:

$$\max_{s_t^0, s_{0t}^0, m^0} \mathrm{E}[\mu^0] = (1-\mu)u(c_{t+1}^{0n}) + \mu u(c_{t+1}^{0d}) \qquad \text{...(7)}$$

$$\text{s.t.} \quad w_t^0 = s_t^0 + s_{0t}^0 - vm^0$$

$$c_{t+1}^{0n} = R_{t+1}^{n} s_t^0 + R_{t+1}^{0} s_{0t}^0$$

$$c_{t+1}^{0d} = R_{t+1}^{d} \in s_t^0 + R_{t+1}^{0} s_{0t}^0 - m^0$$

and the fist-order condition for maximization is

$$\frac{\mu(c_{t+1}^{0n})}{\mu(c_{t+1}^{0d})} = \frac{\mu}{1-\mu}\frac{1-vR_{t+1}^{d}}{mR_{t+1}^{n}} = \frac{\mu}{1-\mu}\frac{1-vR_{t+1}^{0}}{vR_{t+1}^{0}} \qquad \text{...(8)}$$

We will have the equilibrium conditions in capital market and labour market. Besides, equilibrium in the insurance market is given as

$$m(v^{*}) = v^{0}(v^{*}) \qquad \text{...(9)}$$

(3) Intergenerational Disaster Diversification

By setting up disaster reserve and making international loans, the government of LDC would be able to "smooth" the consumptions among generations. If the society's discount rate is *Q*, the social welfare function is usually given by

$$W = \sum_{it} = Q_t (1+\theta)^{-t} \mathrm{E}[(c_t)] \qquad \text{...(10)}$$

If the time horizon is long enough and each generation's life time is relatively short, the social welfare function can be approximated to a continuous one:

$$W = f = \mathrm{E}[u(c_t)] e^{-\theta t} \int_o^{\infty} dt \qquad \text{...(11)}$$

Assuming that the economy is in steady state where each generation behaves in identical economic environment in *ex-ante* sense, the objective function that the government maximizes can be reduced to the expected utility function of the representative generation. Thus, the social welfare maximization problem is equivalent to personal optimization problem of the representative household.

$$\max_{s_t, m} \mathrm{E}[u] = (1-\mu) u\left(c^n_{t+1}\right) + \mu u\left(c^d_{t+1}\right) \qquad \text{...(12)}$$

The funding process of the disaster reserve fund could be denoted as

$$dZ_t = r^{0*}_{t+1} Z_t dt + \gamma dt - n dt - (\sigma - \zeta) dN(t) \qquad \text{...(13)}$$

where Z_t is the total disaster reserve fund raised by the LDC government for diversifying disaster risk. τ is the annual tax imposed on the LDC households to accumulate disaster reserve fund. η is the mean annual repayment from the disaster reserve fund to the DC households. σ is the subsidy to the LDC households after the arrival of disaster. The subsidy σ consists of two parts: σ-ζ from the disaster reserve fund and ζ from the international loan. The sign of σ is given as (+). Once the subsidy includes foreign loans, the following generations will have to pay back the loan, which means that the annual repayment $\eta > 0$. $dN(t)$ denotes the standard Poisson process, which represents the arrival of natural disaster. We could know from the property of Poisson process that $dN(t) . \prod dt$, which means that the expected occurrence of disaster in one unit time is just equal to the intensity of the process, *m*.

In order to discuss the relationship between total loan and annual repayment, we should take into consideration the balance condition of the loan, denoted as

$$dL_t = \gamma^* L_t dt + \eta dt - \zeta dN(t) \quad \text{...(14)}$$

Note that here we use γ instead of r_{t+1}^{0*} for simplicity. Solving for $\mathrm{E}[Z_t]$ and $\mathrm{E}[L_t]$ (for detailed approach of solving, please turn to Ye *et al.*, 2008), we know that

$$\mathrm{E}[Z_t] = \left(\frac{t - \eta - (\sigma - \zeta)\mu}{r}(1 - e^{-\gamma t}) + Z_0\right)e^{rt} \quad \text{...(15)}$$

$$\mathrm{E}[L_t] = \left(\frac{\eta - \zeta\mu}{r}(1 - e^{-\gamma t}) + L_0\right)e^{\gamma t}$$

By No-Ponzi-Game condition (Blanchard and Fischer, 1989), the sustainability constraints of the disaster reserve fund and the balancing condition of the international loan could be given as

$$\lim_{t\to\infty} \mathrm{E}[Z_t]e^{-\gamma t} = 0, \text{ and } \lim_{t\to\infty} \mathrm{E}[L_t]e^{-\gamma t} = 0 \quad \text{...(16)}$$

Hence, the sustainability constraints of disaster reserve and balancing condition for international loan change to

$$\frac{\zeta - \eta - (\sigma - \zeta)\mu}{\gamma} + Z_0 = 0$$

$$\frac{\eta - \zeta\mu}{\gamma} + L_0 = 0 \quad \text{...(17)}$$

By letting the initial amount of disaster reserve and loan both equal to 0, we get the equilibrium condition in disaster reserve and international loan

$$\eta = \mu\zeta,\text{, and } \gamma = \mu\sigma \quad \text{...(18)}$$

Equation 18 implies that the ratio of tax paid to government subsidy is equal to the probability of disaster. If there is no limitation, as a risk neutral funding resources, the disaster reserve will absorb all disaster risk from the households and diversify it perfectly. The LDC households would then pay the amount of tax which equals to the insurance premium of purchasing full coverage when premium rate is fair. Households' lifetime budget constraints change to

$$\begin{aligned} s_t &= w_t - \tau \\ c_{t+1}^{n} &= \left(1 + r_{t+1}^{n}\right) s_t \\ c_{t+1}^{d} &= \left(1 + r_{t+1}^{d}\right) \in s_t \sigma(\gamma) \end{aligned} \quad \text{...(19)}$$

$$\begin{aligned} s_t^0 + s_{0t}^0 &= w_t^0 - \zeta \\ c_{t+1}^{0n} &= \left(1 + r_{t+1}^{n}\right) s_t^0 + \left(1 + r_{t+1}^{0}\right)\left(s_{0t}^0 + \zeta\right) \\ c_{t+1}^{0d} &= \left(1 + r_{t+1}^{d}\right) e s_t^0 + \left(1 + r_{t+1}^{0}\right)\left(s_{0t}^0 + \zeta\right) \end{aligned} \quad \text{...(20)}$$

However, the assumption of no limitation does not stand. As the disaster reserve is kept in the DC, thus the equilibrium in the capital in the DC used to production is changed to

$$k_{t+1}^0 = s_{0t}^0 + Z_t \quad \text{...(21)}$$

Note that the k_{t+1}^0 in (21) would be different from the previous case. When the disaster reserve is kept in the DC, it lowers the rate of return of investing in DC while simultaneously the capital in LDC goes down and the rate of return of investing in the LDC would go higher. Then the DC households would adjust their portfolio by adding investment in the LDC. However, as it is risky investment, the amount would be less than Z_t and thus k_{t+1}^0 is likely to be larger than that in the previous case.

Eq. (20) indicates that DC young households lend money to the LDC government and then get fully repaid in the latter period of their life, both the principle and the interest. In this sense, the DC young households are equivalent to the benchmark case because the money originally used to invest in the DC are lent to the LDC government but returned at the same rate of return as domestic investment. Due to the personal optimization programme, the size of the loan should be not larger than the size of optimum domestic investment of the next young generation, s_{0t+1}^{0*}. This means that there would be an up limit of subsidy. The payment capacity of the disaster reserve fund should equal to the funds kept in disaster reserve plus the maximum willingness of lending of the foreign young generation,

$$s = \zeta_{t+1} + Z_{t+1} \leq s_{0t+1}^{0*} + Z_{t+1} \qquad \text{...(22)}$$

This equation implies that a household would get subsidy of σ = min {σ, σ}, in which *s* is the amount of subsidy a household needed to fully diversify his risk. If the household wants to optimize its expected utility, it must know two pieces of information: the one is the fund kept in disaster reserve and the other is how much the foreign young generation would invest in the DC. Meanwhile, the maximum subsidy capacity from the disaster reserve will also affect the investment behaviour of the DC households. Similarly, in practice, governments could make large amount of loans based on the State credit. This large amount, however, doesn't mean infinite.

(4) Numerical Results

If we specify the probability and damage ratio of disaster as $\mu = 0.2$, $\varepsilon = 0.5$, and instantaneous production function and utility function both in log form, we could get the expected utilities in all three cases. The results are listed in Tables 8.2, 8.3, and 8.4.

Table 8.2: Numerical Results of Transferring Disaster Risk via the Capital Market

No.	w_t	w_t^0	s_t^{0*}	s_{0t}^{0*}	R_{t+1}^0	R_{t+1}^n	R_{t+1}^d	$E[u]^*$	$E[u^0]^*$
1.	5	5	0.00	5.00	1.200	1.200	0.400	1.684	1.792
2.	5	15	0.80	14.20	1.070	1.172	0.372	1.657	2.776
3.	5	25	1.85	23.15	1.043	1.146	0.346	1.631	3.261
4.	6	15	0.00	15.00	1.067	1.167	0.367	1.834	2.773
5.	6	25	0.98	24.02	1.042	1.143	0.343	1.811	3.260
6.	6	35	1.59	33.41	1.030	1.132	0.332	1.799	3.585

From the results of numerical simulation, several important implications can be found. The first is compared to the benchmark case, it improves the expected utility of households a lot either to transfer the risk via the insurance market or to diversify it among generations. The second is the premium rate in the insurance market is approximately 20 per cent higher than the fair premium rate. It is

Table 8.3: Numerical Results of Transferring Disaster Risk via Private Insurance Market

No.	w_t	w_t^0	s_t^{0*}	v	m_t^*	s_t^{0*}	s_{0t}^{0*}	R_{t+1}^0	R_{t+1}^n	R_{t+1}^d	$\mathrm{E}[u]^*$	$\mathrm{E}[u^0]^*$
1.	5	5	4.69	0.207	1.480	0.00	5.31	1.188	1.213	0.713	1.706	1.788
2.	5	15	4.66	0.208	1.637	0.88	14.46	1.069	1.180	0.680	1.678	2.776
3.	5	25	4.63	0.209	1.766	1.96	23.41	1.043	1.152	0.652	1.652	3.262
4.	6	15	5.59	0.208	1.983	0.09	15.32	1.065	1.176	0.676	1.856	2.773
5.	6	25	5.55	0.209	2.132	1.12	24.33	1.041	1.150	0.650	1.833	3.260
6.	6	35	5.53	0.208	2.233	1.77	33.70	1.030	1.137	0.637	1.822	3.585

because the supply side is taking the risk by other means (through the capital market) simultaneously and thus it is not risk neutral. In this sense, the international insurance is typical Malinvaud-Arrow insurance as all households are taking the same risk in a collective way. In this sense, the 20 per cent up of the premium rate is the cost for collective risk, the risk premium.

Table 8.4: Numerical Results of Diversifying Disaster Risk among Generations

No.	w_t	w_t^0	s_t^{0*}	n	s_t^{0*}	s_{0t}^{0*}	R_{t+1}^0	R_{t+1}^n	R_{t+1}^d	$\mathrm{E}[u]^*$	$\mathrm{E}[u^0]^*$
1.	5	5	4.67	1.67	0.00	5.00	1.136	1.214	0.714	1.7096	1.7373
2.	5	15	4.61	1.93	1.40	13.60	1.063	1.166	0.666	1.6683	2.7689
3.	5	25	4.59	2.04	2.37	22.63	1.040	1.144	0.644	1.6486	3.2582
			4.60	2.00	2.36	22.64	1.040	1.144	0.644	1.6486	3.2582
4.	6	15	5.53	2.34	0.67	14.33	1.060	1.161	0.661	1.8463	2.7659
			5.60	2.00	0.61	14.39	1.060	1.161	0.661	1.8459	2.7659
5.	6	25	5.51	2.47	1.58	23.42	1.039	1.141	0.641	1.8286	3.2568
			5.60	2.00	1.49	23.51	1.039	1.141	0.641	1.8279	3.2568
6.	6	35	5.49	2.54	2.16	32.84	1.028	1.131	0.631	1.8194	3.5833
			5.60	2.00	2.06	32.94	1.028	1.131	0.631	1.8185	3.5833

Note: The ratio between tax and subsidy is set at μ. The amount of liquid capital saved in the Disaster Reserve as well as the maximal subsidy amount is assumed to be 2.

It can be easily found that the inter-generational instrument, which is equivalent to the fair insurance programme when there is no liquidity or credit constraint (numerical results No. 1 and 2 in Table (8.4), diversifies the risk fully for LDC individuals. According to our assumption, the subsidy capacity is set to be equal to the capital kept

Table 8.5: Numerical Results of Benchmark Case compatible to the Inter-Generation Case

No.	w_t	w_t^0	s_t^{0*}	s_{0t}^{0*}	R_{t+1}^0	R_{t+1}^n	R_{t+1}^d	EU^{1*}	EU^{2*}
1.	5	5	0.00	5.00	1.125	1.200	0.700	1.684	1.7272
2.	5	15	1.05	13.95	1.059	1.165	0.665	1.650	2.7657
3.	5	25	1.99	23.01	1.038	1.143	0.643	1.628	3.2568
4.	6	15	0.24	14.76	1.056	1.160	0.660	1.828	2.7629
5.	6	25	1.12	23.88	1.037	1.140	0.640	1.808	3.2555
6.	6	35	1.68	33.32	1.028	1.130	0.630	1.797	3.5826

Note: This is not the true benchmark case but one purely for comparison with the inter-generational case. It is assumed that the LDC government is investing in the DC with capital amount to 2.

Table 8.6: Numerical results international insurance case compatible to the inter-generational case

No.	w_t	w_t^0	s_t^{0*}	ν	m_t^*	s_t^{0*}	s_{0t}^{0*}	R_{t+1}^0	R_{t+1}^n	R_{t+1}^d	EU^{1*}	EU^{2*}
1.	5	5	4.67	0.202	1.614	0.00	5.33	1.120	1.214	0.714	1.7086	1.7385
2.	5	15	4.66	0.211	1.610	1.11	14.23	1.058	1.173	0.673	1.6709	2.7695
3.	5	25	4.63	0.210	1.755	2.09	23.28	1.038	1.149	0.649	1.6492	3.2587
4.	6	15	5.59	0.211	1.953	0.30	15.11	1.055	1.170	0.670	1.8501	2.7664
5.	6	25	5.55	0.210	2.120	1.24	24.20	1.037	1.147	0.647	1.8302	3.2573
6.	6	35	5.53	0.209	2.227	1.85	33.62	1.027	1.135	0.635	1.8201	3.5837

Note: This is not the true international insurance case but one purely for comparison with the inter-generational case. It is assumed that the LDC government is investing in the DC with capital amount to 2.

in the reserve, 2. In this sense, in numerical results No. 3~6 LDC individuals cannot meet their first-best demand for diversification. There are two series of result for Nos. 3~6, with the upper one showing the first-best choice while the lower one showing the result binding at the maximal subsidy amount.

In order to check the efficiency of risk-diversification of the inter-generational approach, we have computed the numerical results of the benchmark case and the international insurance case compatible to the inter-generational case. Comparing the welfare states of individuals across Tables 8.4, 8.5, and 8.6, it can be found that the benchmark case exhibits the lowest economic efficiency, as there is no means for risk transfer or diversification for LDC individuals. It is interesting to find out that the inter-generational approach, which is equivalent to fair-premium-rate insurance, does not lead to first-best equilibrium! The reason is not difficult to find. In this small two-country economy, when the risk financing choice of the LDC individual changes, the investment behaviour of the DC individuals will change correspondingly and finally the improvement in the welfare state of the LDC individuals may be offset by such responses.

Another thing worth noting is that DC individuals may not be delighted with the investment from LDC disaster reserve because it causes negative externality on their welfare states. Once the capital in the disaster reserve is invested in the DC, the domestic rate of return of investment of the DC will drop. DC individuals are then forced to restructure their investment portfolios and take more risk. It can be seen that among the welfare state of DC individuals is the lowest in Table 8.4 out of three tables. Here it may raise the doubts that why DC individuals allow such kind of foreign investment. Think the question over and it can be found that only the elder generation of DC is not delighted to accept such investment. The younger generation of DC is happy with it. When capital investment increases, the return to investor drops but the labour income of the young generation increases. From the angle of long-run economic development, the DC government will also be happy to accept this investment.

Issues and Alternatives in Japan and China

Earthquake Insurance Programme of Japan

Japan is a country located on the Circum-Pacific Seismic Zone. In history, Japan experienced several devastating earthquakes, including the well known Great Kanto Earthquake in 1934 and Hansin-Awaji Earthquake in 1995. In order to finance the huge damages induced by earthquake, the national earthquake insurance system of Japan was launched in 1966 and developed and improved during the past years. The system has been regarded as one of the most successful catastrophic insurance programmes in the world, and numbers of reports and papers have investigated and discussed on this system. Therefore, this section will not go through the general matters repeatedly but pick up the essential pieces of information which highlights the contribution of Japanese Government in this system.

The major role of the Japanese Government in the national earthquake system in terms of financial aspect is a reinsurance partner.

The earthquake insurance and reinsurance market in Japan consists of three layers. In the first layer, policyholders purchase insurance coverage from private insurance companies. The liability of primary insurers is then completely reinsured by Japan Earthquake Reinsurance Company Ltd. (J.E.R.). In the third layer, J.E.R. cedes its liability to both private reinsurers and the Government. According to the latest revision in April 2008 (NLIRO, 2008), the liability sharing scheme between the J.E.R. and Japanese Government is given as below (Fig. 8.4).

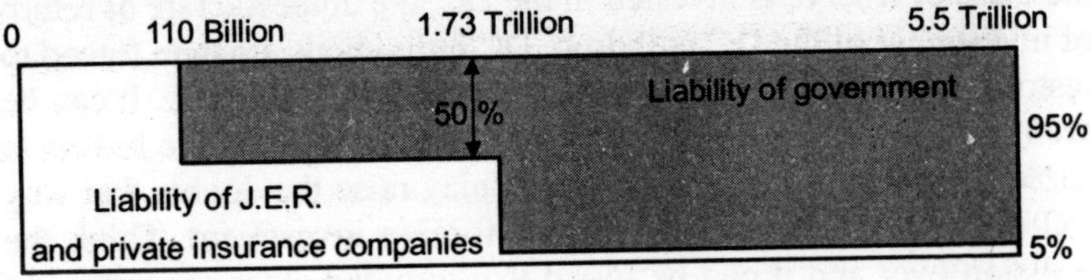

Fig. 8.4: Liability Sharing of Insurance Companies and Japanese Government

Source: NLIRO (2008).

For claims below 110 billion JPY (induced by a single earthquake), Japanese Government is not involved in sharing; for claims between 110 billion and 1.73 trillion JPY, insurance companies and Japanese Government shall each bear 50 per cent of the loss; for claims between 1.73 trillion and 5.5 trillion JPY, the Government shall bear 95 per cent of the loss while the remaining is borne by insurance companies.

Until the Aggregate Limit of 5.5 trillion JPY, the liability of J.E.R. and private insurance companies adds up to 1.1085 trillion JPY while the Government will have to bear up to 4.3915 trillion JPY. In case the insurance claim exceeds the upper limit of 5.5 trillion JPY, the respective insurance claims can be reduced and paid in accordance with the proportion of the Aggregate Limit to the total amount of insurance claims to be paid.

Both insurance companies and the Government are obligated by the law to accumulate premium as liquid reserves, excluding the portion of necessary expenses for contracts. Additionally, it is obligated that all the investment profits from the accumulated liability reserves also be accumulated as liability reserves.

Moreover, concerning with the contribution of Japanese Government and the money from the taxpayer, the premium rate of earthquake insurance is tightly tailored. The premium rate is determined as non-profitable for primary insurers while transaction costs are embodied in, including costs in administration and underwriting. A new discriminated premium rate system was adopted since 2007 and premium rates are given based on administrative divisions of "To-Dou-Fu-Ken". This update further reduces the costs for adverse selection and *ex ante* moral hazard.

The national earthquake insurance programme could be highlighted in following aspects according to the discussion of this paper: (1) the insurance pool is set up at the national level. With the participation of the Government, risk units from different regions of the country and different generations are pooled simultaneously, which largely increases the effect of diversification; (2) the Government as the "last" reinsurer makes inter-temporal diversification viable and further strengthens the confidence of the private sector in operating earthquake insurance.

China Agriculture Policy Insurance Programme (CAPIP)

In the vast rural areas in China, agriculture has been suffering from natural disasters a lot. Tropic cyclones in the south-east coastal provinces, floods in major river basins, and drought in the vast Northern China have been doing huge damage to agriculture. The past ten years has been a decade with intensive arrival of large scale catastrophic events, e.g., the floods in 1998, catastrophic typhoons in 2006 and 2007, and catastrophic snow in Central and South China in 2008. Due to the high vulnerability of Chinese rural and agriculture areas, large numbers of famers lose their yields year by year.

In Chinese mainland, there was agricultural insurance programme from the mid of 1980s to late 1990s. However, that programme encountered all problems that common disaster insurance would face. It was a puzzle: farmers felt premium rates were too high to afford while insurers felt premium rates were too low to maintain the business. When it was closed by the Central Government, the programme was identified as "low insurance penetration with quite high indemnity claim ratio". The People's Insurance Company of China (PICC), a state-operated insurance company at that time, stopped services for agriculture production as agriculture insurance lines were the least profitable products: the annual average indemnity claim ratio was 87.2 per cent, which is much higher than the profitable threshold around 70 per cent (Shi, 2007).

The agricultural insurance programme was re-picked-up by the Chinese Government as a component of agriculture supporting system. After the devastating flood in Yangtze River in 1998, disaster mitigation measures in urban areas and major river basins were strengthened quite a lot. However, agriculture production is still extremely vulnerable to meteorological disasters. Meanwhile, after joining the WTO, a lot of agriculture support measures were restricted according to the WTO Agreement on Agriculture but disaster insurance is an exemption. The new phase of agriculture insurance was then signalized by the No. 1 Document of the Central People's Government of China of 2004. In 2006, the Government issued *Some Opinions of the State Council on the Reform and Development of the Insurance Industry*, which addressed the intention of "to improve multi-layer agriculture catastrophe risk transfer mechanism and seek for establishment of agricultural reinsurance system sponsored by Central and Local Governments" (The State Council of China, 2006). In the following year, six provinces (municipality or autonomous region) were chosen to initiate pilot programmes in agricultural disaster insurance. Compared to the previous programme which is purely market-based commercial disaster insurance, the new programme involves strong government intervention with direct premium subsidy from government budget at four levels, including central, provincial, city and county. For this reason, it is called "Agriculture Policy Insurance" in Chinese, as a contrast to commercial insurance.

The intervention is believed to have learned from agriculture insurance programme of the North America, particularly from the experience of the United States. This kind of agriculture insurance programme is characterized by (Ibarra and Skees, 2007): core products that involve insurance at the farm level for multiple perils; government subsidies that are linked to premiums on a percentage basis; government subsidies or government agencies for the administrative cost of the programme; and a major role for government in pooling and holding some of the most catastrophic

Table 8.7: Operation of 6 Pilot Agriculture Insurance Programmes in China in 2007

Provinces / *Items*		*Hunan*	*Jilin*	*Inner Mongolia*	*Xinjiang*	*Sichuan*	*Jiangsu*
Insured crops		Rice and cotton	Corn, rice, soybean, tobacco, *et al.*	Corn, rice, and soybean	Cotton, corn, rice, soybean and wheat	Rice and corn	Rice, wheat, cotton, cole and corn
Perils		Rainstorm, flood, inundation, wind, hail, frost, and drought			—	Rainstorm, flood, inundation, wind, hail, frost, and drought	
Liability *(CNY/ Mu[a]/ production season)* and Premium rate *(%)*		Rice: 240 (basic[b] 5%, drought 3%, all 7%) Cotton: 300 (8%)	Corn: 200 (10%) Rice: 266.7 (8%) Soybean: 166.7 (8%)	Corn: 230 (10%) Wheat: 300 (8%) Soybean: 170 (8%)	Cotton: 400 (7%)	—	Discriminated premium rate according to risk mapping.
Subsidy rate	Central	50%	25%	25%	25%	25%	—
	Provincial		25%	50%	25%	25%	
	Local	>=10%	30%	10%	—	20%	
	In total	>=60%	80%	85%	>=50%	70%	>= 60%
Summary of 2007	Premium *(CNY)*	750 million	—	—	760 million	74 million	450 million
	Indemnity *(CNY)*	440 million	—	—	—	19 million	150 million

Notes: a. 1 Mu = 6.667 Are;
b. Basic liability means all perils except drought.

risk. Compared to the government-sponsored crop insurance programmes in North America, issues in common of CAPIP are concluded as :

- Multi-peril insurance lines for crop plantations against rainstorm, flood, inundation, strong wind, hail, frost, and drought.
- Premium rates differ from 3 per cent to 10 per cent according to region, crops, and perils. Transaction and administrative costs are not embodied in premiums. Insurance lines are priced as non-profitable for insurers.
- Low premium coupled with low liability. The insurance contract only covers the physical cost of crops, including costs in seeds, fertilizer, pesticide, irrigation, machinery, and mulching film. Costs in labour forces are excluded.
- Programmes are operated at the provincial level. The Central Government and provincial government subsidize 50 per cent of the premium while local governments (city and county level) subsidize around 10~30 per cent. Policyholders will pay the rest of premium.
- Provincial governments extract catastrophic reserve from annual business surplus of agriculture disaster insurance lines. When catastrophic disaster hits and indemnity reaches to a certain threshold, provincial governments will use the liquid fund kept in the reserve to help insurance companies cap the losses.

The details of operation in year 2007 in representative provinces and municipality are given in Table 8.7.

The Agriculture Policy Insurance Programme is a very typical government-sponsored private insurance programme. In this programme, government uses tax revenues to proportionally subsidize policyholders in premium. It has following advantages: (1) Premium rate are seemingly cheaper for farmers. The farming population is more likely to afford. (2) Government involvement makes farmers more confident about the insurance programme. (3) There is no need to worry about excessive coverage purchasing, as the area of cultivated crops that one farmer could insure is fixed. He can at most buy a full coverage but no excessive coverage even if the premium rate is very cheap. (4) The disaster reserve kept by the government helps insurers have easier access to liquid capital at much lower transaction costs.

Conclusion

This article summarizes the challenges faced by disaster insurance industry into three aspects, difficulty in identification of risk curve, insufficient liquid capital allocated for coming peak losses, and high costs for ceding and risk capital sources. The challenges weaken the performance of insurance in financing disaster risk, either induced by the inherent feature of disaster risk itself or the environment of the disaster insurance market and international capital market. As a matter of fact, efforts from governments are called for and private-public partnership is necessary for the financial management of disaster risk.

This chapter advocates proactive and market-oriented approach in financing disaster risk. A government is expected to adopt measure in supporting and intervention. The optimization problem of a government could be described as to increase households' affordability to insurance coverage subject to the sustainability constraint of insurers' business as well as its own fiscal resources. Besides removing loading factors induced by various types of cost, the article proposed a general framework for government to improve the "intra-temporal" social optimum achieved through the exchange of Malinvaud-Arrow type of disaster insurance, which is named as "intergenerational disaster risk diversification". The main structure of the strategy is to set up a liquid reserve through tax revenue accumulation to cushion the random shocks induced by natural disasters. International financial institutions provide contingent loan service when liquid capital is insufficient to cope with disaster losses. With tax and subsidy ratio appropriately given and unlimited loans, the reserve could perfectly smooth consumptions of households from different generations along the time. A two-country model further demonstrates how the intergeneration approach diversifies risk among generations. Numerical examples show that Pareto improvement is achieved with the exchange of Malinvaud-Arrow insurance, the international insurance contract in the two-country model. The premium rate of the Malinvaud-Arrow insurance is around 20 per cent higher than the probability of the event, indicating a 20 per cent risk premium embodied. When the intergenerational framework is introduced into the system, the social welfare is further improved and the extent depends on the maximum amount of loan that the government could access to.

As illustrative cases, the earthquake insurance programme in Japan and the agriculture insurance programme in China are briefly introduced. In Japan's case, Japanese Government uses funds to develop reinsurance programmes to cover the excess-of-loss claimed by earthquake, together with the non-life insurance industry of Japan. The earthquake insurance is categorized as a non-profitable programme with strong government supervision. Premium rates are discriminated based on risk assessment and mapping. In this sense, the intervention from the Government mainly resolves the problem of sustainability of disaster insurance. In China's case, the CAPIP follows another approach that the capital is used to directly subsidize premiums paid by farmers. Similarly, it is also defined as a non-profitable programme. The intervention works in the way that government subsidy increases the maximum willingness to pay for insurance coverage. The premium rate becomes relatively "cheaper" and more farmers could afford. Therefore, the chief purpose of this programme is to resolve the affordability puzzle other than solvent issues.

In conclusion, intervention from the government is necessary and effective in terms of financing disaster risk. Particularly, when it comes to the inherent flaws of disaster insurance, the dependency across risk units, governments must contribute. The framework of intergenerational disaster risk diversification proposed in this chapter gives a very intuitive example of how a government could use its unique advantages to help the market diversify the risk. Governments, however, should also be cautious when conducting intervention especially in the price system of the market. Intensive intervention could induce the price system distorted so much that the demand exceeds the capacity of primary insurers. Meanwhile, the heavily-subsidized premium rate will pass wrong information on the true cost of risk and mislead households' risk perception and mitigation activities.

Acknowledgement

This Study has been financially supported by National Natural Science Foundation of China (NSFC No. 40821140354) "Disaster Risk Governance: a case study of the IHDP-IRG Core Science Project" and DRH (Disaster Reduction Hyper-base)—CASiFiCA (Case Station-Field Campus) project funded by Special Coordination Fund for Promoting Science and Technology, Ministry of Education, Culture, Sports, Science and Technology of Japan.

References

Blanchard, O.J. and S. Fischer (1989): *Lectures on Macroeconomics.* The MIT Press, 1989, pp. 49–50.

Cass, D., G. Chichilnisky, and H.M. Wu (1996): Individual risk and mutual insurance, *Econometrica*, Vol. 64, No. 2, 333-341.

Cummins, J.D. (2007): Reinsurance for natural and man-made catastrophes in the United States: Current state of the market and regulatory reforms, *Risk Management and Insurance Review*, Vol. 10, No. 2, 179-220.

Cummins, J.D. (2008): CAT bonds and other Risk-Linked Securities: State of the market and recent developments, *Risk Management and Insurance Review*, Vol. 11, No. 1, 23-47.

Cummins, J.D., and P.M. Danzo, (1997): Price shocks and capital flows in liability insurance industry: Overview, *Journal of Financial Intermediation*, 6: 3-38.

Cummins, J.D., and N.A. Doherty (2002): Capitalization of the property-liability insurance industry: Overview, *Journal of Financial Services, Research*, 21: 5-14.

Froot, K.A. (1999a): *The Financing of Catastrophe Risk*. The University of Chicago Press, pp. 1~2.

Froot, K.A. (1999b): The evolving market for catastrophic event risk, NBER working paper series, *Working Paper* 7287.

Gollier, C. (2002): Time diversification, liquidity constraints, and decreasing aversion to risk on wealth. *Journal of Monetary Economics*, Vol. 49, pp. 1439-1459.

Guha-Sapir, D., *et al.* (2004): *Thirty Years of Natural Disasters 1974-2003: The Numbers*. Presses Universitaires de Louvain.

Gurenko, N.E. (2007): Transferring national catastrophe risk exposures to the market: Lessons learned, paper presented at the International Conference on Asian Catastrophe Insurance, 2007, December 3-4, Kyoto, Japan.

Guy Carpenter (2007): *U.S. Reinsurance Renewals at January 1, 2007: Smooth sailing Ahead*? New York: Guy Carpenter.

Hoyois, P., *et al.* (2007): *Annual Disaster Statistical Review: Numbers and Trends* (2006). Centre for Research on the Epidemiology of Disasters, School of Public Health, Catholic University of Louvain, Brussels, Belgium. http://*www.emdat.be/Publications/publications*.html (accessed at Jan 23rd, 2008).

Ibarra, H. and J. Skees, (2007): Innovation in risk transfer for natural hazards impacting agriculture. *Environmental Hazards*, Vol. 7, pp. 62-69.

Jaffee, D.M. and T. Russel, (1996): Catastrophe insurance, capital markets and uninsurable risks. Paper presented at the Wharton Financial Institutions Centre's May 1996 Conference on Risk Management in Insurance Firms. *http://fic.wharton.upenn.edu/fic/papers/96/9612.pdf,* accessed on January 28th, 2008.

Jones, K. (2007): Catastrophe insurance in Asia—Where to from here? Presentation at the First International Conference on Asia Catastrophe Insurance, December 3-4, 2007 in Kyoto, Japan.

Kleindorfer, P., and H. Kunreuther, (1999): The complementary roles of mitigation and insurance in managing catastrophic risks. *Risk Analysis*, Vol. 19, No. 4, pp. 727-738.

Kunreuther, H. (2000): Insurance as cornerstone for public-private sector partnerships. *Natural Hazards Review*, Vol. 1, No. 2, pp. 126-136.

Kunreuther, H. (2001): Incentives for mitigation investment and more effective risk management: The need for public-private partnerships. *Journal of Hazardous Materials*, No. 86, 171-185.

Kunreuther, H., R.M. Hogarth, and J. Meszaros, (1993): Insurer ambiguity and market failure. *Journal of Risk and Uncertainty*, Vol. 7, pp. 71-87.

Kunreuther, H., J. Meszaros, R.M. Hogarth, and M. Sprance, (1995): Ambiguity and underwriter decision processes. *Journal of Economic Behaviour and Organization*, Vol. 26, pp. 337-352.

Lewis, C.M. and K.C. Murdock, (1996): The role of government contracts in discretionary reinsurance markets for natural disasters. *The journal of Risk and Insurance*, Vol. 63, No. 4, Symposium on Catastrophic Risk. (December, 1996), pp. 567-597.

Linnerooth-Bayer, J. and R. Mechler (2007): Disaster safety nets for developing countries: extending public-private partnerships. Environmental Hazards, No.7, pp. 54-61.

Munich Re (2007): Topics Geo *Natural Catastrophes 2006*. Munich: Munich Re Group Knowledge Series. *http://www.munichre.com/publications/302-05217_en.pdf*

Mürmann, A. (2001): Pricing catastrophe insurance derivatives. Research paper, The Wharton School. *http://www.huebnergeneva.org/documents/catastrophederivatives.pdf.*

Non-Life Insurance Rating Organization of Japan (NLIRO), (2008): Earthquake Insurance in Japan. *http://www.nliro.or.jp/english/earthquake.html*, accessed on 29th, September, 2008.

Scawthorn, C. (2006): National insurance programmes for natural hazards mitigation. Presentation at the 6th IIASA-DPRI Annual Forum on Integrated Disaster Risk Management, August 13-17, 2006 in Istanbul, Turkey.

Schade, C., H. Kunreuther, K. Kaas, (2002): Low-probability insurance decisions: The role of concern. Wharton Risk Centre Working Paper, Wharton Business School, University of Pennsylvania, *http://edoc.hu-berlin.de/series/sfb-373-papers/2002-23/PDF/23.pdf*, accessed on February 11th, 2008.

Shi, P. (2007): Natural disaster insurance issue and strategy of China. paper presented on the First International Conference on Asia Catastrophe Insurance, December 3-4, 2007 in Kyoto, Japan.

The State Council of China (2006): Some opinions of the State Council on the reform and development of the insurance industry. *http://www.xinhuanet.com*.

World Bank (2006): Hazards of nature, risks to development: An IEG evaluation of World Bank assistant for natural disasters. *The World Bank*, Washington DC.

Yaari, M. E. (1976): A law of large numbers in the theory of consumer's choice under uncertainty, *Journal of Economic Theory*, 12, 202-217.

Ye, T., M. Yokomatsu, and N. Okada, (2008): Combined International and Intergenerational Disaster Risk Diversification: An Innovative Instrument for Government Intervention into the Private Disaster Insurance Programme, 2008 IEEE International Conference on System, Man and Cybernetics, Singapore, Oct. 12~15.

Yokomatsu, M. and K. Kobayashi, (2000): Catastrophe risks and economic valuation of disaster mitigation, paper presented at the Second Euro Conference on Global Change and Catastrophe Risk Management: Earthquake Risks in Europe, IIASA, Laxenburg, Austria.

9

A Framework for Island Disaster Para-Diplomacy

ILAN KELMAN, AND BOB CONRICH

Island disaster para-diplomacy refers to non-sovereign islands dealing with state governments other than their governing state and international agencies for disaster-related activities, covering pre-disaster actions and post-disaster actions. Based on past island-related disaster diplomacy work, this chapter details three case studies in which island disaster para-diplomacy has had potential: Nevis in the Caribbean, Tristan da Cunha in the South Atlantic, and Tikopia and Anuta in the Pacific. Based on these case studies, six issues important to non-sovereign islands are highlighted to provide a starting framework for analysing further case studies: sovereignty, transportation access, natural resources, population size, ability to engage in para-diplomacy, and loyalty to the governing state. Then, the future of island disaster para-diplomacy is suggested as being most relevant for creeping environmental changes within the context that all forms of disaster diplomacy tend to show disaster-related activities catalysing, rather than creating diplomatic activities.

Background for Island Disaster Para-Diplomacy

Island Governance and Disasters

Many islands and island groups are not sovereign states yet have some responsibility for their own governance. Examples are Prince Edward island, Barbuda, New Caledonia, the Faroes, and Zanzibar, each of which represents a different form of governance (see also Baldacchino,

2004). In some literature, these Island entities are collectively termed Sub-National island Jurisdictions (ICS, 2005). An easier approach might be to refer to them as non-sovereign islands. Pedantically, that term encompasses islands across more than one country, such as Hispaniola and New Guinea, along with islands, inhabited or uninhabited, without their own government such as Norway's Jan Mayen and New Zealand's South Island. However, the context of most island governance discussions will be clear about whether or not a government is involved, suggesting that "non-sovereign island" is a more practical term to use than "sub-national island jurisdiction".

One area of interest for island governance is dealing with disasters. Islands and Island groups often experience exacerbated vulnerabilities and disaster impacts (e.g., Howarth, 2005; Lewis, 1999; Pelling and Uitto, 2001), particularly due to their relatively small size in population, area, and land-based resources. Other island characteristics, including marginalisation and remoteness can cause difficulties too.

For non-sovereign island governments, determining responsibility for pre-disaster actions, such as planning and mitigation, and for post-disaster actions, such as response and recovery, is not always straightforward. If a non-sovereign island and its governing state or its governing state's capital are far apart, an event could affect the island without the national authorities realising, or caring to admit, the extent of impacts. Similarly, internationally or nationally-mandated programmes related to disaster risk reduction might be implemented improperly because less attention is given to the island's needs compared to national needs as perceived from the capital. Where perceived or real inadequacies manifest in a state dealing with disaster issues, an island has five principal options, some of them interconnected (after Kelman *et al.*, 2006):

- Do nothing.
- Seek sovereignty from the governing state.
- Improve the state's actions.
- Improve the non-sovereign island's capabilities.
- Deal with international organisations and other governments.

This chapter examines the last point in order to explore one dimension of how non-sovereign islands deal with disasters, before and after events. The focus here is "disaster diplomacy".

Disaster Diplomacy and Disaster Para-Diplomacy

In asking how and why disaster-related activities do and do not reduce political enmity, past disaster diplomacy work (http://www.disasterdiplomacy.org) has covered pre-disaster activities and post-disaster activities. In Kelman and Koukis (2000); disaster diplomacy case studies were Greece and Turkey's responses to the earthquakes in each country in 1999 (Ker-Lindsay, 2000); weather- and climate-related collaboration between Cuba and the USA especially for hurricane monitoring (Glantz, 2000); and preventing a drought disaster across southern Africa despite a severe drought emergency (Holloway, 2000). Other case studies include rapprochement between India and Pakistan following the 26th January, 2001 earthquake disaster in Gujarat (Kelman, 2003) and the 8th October, 2005 earthquake disaster in Kashmir (Kelman, 2006a); the USA providing aid to Iran after the 26th December, 2003 Bam earthquake disaster (Warnaar, 2005); and international aid offered to the USA after the Hurricane Katrina disaster in 2005 (Kelman, 2007a). All these case studies are multilateral, involving two or more sovereign states.

Examples of intra-state case studies are droughts affecting the civil war in Sudan (e.g., Autesserre, 2002; Buchanan-Smith and Christoplos, 2004) and the effect of the 26th December, 2004 tsunamis on internal conflicts in Aceh and Sri Lanka (e.g., Gaillard *et al.*, 2008; Kelman, 2005b; Le Billon and Waizenegger, 2007; Rajagopalan, 2005; Renner and Chafe, 2007). Some limited analysis has been completed for the Philippines, such as the implementation and breaching of a ceasefire between the government and the New People's Army rebel group during the August 2006 Mayon volcano evacuation operations (Kelman and Gaillard, 2007).

The pattern seen from the disaster diplomacy case studies examined so far is that :

(a) Disaster-related activities can, but do not always, have a short-term impact on diplomacy.
(b) An impact on diplomacy occurs only when significant connections already exist, such as trade links or secret negotiations. Where prior connections amongst the parties are minimal, disaster-related activities rarely yield new

diplomatic initiatives. That is, disaster-related activities can catalyse and influence already existing diplomatic endeavours, but tend not to yield new diplomatic initiatives.

(c) Over the long-term, non-disaster factors have a more significant impact on diplomacy than disaster-related activities. Non-disaster factors could be a leadership change, distrust, belief that an historical conflict or complaint should take precedence over present day humanitarian needs, or priorities for action other than conflict resolution and diplomatic dividends.

Additionally, disaster-related activities can sometimes exacerbate conflict (e.g., Brancati, 2007; Glantz, 2001).

One disaster diplomacy spin-off is "environmental diplomacy", investigating whether or not multilateral environmental issues and agreements could lead to lasting, positive diplomatic outcomes beyond the specific environmental issue (Kelman, 2003). The evidence so far suggests that multilateral environmental agreements are most successful, including amongst countries in conflict, when diplomatic interactions occur on only the environmental issue in question, without bringing in wider concerns.

Another disaster diplomacy spin-off is disaster para-diplomacy. Para-diplomacy refers to a non-state government developing a foreign policy and conducting international relations; that is, a non-state government's relations with states other than its governing state and international agencies. Examining disaster para-diplomacy entails analysing how disaster-related activities do and do not affect cooperation between a non-state government and sovereign states or international agencies. Island disaster para-diplomacy refers to disaster para-diplomacy for non-sovereign islands.

Kelman *et al.* (2006) detailed island disaster para-diplomacy for Commonwealth countries. They examined legal regimes through the empirical evidence of countries' constitutions, disaster-related legislation, and inter-governmental organisations. Disaster para-diplomacy is hardly mentioned, so it is legally neither permitted nor denied. Yet an examination of what occurs in practice revealed a few isolated examples of island disaster para-diplomacy, although there were many more possibilities which were not acted upon.

Two reasons were suggested for why island disaster para-diplomacy is not as popular as other island para-diplomacy activities in the Commonwealth, including sports, trade, and cultural links. First, non-sovereign islands enjoy a wide variety of forms of autonomy and find advantages from them. The pattern, in fact, has been for their populations to vote against sovereignty in referenda. The governing state offers a crutch or lifeline, particularly in times of need. Disasters are seen as times of need and, rightly or wrongly, the expectation—or perhaps just the hope—is that the governing state will step in. That suggests that from the non-sovereign island's perspective, there is no need for disaster para-diplomacy.

Second, and equally powerful, is that most governments have traditionally not viewed disaster risk reduction as being a high priority. Most disaster-related measures are put in place to avoid a disaster similar to the one which was just experienced. That statement applies to both the non-sovereign island governments and to their governing states. Disaster para-diplomacy is rarely considered because disaster risk reduction is rarely considered by any government in comparison to endeavours deemed to be of higher priority such as culture, sports, and trade.

Further island disaster diplomacy research, including some para-diplomacy, was reported by Kelman (2006b) who explored how inter-state relationships could be affected if climate change threatens or leads to island evacuation. Possibilities were reviewed for evacuated island communities, including becoming integrated into another state or having their island community recreated on existing land or on newly created land. The resulting operational ethics issues were discussed, incorporating consequent legal questions. The ethical-legal themes covered were the responsibility, funding, decision-making authority, and prioritisation of sovereignty and governance for island evacuees.

These results led to interlinked conclusions. First, islands can lead to significant inter-state concerns and deserve more prominence than they usually receive. Second, the discussion applies beyond climate change because climate change is only one challenge and opportunity facing islands. Third, disaster diplomacy continues to yield mixed results, with disaster-related activities rarely creating new diplomacy, but providing a potential for catalysing existing diplomatic processes. That potential is not always realised. Overall, climate change compounds already existing challenges facing islands and forces those threats onto inter-state relations with mainly failures in subsequent disaster diplomacy. However, climate change does not introduce new or unique island challenges.

This Chapter

This chapter builds on past island disaster para-diplomacy work by moving the theory forward in the form of a framework for analysing case studies. Three case studies are presented in detail: Nevis in the Caribbean, Tristan da Cunha in the South Atlantic, and Tikopia and Anuta in the Pacific. All three case studies involve islands whose governing state is part of the Commonwealth in order to build directly on Kelman *et al.* (2006). Based on this evidence, a framework for analysing island disaster para-diplomacy is proposed followed by remarks on the possible future of island disaster para-diplomacy.

Nevis (Caribbean)

Nevis is an island with its own government within the Caribbean state of St. Kitts and Nevis (termed "St. Kitts-Nevis" here for clarity). St. Kitts-Nevis, with a population of approximately 28,000 on St. Kitts about approximately 10,000 on Nevis, is governed under the 1983 Constitution of St. Kitts-Nevis through the country's capital, Basseterre, on St. Kitts. Nevis retains some autonomy through devolution within the federation. From the Nevisian capital Charlestown, the Nevis Island Administration (NIA) and the Premier of Nevis control some Nevisian affairs, as listed in Chapter X, Section 106 of the Constitution. Examples are education, mineral resources, labour, and fisheries, but a Nevisian ordnance may not affect the power of the St. Kitts-Nevis Government.

Chapter X, Section 113 and Chapter XI, Section 115 of the Constitution give Nevis the right to declare unilateral independence through a process including a referendum in Nevis in which two-thirds of votes cast are in favour. The latest referendum on 10th August, 1998 resulted in 2,427 votes (62%) in favour of Nevis' independence, so the proposal failed, but that has not stymied efforts to continue seeking Nevisian independence.

Disasters are referred to in Chapter II, Section 19 of the Constitution which details NIA's responsibilities and powers regarding declarations of emergency. The St. Kitts-Nevis Government agency responsible for disasters is the National Emergency Management Agency (NEMA) under the Ministry of National Security. Despite a lack of specific reference in the Constitution, Nevis has its own Nevis Disaster Management Office (NDMO) which is accountable to NIA. NEMA, however, is mandated to control all international disaster matters and acts on behalf of both islands within the regional organisation, the Caribbean Disaster Emergency Response Agency (CDERA).

One of CDERA's roles is to provide immediate and coordinated response to a disaster event once the affected state requests such support. In an emergency affecting Nevis only, a request for assistance would have to me made through the St. Kitts-Nevis Government. Where external information is provided, NEMA is the first recipient. Communications are not automatically shared with NDMO.

NEMA is publicised throughout St. Kitts via placards and murals, but not on Nevis because Nevisian policies and agencies take precedence over federal ones—as long as they do not affect the power of the St. Kitts-Nevis government, as noted earlier—and NDMO is the disaster management agency on Nevis. Although NDMO is recognised by Nevisians, knowledge of NEMA's existence is limited (Davies, 2005). NEMA was mentioned in several public survey questions during pilot studies for further research on Nevis, but references to NEMA had to be removed for the later work because respondents consistently questioned its definition and role (Davies, 2005). Despite the lack of knowledge regarding NEMA and despite NDMO's role on Nevis, government representatives in Basseterre assume that NEMA would be the public's primary source of information and trust regarding disasters on Nevis (Davies, 2005).

As one example of the operational challenges which emerge, the Nevis Disaster Plan (NDMO, 2005) details a "Volcanic Disaster Plan" outlining measures to be taken during an eruption of the volcano which forms Nevis (GVP, 2008; Simpson, 2005). The main emergency measure in the plan is evacuation of Nevis' population to St. Kitts. The channel between the two islands is only 3 km at its narrowest point which is between two rural areas without large harbours. The channel is approximately 18 km wide between the two islands' capitals and each has a good harbour, with regular ferry services running between the two. Both islands have airports servicing the Eastern Caribbean but Nevis' airport would face significant, and most likely total, disruption in a volcanic eruption while ash would likely restrict aircraft operations from St. Kitts.

In an evacuation, the entire population of Nevis would be expected to leave, the vast majority of whom would be evacuated to St. Kitts. When the Volcanic Disaster Plan was published in 1989

(NDMO, 1989), Nevis' population totalled 9,428, yet the Plan details that only 6,600 people would seek accommodation on St. Kitts. Pick up points, assembly areas and evacuation routes are described, yet the plan has not been in the public domain. Unless this information is available and known to the evacuees and hosts, the procedures would be difficult to implement in a crisis. Additionally, the plan does not recognise that safety on St. Kitts from volcanic activity, especially ash, would not be guaranteed during an eruption on Nevis.

Could island disaster para-diplomacy play a role for Nevis? Para-diplomacy plays a role for pro-independence Nevisians, but does or could that spill over into disaster-related activities? The Nevisian independence movement often cites a disparity in the sharing of financial resources as a reason for pursuing their separatist agenda. For disaster-related activities, they suggest a consistent bias in the allocation of disaster relief aid with St. Kitts gaining and Nevis suffering. This concern is supported by interviews with Nevisians (Mitchell, 2006) in which respondents perceived that, during hurricane relief efforts in the late 1990s, aid was distributed on a political rather than a need basis. These allegations might or might not be true and little evidence exists to suggest that Nevis is actively seeking disaster risk reduction funding independently of St. Kitts-Nevis. Instead, the alleged disparity in funding seems to be highlighted as a typical political ploy to garner sympathy for independence without having sought evidence to support the allegation. Yet, evidence supporting the allegation could be readily available if it were sought.

Nevertheless, NDMO has its own website (www.nerisdm.com) which is used to communicate and build credibility with external agencies without going through Basseterre. Other media provide similar opportunities. For example, in June 2005, Nevisian Premier Vance Amory was quoted in regional media as searching for funds to repair the island's infrastructure following recent floods. Nevis is implementing disaster para-diplomacy to some extent, although in an *ad hoc* and limited manner.

Those scattered incidents are disaster para-diplomacy precedents, but are not likely to directly affect operations in the case of a major emergency on Nevis. Instead, as usually happens regarding disaster risk reduction, decisions will be made once the crisis strikes. Rather than following the Volcanic Disaster Plan, realistically, Nevisians are likely to be evacuated to several Caribbean islands and to require transitional settlement and shelter in each location (Corsellis and Vitale, 2005). NIA would be involved to some extent regarding communicating with displaced people, host governments, and international agencies, but is unlikely to be involved in immediate decision-making as they, too, will be displaced and would not have the capability to implement and direct emergency evacuation and resettlement operations.

However, once the volcano pacifies, reconstruction would need international support. Would NIA's level of involvement and competence in recovery and reconstruction demonstrate whether or not Nevis is ready for independence? In parallel, would a robust or weak response from Basseterre influence Nevisian independence, including the possibility of a strong response annoying Nevisians because it appears as if Basseterre is trying to control internal Nevisian affairs? Or would the population not mind who controls and provides resources as long as they receive aid?

As another dimension to disaster para-diplomacy for St. Kitts-Nevis, the island of St. Kitts also yields some evidence of disaster para-diplomacy as a reaction to perceived inadequacies in the national structure. Mitchell (2006) describes how some NEMA-run district disaster committees on St. Kitts have sought materials and equipment from the St. Kitts Red Cross and from the International Federation of Red Cross and Red Crescent Societies because they were unhappy with the highly centralised government control over disaster-related resources. Interpretations of such action range from being greedy to grasping opportunities to gaining needed resources rather than relying on government assistance. A concerted para-diplomacy or disaster para-diplomacy strategy is not a main reason for these activities.

Overall, limited and *ad hoc* disaster para-diplomacy occurs within St. Kitts-Nevis, but not as part of any coherent para-diplomacy strategy or with any specific intention of bolstering island para-diplomacy. While continued Nevisian disaster para-diplomacy could theoretically lead to increased power, authority, and confidence for Nevis to deal with national governments or international agencies on non-disaster issues—and perhaps lend support to the independence movement—the reality is that Nevisian governance tends to consider much shorter time scales without much coherence in longer-term disaster strategies or in linking across different governance interests.

Tristan da Cunha (South Atlantic)

Tristan da Cunha, home to approximately 260 people, is the remotest inhabited island in the world and is a UK Overseas Territory. On 21st May, 2001, hurricane-force winds caused extensive damage to Tristan's sole settlement. Despite damage of at least several hundred thousand Pounds Sterling (Brock, 2005; Brock and Glass, 2005; Glass, 2003), the UK Government provided only £75,000 ("Banking News", 2001). Meanwhile, an international appeal was sent out through expatriate Tristanians who, within a few months, raised £79,936.08 for a disaster fund (personal communication from Colin Topping on 27th November, 2001, quoting a letter he received from Tristan da Cunha's Chief islander). The remainder was covered by subsequent international donations as well by the Tristanians, including their volunteer labour for the repairs. The majority of materials were ordered and shipped from Cape Town, South Africa, which is the usual shipping point for any goods coming to Tristan da Cunha.

A situation existed where, according to the Tristanians, the UK Government was not providing Tristan da Cunha with all the needed post-disaster support. Tristanians solicited funds from elsewhere, setting up a disaster fund for this purpose. They might also have approached non-UK State Governments or international agencies for post-disaster supplies and for implementing mitigation. Tristanians, though, are highly loyal to the UK. One of us (Conrich) visited Tristan da Cunha in January 2002 and found a resigned acceptance to the limitations of the UK Government's reconstruction and development assistance with no impetus towards considering looking elsewhere. Another important factor was not wishing to be beggars, but to continue being as self-sufficient as possible. To seek para-diplomacy would also mean opposing the UK Government's representative on the island, an idea which is not part of Tristanian culture. Yet the disaster fund allowed international donors, state and non-state, the opportunity to support the rehabilitation effort on Tristan directly, bypassing the UK Government.

This situation further illustrates the definitional awkwardness of some para-diplomacy instances. When the UK Government's appointed representative is not on the island, a Tristanian becomes the acting UK Government representative. Any actions to solicit external assistance would, therefore, be coming from an islander, making it para-diplomacy, but from the UK Government's representative on the island, so that it would simultaneously not be para-diplomacy. As with Nevis, the difference between reality and academic analysis is demonstrated. When people need assistance, quite rightly, they will frequently seek it without necessarily being interested in formal protocols, legal regimes, or labels such as "para-diplomacy". That might make the academic analysis inconsistent in terms of categorising an action as para-diplomatic or not, but that categorisation is irrelevant in comparison to the need to seek assistance.

Similarly, towards the end of November 2007, several dozen Tristanians contracted a nasty flu virus which hit those with asthma particularly hard. Drug stocks on the island for dealing with flu were getting low, so a radio request was sent to nearby ships asking them to drop off some more supplies. This request was overheard in the UK via the radio traffic and then picked up and exaggerated by the media. The story broke in international headlines of this remote island facing a horrific medical emergency and desperately needing life-saving drugs.

Throughout the incident, both the legitimate request and the media hyperbole, no concern was raised that the Tristanians had appealed for external assistance without going through the proper UK Government channels. That is, island disaster para-diplomacy had occurred for the illness and was assumed to have occurred for the alleged epidemic—except that the appeal had been made with the acquiescence of the UK Government's representative. Was it really para-diplomacy even if formal permission from the UK Government had not been sought or given? In practice, such formalities are pointless and irrelevant for small, isolated communities. Assistance was needed, so Tristanians requested it through the most appropriate, efficient, and effective channels. In the end, social isolation and recovery time in December 2007 helped to stem the flu outbreak without fatalities. The drug stocks were soon replenished.

Then, on 13th February, 2008, a real disaster struck Tristan da Cunha. At about 0400, a fire destroyed the island's fish factory which included the generators used to provide the island with its 24-hour electricity supply. There were no injuries, but power was limited using the backup generator until a new generator arrived. In the response, all interested parties collaborated—the islanders, the factory owners, the UK Government, and suppliers in South Africa. Whether or not the islanders or the UK Government's representative on the island made decisions and directed the efforts is moot, as is the choice to use or not use the label of "disaster para-diplomacy".

Tristan da Cunha also illustrates the potential for disaster para-diplomacy for longer-term environmental disasters, in this case overfishing and marine biodiversity loss. The waters around Tristan da Cunha and its nearby uninhabited islands—Inaccessible island, the Nightingale Islands, and Gough Island—are rich in marine resources. Tristanians are dependent on those resources, but the abundance brings legal and illegal fishers from around the world. Tristanians are also aware of the important biodiversity of their islands and they protect threatened species such as the yellow-billed albatross and the Tristan bunting along with those species' habitats. Sea birds are nonetheless experiencing high mortality due to illegal fishing and marine debris brought by ocean currents (Ryan, 1987; Ryan, 1991; Ryan and Cooper, 1991; Ryan and Fraser, 1988).

Tristanians lack the resources to stop others engaging in poor or illegal practices which affect their islands. The UK Government would need to lead the enforcement of regulations in the vicinity of Tristan da Cunha, including proper fishing techniques, appropriate waste disposal, and prevention of alien species from establishing. Without full support from the UK Government, fishing and biodiversity concerns might eventually lead Tristanians into discussions with international organisations or other governments as long as the Tristanians would accept this radical cultural shift. If not, then the long-term disaster is likely to continue because island disaster para-diplomacy has potential but is not fulfilled.

Overall, limited and *ad hoc* disaster para-diplomacy is seen with regard to Tristan da Cunha, although there is much more potential which is not realised. But this case study demonstrates how the analysis of island disaster para-diplomacy is not straightforward. Realities on the ground dictate needed actions irrespective of theoretical labels of those actions.

Tikopia and Anuta (Pacific)

The small islands of Tikopia and Anuta are located in the far eastern Solomon Islands. Officially part of Temotu province, the islands lack airstrips, jetties and reliable off-island communication. Governance is undertaken by the island chiefs whose powers are recognised in the Solomon Islands' Constitution. Chapter XII, 114(2)(b) of the Constitution states that Parliament shall "consider the role of traditional chiefs in the provinces" which, however, vague a statement, leaves a possibility for chief-based disaster-related activities that could incorporate disaster para-diplomacy.

On 28th December, 2002, Tikopia and Anuta were hit by Category 5 Cyclone Zoë (Anderson-Berry *et al.*, *c.* 2003; Kelman, 2005a; Vettori and Stuart, 2004; Yates and Anderson-Berry, 2004). None of the inhabitants perished, but the devastation made their food, water, and shelter situation dire. The first formal aid supplies arrived by ship from Honiara, the Solomon Islands' capital, despite the distance of more than 1,000 km plus delays due to logistical and political reasons.

The closest location to Tikopia and Anuta from which relief supplies could have been brought belongs to Vanuatu, with Luganville being just 400 km away from Tikopia. This possibility was demonstrated by journalist Geoff Mackley who flew relief supplies to Tikopia from Vanuatu by helicopter ("Islanders' Miracle Survival", 2003).

In principle, due to the constitutional clause quoted earlier, the chiefs might have been able to request assistance by ship or helicopter from Vanuatu. In practice, Tikopia and Anuta had only one radio each and both radios had been broken before Cyclone Zoë, being made operational only after a post-cyclone aid team had arrived (Anderson-Berry *et al.*, *c.* 2003). As well, such action could have had diplomatic implications.

First, Honiara could have lost face because Vanuatu would have helped Solomon Islanders instead of, or before, the Solomon Islands government. Second, aid supplies crossing state lines normally have to be approved by the recipient state, so if that protocol were followed, Honiara would have had to actively accept help from Vanuatu. Third, with the residents of Tikopia and Anuta being ethnically more closely related to the people of Vanuatu than to those in the western part of the Solomon Islands, the Honiara government might have chosen to interpret Vanuatu's assistance as fuelling conflict within the Solomon Islands.

Nevertheless, as demonstrated with Tristan da Cunha, islanders in a post-disaster situation are usually more interested in obtaining relief supplies and rebuilding their communities as soon as possible wherever the help arrives from, rather than playing para-diplomacy and definitional games. Irrespective of the high-level politics and academic debates, the reality is that opportunities for island disaster para-diplomacy are usually enacted or avoided for pragmatic reasons: to gain assistance in the most efficient manner feasible within the current cultural paradigm.

As with Nevis and Tristan da Cunha, disaster para-diplomacy decisions are not necessarily made as part of a longer-term strategy or as a desire to bolster or hinder more autonomy. Instead, the residents of Tikopia and Anuta did not enact post-cyclone para-diplomacy with Vanuatu because they had no means of communication with the outside world. The decision was first made for them by Mackley who independently chose to transport a single helicopter load from Vanuatu. Then, decisions continued to be made for the islanders at the governmental level by choosing to stage the relief mission from Honiara rather than from Luganville.

For Tikopia and Anuta, limited and *ad hoc* disaster para-diplomacy opportunities existed, but were not enacted because practical constraints precluded the islanders from making disaster-related decisions. Realities on the ground dictated actions rather than trying to develop a long-term disaster para-diplomacy strategy within wider para-diplomacy, autonomy, constitutional, and governance contexts.

A Starting Framework for Island Disaster Para-diplomacy

From the three case studies—and building on discussions in Baldacchino (2004), Bartmann (1996), ICS (2005), Kelman (2006b), Kelman (2007b), Kelman *et al.* (2006), and Rainer (2005)—six issues important to non-sovereign islands can be highlighted as being particularly pertinent for disaster para-diplomacy: sovereignty, transportation access, natural resources, population size, ability to engage in para-diplomacy, and loyalty to the governing state. To understand and analyse island disaster para-diplomacy for a case study or for a national government's policy development, these issues are a useful starting framework (Table 9.1). Table 9.1 also summarises the framework's issues for the three case studies described earlier.

The possibilities for a disaster to affect the desire for independence is not a new aspect of disaster diplomacy. Poor response following the 1970 cyclone in East Pakistan contributed towards the subsequent revolution there which created Bangladesh (Lewis, 1999). Not all such instances influence sovereignty politics. The initially inadequate response from the UK Government to the volcanic eruptions starting in 1995 on Montserrat, a UK Overseas Territory in the Caribbean, have not pushed independence (Fergus, 2002).

Rather than waiting passively to see what impact disaster-related

Table 9.1: Island Disaster Para-diplomacy Framework, Applied to Three Case Studies

Issue ↓ Islands →	*Nevis*	*Tikopia and Anuta*	*Tristan da Cunha*
Sovereignty	Strong interest	Significant autonomy exists and full independence would not likely be feasible. Closer affiliation to Vanuatu might be of interest.	No interest.
Transportation access	Reasonable	Limited	Very limited
Natural resources (e.g. fish, minerals, natural heritage, arable land) and disaster para-diplomacy	Not likely to be used as a basis for disaster para-diplomacy.	Limited potential to be used as a basis for disaster para-diplomacy.	A strong potential to be used as a basis for disaster para-diplomacy, but that is unlikely to be fulfilled.
Population size	Largest of the three case studies.	Medium of the three case studies.	Smallest of the three case studies.
Ability to engage in para-diplomacy	Strong ability to seek prominence beyond the governing state.	Became prominent beyond the governing state only with external interest and assistance.	Irrespective of ability, limited interest in para-diplomacy.
Loyalty to the governing state	Mixed	Limited	Strong
Overall analysis	Island disaster para-diplomacy has strong potential.	Aspects of island disaster para-diplomacy are feasible.	Island disaster para-diplomacy is unlikely.

activities might have on a island's sovereignty interests, disaster para-diplomacy could be used as an active tool to promote independence or non-independence. Successful para-diplomacy, such as using external assistance to mitigate disasters or to respond effectively to an event, could garner support for independence. Reliance on external assistance, particularly from or managed by the island's governing state, could illustrate the need for dependency, garnering support to oppose independence.

Considering the opposite, that of moving away from sovereignty, no recent case studies were found where an independent island state lost its sovereignty due to a disaster, although East Timor declared independence in 1975 and nine days later, the disaster of the Indonesian invasion ended their sovereignty. One close analogy is Nauru, a small island state in the south Pacific. Due to phosphate resources, Nauru after its independence was one of the richest per capita countries in the world. Corruption, mismanagement, and incompetence squandered that wealth. With the phosphate now depleted and none of the money remaining, Nauru retains its statehood in name but has effectively become an Australian dependency. Australian officials manage the government and are trying to create a future for the country.

Regarding transportation access, the two characteristics to consider are mode of transport and distance or speed for reaching the island. In Nevis' case, the closest island is St. Kitts, part of the same state and a short flight or boat trip away. For Tristan da Cunha, as well as for Tikopia and Anuta, access is much more difficult. While some argue that proximity and ease of access should increase amity by getting to know and respect one's neighbour, closeness can also breed mistrust and the desire to be different. The case studies here demonstrate the latter with Nevis being the closest to its governing state and the most ardently independent while Tristan da Cunha is the farthest from its governing state and the least inclined towards sovereignty.

One factor not evident in these case studies is the effect of a "fixed link". A fixed link to an island is a physical connection to other islands or to the mainland, most notably bridges, tunnels, and causeways. That increase in access has been welcomed as bringing opportunity to keep island life viable and has been criticised as impinging on islandness and island culture (Baldacchino, 2007). As noted above, increased closeness and access can either augment or diminish interest in island sovereignty depending on other factors.

Given the widely varying effects on island identity of different forms and types of transportation access, it could be that other factors tend to be more important regarding island disaster para-diplomacy. While transportation access is frequently identified as an important island issue and while practical logistics often dictate the potential form of disaster para-diplomacy which could occur (Kelman *et al.*, 2006), this issue is perhaps mainly a key pragmatic constraint and opportunity within which decisions are made, rather than helping to shape strategic policies regarding disaster para-diplomacy.

In contrast, the population size and ability to engage in para-diplomacy of many non-sovereign islands are linked and sometimes mould the disaster para-diplomacy strategies which are used. The smallness in physical size, population, and land-based resources of many non-sovereign islands means that they are frequently marginalised and are relatively powerless beyond their borders. Para-diplomacy might not be effective irrespective of how much proactive effort is put into it.

Assuming that this situation exists in every case would underestimate the prominence which some island disaster para-diplomacy case studies generate. Over the past twelve years, two UK Overseas Territories hit international media headlines and caused difficulties and embarrassment for the UK Government on disaster-related issues :

(a) Montserrat, due to ongoing volcanic eruptions which started in 1995 (e.g., Clay, 1999; Davison, 2003; Pattullo, 2000).
(b) Pitcairn Island, where a crisis resulted when, in April 2003, British authorities charged several men with sex crimes (for background, *see* Trenwith, 2003).

Yet non-sovereign islands rarely have the personnel, knowledge, or experience to deal with disaster-related issues or to conduct para-diplomacy. This situation is a strong barrier towards actively implementing island disaster para-diplomacy even if it desired. Following Cyclone Zoë, the impacts on Tikopia and Anuta garnered attention only because one journalist decided that should happen. For Tristan da Cunha, the non-disaster of the 2007 flu outbreak resulted in international attention and offers of assistance whereas the real disaster of the 2008 factory fire appeared almost exclusively in regional media. The size and para-diplomacy ability of these non-sovereign islands sometimes leave them to the whims of outside forces in terms of actively promoting or actively avoiding disaster para-diplomacy; however, at other times, resourcefulness and creativity can overcome the alleged disadvantages of small size and remoteness (Kelman, 2007b).

Finally, Nevis illustrates the importance of having government agencies which are known and trusted by the population—along with the difference between trust and awareness of the island's government agencies compared to those of the governing state (Davies, 2005; Mitchell, 2006). That knowledge and trust must also extend to external governments and agencies or else para-diplomacy, disaster-related or otherwise, would be unlikely to occur.

Because the framework in Table 9.1 was developed based on limited case studies, caution should be used in applying it. It provides merely a useful starting point based on some empirical evidence interpreted in the context of non-sovereign island governance.

The Future of Island Disaster Para-diplomacy?

In recent decades, long-term environmentally related disasters have gained prominence for non-sovereign island governance. Could they dominate island disaster para-diplomacy in the future? Glantz (1994a,b) refers to the three phrases of "creeping environmental changes", "creeping environmental problems", and "creeping environmental phenomena" as incremental changes in environmental conditions which cumulate to create a major catastrophe or crisis, apparent only after a threshold has been crossed. Creeping environmental changes such as desertification, salinisation of water supplies, and climate change significantly impact all geographical levels and cross borders, making them useful cases for disaster diplomacy (e.g., Kelman, 2006b). These environmental changes are sometimes caused more by human activity than by natural variation, such as salinisation of water supplies occurring due to overextraction and climate change being partly attributed to human fossil fuel use.

Analogies also occur for "creeping social changes", "creeping social problems", and "creeping social phenomena" which would be defined as incremental changes in social conditions which cumulate to create a major catastrophe or crisis, apparent only after a threshold has been crossed. Examples are the prevalence of the English language suppressing local linguistic cultures; the internet slowly changing values and the youth's future goals; and economic globalisation leading to social and cultural globalisation. To some degree, the isolation of many non-sovereign islands is currently stymying the impacts of creeping social changes in comparison to prevalent creeping environmental changes. In the future, the effects of social changes could exceed the effects of environmental changes for non-sovereign islands. For instance, Tristan da Cunha received an internet connection in 2007 connecting the population to the world much more rapidly and cheaply than before while its governing territory of St. Helena is building an airport to eliminate the ship journey of several days from the Ascension Island or Cape Town airports.

With regard to ongoing island para-diplomacy for creeping environmental changes, climate change is currently the most prominent example (Kelman, 2006b). The Alliance of small island States (AOSIS) is an inter-governmental organisation with non-sovereign members of the Cook Islands and Niue. AOSIS "functions primarily as an *ad hoc* lobby and negotiating voice for Small Island Developing States (SIDS) within the United Nations system" on climate change (http://www.sidsnet.org/aosis). Sea-level rise, ocean acidification, salinisation of water resources, changes to marine resources, and a fear of a worsening tropical cyclone regime are strong candidates for precipitating such efforts because they have the potential to threaten the existence of many non-sovereign islands. Kelman (2006b) summarises the island disaster diplomacy potential of climate change incorporating some para-diplomacy examples.

As these creeping environmental changes begin to affect non-sovereign islands more, and perhaps to a greater extent than the governing states, the non-sovereign islands are using the international stage to try to address these issues, thereby effecting disaster para-diplomacy. In addition to AOSIS, the Association of Overseas Countries and Territories of the European Union—a non-profit established under the auspices of an inter-governmental agreement—met in Greenland from 5-7th September, 2006 with discussions including climate change (European Commission, 2006) and they were represented at a climate change meeting in The Hague from 13 to 14 February, 2007 (OCTA Newsletter, 2007). These meetings made it clear that these non-sovereign jurisdictions, most of which are islands, need to take initiatives in addressing climate change and other disasters.

Yet not all such intentions yield specific or effective actions. The Cook Islands and Niue are the only non-sovereign islands which have ratified the Kyoto Protocol as of June 2007. That could be interpreted as indicating a first step towards the possibility of island disaster para-diplomacy on climate change. On the other hand, since these two islands' governing state of New Zealand has also ratified the Kyoto Protocol, and since their lobbying resources and impacts are unlikely to match those of New Zealand or other sovereign states, even if they desired or attempted strong para-diplomacy on the Kyoto Protocol, it would be unlikely to have much effect. As well, the actions demanded of the Cook Islands and Niue in the Kyoto Protocol are so miniscule that no perceptible effect on climate change will result. Therefore, another possible interpretation of this island disaster para-diplomacy is that it is a symbolic gesture which might or might not set a useful precedent, but which is not of any immediate practical value.

These continuing analyses of island disaster para-diplomacy provide further evidence for the three main disaster diplomacy patterns witnessed so far:

(a) Disaster-related activities can, but do not always, have a short-term impact on diplomacy. Disaster-related activities for non-sovereign islands have the potential to yield para-diplomacy, but it is not an inevitable outcome.

(b) Disaster-related activities can catalyse and influence already existing diplomatic endeavours, but do not tend to yield new diplomatic initiatives. To determine the level of already existing connections, an initial assessment could be made with the framework shown in Table 9.1. This quick, first-order checklist might also assist in ranking the relative relevance of issues.

(c) Over the long-term, non-disaster factors have a more significant impact on diplomacy than disaster-related activities. In fact, where para-diplomacy is likely or occurs, it can be used to support independence or to signify that less responsibility and less autonomy would be preferred. That is, the non-disaster factor of the previously determined decision to support or oppose different levels of autonomy usually directs how para-diplomacy opportunities will be used. Para-diplomacy effectiveness influencing autonomy decisions is rarer.

Disasters are not the only concern of non-sovereign islands and their governing states. Para-diplomacy, desire for sovereignty, and intra-state relations are influenced by, amongst other factors, natural resources, the form of representative governance, intra-national and international trade, taxation, infrastructure construction and maintenance, corruption, incompetence, history, nationalist feelings, internal and external politics, and culture. Disaster para-diplomacy has a role to play, but it must be considered simultaneously with the many other activities involved in governing and being governed. Disaster-related activities must be recognised as rarely being prominent—until it is too late because a major catastrophe strikes and must be addressed.

Acknowledgements

With thanks to Tom Mitchell, Megan Davies, and Iain Orr who provided essential material and ideas.

Abbreviations

AOSIS	Alliance of Small Island States
CDERA	Caribbean Disaster and Emergency Response Agency
NDMO	Nevis Disaster Management Organisation
NEMA	National Emergency Management Agency (St. Kitts and Nevis)
NIA	Nevis Island Administration
SIDS	Small Island Developing States

References

Anderson-Berry, L., C. Iroi, and A. Rangi (*c.* 2003): *Tropical Cyclone Zoë, Tikopia and Anuta, Solomon Islands, December 26-29, 2002.* Centre for Disaster Studies, James Cook University, Townsville, Queensland, Australia.

Autesserre, S. (2002): "United States 'humanitarian diplomacy' in

South Sudan". *Journal of Humanitarian Assistance*, online only http://www.jha.ac/articles/a085.htm

Baldacchino, G. (2004): "Autonomous but not sovereign?: A review of island sub-nationalism", *Canadian Review of Studies in Nationalism*, XXXI: 77-91.

Baldacchino, G. (ed). (2007): *Bridging Islands: The Impact of Fixed Links*. Acorn Press, Charlottetown, PEI, Canada.

"Banking News" (2001): "Tristan da Cunha-Disaster relief fund", Press release from Crown Agents Financial Services Limited (25 June 2001).

Bartmann, B. (1996): "Saltwater Frontiers: Jurisdiction as a Resource for Small islands", Keynote Address to the *Annual Conference of the Island Institute*, Island Institute, Castine, Maine, USA.

Brancati, D. (2007): "Political Aftershocks: The Impact of Earthquakes on Intrastate Conflict". *Journal of Conflict Resolution*, 51(5): 715-743.

Brock, J. (2005): "Tristan da Cunha: Flags Half-Mast for Tsunami Victims", *Tristan Times*, 5 January, 2005.

Brock, J. and S. Glass (2005): "Tristan: Poaching Threatens Tristan da Cunha's Hurricane Recovery". *Tristan Times*, 12 June, 2005.

Buchanan-Smith, M. and I. Christoplos (2004): *Natural Disasters in Complex Political Emergencies: Report on a Seminar hosted by the British Red Cross Society*. British Red Cross Society, London, UK.

Clay, E. (1999): *An Evaluation of HMG's Response to the Montserrat Volcanic Emergency*. Department for International Development Evaluation Report EV635, London, UK.

Corsellis, T. and A. Vitale (2005) *Guidelines for the Transitional Settlement of Displaced Populations*. Oxfam, Oxford, UK.

Davies, M. (2005): *Appraisal of Proactive Volcanic Disaster Management on Nevis, West Indies*. Master of Science dissertation, Department of Earth Sciences, University College of London, London, UK.

Davison, P. (2003): *Volcano in Paradise*. Methuen, London, UK.

European Commission (2006): *Report on the Fifth OCT-EU Forum*, 5-7 September, 2006, Nuuk, Greenland D1*4/SV D(2006) D/5692. European Commission, Directorate-General Development and Relations with African, Caribbean and Pacific States, ACP II-West and Central Africa, Caribbean and OCTs, Relations with the countries and the region of the Caribbean and the OCTs, Brussels, Belgium.

Fergus, H. (2002): "Constitutional Modernisation in Montserrat and the Cayman Islands: Taking the British Seriously?" Paper presented at the *Montserrat Country Conference*, 13-14 November 2002, Montserrat.

Gaillard, J.-C., E. Clavé, and I. Kelman (2008): "Wave of Peace? Tsunami disaster diplomacy in Aceh, Indonesia". *Geoforum*, 39(1): 511-526.

Glantz, M.H. (1994a): "Creeping Environmental Problems". *The World & I*, June: 218-225.

Glantz, M.H. (1994b): "Creeping environmental phenomena: Are societies equipped to deal with them?" Pages 1-10 in M.H. Glantz (ed.), *Creeping Environmental Phenomena and Societal Responses to Them*, Proceedings of Workshop held 7-10 February, 1994 in Boulder, Colorado. NCAR/ESIG, Boulder Colorado.

Glantz, M.H. (2000): "Climate-Related Disaster Diplomacy: A US-Cuban Case Study", *Cambridge Review of International Affairs*, XIV(1): 233-253.

Glantz, M.H. (2001): "Climate-related flashpoints: A useful notion for early warning?" *ENSO Signal*, 18: 1.

Glass, J. (2003): "Tristan: Official Hurricane Report". *Tristan Times*, 17 November, 2003.

GVP (2008): *Nevis Peak*. Global Volcanism Programme, Smithsonian Institute, Washington, DC, USA, http://www.volcano.si.edu/world/volcano.cfm?vnum=1600-04=

Holloway, A. (2000): "Drought Emergency, Yes...Drought Disaster, No: Southern Africa 1991-93". *Cambridge Review of International Affairs*, XIV(1): 254-276.

Howarth, R. (2005): "Islands, Isolation and Vulnerability". *Know Risk*, pp. 224-227, Tudor Rose Publications and the International Strategy for Disaster Reduction, Leicester, UK and Geneva, Switzerland.

ICS (2005): *Research Workshop on Sub-National Island Jurisdictions, 18/19 April 2005*, ICS (Institute of Commonwealth Studies, London), London, UK.

"Islanders' Miracle Survival" (2003): *The Australian*, 4 January 2003.

Kelman, I. (2003): "Beyond Disaster, Beyond Diplomacy". *Natural Disasters and Development in a Globalizing World* (M. Pelling, ed.): pp. 110-123, Routledge, London, UK.

Kelman, I. (2005a): "Some Outlying Effects of Cyclone Zoë". *Know Risk*, p. 237, Tudor Rose Publications and the International

Strategy for Disaster Reduction, Leicester, UK and Geneva, Switzerland.

Kelman, I. (2005b): "Tsunami Diplomacy: Will the 26 December, 2004 Tsunamis Bring Peace to the Affected Countries?" *Sociological Research Online* 10(1): http://www.socresonline.org.uk/10/1/kelman.html

Kelman, I. (2006a): "Acting on Disaster Diplomacy". *Journal of International Affairs*, 59(2): 215-240.

Kelman, I. (2006b): "Island Security and Disaster Diplomacy in the Context of Climate Change". *Les Cahiers de la Sécurité*, 63: 61-94.

Kelman, I. (2007a): "Hurricane Katrina Disaster Diplomacy". *Disasters*, 31(3): 288-309.

Kelman, I. (ed.) (2007b): "The Island advantage: Practices for prospering in isolation". *id21 insights*, no. 70 (November).

Kelman, I., M. Davies, T. Mitchell, I. Orr, and B. Conrich (2006): "Island Disaster Para-Diplomacy in the Commonwealth". *The Round Table: The Commonwealth Journal of International Affairs*, 95(386): 561-574.

Kelman, I. and J.-C. Gaillard (2007): "Disaster Diplomacy in the Asia-Pacific Region". *UN/ISDR Informs: Disaster Reduction in Asia Pacific*, 3: 54-57.

Kelman, I. and T. Koukis (eds). (2000): "Disaster Diplomacy". Special Section in *Cambridge Review of International Affairs*, XIV(1).

Ker-Lindsay, J. (2000): "Greek-Turkish Rapprochement: The Impact of 'Disaster Diplomacy'?", *Cambridge Review of International Affairs*, XIV(1): 215-232.

Le Billon, P. and A. Waizenegger (2007): "Peace in the Wake of Disaster? Secessionist Conflicts and the 2004 Indian Ocean Tsunami". *Transactions of the Institute of British Geographers*, 32(3):: 411-427.

Lewis, J. (1999): *Development in Disaster-prone Places: Studies of Vulnerability*. Intermediate Technology Publications, London, UK.

Mitchell, T. (2006): *Building a Disaster Resilient Future: Lessons from Participatory Research on St. Kitts and Montserrat*. Ph.D. thesis, Department of Geography, University College London, London, UK.

NDMO (1989): *Nevis Volcanic Emergency Plan*. NDMO (Nevis Disaster Management Office), Charlestown, Nevis.

NDMO (2005): *Nevis Disaster Plan: Draft*. Annex 1 of *National Disaster Plan 1989* prepared for the Office of the Nevisian

Premier and Stakeholders. NDMO (Nevis Disaster Management Office), Charlestown, Nevis.

OCTA Newsletter (2007): International Climate Change and Vulnerability Conference. *OCTA Newsletter*, 1 (April): 2.

Pattullo, P. (2000): *Fire from the Mountain: The Tragedy of Montserrat and the Betrayal of its People*. Constable and Robinson, London, UK.

Pelling, M. and J.I. Uitto (2001): "Small Island Developing States: Natural Disaster Vulnerability and Global Change", *Environmental Hazards*, 3(2): 49-62.

Rainer, J. (2005): "Are tiny islands viable in the 21st century?" *Small Islands Voice Global Forum*, message 126, http://www.sivglobal.org/?read=126

Rajagopalan, S. (2005): "Post-Tsunami International Relations: A Sea Change?" *Chaitanya Brief*, I(2), Chaitanya Consult, Chennai, India.

Renner, M. and Z. Chafe (2007): *Beyond Disasters: Creating Opportunities for Peace*. World Watch Institute, Washington, DC, USA.

Ryan, P.G. (1987): "The origin and fate of artefacts stranded on islands in the African sector of the Southern Ocean". *Environmental Conservation*, 14(4): 341-346.

Ryan, P.G. (1991): "The impact of the commercial lobster fishery on seabirds at the Tristan da Cunha islands, South Atlantic Ocean". *Biological Conservation*, 57(3): 339-350.

Ryan, P.G. and J. Cooper (1991): "Rockhopper penguins and other marine life threatened by driftnet fisheries at Tristan da Cunha". *Oryx*, 25(2): 76-79.

Ryan, P.G. and M.W. Fraser (1988): "The use of great skua pellets as indicators of plastic pollution in seabirds". *Emu*, 88(1): 16-19.

Simpson, K. (2005): "Nevis". *Volcanic Hazards Atlas of the Lesser Antilles*, pp. 168-177, Seismic Research Unit, University of the West Indies, Trinidad and Tobago.

Trenwith, A. (2003): "The Empire Strikes Back: Human Rights and the Pitcairn Proceedings", *Journal of South Pacific Law*, 7(2): http://www.paclii.org/journals/fJSPL/vol 07no2/3.shtml

Vettori, L. and C. Stuart (2004): "Cyclone in the Pacific". *Oxfam News* (Australia), Autumn: 10-11.

Warnaar, M. (2005): *Shaken, Not Stirred: Iranian Foreign Policy and Domestic Disaster*. Master's thesis at the Universiteit van Amsterdam, the Netherlands.

Yates, L. and L. Anderson-Berry (2004): "The Societal and Environmental Impacts of Cyclone Zoë and the Effectiveness of the Tropical Cyclone Warning Systems in Tikopia and Anuta Solomon Islands, December 26–29, 2002". *The Australian Journal of Emergency Management*, 19(1): 16-20.

10

The Strategy of Information Sharing and Coalition Formation : The Case of the Ganges

MAIKO SAKAMOTO

A hierarchy decision system is modelled with non-cooperative game theory in extensive form, and the way how the coalition evolves as equilibrium is analysed on the case of regulation over the Ganges where Nepal, India and Bangladesh are stakeholders. The result will give required conditions to achieve joint development by all the players.

Introduction

There are a lot of treaties on regulations of international rivers in the world. The number of the treaties is counted to be around 145, and 86 per cent of those were concluded by two countries. Normally, it seems more efficient to conclude an agreement among all concerned stakeholders in a region if the stakeholders are even. As for agreements on regulations of rivers, there already exists topographical unfairness before negotiation begins. This is thought to be one of the reasons why an agreement among all concerned stakeholders is difficult to be fulfilled in negotiation process over international rivers.

In this chapter, the relationship among stakeholders of the Ganges is analyzed in terms of coalition formation. This chapter consists of 6 sections. In section 2, historical background among players, namely India, Bangladesh, and Nepal is summarized. In section 3, methodology is proposed, and payoffs for possible coalitions are calculated. In section 4, using the calculated payoff, equilibrium coalition is analyzed with extensive form non-cooperative game theory. Here, two types of framework are assumed; one is 1-dimenisonal hierarchy system, and the other is 2-dimensional hierarchy system. In 1-dimensional hierarchy, Nepal and Bangladesh cannot negotiate with each other directly, and on the other hand, in 2-dimensional hierarchy, Nepal and Bangladesh can negotiate with each other directly behind India. Finally, the benefit of joint development is explained, and conditions to encourage the players to cooperate with each other are proposed.

Historical Background

The Ganges basin is shared among Nepal, India, and Bangladesh. They have confronted the problem about how to develop the basin of the great Ganges. It is said that there is no doubt to implement basin-wide and joint approach for total benefit and fairness for all of the stakeholders in the river basin. However, it is sometimes difficult for the stakeholders to cooperate with each other because the stakeholders who are situated upstream are less motivated to cooperate than those in the downstream. Basically, upstream countries can use water resources of a river as much as they want, and once they encounter a flood they can make the river flow as it is. As a result, downstream countries sometimes suffer from severe droughts or floods. In the case of the Ganges, Nepal and India are generally considered as upstream countries, and Bangladesh is considered as a downstream country.

An upstream country usually has the strongest power in a basin because it has the right to administrate the river in the first place because of its topographical advantage. In the Ganges, India is the strongest stakeholder although Nepal is the most upstream country. This is because India has better economics, politics and arms in the region. Therefore, the Ganges has been regulated by the initiative of India. In particular, India and Bangladesh have been under strong tension.

India likes to adopt a bilateral approach, not multilateral approach nor an assistance of third party, so that India and Nepal have treaties between them while India and Bangladesh have a treaty between them bilaterally.

The first significant event in their recent history concerning the Ganges is that India unilaterally built the Farakka Barrage across the Ganges River near the border between India and Bangladesh in 1975. Initially, a temporary treaty was concluded between India and Bangladesh. This treaty stipulated that India could withdraw 310-350 m^3/s of water at the Farakka Barrage and discharge 1,245-1,400 m^3/s of water downstream from April 21st to May 30th, when the Ganges River has the least amount of water in a given year. A few months later, the treaty expired, and India began to draw water without any consensus until the two countries concluded a second agreement in 1977. The 1977 treaty was concerned with the Ganges River water resources allocation during the dry season. At first, Bangladesh and India claimed different definitions for what months constitute the dry season. Bangladesh insisted that it was from November to May, while India argued that it was from March to May. As a result of their compromise, the definition for the dry season in this treaty was from January to May. India obtained the right to withdraw more water than what was agreed to in the 1975 temporary treaty. Bangladesh was obliged to compromise more than India. The 1977 treaty required that India withdraw water such that the rate of flow released to Bangladesh should not be less than 80 per cent of the water allocated to Bangladesh. This treaty was in effect until 1984.

After 1984, there was no rule for utilization of the Ganges River water resources between the two countries until a treaty was concluded again in 1996. In the 1996 treaty, Bangladesh made even more compromises than in the treaty covering 1977 to 1984 because the amount of water which Bangladesh can get is sometimes less than 800 m^3/s in the 1996 treaty.

The 1996 treaty has apparently settled the dispute between the two countries for the time being, and this treaty is sometimes treated as a successful case of resolving international water conflicts. However, a visit to the Ganges in the dry season reveals the different scenery upstream and downstream from the Farakka Barrage. In the upper stream, the Ganges River has a generous amount of water, while downstream people sometimes can go across the river on foot. Therefore, it is obvious the conflict is not completely resolved and more work remains to be done.

In fact, the treaty is clearly advantageous to India which is situated upstream, and Bangladesh has many legitimate complaints about the treaty. In particular, the amount of the Ganges River water flowing into Bangladesh is a consequence of the amount of water withdrawn by India at the Farakka Barrage. Hence, a good relationship between Bangladesh and India is important to reduce Bangladesh's vulnerability to droughts and floods. Poor communication between the two countries increases the risk of water shortages and inundations.

This is not the case only between India and Bangladesh. A good relationship between India and Nepal is also important for basin-wide improvement. They have some treaties on electricity development between India and Nepal. The way to use water resources in the upstream region will surely influence the river situation in the downstream region. A third party or legal regime intervention is effective to the situation (Sakamoto *et al*, 2005). To discuss how it is possible to incorporate that kind of legal regime or a third party intervention into the conflict, firstly we must understand the structure of the problem. In the successive sections, a system model of combining river systems optimization and game theoretical decision-making analysis is proposed, and based on the model analysis, it will discuss how the players can be motivated to implement the joint-development.

Methodology

In this chapter, two types of model frameworks are prepared for analyzing the coalition formation among stakeholders :

1. Non-cooperative game theory with 1-dimensional hierarchical system.
2. Non-cooperative game theory with 2-dimensional hierarchical system.

At first, a model to evaluate coalition values is introduced. In cooperative game theory, this kind of coalition value is called a characteristic function. However, in this chapter, the definition of coalition is different from that of cooperative game theory so that we call it just 'coalition value'.

In the case of the Ganges, nine types of coalitions are assumed as shown in Table 10.1. The Figure 10.1 depicts the system.

Table 10.1: Types of Coalitions

Case	*Coalition S*	*Case*	*Coalition S*
1	I, B, N	5	IN, IB
2	I, B, N	6	IB, BN
3	I, B, N	7	IN, BN
4	I, N, B	8	IB, BN, IN
		9	IBN

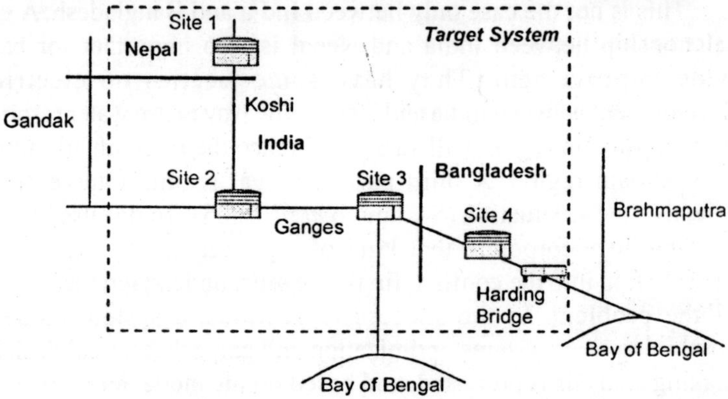

Fig. 10.1: Sketch of the System

For each case of Table 10.1, maximized (aggregate) net benefit of focused player(s) in a coalition is used as the coalition value which is calculated by solving the following problem. Main frame of this model is referred to Roger's work (1969). After showing sets of equations, details of the model are explained.

Object function is modelled as in equation.

$$\max_{S'(\subseteq S)} \sum_{i\in F(S')}\sum_{j\in J_D} ay_{ij} + \sum_{i\in F(S')}\sum_{j\in J_R} pz_{ij} - \sum_{i\in F(S')} cV_i - dE - \sum_{i\in F(S')}\sum_{j\in J_R} b(x_{ij} - G) \quad (1)$$

Constraints are shown in the following:
continuity at each reservoir

$$\sum_{j\in J} x_{ij} \le \sum_{j\in J} I_{ij} \quad for\ i \in N \quad (2)$$

flow continuity between sites (for downstream sites)

1. In rainy season which is non-irrigation season, equation (3) is applied.

$$I_{ij} = \sum_{i' \in I} x_{i'j} \tag{3}$$

2. In dry season which is irrigation season, equation (4) is applied.

$$I_{ij} = \sum_{i' \in I} (x_{i'j} - (1-\alpha) y_{i'j}) \tag{4}$$

storage and flow continuity at a site

$$v_{ij} = v_{i(j-1)} + I_{ij} - x_{ij}^{`} \quad for\ i \in N\ and\ j \in J \tag{5}$$

storage less than capacity

$$\sum_{j \in J} x_{ij} + V_i \geq \sum_{j \in J} I_{ij} \quad for\ i \in N \tag{6}$$

flow to surface irrigation

$$x_{ij} - y_{ij} \geq 0 \quad for\ j \in J_D\ and\ i \in N \tag{7}$$

flow through turbines less than or equal to capacity of turbines

$$\beta V_i - z_{ij} \geq 0 \quad for\ j \in J_R\ and\ i \in N \tag{8}$$

power flow less than or equal to be released

$$x_{ij} - z_{ij} \geq 0 \quad for\ j \in J_R\ and\ i \in N \tag{9}$$

upper limit on size of surface storage

$$V_i \leq \overline{V}_i \quad for\ i \in N \tag{10}$$

budged constraints

1. If Bangladesh is not in a coalition, then equation is used as a budget constraint:

$$\sum_{i \in F(S')} cV_i \leq \sum_{k \in K(S')} \overline{B}_k \tag{11}$$

2. If Bangladesh is in a coalition, then equation (12) is used as a budget constraint. In other words, constructing embankment is an option only for Bangladesh.

$$\sum_{i \in F(S')} cV_i + dE \leq \sum_{k \in K(S')} \overline{B}_k \quad (12)$$

initial condition; dams become empty at the end of dry season (March)

$$v_{i3} = 0 \ \ for\ i \in N \quad (13)$$

All variables should be larger than or equal to zero.

$$x_{ij}, y_{ij}, z_{ij}, V_i, v_{ij}, E \geq 0 \quad (14)$$

The parameters and variables in the equations are defined as follows:

i, *index of sites;*
i', *index of direct upstream sites;*
N, *number of sites;*
S', *subset of coalition S;*
$F(S')$, *single component (site) which belongs to a player in coalition S';*
j, index of months;
J, number of months;
J_R, set of the months in rainy season, i.e., from April to October;
J_D, set of the months in dry season, i.e., from November to March;
k, index of countries (players);
K, set of the countries (players) in a coalition;
p, price of hydro power per unit of flow;
a, value per unit of irrigation water for use in the downstream neighbourhood;
b, value lost by flood in terms of flow unit;
c, cost per unit volume for surface storage;
d, cost of embankment built at flood control per unit flow;
x_{ij}, release from reservoir *i* in the month *j*;
y_{ij}, agriculture diversion at location *i* in month *j*;
z_{ij}, flow through turbines at location *i* in month *j*;
V_j, volume capacity of reservoir *i* in terms of flow units;
v_{ij}, volume of reservoir *i* in month *j* in terms of flow units;
I_{ij}, average inflow into reservoir *i* in the month *j*;

E, size of embankment in terms of flow unit;
G, flood capacity on river system;
$\overline{V}_i$, maximum size of reservoir i;
$\overline{B}_k$, maximum budget of country k;
α, proportion of irrigation water returning to stream;
β, capacity of turbines expressed as a proportion of storage.

The values used for parameters are shown in Table 10.2, and the corresponding hydrology data used in the model is shown in Table 10.3. S', $F(S)$ of each coalition are defined as in Table 10.4, where I_m in case 8 means site m in India so that m takes the number 2 or 3 as seen in the site map of Figure 10.1.

The details of main Idea of the model is explained in the following :

Table 10.2: Settings of Parameters

	Symbol	*Value*	*Unit*
Price of hydro power per unit of flow	p	11.7	Rs./ $m^3 \times 10^3$ /month
Average value product by irrigation	a	53.9	Rs./ $m^3 \times 10^3$ /month
Average lost by flood	b	53.9	Rs./ $m^3 \times 10^3$ /month
Annual cost of surface storage	c	14.1	Rs./ $m^3 \times 10^3$ /month
Maintenance cost of embankment from Aug to Oct	d	7.30	Rs./ $m^3 \times 10^3$ /month
Flood constraint	G	49.3	$m^3 \times 10^9$
Upper limit on reservoirs of site 1 and 2	$\overline{V}_1, \overline{V}_2$	6.17	$m^3 \times 10^9$
Upper limit on reservoirs of site 3 and 4	$\overline{V}_3, \overline{V}_4$	18.5	$m^3 \times 10^9$
Budget constraint for Nepal	$\overline{B}_1$	4.0	Rs. $\times 10^6$ /year
Budget constraint for India	$\overline{B}_2$	480.0	Rs. $\times 10^6$ /year
Budget constraint for Bangladesh	$\overline{B}_3$	38.0	Rs. $\times 10^6$ /year
Proportion of irrigation water returning to stream	α	0.2	-
Capacity of turbines	β	0.2	-

Based on Rogers (1969).

Table 10.3: Hydrologic Date (average flow, m×10⁹/month)

Point / Month(j)	Jan	Feb	Mar	Apr	May	June	Jul	Aug	Sept	Oct	Nov	Dec
Kosi $(= I_{1j})$	1.05	0.88	0.94	1.02	1.88	4.97	10.7	10.1	9.22	4.36	2.10	1.43
Ganges (downstream Of Gandak) $(= I_{2j})$	7.34	5.79	5.35	4.16	3.80	5.88	16.5	92.9	82.76	41.26	16.03	9.42

Based on Rogers (1969)

Table 10.4: Types of Coalition Formations

Case	Coalition S	S'			$F(S')$			Order of Optimization
1	I, B, N	I	B	N	I	B	N	N⇨I⇨B
2	IB, N	IB		N	IB		N	N⇨IB
3	I, BN	BN		I	BN		I	BN⇨I
4	IN, B	IN		B	IN		B	IN⇨B
5	IN, IB	I			IBN			IBN
6	IB, BN	B			IBN			IBN
7	IN, BN	N			IBN			IBN
8	IB, BN, IN	I_2N	I_3B		I_2N	I_3B		I_2N⇨I_3B
9	IBN	IBN			IBN			IBN

Player can decide construction of a dam at own site as well as how much water they release from the dam and how to use it. As shown in Figure 10.4, Nepal owns site 1, India owns sites 2 and 3, and Bangladesh owns site 4.

In the dry season, a player can use water for irrigation for the land which is placed at directly below the dam. In the rainy season, a player can use water for generating hydro electricity at the site. In applying the model to the case of the Ganges, only Nepal is assumed to be able to consider both of irrigation and hydro electricity while other countries, India and Bangladesh, cannot consider hydro electricity. Therefore, if Nepal is not in a coalition, 2nd term in equation (1) is not present. Players try to maximize sum of profits by irrigation and hydro electricity minus sum of losses by flood damage and maintaining the dam and embankment. In application, only Bangladesh is assumed to suffer from floods and have the option to maintain embankment. In calculation, maintenance cost of embankment is considered only for three months from August to October when a flood is the most severe.

We also put an assumption about the strategy of constructing dam; only India can construct a dam by itself, and other players, Nepal and Bangladesh, need to make a coalition to make a dam. Furthermore, notice that we do not assume construction cost of dams, and only cost of surface water storage is considered. This is because all of countries focused on are thought to need financial support for construction more or less. In the following section, the construction cost is not considered for Bangladesh and Nepal, but it is optionally considered for India. This means that we implicitly assume an outside organization gives financial aid to players, particularly Bangladesh and Nepal, when they decide to construct a dam.

Nine types of coalition are considered as shown in Table 10.4.

Case 1 means that India, Bangladesh and Nepal individually maximize their own cost-benefit function [equation (1)] by changing only its own variables under its own cost constraints. In other words, there is no coalition. Under this condition, firstly, Nepal's maximization problem is solved because it is the most upstream country and it can control the river in the first place. Secondly, India's maximization problem is solved under the condition of flow which is released by Nepal as a consequence of Nepal's optimization. Finally, Bangladesh's maximization problem is solved with flow constraints through Nepal and India.

In case 2, firstly, Nepal decides the volume of a reservoir and water which will be released from the reservoir at site 1 by maximizing its own cost-benefit function, and given this condition, India and Bangladesh maximize their joint cost-benefit function under both of their constraints.

In cases 5, 6, 7, all of the players are indirectly connected by two bilateral agreements, but it does not mean there exists a multilateral coalition. Therefore, the player who is in the both coalitions becomes a key player which is called a pivot player in the following. The pivot player is assumed to control the situation as it wants because only the pivot player has all the information. Then, the problem to be solved in cases 5, 6, 7 is maximization of pivot player's payoff with the variables of all the players.

In case 8, in the first place, India and Nepal maximize their cost-benefit function concerning sites 1 and 2 which can be thought as the upstream part of the Ganges. Secondly, given the maximized condition on sites 1 and 2 India and Bangladesh maximize their cost-benefit function concerning sites 3 and 4.

In case 9, India, Bangladesh and Nepal maximize their joint cost-benefit function by changing all their variables under all of their constraints.

The summary of results is shown in Tables 10.5 and 10.6.

Value of coalition means aggregate net benefit among the players in the coalition. Net benefit means benefit minus cost. For example, in case 2, coalition value means aggregate net benefit of India and Bangladesh. In case 8, coalition value means aggregate net benefit of India, Bangladesh and Nepal. As for case 1, there is no coalition so that value of coalition is not able to define. In this case, aggregate value of individual net benefit of all the players is given with ( ).

Total benefit means aggregate benefit of all the players. Total cost means aggregate cost of all the players. Then, total net benefit means total benefit minus total cost. Individual net benefit means benefit minus actual cost for a player. Individual benefit from irrigation means benefit generated from irrigation for a player. Hypothetical individual cost means cost of constructed objects in player's site(s). Actual individual cost is the money which a player actually pay. Therefore, if a player can get more objects than what the player can construct by its own budged, hypothetical individual cost becomes larger than actual individual cost.

Analysis on Coalition Formation Process

In this section, negotiation process among 3 players, India, Bangladesh and Nepal, is modelled with extensive form non-cooperative game theory in 1-dimensional hierarchy system and 2-dimensional hierarchy system. The hierarchy structure is modelled by the order of making decisions, and this is why extensive form non-cooperative game theory is applied, which can consider the order of decision-making.

The payoff for each coalition is set based on the results in the previous section. The values of individual net benefit are used as payoffs of the players. In the successive subsections, firstly, the brief introduction of non-cooperative game theory is explained. Secondly, equilibrium in 1-dimensional hierarchy system is analyzed, where only India can negotiate with other players while Bangladesh and Nepal cannot make a coalition between them. Thirdly, equilibrium in 2-dimensional hierarchy system is analyzed, where Bangladesh and Nepal can negotiate with each other behind India so that India does not know whether they make a coalition or not when India talks to either of them.

Non-cooperative Game Theory in Extensive Form

Game theory is used to model a conflict situation and to help understand the phenomenon in logical ways. In this chapter, the Ganges conflict is modelled with extensive game form. Game theory is a powerful tool of analyzing ongoing conflicts. It provides probable outcomes which are based on certain assumptions. In this subsection, a general introduction about game theory in extensive form is given with mentioning fundamental concepts and essential assumptions (Grints, 2000).

An extensive form game consists of a number of players, a game tree, and a set of payoffs. A game tree consists of a number of nodes connected by branches. A path from node *a* to node a′ in the game tree is a sequence of moves starting at *a* and ending at a′. If there is a path from node *a* to *a*′, we say *a* is an *ancestor* of a′, and *a*′ is a *successor* to *a*. We call *k* the length of the path. If a path from *a* to *a*′ has length one, we call *a* the parent of *a*′, and *a*′ is *child* of a. We require that the game tree have one node *r*, called the *root node*, that has no parent, and a set *T* of nodes called terminal nodes or leaf *nodes*, that have no children. We associate with each terminal node *t* ∈ *T*, and each player *i*, a *payoff,* (t) ∈ R (*R* is the set of real numbers). We say the game is finite if it has a finite number of nodes. We assume all games are finite, unless otherwise stated.

We also require that the graph have the following tree property. Tree must be exactly one path from the root node to any given terminal node in the game tree. One obvious but important implication of this property is that every node except the root node has exactly one parent.

Players relate to the game tree as follows. Each nonterminal node is assigned to a player who moves at that node. Each branch from a node represents a particular action that the player assigned to that node can take there, and hence determines either a terminal node or the next point of play in the game—the particular child node to be visited next.

The tree property thus means that there is a unique sequence of moves by the players leading from the root node to any specific node of the game tree, and for any two nodes, there is at most one sequence of player moves leading from the first to the second.

Table 10.5: Summary of Results (1 of 2)

Case	Coalition	Value of Coalition	Total Net Benefit	Total Benefit	Total Cost	V_1	V_2	V_3	V_4	E
1	I, B, N	(-276)	-276	111	387	0.00	6.17	18.50	0	7.81
2	IB, N	3,386	3,212	3,730	518	0.00	2.57	13.37	0	40.09
3	I, BN	-4,310	-691	-300	391	2.97	6.17	18.50	0	0.00
4	IN, B	3,704	-1,090	-668	422	6.17	6.17	0.68	0	7.81
5	IN, IB	-242	-242	280	522	6.17	6.17	18.50	6.09	0.00
6	IB, BN	3,197	3,197	3,719	522	0.00	4.37	0.00	10.79	42.16
7	IN, BN	3,120	3,120	3,641	521	6.17	1.81	6.92	0	42.66
8	IB, BN, IN	2,865	2,865	3,374	509	6.17	6.17	15.02	0	18.53
9	IBN	3,145	3,145	3,667	522	6.17	5.79	15.04	0	18.50
Unit		Rs. $\times 10^6$ /year								$m^3 \times 10^9$

Table 10.6: Summary of Results (2 of 2)

Case	Coalition	Individual Net Benefit			Individual Benefit from Irrigation			Hydro Electricity	Hypothetical Individual Cost (Actual)			Damage by Flood
		I	B	N	I	B	N		I (480)	B (38)	N (4)	
1.	I, B, N	3,971	-4,204	344	4,320	310	344	0	349	38	0	4,476
2.	IB, N	3,313	73	344	3,793	247	344	0	225	293	0	136
3.	I, BN	4,010	-4,854	544	4,359	311	504	48	349	0	42	5,127
4.	IN, B	2,933	-4,372	771	3,413	142	677	98	297	38	87	4,476
5.	IN, IB	3,893	-4,384	771	4,373	644	677	98	349	86	87	4,990
6.	IB, BN	2,713	662	344	700	344	0	62	460	0	0	0
7.	IN, BN	2,978	-108	771	3,458	177	677	98	123	311	87	247
8.	IB, BN, IN	3,570	-967	771	4,050	270	678	98	287	135	87	1,199
9.	IBN	3,238	-342	771	3,718	208	677	98	178	257	87	512
Unit		Rs. $\times 10^6$ /year										

Suppose each player $i = 1,..., n$ choose strategy s_i from their strategy set S_i, hence $S_i \in S_i$. We call $s = (S_1,..., S_n)$ a strategy profile for the game, and we define the *payoff function* of player *i*, given strategy profile *s*, as $\pi_i(s): S \rightarrow R$.

We say a strategy profile $s^* = (s_1^*,..., s_n^*)$ is a *Nash* equilibrium if, for every player $i = 1, ..., n$, and every s_i, we have $\pi_i(s^*) \geq \pi_i(s_i, s^*_{-i})$ where the player *i* chooses the different strategy from s^* and all the other players which is represented by—*i* chose the strategy profile s^*. Choosing s_i^* is at least as good for player *i* as choosing any other s_i given that the other players choose $s\text{-}i^*$. Nash equilibrium is important because we can know how people will play a game if they are rational.

A powerful way of finding Nash equilibrium is to eliminate what are called *dominated strategies*. Suppose s_i and s'_i are two strategies for player *i*, and we say S'_i is *strictly dominated* by S'_i if, for every choice of strategies of the other players, *i* 's payoff from choosing s_i is *strictly greater* than *i*'s payoff from choosing, S'_i. We say s_i is *weakly dominated* by s_i if, for every choice of strategies of all the other players, *i* 's payoff by choosing s_i is *at least as great as* *i*'s payoff by choosing S'_i. It is clear that a strictly dominated strategy s_i is never part of Nash equilibrium, since the player *i* could do better by switching to another strategy that dominates s_i. We can, therefore, eliminate such strategies without losing any Nash equilibrium. We call this process the elimination of strictly dominated strategies. This procedure is formally called backward induction in extensive form game because we start the procedure at the end of the game and move backward to the root node.

The detailed procedure of backward induction can be explained as follows. Choose any terminal node $t \in T$ and find the parent node of this terminal node, say node *a*. Suppose player *i* chooses at *a*, and suppose *i*'s highest payoff at *a* is attained at node $t' \in T$. Erase all the branches from *a* so that *a* becomes a terminal node, and attach the payoffs from t' to the new terminal node *a*. Also record *i*'s move at *a*, then we can specify *i*'s equilibrium strategy when we have finished the analysis. Repeat this procedure for all terminal nodes of the original game. After that, we will have an extensive form game that is one level less deep than the original game. Now repeat the process as many times as is necessary, until the game tree has just one node. When we reassemble the moves we have recorded for each player, we will have subgame perfect Nash equilibrium which is peculiar equilibrium concept in extensive form game basically corresponding to Nash equilibrium in normal form game (note that this is not strict definition). In extensive form game with perfect information and pure strategy sets, at least one subgame perfect Nash equilibrium can be obtained by backward induction. Perfect information is the situation where all of the players exactly know which node is now reached. Perfect information means player does not use probabilistic strategy but they choose one certain strategy at their decision-making.

Equilibrium in 1-dimensional Hierarchy System

Along the Ganges, Nepal, India, and Bangladesh are recognized as players whose topographical relationship is depicted in Figure 10.1. All the players are assumed to be thinking about whether they make a coalition with other players or not. They are equally assumed to have two strategies concerning coalition formation; Coalition or Denial.

Among the players there may exist hierarchy structure, and the structure is though to be different depending on the situations. In this subsection, the case where Nepal and Bangladesh cannot negotiate with each other directly is assumed. Normally, the most upstream county has a strong power of regulating the river. However, India is thought to be placed on the top of the hierarchy although Nepal situates in the most upstream part of the Ganges. The second highest player in the hierarchy is assumed to be Nepal, and the third is Bangladesh because of the topographical reasoning.

The hierarchy structure is modelled by the order of making decisions. Therefore, India can decide whether India makes a coalition with other players or not at first, and Nepal can decide next and Bangladesh is the last. The model of the negotiation process is shown in Figure 10.2. As it is seen in Figure 10.2, firstly, India talks to only Nepal, and Bangladesh is not considered to be negotiated by India. In this sense, the hierarchy in Figure 10.2 can be said as the strict hierarchy because there is strict transition order among players. Therefore, Bangladesh can decide its behaviour only if it is asked to make a coalition by the higher player.

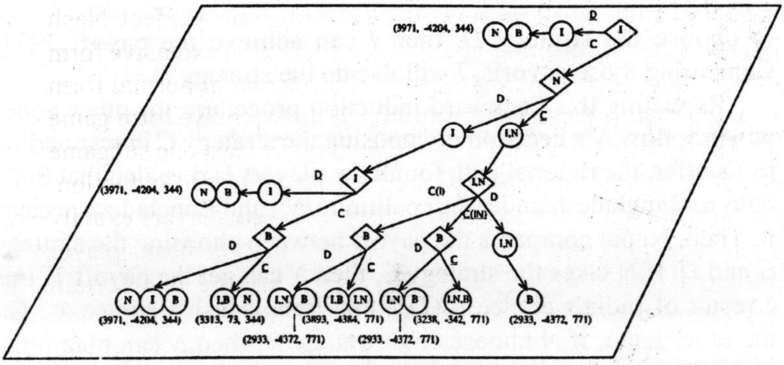

Fig. 10.2: 1-Dimensional Hierarchy System

In Figure 10.2, India is represented by I, Bangladesh by B, and Nepal by N. Lozenges show stages of decision-making by the written player(s) whose names are represented inside of the lozenges. Coalitions are represented by circles. For example, the coalition of India and Bangladesh is represented by 'BI' with the circle. *C* means the strategy Coalition, and *D* means the strategy Denial. The notation as *C(IN)* means that there already exists the coalition '*IN*' and the stronger player in the coalition, which is India, can decide whether India talks to Bangladesh by itself or together with Nepal. If India decides to negotiate with Bangladesh by itself, the strategy is represented with *C(I)* while *C(IN)* is used if India decides to talk to Bangladesh together with Nepal. The numbers as (3972, –4806,344) mean payoffs for each coalition, where the first figure shows the payoff of India, the second for Bangladesh and the third for Nepal.

In this case, since perfect information is assumed, at least one equilibrium can be obtained by backward induction. Figure 10.2 shows the rational decisions of players at each stage, which are shown by underlined *C* or *D*. For example, at the most left and lowest stage in Figure 10.2, where *B* is going to make a decision, comparing the payoffs of *B* between the coalition '*N*', '*I*', '*B*' and the coalition '*IB*', '*N*', the strategy Coalition can be concluded to be better than Denial because Bangladesh's payoff for the coalition '*N*', '*I*', '*B*' is -4806 while the payoff of the coalition '*IB*', '*N*' is 73.

Based on *B*'s decision, now we are focusing on the ancestor node where *I* is making a decision whether *I* will talk to *B* or not. If *I* decides to use the strategy *C*, since *B* is supposed to choose the strategy *C*, then *I* can obtain the payoff 9315. On the other hand, if *I* decides to choose the strategy *D*, then *I* can achieve the payoff 3971. Comparing those payoffs, *I* will decide the strategy *D*.

Repeating this backward induction procedure for other nodes which follow *N*'s decision of choosing the strategy *C* in responding to *I*'s offer, the rational path for all the players is revealed that India talks to Bangladesh under the coalition '*IN*', and Bangladesh accepts it. Then, Nepal compares the payoff between choosing the strategy *C* and *D*. If N takes the strategy *C*, then *N* can get the payoff 771 as a result of India's choice, *C*(*IN*), and Bangladesh's choice, *C*. On the other hand, if N chooses the strategy *D*, then *N* can obtain the payoff 344 as a result of *I*'s choice, *D*. Therefore, *N* will choose the strategy *D*.

Going up to one upper node from *N*'s decision node, *I* is facing at the decision whether *I* chooses the strategy *C* with *N* or the strategy *D*. *I* can get the payoff 3971 if *I* chooses the strategy *D* while *I* can get the payoff 3238 if *I* selects the strategy *C*. Therefore, *I* will decide to select the strategy *C*, and as a whole, an unique path and unique coalition '*I*', '*B*', '*N*' are obtained as subgame perfect Nash equilibrium in the *1*-dimaesional hierarchy system. In other words, there would not exist a coalition among the players and they will make a decision individually.

Now, we assume to incorporate conditional construction cost of dams. That is, only if a player constructs a dam by itself, then the player should pay the construction cost which is estimated Rs. 2.5 billion per a dam. If the player makes a coalition with other players, the construction cost is fully covered by an outside organization. Under this condition, only India can have dams by its own budget. Then, some of payoffs in Figure 10.2 are needed to change so that the payoff of India for the coalition '*N*', '*B*, '*I*' changes from 3971 to –1029. In this case, a unique equilibrium coalition becomes '*I*, *B*, *N*' and the corresponding equilibrium path will be *C*⇨*C*⇨*C*(*IN*)⇨*C* where the first decision belongs to India, the second is Nepal and the last one is Bangladesh. The payoff which is calculated in the section 3 is one-year estimation at the year when dams are constructed. Then, if long term payoff is considered, the equilibrium may be different. However, players are thought to estimate their payoffs with a high discount rate so that the assumption is considered not so far from the reality.

Equilibrium in 2-Dimensional Hierarchy System

In this subsection, 2-dimenisonal hierarchy is assumed as shown in Figure 10.3 and Figure 10.4. Here, Nepal and Bangladesh can negotiate with each other without India's interference. In Figure 10.3 and Figure 10.4, the same shadowed lozenges mean that they are in the same decision stage. For example, the most left and lowest node where '*B*' is written in Figure 10.3 and '*NB*' is written in Figure 10.4 means that Bangladesh is facing at the decision whether *B* will accept *I*'s offer and *N*'s offer at the same time.

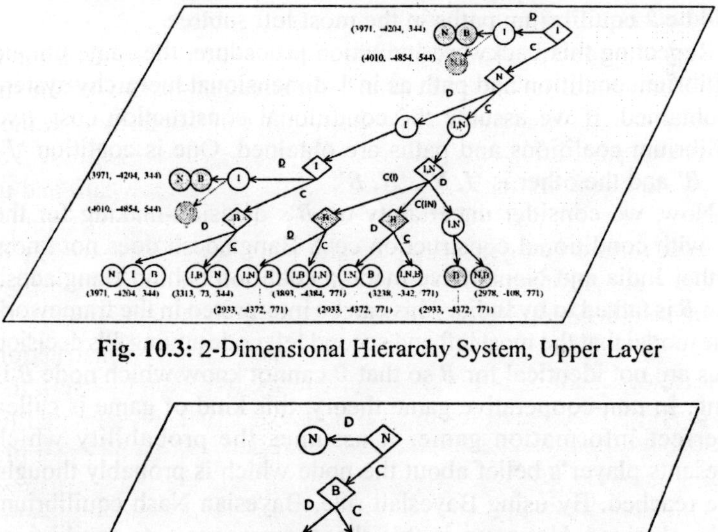

Fig. 10.3: 2-Dimensional Hierarchy System, Upper Layer

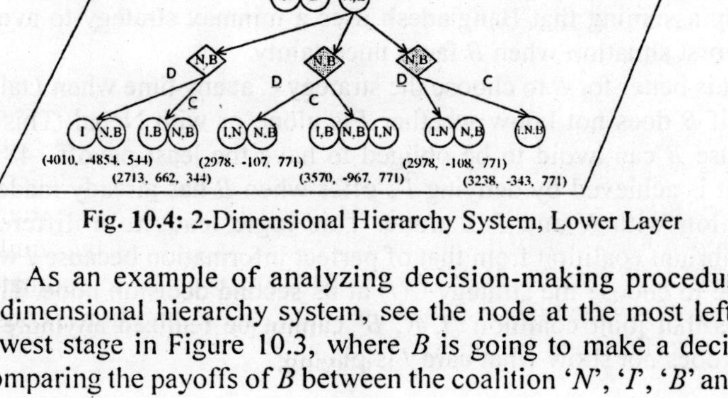

Fig. 10.4: 2-Dimensional Hierarchy System, Lower Layer

As an example of analyzing decision-making procedure in 2-dimensional hierarchy system, see the node at the most left and lowest stage in Figure 10.3, where *B* is going to make a decision, comparing the payoffs of *B* between the coalition '*N*', '*I*', '*B*' and the coalition '*IB*', '*N*'. The strategy Coalition can be concluded to be better than Denial because Bangladesh's payoff for the coalition '*N*', '*I*', '*B*' is 4204 while the payoff of the coalition '*IB*', '*N*' is 73. At the same time, Bangladesh is also facing at the decision about the offer from *N*, which is depicted at the most left node in Figure *10.4*. At this stage, the strategy *C* is better for Bangladesh as well as in upper layer. Now, Bangladesh has two choices; one is to accept *I*'s offer on the condition of non-coalition with Nepal; another is to accept *I*'s offer on the condition of being tied-up with *N*. Comparing to both *B*'s payoff, accepting the offer from *N* is better if Nepal talks to Bangladesh. However, it is not sure whether *N* will make an offer to *B* or not because *N*'s payoffs are same in both situations. Then, there could be 2 equilibrium paths in the most left subtree.

Repeating this backward induction procedure, the same unique equilibrium coalition and path as in 1-dimensional hierarchy system are obtained. If we assume the conditional construction cost, two equilibrium coalitions and paths are obtained. One is coalition '*I*', '*N*', '*B*' and the other is '*I, N*', '*N, B*'.

Now, we consider uncertainty on *B*'s decision-making for the case with conditional construction cost. Bangladesh does not know whether India and Nepal have made a coalition behind Bangladesh when *B* is talked to by India. This can be interpreted in the framework of the model that the most left and second left node among *B*'s decision nodes are not identical for *B* so that *B* cannot know which node *B* is facing. In non-cooperative game theory, this kind of game is called imperfect information game. It assumes the probability which represents player's belief about the node which is probably thought to be reached. By using Bayesian rule, Bayesian Nash equilibrium can be obtained. However, in this chapter, we speculate equilibrium briefly assuming that Bangladesh uses a minmax strategy to avoid the worst situation when *B* faces uncertainty.

It is better for *B* to choose the strategy *C* at any time when *I* talks to *B* if *B* does not know whether *I* is alone or with Nepal. This is because *B* can avoid to be obliged to have the least payoff –4854 which is achieved by denying *I*'s offer when *B* has already made a coalition with *N* and *I* is alone. This logic leads to a different equilibrium coalition from that of perfect information because *I* will decide to choose the strategy *C*(*I*) at its second decision node. This means that joint coalition '*I, N, B*' cannot be realized anymore if India does not show what card *I* is playing.

Conclusion

The hierarchy decision system is modelled with non-cooperative game theory in extensive form, and the way how the coalition evolves as equilibrium is analyzed on the case of the Ganges where Nepal, India and Bangladesh are stakeholders. As a conclusion, the required conditions to achieve the joint development by all the players are revealed that an outside support should be given to united stakeholders not to single stakeholder, and the players should share information about their negotiation process. Both of the two conditions need to be satisfied for the whole basin development.

In this chapter, numerous aspects remain ongoing work; one is to modify the payoff calculation model; second is to establish a payoff allocation rule; third is to incorporate uncertainty on decision-making by more theoretical way. In addition to those, an aspect of governance needs to be considered more for the discussion about players' payoff structure. After those improvements, there will be more to say about how to motivate the players naturally to cooperate with each other.

References

Gintis, H. (2000): *Game Theory Evolving : A Problem-Cenosred Introduction to Modelling Strategic Interaction*, Princeton Univ. Press.

Rogers, P. (1969): A Game Theory Approach to the Problem of International River Basins, *Water Resources Research*, Vol. 5, No. 4, pp. 749-760.

Sakamoto, M., Y. Hagihara, and K.W. Hipel, (2005): Coordination Process by a Third Party in the Conflict Between Bangladesh and India over Regulation of the Ganges River, IEEE International Conference on Systems, *Man and Cybernetics*, pp.1119-1125.

11

Shaken, Not Stirred : Iran's Foreign Relations and the 2003 Bam Earthquake

MAAIKE WARNAAR

After the December 2003 earthquake in Bam, Iran, the international community showed tremendous compassion towards the survivors by sending in huge amounts of relief aid. The Iranian Government's decision to welcome aid from all countries but Israel was unprecedented, and the United States was among the first countries to respond. However, only a few weeks after the disaster, the Iranian Government closed the door on a United States aid delegation. And, as the most urgent phase of the relief effort was over, the cooperation between aid organizations and the Iranian Governments also became more problematic. When South and South-East Asia were hit by a tsunami on December 26, 2004, precisely a year after a devastating earthquake struck the city of Bam in Southern Iran, Iranian President Mohammad Khatami made an interesting remark. As the international community was pledging unprecedented amounts of aid money, he reminded the world of the pledge made to Bam: over 1 billion U.S. dollar. One year later, only a fraction of the promised money had been delivered.[1]

Studies of 'disaster diplomacy' shed light on why the Islamic Republic did not take advantage of the thaw in U.S.-Iranian relations to improve ties. First of all, it seems that disaster diplomacy can only be successful if efforts to improve ties are already on their way. Secondly, disaster diplomacy can only be successful if it happens on a give-and-take basis. An unreciprocated relationship cannot be a sufficient basis for rapprochement. The need for reciprocity may be even more urgent in the case of Iran, as its regime strongly adheres to the principle of independence from other countries.

To help understand the initial success and eventual failure of international cooperation after the Bam earthquake, this chapter will outline the cooperation efforts in the context of the foreign policy of the Islamic Republic and of the donating governments. The case of the international cooperation after the Bam earthquake sheds light on the possibilities for disaster diplomacy: the idea that a rapprochement between countries can be induced by disaster cooperation. An increasing body of literature has been written on this concept, which was coined by Kelman and Koukis (2000). Iran's refusal of the American aid delegation, and the failed delivery of the aid money pledged to Bam, will be analysed in the context of this body of literature. Before this can be done, the concept of humanitarian aid and its role in foreign policy needs to be explained. The process of politicisation of humanitarian aid that started after the Cold War is part of this understanding. This chapter accept the inherently political character of humanitarian aid. In doing so, it challenges a taboo of associating humanitarian aid with politics. Development aid and humanitarian aid are usually treated as separate fields by donating and receiving government, as well as a large chunk of international aid organisations, and even in scholarly literature. Humanitarian aid is seen as the direct consequence of the principle of humanity[1], addressing immediate needs rather than root causes and long-term development. It is perceived as being of a different kind than development aid, which is recognized as an enterprise with political dimensions.

Ideally, humanitarian aid would be based on a humanitarian imperative, free from political considerations. However, understanding a multitude of humanitarian aid problems, dilemmas and disappointments, requires the recognition that humanitarian aid is political. This chapter argues that humanitarian aid, like development aid, is often influenced, if not determined, by political motivations. While this is the case, denying links between humanitarian aid and politics fail to address the root causes of much miscommunication in the field of humanitarian aid. The case of Bam illustrates this.

---

1. The International Federation of Red Cross and Red Crescent Societies (IFRC) defines the principle of humanity as "The desire to prevent and alleviate human suffering wherever it may be found… to protect life and health and to ensure respect for the human being". It is the first principle in the IFRC Code of Conduct. *Source*: http://www.ifrc.org/WHAT/values/principles/humanity.asp. Accessed February 28, 2007.

The Humanitarian Aid System

There appears to have been an increase in humanitarian crises after 1990, and these crises have been posited high on the international political agenda. This has translated into an increase of donations in the field of humanitarian aid, and the concentration of these donations in the hands of a select group of wealthy donors.[2] An important consequence of the increased international interest in humanitarian aid, and with it the increase in aid money donated to humanitarian disasters, is the effect that the political considerations of the prime donors have on the way aid is conducted. Before the 1990s, the humanitarian community had the benefit of relative autonomy; as international governments' humanitarian aid expenditures took up a larger part of their budget, throughout the 1990s, however, the relationship between the state and humanitarian organizations became more and more of a principal-agent kind. Michael Barnett argues that states increasingly came to see aid organizations as carrying out their foreign policy objectives. This resulted in considerable tension. "States see themselves as principals that are providing a temporary transfer of authority to their agents, humanitarian organizations. Yet humanitarian organizations do not see themselves as agents of states or operating with delegated authority; instead they see themselves as agents of humanity and operating with moral authority."[3] The trust between states and humanitarian organizations that had been unchallenged before the 1990s began to erode; as humanitarian organizations depended on the resources to do their work, they needed to respond adequately to this development.[4] This had some positive results, as humanitarian aid organizations became more efficient and better accountable to both donors and receivers. However, at the same time humanitarian aid organizations saw the need to alter their underlying rules to meet the requirements of states, and in doing so, compromised the effectiveness of aid.

Obedience of humanitarian aid organizations to the wishes of the donating governments has made them part of the political process. Part of this is the result of resource dependency of the aid organisations. Governments now decide for themselves where, when, how and by whom their aid money is spent. This is problematic. In their decision to provide humanitarian aid, governments are guided not only by the humanitarian imperative to relieve suffering, but also by other, possibly more decisive motivations. These are political considerations in the domestically defined interest of a state. This 'national interest' is not something objectively given and, therefore, not necessarily the outcome of economic or security interest, but a trade-off between international threats and opportunities, and domestic constraints.

A Two-Level Game

By nature, states are not self-sacrificing humanitarian organizations, but calculators, acting in the best interest of those in power. As states have become the most important donators in the field of humanitarian aid, we cannot explain the outcomes of this practice without taking into account the political motivations of donating governments. As the main donators to humanitarian aid, these actors have tremendous power, which they use to their advantage, even if they would not publicly admit this. Governments are institutions that constantly try to find a balance between the demands and opportunities domestically on the one hand, and those in the international sphere on the other. The model of two-level game (Putnam, 1988) can give us insight in the foreign policy decision-making in the field of humanitarian aid. At the domestic table, we find how civil society and public opinion, in close relation to the media, influence the choices that governments make. Of decisive importance, however, seem to be the considerations at the international table.[5] This is where international governments use humanitarian aid as a tool of foreign policy.

The International Table

After the 1980s there was a substantial increase in international donations to humanitarian situations. This increase had two important characteristics. First of all, a shift took place from multilateral aid to bilateral aid.[II] Increasingly, this bilateral aid was earmarked for specific projects. Barnett explains how as a consequence, "state interests, rather than the humanitarian principle of relief based on need, increasingly drives funding decisions."[6] Studies have shown that foreign policy considerations strongly influence the allocation of disaster assistance

---

II. If a government chooses to donate on a bilateral level, it can choose whether to give money to the government of the affected country directly, or to an aid organization working in the country. When money is donated to a certain country by a multilateral organization like the UN, it is called multilateral aid, but when it is labelled for allocation in one specific country by the donating government, it is mainly bilateral in character and, therefore, called multi-bilateral aid.

by donating states. Drury, Olson and Van Belle even argue that, in the case of the United States, foreign policy considerations and domestic factors are the overriding determinant in deciding *where* to allocate disaster assistance and *how much*.[7]

Secondly, aid is now controlled by a smaller group of international donors. These donors are more inclined to impose conditions and, in doing so, direct aid towards their priorities.[8] Donating governments no longer see the need to rely on aid organizations for their information, and have become directly involved in humanitarian aid situations, by sending representatives into the field to make independent needs assessments. During some complex emergencies, governments have taken up the coordination of humanitarian aid efforts, like the United States in Afghanistan. As humanitarian aid in these instances was an integral part of the warfare and 'winning the hearts and minds of the people,' it proved to be a highly political exercise for the humanitarian organizations involved.[9]

Especially when it comes to disaster aid, donating governments like to see the practice of giving aid as the fulfilment of the ideal of humanitarianism.[10] Tomisha Hattori has taken a critical look at the practice of giving foreign aid, whether development aid or humanitarian aid, and has concluded that ethical claims do not explain the behaviour of donating states, simply because the outcomes of their behaviour do not support this premise. "[W]hile all of these ethical justifications identify with liberal ideals of rights, humanitarianism, and improvement, the aid practice they justify tends towards the opposite effect, anticipating neither the eventual perfection of donors' obligation into a right, the mitigation of a material hierarchy, nor the remedy of a diseased condition."[11] In other words: if (humanitarian) aid was guided by the principle of humanity, it would not look the way it does. Or, as Barnett puts it, "If funding decisions were based solely on need then places like Sudan, Congo, Northern Uganda, and Angola would leapfrog towards the top of the list rather than remain neglected at the bottom."[12]

In other words, the humanitarian principle is not the most important guide for governments when it comes to foreign policy decision-making on humanitarian aid. Governments are calculating actors, bound by a need to maximize economic and political benefit in order to guarantee political survival. Reciprocal transactions fit the frame, and altruism does not.

The Domestic Table

To say that political considerations guide governments in their decision to allocate aid, and how much, is not to say that humanitarian considerations have no influence on the decision-making process. After all, governments consist of people and represent people, and can, therefore, be expected to express human virtues, such as compassion. At the domestic table, representatives of civil society, among whom the domestic counterparts of international humanitarian organization, religious groups and human rights organizations, as well as parts of the electorate, try to appeal to these human qualities. In other words, influenced by domestic actors and domestic public opinion, governments adapt their foreign policies to the ideas and considerations at the domestic table.

The downside to humanitarianism that is encouraged by public opinion is that it hardly ever outlasts the humanitarian phase of the disaster. When public attention shifts away from a disaster, irrespective of the continuing urgency of a post-disaster situation, government attention shifts along with it. The true motivation of donating governments then becomes apparent: if a humanitarian imperative would guide donors, they would donate based on needs, rather than on public opinion. The facts show that the reverse is closer to the truth. To use the Iranian example: for as long as Bam was in the international spotlights, hundreds of millions of dollars in aid were pledged. But, as soon as public attention shifted to other areas of the world, the focus of the international aid regime was redirected.

Disaster Diplomacy

Little research has been done on the relationship between disaster aid and foreign policy. However, there is an interesting article by Drury, Olson and Van Belle (2005), which discusses the influence of political factors on United States' foreign disaster assistance. Drury *et al.* identify realist calculations as the most important determinant in the granting of aid by top U.S. decision-makers, and emphasizes their sensitivity to public opinion in deciding how much to allocate. Drury *et al.* concluded that the results of their study paint a picture of "high U.S. foreign policy makers as Realists at heart, seeing disasters as opportunities to enhance security."[13] The authors draw this conclusion mainly from the U.S. tendency to secure existing bonds by granting aid to friendly countries. The argument could possibly be extended to relations with unfriendly countries: the U.S. aid granted to Iran after the Bam earthquake could perhaps be explained in terms of an effort by the United States to improve relations with Tehran. American policy makers may have contemplated that granting disaster aid may have helped to appease an enemy like Iran.

A field of research has developed that investigates just this. "Disaster diplomacy" theory centres on the idea that disasters may induce international cooperation amongst countries that have traditionally been enemies.[14] Based on the idea that "the cooperative spirit generated from common efforts to deal with disasters... has the potential to override pre-existing prejudices, and break down barriers which then may never be rebuilt".[15] "Kelman and Koukis asked a question, which for the purpose of this chapter will be paraphrased as: "Does disaster diplomacy induce rapprochement between enemy countries?"[16]

Rapprochement is a mutual effort by the governments of enemy countries to work towards normalization of relations. Disaster diplomacy will be defined here as the diplomacy that takes place between countries that are cooperating as a consequence of, or in anticipation of, a disaster. Not every form of disaster cooperation necessarily leads to disaster diplomacy, as "diplomacy refers to politically directed interactions, whereas cooperation involves interactions that are positive but do not necessarily lead to a political pay-off for either party."[17] Theory on disaster diplomacy explores the idea that disaster cooperation between enemy countries can lead to disaster diplomacy, and whether this disaster diplomacy can lead to diplomacy in other fields through a spill-over effect.[18]

Disaster cooperation (→) Disaster diplomacy (→) Diplomacy (→) Normalization of ties.

The logic behind the anticipation of an improvement of ties through disaster cooperation may be based on the idea that "disaster tends to shatter existing norms and practices among states, creating a (momentary) opportunity for fresh recognition of the fragility of life and common humanity that bonds all people."[19] However, case-studies of disaster diplomacy show that disaster cooperation may help to catalyze existing efforts to improve ties, but that disaster cooperation cannot by itself lead to a normalisations of ties. Ker-Lindsay studied the earthquakes in Greece and Turkey in September 1999 in the light of the Greek-Turkish rapprochement that took place around the same time.[20] He explained how disaster-mitigating efforts had an effect on the public perception of the "enemy" among Greeks and Turks. This seems to have spurred the reestablishment of friendly bilateral relations. Though the disaster mitigating efforts on both sides attributed to a rapprochement, the process that led towards a rapprochement was started earlier in the form of the Cem-Papandreou process. "The innovation of the Cem-Papandreou process is that it is based upon recognition of mutual interests and centres on trying to find concrete measures to strengthen contact and cooperation in non-contentious areas."[21] Ker-Lindsay explains. The disaster mitigating cooperation fit this frame. This example of disaster diplomacy should therefore "[...][22] be seen as a way in which two peoples came to a point at which they wished to understand one and another far better and put aside past prejudices. In doing so, this mutual recognition among Greeks and Turks of the equality and humanity of the other allowed the two governments to strengthen, and deepen, a process that had already been put in place." In other words, the disaster diplomacy between Turkey and Greece did not put the process of rapprochement in place, but helped to develop it. The supposition that disaster cooperation may spur existing ties, but not induce disaster diplomacy by itself, is supported by a study of the climate-related cooperation between the United States and Cuba. Though cooperation had taken place between academics on both sides,[23] in 2000 Glantz drew the conclusion that in the absence of a rapprochement between the leadership of Cuba and the leadership of the United States, this cooperation had little chance of inducing further cooperation.[24] This became apparent when in 2001 and 2005 major hurricanes did not lead to disaster cooperation between the countries.[25]

A study of rapprochement between Southern African countries in the early nineties also supports the hypothesis that disaster cooperation can only lead to improvement of ties, if efforts to improve ties are already underway. Disaster cooperation was not identified as the main driving force behind normalization of relations between the South African countries.[26] It did have a catalyzing effect as it "provided the first opportunity for the former adversaries to successfully cooperate on (non-military) security matters."[27]

Two other case-studies offer further insight in this matter. First, in North Korea floods and droughts cumulated in a famine between 1995 and 2000. The need for aid was unquestionable, which gave the international community tremendous leverage over North Korea. This made it possible for Korea's enemies to use food aid "to force diplomatic issues as part of a complex series of negotiations involving aid, diplomatic ties and military capability."[28] This development may have helped better ties between North Korea and the international community develop. However, Kelman argues that any potential for the disaster diplomacy resulting from this situation was lost when George W. Bush termed North Korea as part of an 'Axis of Evil' in 2001. Political considerations on a global scale inhibited the possibilities on a bilateral level.

Second, when India and Pakistan were hit by an earthquake in 2001, Pakistan suffered some damage, but the Indian province of Gujarat was devastated. As a result, disaster cooperation between Pakistan and India was not one of mutual benefit, but an offer from Pakistan to India. India's Prime Minister Vajpayee and Pakistan's *de facto* ruler General Musharraf spoke with each other on the phone personally and publicly for the first time and negotiations on aid were agreed. But when Musharraf deposed of Pakistan's President Rafiq Tara,[29] the Indian leaders became worried that Musharraf's "actions and sudden interest in diplomacy may have had underlying reasons other than to help a neighbour suffering disaster."[30] Negotiations still took place, but no agreement was reached.

The examples show that even if disaster cooperation may initially help to improve ties, this development is very fragile. Despite this, after 2002 the diplomatic relationship between India and Pakistan started to improve. When an earthquake hit Pakistan and India in 2005, India immediately offered aid to Pakistan, which had suffered far worse. To facilitate the aid operations, Pakistan and India collaborated by opening locations along the Kashmiri line of control.[31] Though violence between Pakistan and India over the Kashmir province continued, partly because of conflict between actors beyond the reach of the respective governments, the Kashmir initiatives helped to catalyze an ongoing rapprochement between India and Pakistan.[32]

The case studies for disaster diplomacy remain limited. Some have written about the prospects for disaster diplomacy after the 2004 Tsunami; however, with the exception of a preliminary study of US-Indonesian relations,[33] this literature is concerned mainly with civil war.[34] Other studies have been concerned with Hurricane Katrina, after which aid offers were made to the United States by Iran and Cuba. The United States did not respond to these offers, which means no disaster cooperation could take place.[35] Another case, in which there was a clear opportunity for disaster cooperation, was between Ethiopia and Eritrea in 2002. Ethiopia declined the Eritrean offer to

Ethiopia through Eritrean ports.[36] An investigation into the reasons why offers for disaster aid have not led to cooperation should provide an interesting study. That kind of study, however, would go beyond the scope of this chapter.

The analysis of the aforementioned case studies, limited as they are, help to paint a picture of the potential prospects of disaster diplomacy. In trying to answer the question "does disaster diplomacy induce rapprochement between enemy countries?", it is possible to differentiate between factors that possibly influence the prospects of disaster diplomacy. Four out of five of the case studies discussed above concern neighbouring countries that are facing the same threat. Possibly, the prospects for disaster diplomacy would be entirely different if cooperation took place between enemy countries that were not neighbours. The peace imperative between neighbouring countries is arguably more urgent than between countries far apart. More important, perhaps, is the question of whether countries are facing the same threat. When they do not, instead of a mutually beneficial relationship, disaster diplomacy would take place within a donor-recipient relationship. Inequality and dependency can then become important issues, which may hamper the possibilities for rapprochement.

Another distinction that can be made is between cooperation taking place after a disaster has taken place, as in the example of Greece and Turkey, and disaster diplomacy that takes place to prevent disaster from striking, as is the case between the U.S. and Cuba. The latter kind of disaster diplomacy may not be very different from other kinds of cooperation, such as cooperation in the field of sports or trade. Relief efforts, however, are different because of the evident humanitarian imperative. Potentially, the humanitarian imperative means that the boundary-breaking effect of disaster cooperation may be stronger, as "the reality of providing any kind of disaster assistance in such a situation must overcome many obstacles, mostly political."[37] In practice it seems, however, that if efforts to take down these obstacles are not yet underway, disaster cooperation by itself cannot induce this process. This is the fourth variable that this study will look at. To summarize the variables :

i. Are the cooperating countries near each other?
ii. Are countries cooperating to counter a common disaster or threat, or is there a donor-recipient relationship?

iii. Are efforts to improve ties between enemy countries already underway?
iv. Is the cooperation preventative or does it take place within the framework of disaster relief?

A helpful method of analysing the data of an extended set of case studies, combining the virtues of both qualitative and quantitative methods, is Quantitative Comparative Analysis (QCA).[38] An expansion of the Table 11.1 could offer us insight into conditions that are necessary for disaster diplomacy to be successful. A capital letter indicates the presence of a factor, and the small letter shows the absence.

Table 11.1: Truth Table Disaster Diplomacy Prime Implicant

Case study	*(P)roximity*	*(R)eciprocity*	*(E)fforts to improve ties underway*	*Disaster cooperation (B)efore disaster*	*Success disaster Diplomacy*
Greece-Turkey	P	R	E	b	D
U.S.-Cuba	P	R	e	b	d
Southern Africa	P	R	E	B	D
Pakistan-India 2001	P	r	e	b	d
North Korea	P	r	e	b	d
Iran-U.S.	p	r	e	b	d
Pakistan-India 2005	P	R	E	b	D

PRE

PRE is the combination of (P)roximity of the threat, (R)eciprocity of the relief effort, and (E)fforts for rapprochement underway before the disaster cooperation took place. Two hypotheses can be derived from the truth table. As researchers on disaster diplomacy have already concluded, disaster diplomacy is only successful if efforts to improve ties are already on their way (hypothesis 1). Secondly, disaster diplomacy can only be successful if it happens between countries facing the same threat (hypothesis 2a). This hypothesis could possibly be generalized into the hypothesis: disaster diplomacy can only be successful if it happens on a give-and-take basis (hypothesis 2b). An unreciprocated or unequal donor-recipient relationship seems to be an insufficient basis for rapprochement. Moreover, only a combination of the conditions of proximity and reciprocity (a combination of hypothesis 1 and 2) seems to lead to a rapprochement. Though more research needs to be done, it seems that success stories of disaster diplomacy have always been the result of a reciprocal relationship between the cooperating countries.

The need for rapprochement before disaster diplomacy becomes even clearer when we deduct the prime implicants that account for absence of rapprochement, namely PReb and preb. Combined with the prime implicant for success, PRE, these implicants show that 'proximity' and 'reciprocity' are by themselves insufficient determinants for success, and that 'rapprochement before disaster' is a necessary precondition. However, when disaster diplomacy is successful, it has been in a situation between neighbouring countries, with a certain degree of reciprocity.

The remainder of this chapter will look at the international cooperation after the earthquake in Bam, particularly between the United States and Iran. The cooperation between the United States and Iran after the Bam earthquake can serve as a test case for the abovementioned hypothesis. The United States and Iran broke diplomatic relations after the 1979 hostage crisis, when Iranian students took over the US Embassy in Tehran and held 52 American diplomats hostage for 444 days. The American military aircrafts that supplied aid to Bam in 2003 were the first to enter Iranian airspace after a failed attempt to free the hostages in April 1980.[39]

Bam

In December of 2003, Iran's relations with the West were typically troubled. This seemed to change when the city of Bam, in the south of Iran, was struck by an earthquake. The entire international humanitarian community came to Iran's aid, and the amounts of aid pledged to Bam quickly rose to approximately $ 1.1 billion. Some media suggested that the enthusiasm of the donating countries could be explained in terms of a perceived 'window of opportunity'[40] that some donating governments were taking advantage of. In other words, some governments may have seen the humanitarian disaster and the subsequent Iranian 'open door' policy as an opportunity to improve ties with the Islamic Republic of Iran.

The earthquake that struck Bam on December 26th of 2003 took place in the early morning on a Thursday, the first day of the Iranian weekend, when the city was asleep. The epicentre of the earthquake was in the centre of the urban area, and the traditional construction of houses made sure that when disaster struck, most victims died instantly of suffocation from dust. These different factors contributed to the enormous death toll of approximately 26,000 people. Initial estimations were around 50,000.

During the acute phase of the emergency response, the Government of Iran swiftly and straightforwardly waived visa requirements for foreign aid workers and opened up Iranian airspace to foreign countries. More than 1,600 aid workers from 44 countries were flown into Bam.[41] This produced some remarkable scenes: a team of American search and rescue workers flew the Stars and Stripes from their camp in Bam, and female nurses without Islamic dress gave medical treatment to survivors.

It was extremely difficult to coordinate the relief efforts, as huge amounts of commodities were flown in from all over the world. During the early days foreign airplanes arrived every ten minutes. This was particularly challenging for the Iranian Government, being relatively inexperienced in dealing with outside actors since the 1979 Revolution.[42] Despite this, the Interior Ministry's Disaster Task Force responded quickly and effectively. The Task Force had identified the Iranian Red Crescent as the coordinator of the relief effort. As this organization has a great deal of international disaster experience it was a very effective coordinator. As many victims had died instantly after the earthquake, many search-and-rescue teams were sent back home, and the focus was placed on finding immediate shelter, food, water and medical treatment to those left homeless.

Soon considerable tension rose between international aid workers and Iranian officials. Whereas the cooperation with the Ministry of Foreign Affairs was often encouraging (visa requirements were waived), aid organizations experienced opposition and distrust in their cooperation with the Ministry of Interior. Also, there was disagreement between the Iranians and Western aid organisations over the needs of the survivors. Much assistance was given outside the needs that were established and communicated by the Government of Iran and by the United Nations. Also the timeliness of the delivery was sometimes lacking (heaters were provided when winter was over), and there was disagreement over the quality of the commodities (25% broken rate rice was, according to the Iranians, 'unacceptable for consumption').[43]

Added to this, the international organizations' poor cultural knowledge and sensitivity was a source of miscommunications. "Even humanitarian organizations sometimes have the completely wrong mentality," one aid worker complained. "They just want to do their thing, especially the government based organizations. People, who try to implement things on Iran, without taking into account the history and ideas of the people in Iran, are often left disappointed. From the United States you can almost expect such an attitude. But even European countries that one would think would be more understanding often are not. This also counts for the United Nations."[44]

Tensions between aid organisations and the governments of receiving countries are however not unusual. The Bam relief effort showed that the Islamic Republic of Iran and the West were able to come to cooperation beyond what anyone would have expected, considering their troubled political relationship. Despite this positive development, Iran's 'open door' policy did not outlast the most critical phase of the emergency response. As survivors' immediate needs became less urgent, the cooperation was scaled down. In February 2004, the troubled relationship between Iran and the West was resumed. Aid donations to the Bam earthquake seem to reflect this development: Of the $1.1 billion of aid pledged after the earthquake, only $32 million was delivered by the end of 2004.[45] However, one can only speculate that this gap reflects disillusionment of donating governments, as a large gap between initial pledges and actual eventual donations are commonplace.

Why did Iran not take advantage of the détente, to improve their ties with the EU and the United States? To answer this question, a closer look will be taken at the character of international aid, on the one hand, and at the consequences of accepting this kind of aid on the national level, on the other.

International Opportunities

After the earthquake, the city of Bam became the scene of a number of unique political events. When Britain's crown Prince Charles paid a visit to the disaster-struck city, it was the first visit to the country by a member of the British royal family since the Islamic Revolution. Also the United States' offer to send in an aid delegation headed by Senator Elizabeth Dole, accompanied by former American First Lady Barbara Bush, would have been the first official public visit to Iran since the Revolution. However, it was turned down by the Iranian Government because, according to Government spokesman at the time Abdollah Ramezanzadeh, it was neither the time nor place for a political mission.[46]

The political motivations of the donating governments are open to speculation. In the first weeks after the relief effort the media's attention was mainly focused on the United States and the United Kingdom. Prince Charles's visit to Bam was seen as inappropriate at a time when Iran's conservatives appeared to be gaining the upper hand in domestic politics through disqualification of reformist candidates for the February 20th elections. It was seen as reflecting Britain's keenness to improve ties with Tehran and was regarded as a support to an authoritarian regime.[47]

The prime suspect of attempted 'disaster diplomacy' however, was the United States. The United States' Government was quick to respond to the disaster, and did not hesitate to link the 'open door' policy of Iran to possibilities for improvement in ties. A day after the earthquake in Bam took place, the United States responded with the deployment of humanitarian assistance.[48] On December 29th Secretary of State, Colin Powell commented on the deployment of American aid:

> "This was a humanitarian issue... And in this case, to show them that we were serious and that we were seeing it as a humanitarian issue, [President Bush] had [Deputy Secretary of State] Rich Armitage call the Iranian Perm Rep directly [ignoring the diplomatic custom of relaying through third parties],[49] so he knew it was not just a routine, diplomatic exchange. What was surprising here, Robin, is that within half an hour to an hour, Rich got an answer back from the Permanent Representative, who was in Tehran at that time, and within hours, we had started to assemble relief supplies, planes and rescue workers. Now all those things taken together show that there are things happening, and therefore, we should keep open the possibility of dialogue at an appropriate point in the future."[50]

In the most urgent stages of the disaster aid, Colin Powell did not hesitate to link a humanitarian issue with the possibility of dialogue in the long term. Iranian President, Mohammad Khatami watched these developments with scepticism. "Humanitarian issues should not be intertwined with deep and chronic political problems," he told the international press. "If we see change both in tone and behaviour of the U.S. administration, then a new situation will develop in our relations."[51] However, several Iranian officials were more optimistic. President Khatami's brother Mohammed Reza Khatami, the Deputy Speaker of Parliament, told Reuters that "goodwill will be answered with goodwill." Foreign Minister, Kamal Kharrazi[52] as well as former President and current head of the Expediency Council Hashemi Rafsanjani also responded vaguely positive. "We must look at it more closely," Rafsanjani said, "but they are in the process of sending positive signals for several months now."[53]

In the first weeks of the disaster, the Uniteds States was one of the most generous international aid donors to the Bam disaster.[54] Washington lifted sanctions against Iran for 90 days so that items such as transportation equipment, radios, satellite telephones and computers necessary for rescue and relief operations could be sent to Iran by American NGOs. For American citizens and non-profit groups it became possible to donate money to humanitarian organizations providing relief in Bam now that the sanctions had been relaxed.[55] However, after the offer of a high-level humanitarian delegation was turned down, cooperation between the Iranian and American Governments quickly deteriorated. The proposed mission would have assessed aid priorities for victims of Bam. The Iranian Government explained that the proposal for a humanitarian visit led by Elizabeth Dole was turned down because they preferred a direct approach to political differences. "Political issues must be examined and resolved in their own place, for which there are conditions," Foreign Minister Kharrazi said.[56]

The Iranian 'open door' policy came to an end when the acute phase of the emergency was over. International donors that had wanted to take advantage of a political thaw were left disappointed. Perhaps the disillusionment of those who had hoped for improvement of ties through aid cooperation can partially explain why much of the pledged aid money was not delivered. However, that only a small amount of the aid that was pledged to Bam was delivered requires some examination.

Table 11.2 list the natural disasters for which the United Nations developed Flash Appeals. If the assessment by the United Nations can be used as an indicator of the needs of the survivors, the disasters are listed from most urgent to least urgent. We see that, while on average approximately only 40 per ccent of the UN requirements are met, the Grenada hurricanes and the Philippines floods appeals were covered by international aid contributions respectively for only 14 per cent and 13 per cent. Also, in the case of Iran, the Flash Appeal requirements were not met; compared to the other disasters, however, the international community did fairly well in the case of Iran. With a difference of only one per cent with the Islamic Republic, the most successful appeal of 2004 was the Kenya Flash Appeal.

Table 11.2: Needs *versus* International Aid Contributions[65]

Disaster	*Flash Appeal requirements (revised)*	*Donations within appeal*	*In % of UN Requirements*	*Donations outside appeal*	*Donations Total*
Bangladesh Floods[57]	209,905,410	64,846,945	31%	40,334,065	105,181,010
Kenya Drought[58]	83,249,327	47,342,639	57%	3,319,308	50,661,947
Haiti Floods[59]	37,363,304	13,783,349	37%	26,299,554	40,082,905
Iran Earthquake[60]	32,668,877	18,426,703	56%	112,424,974	130,851,677
Grenada Hurricane[61]	27,640,760	3,957,505	14%	14,087,021	18,044,526
Madagascar Cyclone[62]	15,724,318	7,350,576	47%	4,915,386	12,265,962
Philippines Floods[63]	6,395,635	832,602	13%	16,444,950	17,277,552
Bolivia Drought[64]	1,809,217	763,358	42%	0	763,358
Total	414,756,848	157,303,679	38%	217,825,258	375,128,937

Source: OCHA Natural Disaster in 2004

When looking at the *total* of aid contributions to disasters in 2004, the picture changes. While Kenya received a relatively large amount of donations through the United Nations, outside of the UN Flash Appeal Kenya received only $3 million. However, in the case of Bam, 86 per cent of the donations made to the city were made through organizations other than the UN, adding up to a total that is four times the amount required by the United Nations. Also, the Philippines received a relatively large amount of aid money through channels other than the United Nations. However, while the international community covered 56 per cent of the UN Flash Appeal to Bam, only 13 per cent of the Philippines were covered by international donations.

The relatively large amounts contributed to Bam after the earthquake means neither that the UN requirements were met, nor that all of the needs of the surviving populations were met. It does show two things. First of all, as compared to other natural disasters, the international community has been relatively generous in their contributions to the aid efforts in Bam. In other words, whereas needs are almost never met by international contributions, in the case of Bam the international community came closer to meeting needs than in any other disaster in 2004. Secondly, while the international community contributed a relatively large amount through the United Nations, overall the international community chose to donate through organizations other than the United Nations.

Table 11.3: Allocation of aid Money by the E.U., U.S. and Canada as compared to UN Needs Assessment

Disaster	*Flash Appeal requirements*		*E.U. incl. Members*		*United States*		*Canada*	
Bangladesh Floods[66]	209,905,410	1	65,187,318	1	7,628,170	4	1,038,790	3
Kenya Drought[67]	83,249,327	2	11,912,668	4	26,155,300	1	761,879	4
Haiti Floods[68]	37,363,304	3	16,625,312	3	11,242,648	2	2,554,929	1
Iran Earthquake[69]	32,668,877	4	58,163,128	2	4,796,502	6	1,300,211	2
Grenada Hurricane[70]	27,640,760	5	8,331,008	5	6,031,814	5	166,366	7
Madagascar Cyclone[71]	15,724,318	6	6,137,200	6	1,335,040	7	186,567	6
Philippines Floods[72]	6,395,635	7	4,648,270	7	8,611,840	3	466,102	5
Bolivia Drought[73]	1,809,217	8	765,358	8	0	8	0	8
Total	414,756,848		171,770,262		60,372,614		6,474,844	

The contributions to Bam were relatively high, despite the fact that the initial pledge of $1.1 billion was not met. Is this a result of the fact that the major donors prioritized aid to Bam? Table 10.3 takes a closer look at the donations to Bam by the United States, Canada and the members of the European Union. The disasters are again listed in order of most urgent need as assessed by the United Nations. Some differences in prioritizing between the United Nations and individual donors are expected. Many donating countries or international organizations like the E.U. make their own assessments. However, on the whole the differences in needs assessment should be relatively small. Therefore, only substantial differences in prioritizing between the United Nations and individual donors are of importance.[III] Only Canada and the European Union donated more to Bam than would have been expected when the needs assessment by the United Nations is taken as a starting point. The European Union's priorities are very close to those of the United Nations. The only two countries that switched in the E.U. list as compared to the UN list are Kenya and Iran. It seems that Canada has been most idiosyncratic in their choice of priorities. However, the four most urgent disasters are Canada's four prime receivers, and, consequently, the four least urgent disasters had also Canada's lowest priority. The United States is off on three occasions: the floods in Bangladesh and the Philippines, and the earthquake in Bam. While the Philippines had a higher priority in the UN than among U.S. decision makers, both the Bangladesh floods and the earthquake in Iran received less aid from the U.S. than would have been the case if the U.S. had based their decision where to allocate aid and how much on the U.N. needs assessment. In the case of Bam this is especially surprising, as immediately after the disaster the United States emerged as the biggest donor.

The contributions to natural disaster aid of the United States, Canada and the countries of the European Union are analysed in Table 11.4. The first column shows the contributions of these countries to the disaster in Bam in U.S. dollars and percentages, the second columns shows the contributions of these countries to natural disasters worldwide in 2004 in U.S. dollars and percentages. Table 11.4 reaffirms that the donations made by the United States were relatively

III. For example: Bangladesh Floods is priority number 1 according to the United Nations Needs Assessment, priority number 4 for the United States.

small: whereas the United States contributed 17.3 per cent of international natural disaster aid in 2004, to Bam the United States contributed only 3.7 per cent of the international total.

Table 11.4: Distribution of Disaster aid Money[74]

	Contributions to Bam (through UN and other)[IV]		*Contributions to natural disaster aid in 2004*	
Donating country	*Amount in U.S.$*	*Percentage of total international disaster aid to Bam*	*Amount in U.S.$*	*Percentage of total international disaster aid*
Canada	1,300,211	1.0	13,665,651	2.4
U.S.	4,796,502	3.7	97,412,343	17.3
EC/ECHO	11,373,130	8.7	74,973,092	13.4
UK	5,314,505	4.1	64,633,678	11.5
Belgium	3,274,154	2.5	8,123,136	1.4
Sweden	2,596,189	2.0	11,075,914	2.0
Denmark	2,692,139	2.1	3,223,235	0.6
Ireland	1,647,750	1.3	5,168,755	0.9
Germany	1,861,084	1.4	9,546,341	1.7
Italy	100,416*	**	2,951,535	(0.5)
Spain	25,491,119	19.5	28,239,782	5.0
France	1,237,750	0.9	12,881,726	2.3
Netherlands	1,280,466	1.0	24,148,872	4.3
Lithuania	50,034*	**	**	**
Finland	1,187,648	**	**	**
Latvia	36,798*	**	**	**
Estonia	19,946*	**	**	**
Total E.U.	58,163,128	43,5	267,405,317	43,1
Total E.U. + Canada + U.S.	64,259,841	49	356,044,060	63
Other countries	66,591,836	51	207,306,929	37
International total	130,851,677	100	563,350,989	100

* FTS financial tracking table: no donations outside of UN appeal were found.

** Insufficient information available.

IV. Contributions by March 5, 2005. The information on countries' contributions to particular disasters that is available on the Reliefweb website represents the situation as it is on the day the website is accessed. Earlier numbers are not available.

The European Commission also contributed less of the total of Bam earthquake donations (8.7) than average (13.4). However, the European Union's contributions to the disaster aid in Bam were proportionate compared to their contributions to natural disaster aid (both 43%). While most E.U. members donated around their average, apart from the EC, the United Kingdom spent less than average, and only Spain much more than average on the relief aid in Bam.

In other words, most interestingly, those countries that were initially on the forefront of the international aid effort, namely the United States and the United Kingdom, are the same countries that donated much less to the Bam earthquake relief than would have been expected from their spending records. It could be argued that these countries, having high hopes of the political spin-offs, pledged more than they could deliver when it proved that the Iranian Government was not interested in a political rapprochement based on humanitarian cooperation.

Canada also donated less aid money to Bam than would have been expected from their aid record; however, they lived up to their pledges.[75] According to the judgment of one Canadian newspaper "Canada [...] put aside the recent diplomatic dispute over the murder of journalist Zahra Kazemi in Iran and donated $1.3 million to the Red Cross/Red Crescent, including a planeload of emergency supplies."[76] However, much larger donations would have been expected if Canada and Iran were on friendly terms at the time of the earthquake. As the Iranian-Canadian relations had cooled after the death of Kazemi, Canada seemed to keep a low profile in the Bam relief efforts. Just as much as political hopes can spur aid donations, political disillusionments may be able to discourage contributions.

Domestic Constraints

The seismic hazard map of Iran[77] illustrates how earthquakes have been an everyday reality in the region for thousands of years.[V] The first major earthquake after the Revolution took place in The Manjil area in the North-West of Iran in June 1990. It left 10 cities in ruins and killed between 40,000 and 50,000 people. The earthquake in 1990 took place in a period of political change after the death of

V. The International Institute of Earthquake Engineering and Seismology in Iran reports new earthquakes everyday: www.iiees.ac.ir. In the 20th century only, Iran was hit by earthquakes causing over a thousand deaths 16 times.

Ayatollah Khomeini. Hardliners still dominated the Parliament, but President Rafsanjani and other pragmatists had been elected to government. The acceptance of international aid by President Rafsanjani unleashed a heated domestic debate. The national media reflected the split between proponents and opponents of international assistance to The Manjil area. The *Tehran Times* was positive about the possibility of a positive political spin-off of the relief efforts. The conservative newspaper *Jomhuri Islami,* however, reported that the people buried under the rubble were chanting "death to America" and that these people refused help from "Iran's enemies."[78]

Rafsanjani tried to tone down the signals of enmity at the Friday Prayer at Tehran University a week after the earthquake. "I don't think we see the people who are under the debris saying, 'no, we don't want foreign aid,'" he declared. "Logic says that if our people have no tents and the weather is bad, we should accept foreign aid."[79] Rafsanjani, however, was unable to gain domestic support for an international relief effort and had to turn down much foreign assistance. As a result, the aid that reached the survivors of The Manjil earthquake was insufficient.

At the time of the Bam earthquake, the memory of the failed relief effort after the earthquake in The Manjil area made the government of the Islamic Republic realize that a reliance on domestic capacity in disasters of this scope would be inadequate. The scope of the Bam earthquake, like the one in The Manjil area, surpassed the capacity of the Iranian Red Crescent and other domestic humanitarian actors. Politically, a different approach to international relief was made possible by a considerable change in the political environment since 1990. Since 1996, Khatami's reformists had dominated the democratic institutions in the Iranian Government. Khatami and his coalition had managed to create an international atmosphere of dialogue. This had had a positive influence on the relationship of Iran with Saudi Arabia, the European Union, and to some extent even the United States. Within this atmosphere of dialogue, positive cooperation after the Bam earthquake was made possible. However, any explanation for the 'open door' policy that concentrates on the reformists is incomplete, as it is not the government, but the theocracy which has the final word in foreign policy decision-making.

The Iranian political system comprises an elected government that is supervised by theocratic institutions. The Supreme Leader has the final word in all issues of foreign policy. In the case of the Bam earthquake, the foreign policy process took the shape of an emergency meeting of Iran's most important decision-making institution, the National Security Council (NSC). When the NSC reaches a consensus, it is sent to the Supreme Leader for approval. It was through this process that was decided that foreign aid was welcome. But not only did the Supreme Leader allow international aid, he also gave a high level of authority to the Disaster Task Force, in which people known to have reformists' sympathies were represented.[80]

Foreign Policy Outcome

Why did the Islamic Republic not take advantage of the thaw in U.S.-Iranian relations to improve ties with this country? Earlier studies of disaster diplomacy result in two hypotheses. First of all, it seems that disaster diplomacy can only be successful if efforts to improve ties are already on their way. This is a result of the idea that by itself disaster diplomacy is not powerful enough to break down the boundaries that exist between enemy countries. The United States and Iran had not made efforts to improve ties thus far. Though high-level representatives of the United States and Iran met before the wars in Afghanistan and Iraq, these served the strategic purpose of both countries rather than an effort to improve ties. If ties would have been friendlier before, the events after the Bam earthquake may have sped up those developments. However, the disaster cooperation by itself did not spur positive relations, but rather emphasized the existing hostility.

However, hypothesis 2 may offer us more explanation into why the cooperation after the Bam earthquake had so little positive political spin-off. Hypothesis 2 holds that disaster diplomacy can only be successful if it happens on a give-and-take basis. An unreciprocated relationship cannot be a sufficient basis for rapprochement. This especially counts in the case of Iran, as its regime strongly adheres to the principle of independence from other countries. In that light it is understandable why the Iranian Government could not accept the United States offer for an aid delegation. The Iranian government has always insisted that negotiation with the United States should take place on an equal basis.

Bam was the wrong place at the wrong time for a rapprochement; the wrong time, because efforts for rapprochement had not yet been put in place. Disaster cooperation could not have possibly broken down the barriers that had kept the Islamic Republic and the United States apart for 25 years. The wrong place, because a rapprochement should be based on an equal relationship, not on a donor-recipient relationship.

However, the acceptance by Iran of American aid after the Bam earthquake clearly shows that something was changing in the relationship between Tehran and Washington. Especially when we compare the situation in Bam to the situation 14 years earlier in the The Manjil area, we see that trust between the two countries has grown. After the high-level talks on Afghanistan and Iraq, the Bam cooperation may have contributed to a growing confidence on both the Iranian and American side that these countries could grow towards normalization of ties. The cooperation between Iran and the United States did not provide a breakthrough in the Iranian-American rapprochement. Rather, it should be seen as part of a development towards settlement that was started by Iranian pragmatists in the early 1990s. Between 1996 and 2005 this development has been one of 'two steps forward, one step back.' Since Mahmoud Ahmadinejad was elected President in 2005, this process seems to have been reversed. However, beyond Ahmadinejad's empty rhetoric operates the same theocracy that has shown itself to be capable of pragmatic decision-making. As discouraging as the current rhetoric may sound, it is likely that we will see more of this pragmatism in the future.

Discussion and Conclusion

The case of Bam illustrates that the possibilities of disaster cooperation to produce rapprochement are, at best, extremely fragile. The US attempt to force a rapprochement through a political delegation proved to be more than this delicate detente could take, especially as it challenged Iran's insistence on keeping aid and politics separated. Accepting aid with 'strings attached' would have put Iran in a dependency relationship with the United States that would have been hard to legitimate domestically. Moreover, this kind of dependency could hardly have been a stable basis for relations over the long run.

Still, a more positive scenario is imaginable. In this scenario, the United States would have made different choices in their approach towards Tehran, without having to compromise their political reservations towards Tehran. These alternative choices could have helped to build trust between Iran and the United States, which may have helped to improve relations. These different choices are the following.

First, the United States would not have offered to send a political delegation, thereby respecting a separation between politics and humanitarian aid that Iran insisted on. This way, the US would have been able to present a positive, self-sacrificing image of themselves to the Iranian people. Conversely, the US' offer of a political delegation merely emphasized prejudice against the United States as power-hungry.

Secondly, when Iran offered aid to the United States after it had been hit by hurricane Katrina in 2005,[81] the United States did not respond to this offer. This kind of behaviour confirmed a prejudice that sees the United States as an arrogant power. Accepting Iranian aid would have given a different, more sympathetic image of the United States. Moreover, acceptance of Iranian aid would have made the disaster cooperation after the Bam earthquake more reciprocal. Whereas reciprocity at the time of the Bam disaster was impossible, due to the donor-recipient character of the aid effort, throughout the years Iran and the United States could have developed positive disaster cooperation by mutually aiding each other in times of need.[82]

If efforts towards an improvement of ties between Tehran and Washington had already been in place, the story that unfolded after the Bam 2003 earthquake may have looked different. Under the existing circumstances, however, only a political and reciprocal aid cooperation would have helped to build the trust that is needed for rapprochement in the future. In other words, ironically enough, only a complete separation of humanitarian aid from politics could possibly and over the long run have had the so desired positive diplomatic spin-offs.

Notes

1. "Aid is often fleeting at scenes of disasters", In: *The International Herald Tribune*. January 12, 2005.
2. Barnett 2005, 727.
3. *Ibid.*, 731.
4. *Ibid.*, 729-30.
5. Drury *et al.*, 2005, 20
6. Barnett, 731.
7. Drury *et al.*, 2005, 20.
8. Barnett, 727.
9. *Ibid.*, 731.

10. Hattori, 2003, 230-1.
11. *Ibid.*, 246.
12. Barnett, 2005, 727.
13. Drury *at al.*, 2005, 20.
14. Kelman and Koukis, 2000, 214.
15. *Ibid.*
16. *Ibid.*
17. Glantz, 2000, 240.
18. *Ibid.*, 234.
19. Comfort, 277.
20. Ker-Lindsay, 2000.
21. *Ibid.*, 228.
22. *Ibid.*, 230.
23. Glantz, 2000.
24. *Ibid.*, 250.
25. Kelman, 2007, 2.
26. Holloway, 2000.
27. *Ibid.*, 254.
28. Kelman, 2003, 115.
29. http://archives.cnn.com/2001/WORLD/asiapcf/south/06/20/pakistan.musharraf/ Accessed: February 28 2008.
30. Kelman, 2003, 114.
31. Kelman, 2006, 223.
32. *Ibid.*, 224.
33. Kelman, 2005.
34. Kelman, 2005; Kelman and Gaillard, 2007; Le Billon and Waizenegger, 2007.
35. Kelman, 2007a, Kelman and Gaillard, 2007.
36. Kelman, 2006, 225.
37. Glantz, 2000, 233.
38. Ragin, 2004.
39. Molavi, Afshin; Hanley, Delinda C., March 2004. U.S. "Humanitarian Response to Iran Earthquake Sparks New Debate on Relations", In: *Washington Report on Middle East Affairs*, Vol., 23, Iss. 2. page 1.
40. *The Washington Post*, February 1, 2004. "Activity Heats Up as U.S. and Iran Flirt with Closer Ties"; *International Harald Tribune*, January 5, 2004. "Iran may be primed for reconciliation; Grappling with U.S. power"; *The Economist*, December 30, 2003: "Now wait for the political tremors."

41. UN OCHA Integrated Regional Information Networks (IRIN). January 2, 2005. Iran: Special report on Bam—one year after the devastating earthquake.
42. Workshop of Lessons Learnt on the National and International Response to the Bam Earthquake, 2004, 9.
43. Workshop of Lessons Learnt on the National and International Response to the Bam Earthquake, 2004, 14.
44. Anonymous aid worker in Bam.
45. Table 7: Islamic Republic of Iran 2004 Flash Appeal.
46. BBC, January 3, 2004, "Iran rejects U.S. delegation plan".
47. BBC, February 9, 2004, "Prince meets Iran quake Victims".
48. Government of the United States of America, 27 Dec., 2003. "U.S. to deploy humanitarian assistance to people of Iran."
49. Molavi, Hanley 2004, 1.
50. Wright, 2003.
51. *NewYork Times*, December 30, 2003: "Iran President thanks U.S. for aid following earthquake."
52. Knowlton, 2004.
53. *Ibid.*
54. Srebrnik, 2004.
55. Taghavi, 2004.
56. Asgari; Smyth, 2004.
57. OCHA Table 7: Bangladesh Flash Appeal, 2004.
58. OCHA Table 7: Kenya Flash Appeal, 2004.
59. OCHA Table 7: Haiti Floods Flash Appeal, 2004.
60. OCHA Table 7: Islamic Republic of Iran 2004 Flash Appeal.
61. OCHA Table 7: Grenada Flash Appeal, 2004.
62. OCHA Table 7: Madagascar Flash Appeal, 2004.
63. OCHA Table 7: Philippines Flash Appeal, 2004.
64. OCHA Table 7: Bolivia Flash Appeal, 2004.
65. OCHA Natural Disasters in 2004; OCHA Consolidated Appeals, 2004.
66. OCHA Table 7: Bangladesh Flash Appeal, 2004.
67. OCHA Table 7: Kenya Flash Appeal, 2004.
68. OCHA Table 7: Haiti Floods Flash Appeal, 2004.
69. OCHA Table 7: Islamic Republic of Iran, 2004, Flash Appeal.
70. OCHA Table 7: Grenada Flash Appeal, 2004.
71. OCHA Table 7: Madagascar Flash Appeal, 2004.

72. OCHA Table 7: Philippines Flash Appeal, 2004.
73. OCHA Table 7: Bolivia Flash Appeal, 2004.
74. Compiled from information from UN OCHA Financial Tracking Service www.reliefweb.int/fts
75. Canadian International Development Agency. January 23, 2004: "Canadian aid to earthquake victims in Iran rises to $1.55 million."
76. *The Toronto Sun*, January 2, 2004: "Goodwill grows in the ruins."
77. International Institute of Earthquake Engineering and Seismology.
78. The Associated Press, June 29, 1990: "Iranian President Urges Thanks for Quake Aid in Rebuff to Hard-Liners".
79. The Associated Press, June 29, 1990: "Iranian President Urges Thanks for Quake Aid in Rebuff to Hard-Liners".
80. Workshop of Lessons Learnt on the National and International Response to the Bam Earthquake, 2004, 6.
81. BBC, September 6,2005, "Iran offers US Katrina oil relief".
82. Kelman, 2007, 300-302.

References

Asgari, M.; G. Smyth. January 5, 2004. "Iran gives view on talks with U.S.." In: *Financial Times*. Page 6.

Badri, S. Ali; Ali Asgary; A.R. Eftekhari; and Jason Levy, 2006, "Post-disaster resettlement, development and change: A case study of the 1990 Manjil earthquake in Iran". In: *Disasters*. Volume 30, No. 4. pp. 451-468.

Barnett, Michael. "Humanitarianism transformed." In: *Perspectives on Politics*. December 2005, Vol. 3, no. 4. pp. 723-740.

BBC news archive: *http://news.bbc.co.uk*.

Brancati, D. 2007. "Political Aftershocks: The Impact of Earthquakes on Intrastate Conflict". *Journal of Conflict Resolution*, Vol. 51, No. 5, p. 715-743.

Comfort, L.K. 2000. "Disaster: Agent of Diplomacy or Change in International Affairs?" In: Kelman, I. and T. Koukis (eds). 2000. 'Disaster Diplomacy', special section in *Cambridge Review of International Affairs,* Vol. XIV, No. 1. pp. 214-294.

Disaster Diplomacy: *www.disasterdiplomacy.org*.

Drury, A.C.; R.S. Olson; D.A. Van Belle. 2005. "The Politics of

Humanitarian Aid: U.S. Foreign Disaster Assistance, 1964-1995". In: *The Journal of Politics.* Volume 67, Issue 2.

Gaillard, J.C., E. Clavé, and I. Kelman. 2008. "Wave of peace? Tsunami disaster diplomacy in Aceh, Indonesia". Geoforum, Vol. 39, No. 1. pp. 511-526.

Glantz, M.H. 2000. "Climate-Related Disaster Diplomacy: A U.S.-Cuban Case Study." In: Kelman, I. and T. Koukis (eds), 2000. 'Disaster Diplomacy', special section in *Cambridge Review of International Affairs* (edited by Charlotte Lindberg Clausen), Vol. XIV, No. 1. pp. 214-294.

Hattori, T. 2003. "The moral politics of foreign aid." In: *Review of International Studies* Vol. 29. pp. 229–247.

Holloway, A. 2000. "Drought Emergency, Yes...Drought Disaster, No: Southern Africa 1991-93." In: Kelman, I. and T. Koukis (eds.). 2000. 'Disaster Diplomacy', special section in *Cambridge Review of International Affairs*, Vol. XIV, No. 1. pp. 214-294.

International Red Cross and Red Crescent Movement: *www.ifcr.org*.

Kelman, I. 2003. "Beyond Disaster, Beyond Diplomacy". Chapter 7 in Mark Pelling (ed.), *Natural Disasters and Development in a Globalizing World,* Routledge, U.K.

Kelman, I. 2005. "Tsunami Diplomacy: Will the 26 December, 2004 Tsunami Bring Peace to the Affected Countries?". *Sociological Research Online*, Vol. 10, Issue 1.

Kelman, I. 2006. "Acting on Disaster Diplomacy". *Journal of International Affairs*, Vol. 59, No. 2. pp. 215-240.

Kelman, I. 2007. "Hurricane Katrina Disaster Diplomacy". *Disasters*, Vol. 31, No. 3. pp. 288-309.

Kelman, I. and J.C. Gaillard. 2007. "Disaster diplomacy in Aceh". *Humanitarian Exchange*, No. 37 (March 2007), pp. 37-39. Full text (77 kb in PDF).

Kelman, I. and T. Koukis (eds,). 2000. 'Disaster Diplomacy', special section in *Cambridge Review of International Affairs* (edited by Charlotte Lindberg Clausen), Vol. XIV, No. 1.

Kelman, I. and T. Koukis. 2000. "Disaster diplomacy: Discourse Disintegrated?." In: Kelman, I. and T. Koukis (eds.). 2000. 'Disaster Diplomacy', special section in *Cambridge Review of International Affairs* (edited by Charlotte Lindberg Clausen), Vol. XIV, No. 1. pp. 214-294.

Ker-Lindsay, J. 2000. "Greek-Turkish Rapprochement: The Impact of 'Disaster Diplomacy'?" In: Kelman, I. and T. Koukis (eds.). 2000. 'Disaster Diplomacy', special section in *Cambridge Review of International Affairs,* Vol. XIV, No. 1. pp. 214-294.

Knowlton, B. January 2, 2004. "Iran hints ties to U.S. may thaw over quake." In: *International Herald Tribune.*

Le Billon, P. and A. Waizenegger. 2007. "Peace in the Wake of Disaster? Secessionist Conflicts and the 2004 Indian Ocean Tsunami". *Transactions of the Institute of British Geographers,* Vol. 32, No. 3. p. 411-427.

Lexis Nexis news archive: *www.lexisnexis.com.*

Molavi, A.; D.C. Hanley. 2004. "U.S. Humanitarian Response to Iran Earthquake Sparks New Debate on Relations." In: *Washington Report on Middle East Affairs*. Vol. 23, Iss. 2. p.1.

Putnam, R.D. 1988. "Diplomacy and Domestic Politics: The Logic of Two-Level Games." In: *International Organisation.* Vol. 42, No 3, pp. 427-460.

Ragin, C.C. 1994. "Introduction to qualitative comparative analysis." In: Thomas Janoski and Alexander M. Hicks (eds.): *The Comparative Political Economy of the State*. Cambridge: Cambridge University Press, 1994.

Srebrnik, H. January 29, 2004. "Are Iranian rulers ready for democracy and rapprochement with the U.S.?" In: *Guardian*, p. A.7.

Taghavi, 14 January 2004. "Earthquake aftermath". In: *Al-Ahram Weekly* 8-14 January 2004, Issue No. 672.

UN OCHA Financial Tracking Service: *www.reliefweb.int/fts.*

Warnaar, M. 2005. *Shaken, Not Stirred. Iranian Foreign Policy and Domestic Disaster.* Unpublished Master's thesis.

Workshop of Lessons Learnt on the National and International Response to the Bam Earthquake, 2004. *Report*. April 14-15, 2004.

Wright, R. 2003. "Post Interview with Secretary of State Colin Powell, December 29th". In: *Washington Post.*

12

Roles of Cooperation to Reduce Climate Change Related Disaster Risk

ATANU SARKAR

Global climate change is no more a speculation, rather it is an established fact. The fourth assessment report of Intergovernmental Panel on Climate Change (IPCC) has clearly mentioned the imminent danger due to climate change and extreme weather condition, such as global warming, change of precipitation, melting of glaciers, sea level rise. The major possible disasters on account of climate change are flood, drought, storm and irregular monsoon. Apart from life loss, people will suffer from displacement, economic loss, starvation and outbreak of diseases. Developing countries would be the worst sufferers due to poor adaptation capacity, high population and their location in the most vulnerable zones. Climate change is believed to be due to emission of green house gases. According to the scientists, even any drastic measures to curb green house gas emissions would not bring any perceivable benefits before several decades. Hence, disaster preparedness as preemptive measures is extremely important to reduce human suffering. As several disasters have wide scale impact across the state and country boundaries, there is a need to develop cross boundary strategic plan. For instance, sea level rise will mostly affect low lying deltaic region shared by multiple countries and small islands across the world. Therefore, cooperation among the countries and also at sub-national level is necessary to reduce the disaster risk and adaptation to promote sustainable development.

Introduction

Climate change is no more confined to academic discourse; rather it has become are obvious phenomenon across the world. It is now widely accepted that human activities, in particular fossil fuel use and changing land-uses, are the dominant factor in this growth and are responsible for the climate change observed over the past 50 years (IPCC a). Climate change is distinctly different from weather change. *Weather* is the set of meteorological conditions, such as wind, precipitation, snowfall, sunshine, temperature and so on at a particular time and place. On the other hand, the term *climate* describes the overall long-term characteristics of the weather experienced at a particular place. Therefore, the climate is a long-term summary of weather conditions, taking account of its average and variability of the conditions (UN, 2008). The recent spurts of natural disasters such as droughts, floods and cyclones are believed to be due to global climate change, resulting in huge loss of lives, properties and livelihoods (Cipryk, 2009). In fact, following the current pattern of climate change, it can be anticipated that more extreme weather events in future are likely to occur and eventually would increase the number and scale of disasters. Since the dawn of civilization, humans are familiar with all kinds of natural disasters; however, managing additional burden of disasters is the major challenge of this century (Alfsen, 2001). The situation has become further complex, as the majority of the natural disasters have been taken place in the developing world, where more than three-fourth populations live with minimum adaptation capacity. Majority of the countries lack appropriate strategy pertaining to Disaster Risk Reduction (DRR) (Weinhold, 2004; Fields, 2005). But, there are also several success stories, which are worth replicating elsewhere. However, in the majority of the countries, lack of collective actions and poor cooperation among various sectors are responsible for repeated failure to protect the vulnerable population.

Climate Change and Disaster Linkages

In 1990, the United Nations (UN) General Assembly initiated climate change convention and this led to 154 countries signing the UN Framework Convention on Climate Change (UNFCCC) at the UN Summit in Rio de Janeiro in 1992. Since then, 192 countries including the USA have ratified the convention. The goals of the UNFCCC are to stabilize the amount of greenhouse gases in the atmosphere at a level that prevents dangerous man-made climate changes (UN 2008,

UNFCCC a). IPCC was established in 1988 by the special UN organizations for environment (United Nations Environmental Programme or UNEP) and meteorology (World Meteorological Organization or WMO) following the Brundtland report *Our Common Future*. The goal of IPCC has been to use scientific literature to evaluate the extent and understanding of climate changes and their effects, as well as the potential to adapt to or counteract anticipated climate changes (Pachauri, 2006). IPCC has published four assessment reports in 1990, 1995, 2001 and 2007. The fourth assessment report has contributed stronger evidence ever on climate changes as a reality and anthropogenic roles as the prime causal factors. This report has gained both the public and politicians' awareness on climate changes frequently and quoted for any climate change related debates. Due to scientific and political support, the IPCC's reports have been used as the foundation upon which the UNFCCC acts (UN 2008; IDS, 2008).

Climate Change and Disasters

There is a growing evidence showing increase in frequency and intensity of natural hazards due to climate change, for instance a global increase of 87 per cent in the number of droughts, floods and hurricanes in the last twenty years. The return period (the period of time between two climatic extreme events) and the severity of certain weather events do not follow the conventional trends and hence this is further eroding actual coping mechanisms and raising new challenges for the reduction of social and economic impacts of natural disasters on vulnerable populations (Pierro and Desai, Tibbetts, 2007). Natural hazards cannot be the precursors of disasters unless these are combined with exposed, vulnerable and ill-prepared population or community. Therefore, climate change affects disaster risks in two ways: (a) through increase in weather and climate hazards, and (b) through increases in the vulnerability of communities to natural hazards, particularly through ecosystem degradation, reductions in water and food availability, and changes to livelihoods (Cipryk, 2009; Fields, 2005). It is important to note that climate change has added yet another stress to those of environmental degradation and rapid unplanned urban growth, further reducing communities' coping abilities with even the existing levels of weather hazards. Global development is facing a growing threat from the impact of more extreme events due to changing climate and Organization for Economic Cooperation and Development (OECD) has estimated that up to 50 per cent of development assistance may be at risk because of climate change (Mitchell and van Aalst, 2008). The amplified frequency and intensity of natural disasters has threatened to achieve the Millennium Development Goals and putting more pressure on aid agencies, already overburdened by what has been referred to as "fatigue" in humanitarian response (Pierro and Desai).

It is estimated that, while some mid-latitude and high-latitude areas will initially benefit from higher agricultural production, for many others at lower latitudes, especially in seasonally dry and tropical regions, the rising temperature and the frequency of droughts and floods are likely to reduce crop yield, which could eventually increase hunger and displacement. For instance, significantly increasing trend of precipitation has been witnessed in eastern parts of North and South America, Northern Europe and Northern and Central Asia, and on contrary, drier conditions in the Sahel and Southern Africa, throughout the Mediterranean region, and in parts of Southern Asia. The frequency of heavy precipitation events has increased over most land areas, which is consistent with global warming and the observed increases of atmospheric water vapour (IPCC, c, f). The pattern of rainfall has changed significantly in many places and intensified the suffering of the people. For instance, in 2009, heavy rainfall and flood have affected nearly 350,000 people across West Africa. In many places, the amount of rain that fell in one day was equal to a quarter of the whole country's annual rainfall (BBC, 2009). However, UN has declared this region as drought prone because IPCC has reported 20 to 40 per cent drop in rainfall from the mid to late twentieth century (UNNS, 2009). Coexistence of two opposite extreme weather conditions in a same area have become a common feature due to climate change and make the DRR more challenging. There is evidence for an increase of more damaging intense tropical cyclone activity in the North Atlantic since about 1970, which is correlated with increases in tropical sea surface temperatures. However, according to the IPCC, to date there is no clear trend evident in the global annual number of tropical cyclones (IPCC, c, f).

Impacts of Climate Change Related Disasters

Although climate change will affect every part of the world, people in the poorest countries and poor people in richer countries are more likely to suffer the most. They tend to live in high risk areas such as unstable slopes and flood plains, and often cannot afford to live in well-built houses (Tibbetts, 2007). Many of their livelihoods depend on climate sensitive sectors, such as agriculture with little or no means to cope with climate change, for example owing to low savings, no property insurance and poor access to public services. Climate change is expected to reduce already low incomes and increase illness and death rates in many developing countries. Table 12.1 shows the nature of vulnerability due to climate change in different parts of the world (UN, 2008).

Table 12.1: Vulnerability due to Climate Change in Different Parts of the World

Region	*Vulnerability*
Africa	• Multiple stresses and low adaptive capacities, arising from endemic poverty, weak institutions, and complex disasters and associated conflicts • Drought will continue to be a primary concern (Sahel and Southern Africa) • Water supplies and agricultural production will be terribly affected (by 2020, in some African countries agricultural yields could be reduced by as much as 50%) • By the 2080s, the area of arid and semiarid land in Africa will likely increase by 5-8% • Heavy rain and flash flood
Asia	• Melting of Himalayan glaciers resulting in increase flooding and rock avalanches • Non-availability of adequate fresh water, which by the 2050s will be a concern for possibly more than one billion people • The pressures on natural resources due to high population, rapid urbanization, industrialization, and economic development have been compounded by climate change • Heavy rain and flash flood • Heavily populated coastal areas and delta regions becoming more prone to increased flooding due to rising sea levels and river flooding

(*Contd.*)

Region	*Vulnerability*
Australia & New Zealand	• More frequent extreme events such as heat waves, droughts, forest fires, floods, landslides and storm surges • Increase stresses on water supplies and agriculture • Less seasonal snow cover and shrinking glaciers • Coastal areas to be threatened by the consequences of rising sea levels and increasingly severe and more frequent storms and coastal flooding by 2050
Europe	• Retreating glaciers and extend of permafrost • Reduced precipitation in Southern Europe and the possibility of more droughts in some areas, as well as increased risk of flash floods and reduced crop production • Higher temperatures and heat waves • Increase the frequency and severity of wildfires • Reduced forest area and agricultural productivity • Greater vulnerability of low-lying coastal areas due to rising sea levels
Latin America	• Changes in precipitation patterns and the disappearance of glaciers will significantly reduce the amount of water available • In drier areas, increased salinization and desertification of agricultural land • Rising sea levels will cause increased risk of flooding in low-lying coastal areas
North America	• Further decrease of mountain snow due to rising temperatures resulting in increased winter flooding, reduced summer flows, and altered seasonal availability of water • More, longer and hotter heat waves • Sustained higher temperatures also will increase the risk of forest fires • Coastal communities will be increasingly threatened if the intensity of tropical storms increases
Small island states, coastal systems	• Floods, storm surges, erosion and other coastal hazards every year due to rising sea levels by the 2080s • Reduced water resources are expected in many small islands
Polar Regions	• Reductions in the thickness of glaciers and the extent of ice sheets, and changes in natural ecosystems

Climate change related disasters mostly affect human health and their livelihood. Health and livelihood are also interlinked as health seeking behaviour and access to health care are dependent on economy, livelihood and displacement.

(a) *Impact on health:* The changes in climate are likely to alter the health status of the vulnerable population, including through increased deaths, disease and injury due to heat waves, floods, storms, fires and droughts. Increased malnutrition, diarrhoea and malaria in some areas will significantly increase the morbidity and mortality of the affected population (Tibbetts, 2007; Sarkar, 2008). More heat waves will increase the number of deaths, particularly among the elderly, the very young, or among people who are chronically ill, socially isolated or otherwise especially vulnerable. Displacement of the population due to climate change (also known as environmental refugees) will further take place due to extreme weather condition, loss of livelihood and in turn will increase health hazards, such as infectious diseases, malnutrition and injuries (Fields, 2005; Phillips, 2008).

(b) *Impact on livelihood and quality of life:* Increased drought and flood will likely to lead land degradation, damage to crops or reduced yields, more livestock deaths, and an increased risk of wildfire. Higher temperatures and melting glaciers may cause glacial lake outbursts that could flood downstream settlements. Such situations will increase the risks for populations dependent on subsistence agriculture and may lead to their displacements. These events will disrupt agriculture, settlements, trade and transport and may further increase pressures on urban and rural infrastructure. Increases in the number and intensity of very strong cyclones (typhoons and hurricanes) will affect coastal regions and river basins, with potentially large additional losses of lives and properties, such as agriculture lands and fishing. It is important to note that the most vulnerable industries, settlements and societies are generally those located in coastal areas and river flood plains, and hence those economies are closely linked with climate sensitive resources. And, therefore, where extreme weather events become more intense or more frequent, the economic and social costs of those events will increase [IPCC c, f, Cipryk, 2009].

It is estimated that from 1991 to 2005, 3,470 million people were affected by disasters, 960,000 people died, and economic losses were US$ 1,193 billion (CRED). Poor countries and particularly the small countries are disproportionately affected, owing to intrinsic vulnerabilities to hazards and comparatively low capacities for risk reduction measures. For example, as a result of Hurricane Ivan in 2004, Grenada lost 919 US$ million, equal to 2.5 times its GDP. Since 1988, 76 per cent of all disaster events were hydrological, meteorological or climatological in nature; these accounted for 45 per cent of the deaths and 79 per cent of the economic losses caused by natural hazards (IPCC e). Poor management of local environment has further aggravated the impact of climate related disaster. For example, volatile weather patterns along with poor drainage system, illegal settlements and insanitary conditions are increasingly affecting urban slums in poor countries. When floods occur, residents of marginalized areas have only a limited set of options. They need urgent help to reduce risk and improve prospects for emergency action and safe evacuation (IDS, 2008).

Current Responses

Many countries are actively discussing and negotiating ways to deal with the climate change problem, within the UNFCCC. The primary objective is to mitigate the climate change impacts by addressing the root cause to reduce greenhouse gas emissions from human activity. However, the means to achieve this are very contentious, as it will require radical changes in the way many societies are organized, especially in respect to fossil fuel use, industry operations, urban development and land use. IPCC has defined mitigation by *an anthropogenic intervention to reduce the anthropogenic forcing of the climate system; it includes strategies to reduce greenhouse gas sources and emissions and enhancing greenhouse gas sinks*. Examples of mitigation actions include more efficient furnace systems, developing new low-energy technologies for industry and transport, reducing consumption of energy-intensive products, and switching to renewable forms of energy, such as solar and wind power. Natural carbon sinks, such as forests, vegetation and soils, can be managed to absorb carbon dioxide, and technologies are being developed to capture carbon dioxide at industrial sources and to inject it into permanent storage deep underground (IPCC g).

However, mitigation is a slow process and will take a long time to get any perceivable change. Therefore, management of impacts of climate change to cope with the changed climate conditions (also known as adaptation) has become more imperative to minimize the loss of life and economy. Adaptation is defined by the IPCC as *the adjustment in natural or human systems in response to actual or expected climatic stimuli or their effects, which moderates harm or exploits beneficial opportunities* (IPCC g).. It includes preparing risk assessments, protecting and development of ecosystems, agriculture, water resources, human settlements, developing early warning systems and improving social safety nets. These measures are intrinsically linked to sustainable development, as they reduce the risk to lives and livelihoods and increase the resilience of communities to all hazards. Ideally, adaptation and mitigation should be considered jointly, as some adaptation measures can contribute to reducing greenhouse gas emissions, while conversely mitigation measures can be planned to help reduce, and not inadvertently exacerbate, disaster risks.

DRR is the development and application of policies and practices that minimize risks to vulnerabilities and disasters and it is an essential part of adaptation, in other words, the first line of defense against climate change impacts, such as increased flooding or regular droughts. DRR can be defined as *action taken to reduce the risk of disasters and the adverse impacts of natural hazards, through systematic efforts to analyze and manage the causes of disasters, including through avoidance of hazards, reduced social and economic vulnerability to hazards, and improved preparedness for adverse events*. DRR is now providing its expertise and humanitarian experience to climate change adaptation programmes. For instance, DRR's rich experience on building resilience to existing climate variability is a useful starting point for developing adaptation policies. Climate change related disasters are essentially the high intensity and frequency of the existing natural disasters. Hence, there is significant overlap between the practice and theory of DRR and climate change adaptation. However, there is lack of coherence and convergence in institutions, organizations and policy frameworks and eventually results in duplicated activities and ineffective use of resources. Within multilateral, bilateral and national institutions, climate change adaptation and DRR departments are often disconnected and both sectors suffer from regular development resources. So the poor people have to find a way to cope on their own and encounter huge casualties. It is believed that apart from reduction of climate related losses, DRR and adaptation collaboration can lead to more efficient use of financial, human ; ·d natural resources, increased effectiveness and sustainability (IDS, 2008). Within the next two to three years international climate change policy making body has to provide a strategic opportunity for promoting coherence between DRR and adaptation. During this critical period, such convergence should result in improved integration of both DRR and adaptation in regular planning and programming at all dimensions, resulting in better development outcomes, even in the face of a changing climate (Mitchell and van Aa' t M., 2008). Table 12.2 shows the common DRR strategies in various sectors (UN, 2008; McMichael, 2008b).

Table 12.2: Disaster Risk Reduction Policies in Various Sectors

Sectors	*DRR policies*
Agriculture & food security	• Altering crop strains to enhance their drought and pest resistance • Changing planting times and cropping patterns, and altering land topography to improve water uptake, less dependence on irrigation and reduce wind erosion • Diversification, such as combining food crops, livestock and agro-forestry • Crop insurance
Water	• Protecting water supply infrastructure and traditional water supply sources • Developing flood ponds, water harvesting, improved irrigation, desalination, non-water-based sanitation and improved watershed and trans-boundary water resource management • Integrated water resource management
Health	• Action on water and vector-borne diseases • Early warning systems to address extreme weather events • Raise public awareness of watershed protection, vector control, and safe water and food handling • Enforcement of relevant regulations (food safety, water quality) • Education, research and development on climate-related health risks

(Contd.)

Sectors	*DRR policies*
Awareness & education	• Curriculum development for schools and higher institution • Dissemination of information to various community groups (women, NGOs), public figures, communication channels (radio, television, news paper, internet) • Awareness-raising for strategic intermediaries (teachers, journalists and politicians) • Support to technical experts
Environment	• Maintain healthy ecosystem by strengthening of environmental management in areas of greatest risk from climate hazards • Special emphasis on protecting specific ecosystems (coral reefs, mangrove forests) to protect communities from coastal hazards • Supporting transitions of livelihoods to the displaced population in order to restore the degraded environment • Enforcing regulations to stop hazardous practices
Early warning	• Use latest technology to improve the early warning system • Disseminate warnings to the population at risk in a timely, useful and understandable way • Providing advice to take appropriate actions upon receiving warnings
Development planning	• Making DRR as a formal part of development processes and budgets and programmed into relevant sector projects, such as settlements, infrastructure, coastal zone development and forest use • Avoid hazardous areas, and build environment friendly and hazard resistant schools, hospitals, rods and other public facilities

Cooperation Framework (Local, National, International)

As mentioned earlier that climate-related risks come not only from direct exposure to natural hazards such as floods or droughts, but also from the vulnerability of social and economic systems to the effects of these hazards. So responses to these risks should combine two approaches: short-term measures to react to hazards when they occur, and structural reforms that enhance the capacities of communities to cope (IDS, 2008).

Adaptation through Disaster Risk Reduction and the Hyogo Framework

The Hyogo Framework for Action (HFA), adopted by the member states of the UN provides the foundation for the implementation of Disaster Risk Reduction (DRR). Its overarching goal is to build resilience of nations and communities to disasters, by achieving substantive reduction of disaster losses by 2015 in terms of lives, social, economic, and environmental assets of communities and countries. The HFA offers five areas of priorities for action, guiding principles and practical means for achieving disaster resilience for vulnerable communities in the context of sustainable development. Since inception of the HFA, it has included in many global, regional, national and local efforts to address disaster risk reduction more systematically. Many regional bodies have formulated strategies at regional scale for disaster risk reduction in line with the HFA, in the Andean region, Central America, the Caribbean, Asia-Pacific, Africa and Europe (UNISDR c). Although the UN General Assembly has called for the implementation of HFA, reconfirmed the multi-stakeholder international strategy for disaster reduction (ISDR) system and the global platform for disaster risk reduction to support and promote it, much however, remains to be done. Several countries are yet to implement the HFA framework or to reach at community level. In May 2009, Bangladesh was badly hit by cyclone Aila, which killed hundreds of people and displaced millions. Despite being a cyclone prone country, lack of preparedness at community level is believed to be responsible for extent of damage (Forestpeoples, 2009). In fact, when cyclone Sidr hit Bangladesh in 2007, the recovery was large and quick. However, cyclone Sidr was bigger than Aila and its damage was extensive, but due to international cooperation and proper management recovery was quicker. It is argued that the hesitance of Bangladesh Government to seek foreign support after cyclone Aila is one of the reasons for extensive human suffering (Preventionweb, 2009).

Hyogo Framework in Climate Change related Disaster Risk Reduction

The Hyogo Framework sets out five priorities for action, each elaborated into a number of specific areas of attention. These offer a strong basis for developing concrete risk-reducing adaptation measures. It is important to note that HFA is not specific to climate change; rather it has addressed all existing disasters. But HFA can be extensively utilized in climate change related disaster reduction. The UNFCCC Parties have acknowledged that the current knowledge and capacities to cope with extreme weather events must be harnessed to adapt to climate change. The Bali Action Plan (2007) has listed many of the general principles and requirements for adaptation that are highly relevant to DRR, particularly vulnerability assessments, capacity-building and response strategies, as well as integration of actions into regional and national planning (UNFCCC b, 2008). The Bali Action Plan has emphasized to support climate action in country-led development processes, which in turn supports the adaptation and risk reduction (World Bank, 2009; Mead *et al.*, 2008). Later Stockholm Plan of Action for *Integrating Disaster Risk and Climate Change Impacts in Poverty Reduction* and Oslo policy forum on *Changing the Way We Develop: Dealing with Disasters and Climate Change* reiterated the view of integration of DRR and climate change. In support of the Bali Action Plan, UNFCCC Parties and the UNISDR have been promoting all five of the Hyogo Framework implementation, adaptation programmes, and national risk transfer mechanisms (UNISDR b). In fact, Ban Ki-moon, Secretary-General of the UN has mentioned, '*Climate change is expected to cause more severe and more frequent natural hazards ...... We have a moral, social and economic obligation to build resilience by 2015. Implementing the Hyogo Framework for Action will also help us reach the Millennium Development Goals*' (UNISDR c).

The five priorities of HFA are as follows :

(a) *Ensure that disaster risk reduction is a national and local priority with a strong institutional basis for implementation:* Institution building is critical to ensure both adaptation and risk reduction. Both at federal and provincial level a core ministry with a broad mandate including finance, agriculture, health, environment and other related departments to be responsible for mainstreaming climate change adaptation policies and activities; organizing national and regional level policy dialogue to prepare the adaptation strategy linking with disaster risk reduction strategies. This collaboration is expected to coordinate the climate-related risk reduction activities through a multi-sector mechanism such as a platform for disaster risk reduction; and developing mechanisms to actively engage women, communities and local governments in the assessment of vulnerability and impacts and the formulation of local adaptation activities. The national body of a country can engage in collaborative effort with neighbouring countries and international bodies for resource mobilizations and technical supports. Often, the climate related natural disasters are transnational and cooperation of neighbouring countries enhances the capacity of relief work and adaptation capacity. India for instance has well developed satellite network, which can be well utilized by all South Asian countries for disaster forecasting and preparedness. But this can be only possible if a well established proactive national body is constituted and formal memorandum of understanding is constituted. In fact, the SAARC Disaster Management Centre (SDMC) was set up in October 2006 in New Delhi to serve eight member countries (Afghanistan, Bangladesh, Bhutan, India, Maldives, Nepal, Pakistan and Sri Lanka) of the South Asia Association of Regional Cooperation (SAARC) by providing policy advice and facilitating capacity building services including strategic learning, research, training, system development and exchange of information for effective disaster risk reduction and management in South Asia. The Centre is networking through the national focal points of the member countries with the various ministries, departments and scientific, technical, research and academic institutions within and outside the Government working on various aspects of disaster risk reduction and management (SAARC-SDMC, 2009a). In 2008, SAARC action plan on climate change was adopted during the SAARC ministerial meeting on climate change and formulated the *Dhaka declaration*. The action plan (from 2009 to 2011) has mainly focused on adaptation strategies, policies and actions for technology transfer and mitigation, finance and investment, education and awareness, management of impacts, capacity building for international negotiation (SAARC-SDMC, 2009b, c).

(b) *Identify, assess and monitor disaster risks and enhance early warning*. This action includes development and dissemination of high quality information about climate hazards and their likely future changes (*in situ* and space-based earth observations, remote sensing, geographic information systems, hazard modelling and prediction, weather and climate modelling and forecasting); to conduct national and local level climate change related risk assessment (by developing climate change and disaster risk and vulnerability indicators at national and sub-national scales); to conduct assessments of vulnerability (physical, social, economic and environmental) and specially vulnerable groups; to prepare briefings for policy-makers and sector leaders on regular basis and also updating periodically and disseminating the risk maps to general public and communities; to review the effectiveness of early warning systems (based on through research, partnerships, training and technical capacity building); to implement procedures to ensure warnings reach vulnerable groups; and to undertake public information programmes (through international, regional, national and local mechanisms) to help people understand the risks they face and how to respond to warnings; to forecast emerging risks due to land use (such as coastal or river basin).

(c) *Use knowledge, innovation and education to build a culture of safety and resilience at all levels*. The term *all levels* encompasses community, municipal, province, national, regional and international levels. This action includes collating and disseminating good practices; undertaking public information programmes on local and personal actions that contribute to safety and resilience (in local vernacular); publicizing community successes; training the media on climate related issues; developing education curricula on climate adaptation and risk reduction in school level; supporting research programmes on resilience; and improving mechanisms for knowledge transfer from science to application for risk management in climate-sensitive sectors; encourage partnerships among stakeholders (scientific communities, development practitioners, decision, makers; promote community-based training initiatives and volunteers to enhance local capacities to mitigate and cope with disasters.

(d) *Reduce the underlying risk factors.* This covers several environmental, developmental and societal factors that create or enhance the risks from natural hazards. The interventions can include incorporating climate risk-related considerations in development planning processes by integrating environment and natural resource management; requiring the use of climate risk-related information in city and land-use planning; strengthening and maintaining protective works such as coastal wave barriers, river levees, flood ways and flood ponds; requiring routine assessment and reporting of climate risks in infrastructure projects to protect and strengthen critical public facilities and physical infrastructure, particularly schools, clinics, hospitals, water and power plants, communications and transport lifelines, disaster warning and management centres, and culturally important lands to render them adequately resilient to disaster; developing risk transfer mechanisms and social safety nets; supporting programmes for diversification of livelihoods; and instituting adaptation activities in plans for recovery from specific disasters. It is important to promote food security to ensure the resilience of the affected communities to hazards, particularly in areas prone to drought, flood, cyclones and other related risks that can weaken agriculture-based livelihoods. Disconnect between disaster risk reduction planning and the health sector is a chronic problem and, therefore, there is need to ensure building new hospitals with a level of resilience that strengthens their capacity to remain functional in disaster situations and implement mitigation measures to reinforce existing primary health care facilities. Through health care facilities psycho-social training programmes can be conducted to recover the victims (particularly children) from the psychological damage. The social fall out of the vulnerable population is trafficking and gender based violence, which need effective mechanism to control, such as security and rehabilitation. Mainstream disaster risk considerations into planning procedures for major infrastructure projects, including the criteria for design (such as large dams, ports, fish cultivation, tourist resort, etc.) (OCFP, 2008; McMichael *et al.*, 2008a).

(e) *Strengthen disaster preparedness for effective response at all levels.* Resilience building and early warning systems contribute to significant reduction of impacts due to disaster. Other specific actions can include revising preparedness plans and contingency or emergency funds to account for the projected changes in existing hazards and new hazards not experienced before; building evacuation mechanisms and shelter facilities with the help of local community and regular disaster preparedness exercises; and developing specific preparedness plans for areas where settlements and livelihoods are under threat of permanent change. As poor in developing countries are mostly exposed to and affected by natural hazards and they have limited or no access to insurance and financial services, disaster is often seen as a primary cause for what has been called the 'poverty trap'. Therefore, insurance of assets, particularly the land and crop is necessary to sustain their livelihood (Pierro and Desai).

Evidence of Some Pragmatic Initiatives

DRR offers cost-effective approaches to reduce the negative impacts of flooding, landslides, heat waves, temperature extremes, droughts and intense storms. But the benefits are not limited to money saving, it takes into account the secure livelihoods and lives. For example, China spent US$ 3.15 billion on flood control between 1960 and 2000, which is estimated to have averted losses of about US$ 12 billion. While the disaster mitigation and preparedness programmes in Andhra Pradesh (India) yielded a benefit/cost ratio of 13.38, mangrove planting project in Vietnam to protect coastal populations from typhoons and storms yielded an estimated benefit/cost ratio of 52 over the period 1994 to 2001. Hurricane Katrina caused devastating damage in the affected states of US, however, the property owners who implemented hurricane protection methods saved US$ 500 million in property losses, after customer investments of only US$ 2.5 million (Mills, 2006). A study in Cayman islands (tropical cyclones prone) and Ceará in northeast Brazil (drought prone) has shown that focusing on specific adaptations and increasing the adaptive capacity of vulnerable groups improved the collective actions, peoples' participation and self-reliance in DRR (IDS, 2008). In response to Kenya's long periods of drought that have killed many of their domestic animals in recent years, camels have been introduced to the semi-nomadic Masai community in the Great Rift Valley. It was expected that the camels would be more resilient than the Masai's traditional livestock and able to survive in harsh dry conditions and will in turn help the tribes adapting to climate change (IDS, 2008).

Conclusion

DRR and climate change adaptation are of critical importance to the security of millions of people, and that vulnerability reduction can serve as a cornerstone for strategies to reduce the negative outcomes of climate change. The issue of vulnerability to natural hazards and disaster risks must remain central to the discussions, and progress must be made to effectively and fairly address the increased risks. For successful adaptation and DRR, the attention should be made to effective development planning and programming: managing risks and uncertainties for all shocks and stresses. However, there is often little political will or financial incentive to invest resources to prevent any anticipated danger due to natural disaster, particularly on account of climate change. Rather, there is more interest in investing in visible infrastructure or social programmes, which might give instant recognition. As a result, the incentives are more skewed given that the donor community provides generous humanitarian assistance after a disaster but fails to provide similar kind of support for risk reduction.

In developing countries, adaptation and DRR mostly run by two separate institutions, each with their own coordination groups, funding, and separate negotiations both at national and international level. This is the major obstacle while sharing very similar objectives, and challenges in raising the profile of their agendas and they often fail to coordinate. This organizational set-up engender duplication of efforts, administrative inefficiencies and even competition among various groups resulting in hampering DRR and adaptation efforts and compromises the overall efficiency.

The major challenges of HFA is unlike UNFCCC, it does not contain an inherent financial mechanism and is not legally binding. For example; the Least Developed Countries Fund (LDCF) and the Special Climate Change Fund (SCCF), two financing mechanisms set up under the UNFCCC and managed by the Global Environment Facility (GEF), pay special attention to DRR in their guidance. The guidance for the SCCF indicates of supporting the capacity-building, preventive measures, planning, preparedness and management of disasters relating to climate change, including contingency planning for extreme weather events (UNFCCC b, 2008; Mitchell and van Aalst, 2008). The World Bank has initiated the strategic climate fund which includes Pilot Programme for Climate Resilience (PPCR) to help the most vulnerable developing countries to explore practical ways to increase climate resilience in core development planning and budgeting. This programme is essentially built on National Adaptation Programmes of Action (NAPA), the World Bank initiative to support the least developed countries (World Bank, 2009). However, the financing mechanism for adaptation under the Kyoto Protocol, specific guidance for the Adaptation Fund has not been developed yet and the amount is too little to bring any perceivable change (Mead *et al.*, 2008). There are few instances where bilateral or multilateral donors have integrated their support for DRR and adaptation and many DRR programmes were funded from humanitarian budgets and coordinated from humanitarian aid departments. But often it makes the situation more difficult as it may increase separation of DRR projects from regular sectoral development. Also some donors have concerned that combining DRR funding with humanitarian assistance budgets turned the humanitarian assistance complicated. Despite difficulties and administrative complexities, several donors tried to coordinate these different dimensions such as, where early warning signals a potential disaster, the best humanitarian response is likely to combine humanitarian preparedness to respond with community-based awareness raising and organization, and DRR integrated into development, including infrastructure design and spatial planning. It is being felt that unsustainable DRR resulting in mal-adaptation. In other words, reduction of climate-related losses, through more widespread implementation of DRR measures linked with adaptation (Venton and La Trobe, 2008). Several agencies are trying to make the case for integration of adaptation into development through a risk-based approach, screening development activities and portfolios for climate risk. Success can be achieved by improving communication and collaboration between the climate change adaptation and disaster risk management communities in all levels. Assessment of vulnerability by using a systematic methodology to study climate change vulnerability in the context of multiple stressors is an important step to integrate DRR and adaptation and to identify those locations where policy intervention is most critical both geographically (e.g., double exposed) and thematically (e.g., access to irrigation, credit, alternative crops). The method needs to rely on both vulnerability mapping and local-level case studies with the help of community based organizations, may be used to assess differential vulnerability for any particular sector within a nation or region. As a standard guideline, IPCC framework to map regional vulnerability as a function of adaptive capacity, sensitivity, and exposure to climate change and another global stressor can be utilized. By combining regional vulnerability mapping with local-level case studies, we can capture factors and processes operating and interacting at different scales, and to understand how local-level decisions are shaped by factors at the national and international level (TERI, 2003, O'Brien *et al.*, 2004; Ebi *et al.*, 2006).

Lastly, new interdisciplinary research is needed to address the increasing occurrence of *complex extremes* and *complex emergencies* posing pressing challenges for the climate change adaptation and disaster risk communities and the development community at large. The research efforts must focus the critical role that non-climatic factors, such as development levels, inequality, and cultural practices play in these complex extremes. It is becoming clear that neither DRR nor climate change adaptation is about addressing disasters or climate change alone, but rather about confronting the societal context in which these changes are occurring (GECHS, 2008).

References

Alfsen, KH. (2001): Climate change and sustainability in Europe, CICERO Policy Note 2001: 03, Centre for International Climate and Environmental Research, Oslo, Norway.

BBC (2009): UN warns on West Africa floods, http://news.bbc.co.uk/2/hi/africa/8239552.stm as viewed on March 2010.

Cipryk, R. (2009): Impacts of climate change on livelihoods: What are the implications for social protection? CDG Working Paper 1, Climate and Disaster Governance (CDG) Programme, Institute of Development Studies, University of Sussex, UK.

CRED, Centre for Research on the Epidemiology of Disasters (CRED), http://www.emdat.be/ as viewed on March 2010.

Ebi, K.L.; R. Sari Kovats; B. Menne (2006): An Approach for Assessing Human Health Vulnerability and Public Health Interventions to Adapt to Climate Change, *Environmental Health Perspectives*, 114(12):1930–1934.

Fields, S. (2005): Continental Divide: Why Africa's Climate Change Burden is Greater, *Environmental Health Perspectives*, 113(8): A 534–537.

Forestpeoples (2009): Cyclone Aila's devastation of the Bangladesh coast-another victim of climate change? *http://www.forestpeoples.org/documents/asia*_pacific/bangladesh_cyclone_rep_jul09_eng.shtml as viewed on March 2010.

GECHS (2008): *Disaster Risk Reduction, Climate Change Adaptation and Human Security* (Report, 2008:3), Global Environmental Change and Human Security Project, University of Oslo, Norway.

IDS (2008): *Climate change and cities* (id21 insights 71) www.id21.org/insights/insights71/index.html as viewed on March 2010.

IPCC (a) Fourth Assessment Report, Working Group I, Frequently Asked Questions: http://www.ipcc-wg1.unibe.ch/publications/wg1-ar4/wg1-ar4.html as viewed on March 2010.

IPCC (b) Fourth Assessment Report, Working Group I, *Glossary of Terms*: http://www.ipcc-wg1.unibe.ch/publications/wg1-ar4/ar4-wg1-annexes.pdf as viewed on March 2010.

IPCC (c) IPCC Fourth Assessment Report, Working Group I, Summary for Policy-makers: http://www.ipcc-wg1.unibe.ch/publications/wg1-ar4/ar4-wg1-spm.pdf as viewed on March 2010.

IPCC (d) Fourth Assessment Report, Working Group II Report: http://195.70.10.65/ipccreports/ar4-wg2.htm as viewed on March 2010.

IPCC (e) Fourth Assessment Report, Working Group I Report: http://195.70.10.65/ipccreports/ar4-wg1.htm as viewed on March 2010.

IPCC (f) Fourth Assessment Report, Working Group II, Summary for Policy-Makers: http://www.ipcc.ch/pdf/assessment-report/ar4/wg1/ar4-wg1-spm.pdf as viewed on March 2010.

IPCC (g) Fourth Assessment Report, Working Group II, Glossary of Terms: http://www.ipcc.ch/ipccreports/ar4-wg1.htm as viewed on March 2010.

McMichael; A.J., S.; Friel A. Nyong; Corvalan (2008a): Global environmental change and health: impacts, inequalities, and the health sector, *BMJ*, 336:191-194.

McMichael, A.J. (2008b): Environmental change, climate and population health: A challenge for inter-disciplinary research, *Environ Health Preventive Medicine*,13:183–186.

Mead L.; H. Gitay; L. Noble (2008): Bali Climate Conference and Its Main Outcomes, *Development Outreach* 10(1): pp. 41–43.

Mitchell, T., M. van Aalst (2008): 'Convergence of Disaster Risk Reduction and Climate Change Adaptation: A Review for DFID', DFID, UK.

Mills, E.: E. Lecomte, (2006): From Risk to Opportunity: How Insurers Can Proactively and Profitably Manage Climate Change. http://eetd.lbl.gov/emills/pubs/pdf/ceres_report_090106.pdf as viewed on March 2010.

O'Brien, K.; Rleichenko; U. Kelkar; H. Venema; G. Aandahl; H.Tompkins; A. Javed; S. Bhadwal; S. Barg; L. Nygaard; J. West (2004), Mapping vulnerability to multiple stressors: Climate change and globalization in India, *Global Environmental Change* 14:303–313.

O.C.F.P. (2008): *Addressing the Health Effects of Climate Change: Family Physicians Are Key*, The Ontario College of Family Physicians, Toronto, Canada.

Pachauri, R.K. (2006): Perspectives of IPCC on Adaptation, In: The Proceedings of the International Conference on Adaptation to Climate Variability and Change, Jan 5–7, 2006, New Delhi, India, pp. 4–6.

Phillips, M.L. (2008): Dengue Reborn Widespread Resurgence of a Resilient Vector, *Environmental Health Perspectives*, 116(9): A 382–388.

Pierro, R.; B., Desai. *The potential role of Disaster Insurance for disaster risk reduction and climate change adaptation*, Climate and Disaster Governance and Christian Aid, http://cdg. lathyrus

.co.uk/docs Disaster %20 Insurance_CCA_DRR_Christian Aid. pdf as viewed on March 2010.

Preventionweb (2009): Bangladesh: Cyclone Aila recovery slower than Sidr. http://www.preventionweb.net/english/professional/news/v.php?id=10536 as viewed on March 2010.

SAARC-SDMC 2009a, SAARC Disaster Management Centre, http://saarc-sdmc.nic.in/home.asp as viewed on March 2010.

SAARC-SDMC 2009b, SAARC Action Plan on Climate Change http://www.slmfa.gov.lk/saarc/images/stories/saarc Action_Plan_Climate_Change.pdf as viewed on March 2010.

SAARC-SDMC 2009c, Dhaka Declaration on Climate Change, *http://saarc-sdmc.nic.in/pdf/publications/climate/chapter-1.pdf* as viewed on Sep 2009.

Sarkar, A. (2008): Climate Change and Health: Methodological Issues and Introduction to Climate Epidemiology, *Ind J, Pub. Health,* 52(2): 100-106.

TERI 2003, *Coping with global change vulnerability and adaptation in Indian agriculture*, The Energy and Resources Institute, New Delhi, India.

Tibbetts, J. (2007): Driven to Extremes: Health Effects of Climate Change, *Environmental Health Perspectives*,115(4):A 197–203.

UN (2008): Climate Change and Disaster Risk Reduction (Briefing Note 01), International Strategy for Disaster Reduction (ISDR), Geneva.

UNFCCCa Article 1, Definitions:h t t p : / / u n f c c c . i n t / essential_background/convention/background/items/*1349*.php as viewed on March 2010.

UNFCCC (b) 2008. Bali Action Plan, http://unfccc.int/files/meetings/cop_13/application/pdf/cp_bali_action.pdf as viewed on March 2010.

UNISDR Framework for Action 2005-2015: Building the resilience of nations and communities to disasters (HFA), see Part B, paragraph 4 (i) (c): http://www.unisdr.org/eng/hfa/hfa.htm as viewed on March 2010.

UNISDR (b).Stockholm Plan of Action for Integrating Disaster Risks and Climate Change Impacts in Poverty Reduction: http://www.unisdr.org/eng/risk-reduction/climate-change/docs/Climate-Change-DRR.pdf as viewed on March 2010.

UNISDR (c): Hyogo Framework for Action 2005-2015: Building the Resilience of Nations and Communities to Disasters, Geneva,

Switzerland, http://www.unisdr.org/eng/hfa/docs/HFA-brochure-English.pdf as viewed on March 2010.

UNNS 2009, UN gathers experts to help West African farmers cope with climate change, *UN News Service*, http://www.un.org/apps/news/story.asp?NewsID=30623 as viewed on Sep 2009.

USEPA (2006): *Excessive Heat Event Guidebook*. United States Environmental Protection Agency Office of Atmospheric Programmes, Washington D.C. http://www.epa.gov/heatisland/about/pdf/EHEguide_final.pdf as viewed on March 2010.

Venton P.; S.La Trobe (2008): *Linking climate change adaptation and disaster risk reduction,* T:earfund, Teddington, UK.

Weinhold, B, (2004): Infectious Disease: The Human Costs of Our Environmental Errors, *Environmental Health Perspectives* (112)1: A32-A39.

World Bank (2009): *Development and Climate Change*: The World Bank Group at Work, The World Bank Group, Washington, DC, US.

13

Social and Health Impacts of Recurrent Floods and Cooperation among different Stakeholders : A Case Study of Murshidabad District in West Bengal

SOUMITRA ROY

Some parts of India are highly susceptible to recurrent flooding. Southern parts of Murshidabad District in West Bengal faced more than 10 flooding in last two decades. Floods cause great economic and health hardships to its victims. Apart from immediate outbreak of communicable diseases (proximate impacts), communities also suffer consequential health impacts. Recurrent flooding makes great damage to lives of the people in rural areas and often force them to migrate for livelihood and safety purposes to other places. This often impacts through physical and mental health problems.

This chapter explores flood impacts on rural households selected through stratified proportionate random sampling from one of the worst affected villages in eastern part of India that was inundated more than 10 times between 1991 and 2009, and analyses the health problems and other social issues, requirement of relief in the context and cooperation among various stakeholders. The study used both quantitative and qualitative empirical data collected through 2001 to 2004.

Acute Respiratory Infections and Acute Diarrhoeal Disease were the most frequent proximate health impacts of flooding. The study found significant out migration of male members of the flood-affected families owing to economic deterioration and loss of agricultural lands. Lacking in education and skills, they got engaged in lowly paid and laborious jobs in major urban centres. These migrant labourers generally live without their families in the cities in infrastructurally deficient living conditions. Diseases that were most prevalent among these migrant labourers included jaundice, malaria, peptic ulcer syndrome and Sexually Transmitted Infections (STIs). STI was found to be transmitted heterosexually to their wives as well.

Following some devastating natural disasters in India, Government took some-long term initiatives in mitigating the impacts at the community level. The initiative took a broader approach by setting up disaster management units as the district level, involving mid-level government. executives, and International level NGOs, local governments (Panchayats at various level) and communities, particularly the women of self-help groups. The aim has been to build capacities at the household level to mitigate the immediate impacts of the disasters and reduce over dependence on the government relief department. However, the initiative is only at its nascent stage and there is long way to go to provide functional empowerment to the communities.

Introduction

Floods are among world's most frequent and damaging disasters (IFRCRCS, 1998: 147). Due to its geographical nature, the occurrences of flood in India are higher than other natural disasters. Within India some States like West Bengal, Bihar, Orissa, Assam and parts of Uttar Pradesh flood occurrences have almost been annual affair. In the last 40 years, the country has faced moderate to severe flood situations every year and more than 40 million hectares of land are considered to be prone to flooding, the average area affected by floods annually is about 8 million hectares (Director General of Health Services, GoI, 1992).

West Bengal is located in the eastern part of the country and is gifted with dynamic river systems. These rivers are integral part of Bengal's geography and they have always shaped its history and social development. Bengal has been known for its riverine civilization as its agriculture, commerce, external trade, agro industries, forestry depended heavily on its rivers. Bernier wrote in 1667 that Bengal seemed to him richer than Egypt, thanks to its rivers. Rivers had contributed to Bengal's growth and prosperity to a large extent and will continue to do so (Majumdar, 1941 in Biswas, 2001: 42).

However, this river system has become the victim of modern civilization. Irreversible changes have occurred in the river system due to laying of railways, construction of dams and barrages and an ever-increasing density of population in the State and their encroachment of the flood plains have resulted into choking and congestion in the natural drainage system (Majumdar, S.C., 1941 in Biswas, K.R., 2001). It is certain that West Bengal has become one of the most flood prone areas in the country. The extremity of the situation can be judged from the fact that between 500 to 20,000 square kilometres of land in the State have been inundated every year since 1960 (SSUP, 2000).

Floods leave differential impacts on human lives, which can be attributed to various geographical, socio-economic and political factors. Health impacts, both physical and mental, changes in social structure, employment patterns and agricultural practices are the visible ones. There are very few studies that exclusively deal with these issues, particularly in the context of developing countries. In this background an empirical research was initiated to study the health and other social impacts on a community in the Murshidabad District of West Bengal in India that has been facing annual flood inundation for over a decade.

Methodology

The broad objective of this study was to gain a holistic understanding of the problems arise in a disaster situation with a focus on health. The research was designed to be an *ex post facto* exploratory study based on empirical data that was both qualitative and quantitative in nature. The victims of a flood prone area were purposively chosen for the study.

The study was conducted in Saspara village, located within the administrative boundary of Andulia *Gram Panchayat* (Local Self-Government) in Murshidabad district of West Bengal [Latitude between N 24°50′20″ (North) and N 23°43′30″ (South) and Longitude between E 88°46′00″ (East) and E 87°49′17″ (West) (*West Bengal District Gazetteer*, 2003:1)].

The Proportionate Random Sampling method was used to determine the exact sample size from stratified households on the basis of their economic status. The number of active respondents was 226 from very poor, 108 from not so poor and 13 from the well off categories out of the 842 dwelling units in the village. The average annual family income of the 'very poor' household was Rs. 21,600, for the 'not so poor' category households it was between Rs. 21,601 and Rs. 60,000 and for the 'well off' households it was more than Rs. 60,000. However the average annual family income was calculated was Rs. 2,30,770 for the samples included in the study for this category of household.

Apart from the above-mentioned flood affected families, community leaders representative in local governments, directly involved in the post-flood emergency relief and reconstruction process, government officials responsible for the disaster management policy making and implementation in the State and non-governmental organisations involved in post-flood relief and pre-disaster preparedness activities in the area were also interviewed through structured and semi-structured interview schedules and focus group discussion guidelines. In-depth interviews were conducted with the flood affected families, which were subsequently developed into case studies, to express the traumatic experiences of the victims, their visible emotional outbursts while recalling the miserable days of floods, the health problems they suffered and various other issues that are still lingering in their mind. The span of data collection was more than three years-starting in December 2000 and continued till February 2004. Extensive review of relevant literature, Census various government documents and flood reports in the vernacular media was carried out while conducting the research.

Economic and Social Background of the Study Area

Land Holding Pattern

Economy of the district of Murshidabad has been predominantly agriculture based, people's lives revolve around the cultivation and related activities. In the agrarian society the land is not only considered as a source of the livelihood, but also an asset that can easily be converted into cash (through sale, mortgage etc.) at the time of distress.

In the post-flood scenario it was observed that the land ownership was in the hand of particular economic classes we find that there has been a definite isolation in the ownership of the lands. Around 90 per cent of the respondents from 'Not So Poor' class and over 92 per cent of the 'Well Off' class respondents have possession over the agricultural lands. In contrast, two-third of the 'very poor' households do not own lands. This makes already distressed people more vulnerable at the time of emergency (Table 13.1).

Table 13.1: Number of Households owning Agricultural Lands

If possessing own agricultural land	*Economic Classification of HHs*						*Total*	
	Very Poor		*Not so Poor*		*Well off*		*No.*	*%*
	No.	*%*	*No.*	*%*	*No.*	*%*		
Yes	78	34.5	97	89.8	12	92.3	187	53.9
No	148	65.5	11	10.2	1	7.7	160	46.1
Total	226	100	108	100	13	100	347	100

A closer look at the size of land holdings among the different class of households showed that about 95 per cent of 'very poor' were having less than 132 decimals (4 bighas). Whereas, more than 58 per cent of the 'well off' respondents possessed more than 264 decimals and 75 per cent of 'not so poor' class had between 66 to 264 decimals (Table 13.2).

Table 13.2: Land Owning Pattern Among Different Classes

Land Size	*Economic Classification of HHs*						*Total*	
	Very Poor		*Not so Poor*		*Well off*		*No.*	*%*
	No.	*%*	*No.*	*%*	*No.*	*%*		
Less than 66 decimals	34	43.6	13	13.4	1	8.3	48	25.7
66 to 132 decimals	40	51.3	38	39.2	2	16.7	80	42.8
133 to 264 decimals	4	5.1	35	36.1	2	16.7	41	21.9
More than 265 decimals	—	—	11	11.3	7	58.3	18	9.6
Total	78	100	97	100	12	100	187	100

It is mentioned earlier that the agriculture and related activities have always been the main source of employment in the study area, owning cultivatable land has significant meaning both in social and economic terms. Seventy-two years old Abdul Makid remembers,

"Eighteen to twenty years ago people of this village used to have more land. Many more people had 'Khajna lands' (lands for which people used to pay taxes to the local Landlord) under their possession". Samsul Sheik who was a participant of group discussion in the village sadly expressed that, "The increase in occurrences of flooding in last one decade or so has destroyed us. I have lost my 66 decimals of land. I had to sale those to a businessman of Hizole due to my loss of income and impending poverty. I had no other option except to sale those precious possessions." Another respondent in the group discussion Bhutun Sheik expressed similar concerns, "Lands in Hizole area are considered to be prime possessions as they produce 'gold'. But we are losing our lands there. Before we initiate recovering the mortgaged lands another flood comes and destroys us again." Lands in Hizole were not only considered as prime property to a farmer in the village, but also a place where employment was available aplenty.

Safikul Islam recalled "Only 15 years ago the people in this village used to be wealthy and happy. The village used to look very neat and tidy." Then things started changing from the beginning of the 90s. "The water sharing treaty of the River Ganges between India and Bangladesh has changed our life. This is a Beel (lake) area and water will be naturally deposited here before it is finally released into the river Bhagirathi. The water from Rajmahal Hills flows down through the rivers of Mayurakshi, Bele, Kuiya, Dwarka, etc., and because of the low gradient of the earth and concave surface of the beel water gets accumulated here for a short time, before getting released into the river Bhagirathi (bifurcation of the river Ganges into Indian side)", informs Kasem Seikh (an employee in the Irrigation and Waterways Department of the Goverment of West Bangal). Fifty-year-old Fayaz Mullah supports this remembering, "During those days time water used to get released from this area very fast. Water logging was never for more than 5-6 days around our village, except for some odd years like 1978. In spite of that short duration of flooding we used to get some rice because the plants used not to be submerged for a long period." But now the duration of flood has been much longer. Now water gets stagnated in the Hizole beel for more than 60 days, sometimes even more.

A by stander Sohagi Bibi informed, "I have sold all my 4 bighas of land in 'Ahiri Moroler Gher' (Embanked area for Cultivation, named after some Ahiri Morol, within the Hizole beel), I lost paddy for five consecutive years from 1991. I had no other option left (except to sale the land)." These give a fair idea on the reasons for the distress among the people here. Further discussions revealed that a significant number of villagers had sold their land to fight distress that occurred as a result of recurrent flood in the recent times.

Apart from the agricultural landholders, the people who earn employment from the agricultural activities there too bear the brunt of the situation. For example, the employment of the power tiller/ tractor operator, helper in the pesticide shops etc. are also at stake because of the reduced agricultural activities in the area. Such people are also facing hard times as a result of the recurrent flood in the area. The example of Parimal Pal would stand testimony to the reality of the area.

Parimal Pal 32, of Kamarpara in Saspara had two other members in his family to look after, including a six months old girl child. He was a daily wage labourer during the period of cultivation, and in the other months he worked in a cooking gas warehouse in Kandi. He did not possess any land and earned their living depending on the daily wage income. His monthly income used to be Rs. 2000 to Rs. 2400 in the normal times. But the flood in 2000 had brought a lot of hardship for him and his family. During the flood his house was totally destroyed and the daughter started suffering from fever and diarrhoea. After a lot of struggle he could take her to Kandi Hospital and there she was admitted for three days. In the process Parimal had to spend more than Rs. 500. His struggle did not end there, and following the flood he could not find a job for next four months (this cost him another 2000 × 4 = Rs. 8000 at least). The hardship continued for the family and he had to take a loan of Rs. 2000 to build the house and keep the family expenditure going, from his well off neighbour at the rate of Rs.10 per month interest. To strike a balance he had to reduce the expenditure on food and gradually started selling his assets like wrist watch, bi-cycle and lastly the only cow (for Rs. 600, which otherwise could have been sold for Rs. 1200) which they used to milk for their little baby. As on October 2001 Parimal owed Rs. 1000 to his neighbour and still struggling to cope with the loss he incurred due to the flood. He could not find his job at gas warehouse back and started working in a grocery shop at Kandi and earns only Rs. 900 per month.

The daily wage earners, who were solely depending on the

agriculture related activities became major victims of the situation. As it is mentioned earlier, due to the longer period of stagnation of the water in the low lying areas in Kandi, a large area of cultivatable land had become unusable particularly during the monsoon. The Hizole beel area, where most of the agricultural activities are carried out and stands as the major source of livelihood in the area, had been affected most.

A further enquiry into the affected land in the Hizole area, it was found that this beel contains 3500 hectares of cultivatable land, out of which 15,00 hectares (11,250 bighas) had become un-cultivatable during the monsoon since 1990. "Submergence of the land is the reason", cited Mr. Tarun Kumar Trivedi, Sub-Divisional Agricultural Officer. He further explained, "The submergence of the land is not only hurting the landowners but also eating up the employment of large number of agriculture labourers." Given recurrent flood phenomenon, cultivation of about 200 hectares (about 50,000 decimals) of land adjacent to the study village resulted into the loss of 6000 mandays per month. A conservative calculation showed.

For each hectare (1 hectare = 247.5 decimals) of Aman paddy cultivation about 150 labourers are required (seed to seed). The average cultivation time of aman is 160-170 days (150 days in case of high yield). So, the total loss of mandays for 200 hectares of cultivable land would be: 200 × 150 = 30,000 mandays for approximately 5 months. This makes at least 6,000 agricultural labourers unemployed in the area.

Trends of seeking Employment through Temporary Migration

The occupation patterns of the respondents showed that almost around 16 per cent of the total respondents had been migrant workers. Understanding of the migration patterns of the respondents and their family members would be important in analyzing the impact of flood disasters on the overall well-being and health of the respondents and their families. Interviews reveal that going away from the village in search of employment has been one of the very important avenues to earn living for the family and the magnitude of the trend could be understood from the fact that out of 842 families living in the village there were 600 males out on migration to various parts of the country at any given point of time.

From the in-depth enquiry it is noticed that there are six unskilled occupations namely Rickshaw Pulling, Earthen Work, Kabari (buy and sale of old items) Business, Daily Wage Labourers, Petty Helpers and Rag picking that attracts people who are most illiterates and possess no vocational skills. Almost 47 per cent of these temporary migrants were either Rickshaw Pullers or construction workers.

These temporary employment seeking migrations were always forced and unaccompanied by the female partner and other family members due to very harsh and poor living condition and low earning that is just not enough to maintain the family there. Enquiry into the marital status of the migrants show that 75.5 per cent of them were married and in the age group of 24 to 43 years. The duration of stay away from home is about 9-10 months in the year.

Gulam Gosh, 27, a rickshaw puller who generally goes to Varanasi, was married 8 years ago. He had been to different other places like Delhi, Jamshedpur, Mumbai etc. to earn his living by pulling rickshaw. He earned about Rs. 3,000 to 3,500 per month. "I live there in a small room, shared by nine other persons. The monthly rent of the room at Varanasi is Rs. 800, for each person. Renting of a family accommodation will cost much more, and considering my income it is only next to impossible to maintain another family establishment there", said Gulam. "The living cost in Delhi and Mumbai is much higher than Varanasi, therefore, we just can't even think of taking our families there", he further whined. It was observed that, the phenomenon might lead to certain behavioural practices among the migrants, which may cause certain health impacts.

Dilapidated Dwelling Units

It is a well-established fact that floods have direct impact on the dwelling units. The houses in the study village suffered a severe damage during each flood. The present housing condition showed that there were about 64.7 per cent of them had mud houses that include scanty and temporary mud structures and possessed by 14.7 per cent were Pukka houses. It has been observed that in certain parts of the village, the houses were destroyed for as many as four times in last one decade of repeated flood along with their other valuables. Most of them now live in scanty structure with a thatched temporary roof over the head. We tried to make an insight into the indigenous coping mechanism as far as houses in the area are concerned. Some illustrations are given here to provide understanding of the readers to some extent about the housing conditions in post-flood days and coping mechanisms are being employed by the economically better off households to save the houses from falling during the days of inundation.

Direct and Indirect Health Problems

There were mainly four types of health problems reported during the days of flooding. The class differential of the suffering of the disease shows that morbidity due to fever, cough and cold had been the highest across all the classes, which was followed by diarrhoeal diseases (Table 13.3).

Table 13.3: Disease Pattern among the Different Classes

Health problems reported	*Economic Classification of HHs*						*Total*	
	Very Poor		*Not so Poor*		*Well off*		*No.*	*%*
Year	No.	%	No.	Months		%		
Acute Respiratory tract Infection (ARI)	94	41.6	51	47.2	12	92.3	157	45.2
Swelling of legs and body	18	8.0	3	2.8	—	—	21	6.1
Diarrhoea	95	42.0	38	35.2	—	—	133	38.3
Sickness of children	2	.9	2	1.9	1	7.7	5	1.4
No sickness reported	17	7.5	14	13.0	—	—	31	8.9
Total	226	100	108	100	13	100	347	100

Though diarrhoeal diseases among the 'very poor' class had been very high, there was general increase in the reported cases of diarrhoea during rainy season. The conclusion drawn from the above observation is that with the arrival of monsoons, the cases of diarrhoea increase but floods are definite reasons that trigger an abnormal rise in incidence of the disease in the affected area (October in 1998, 1999 and 2000 being the month when there was flooding).

Disease reporting at the health centre in the study area showed a general increase in cases of diarrhoea during the rainy season, i.e., from May-June to September-October every year. Floods increased the diarrhoeal cases by five times as compared to the trend shown in different years. This was observed in 2000 when exceptionally high intensity floods hit the study area. Further, the reported cases in year 2000 were almost 2.5 times more than the cases reported in the same month of the previous year which had lower intensity floods. The year 2001 being an active year of follow-up of the cases, there was an increase in the number of reported cases. (Graph 13.1).

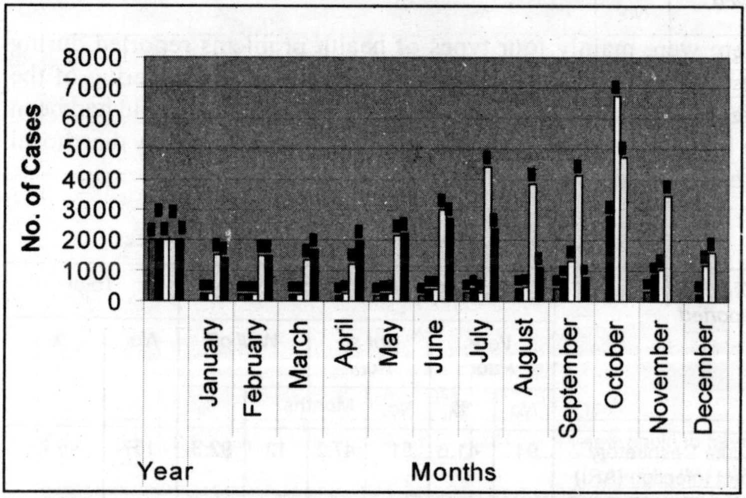

Graph 13.1: Monthly Variation in Reported Cases of Diarrhoeal Diseases (*Source*: Gokarna BPHC, 2004)

Table 13.4 shows that people from 'very poor' and 'not so poor' households had been the main victims of floods. More than 70 and 72 per cent of the respondents from 'very poor' and 'not so poor' categories respectively reported water stagnation around their living places for more than 15 days. Around 70 per cent of the 'well off' households faced flooding in and around their houses only for five days, as their dwelling places were located at a higher ground.

A possible association between the consumption of drinking water and suffering from diarrhoeal diseases could be observed from the data collected. The study showed that almost 70 per cent of the 'well off' and 31 per cent of the 'not so poor' people could take precautionary measures in terms of storing proper drinking water and accessing it during the period of emergency. About a third of the 'well off' households were prepared with water purification tablets and maintained all precautions. In contrast, a majority of the 'very poor' people had no access to drinking water, and often consumed unsafe floodwater (Table 13.5).

Table 13.4: Approximate Days of Inundation of the Dwelling Places

Duration of inundation of living place	*Economic Classification of HHs*						*Total*	
	Very Poor		*Not so Poor*		*Well off*		*No.*	*%*
	No.	*%*	*No.*	*%*	*No.*	*%*		
2 days	—	—	—	—	1	7.7	1	0.3
5 days	11	4.9	—	—	8	61.5	19	5.5
10 days	56	24.8	30	27.8	3	23.1	89	25.6
More than 15 days	159	70.4	78	72.2	1	7.7	238	68.6
Total	226	100.0	108	100.0	13	100.0	347	100.0

Table 13.5: Drinking Water used during the Floods

Type of drinking water	*Economic Classification of HHs*						*Total*	
	Very Poor		*Not so Poor*		*Well off*		*No.*	*%*
	No.	*%*	*No.*	*%*	*No.*	*%*		
Reserved drinking water	16	7.1	34	31.5	9	69.2	59	17.0
Collected rain water	17	7.5	5	4.6	—	—	22	6.3
Procured water from tube well located at a higher place	20	8.8	12	11.1	—	—	32	9.2
Flood water purified using halogen tablets	—	—	3	2.8	4	30.8	7	2.0
Both rain water and flood water	68	30.1	21	19.4	—	—	89	25.6
Flood water	105	46.5	33	30.6	—	—	138	39.8
Total	226	100	108	100	13	100	347	100

When we consider the type of water consumed by the respondents during the days of emergency, it is noticed that about 90 per cent of the cases reported for diarrhoea had consumed unsafe drinking water. This shows a strong association between the quality of drinking water and diarrhoeal diseases in case of flooding (Table 13.6).

The case reports from the area stood testimony to the fact that drinking of the unsafe water often caused health emergency during the days of inundation. This Dawood Seikh 40, is a very poor agricultural landless person earns livelihood by preparing per boiled rice and selling it in the nearby market. Occasionally, he goes to Kolkata as a helper, which brings some extra income for the family.

Table 13.6: Association between Cases of Diarrhoea in relation to the Source of Drinking Water during Floods

Health problems reported	*Kind of water consumed during floods*												*Total*	
	Preserved Drinking water		*Rain water after collection*		*Unsafe Flood water*		*Flood water after purified with halogen tablets*		*Non-affected tube well*		*Both rain water and flood water*		*No.*	*%*
	No.	*%*	*No.*	*%*	*No.*	*%*	*No.*	*%*	*No.*	*%*	*No.*	*%*		
Diarrhoea	7	5.3	6	4.5	93	69.9	—	—	—	—	27	20.3	133	100.0

His family consists of 6 members, including 4 children. Two elder daughters are 17 and 15 years old. Younger ones are sons, aged 14 and 9 years. In the 2000 flood, he lost his house immediately after the water entered into the village. "This time the force of water was too great, my house could withstand the flood of 1999, but this time in 30 minutes it collapsed". He keeps telling, "I am a regular listener of radio news, I learned from it that it was raining heavily in the hills of Chota Nagpur. The rain here was also torrential, we never show that kind of rain in our life. So, the flood was evident. We were just waiting for that to come. I know preparing *machan*, and we acted immediately, put all our valuables on it. But this time flood came with enormous speed and much before than we expected. Although we could take some food with us, but could not manage to take much drinking water, soon started running short of this. Our problem aggravated when a family of the nearby house, whose husband was on migration, too landed on our machan without any food and water. All the nearby hand pumps went under water immediately. There was no way we could procure drinking water and due to the high speed of the water flow it was not possible for me to go around, swimming. First four days it was raining, and we used to take rain water, and after the rain stopped it took too long, more than 10 days to recede the floodwater. We were staying in the *machan* and having floodwater and did not receive any relief from anywhere. We had a hard time in accommodating 11 people on that small *machan*. The condition was getting worse. On the sixth day my 6 years old son vomited twice in the morning. He had some stomachache and by the evening he passed loose stool more than 10 times. Next day in the morning his health condition went really bad. Everything was under water; I did not know where a doctor would be available. We had no other option except to wait for the water to recede. From the radio I learned that in case of diarrhoea the patient should be given ORS, which can also be made in the home by mixing a pinch of salt and sugar. We started applying that. But the water was very bad. Next day morning I found a small boat with people from our next village and requested them to take my son to a doctor. We went to Debu doctor, a RMP, who practiced at the nearby place. Being a low-lying place, we found the whole house was submerged. But the doctor was still there on the rooftop and it was our good luck that he could save some medicines too. Immediately he gave two injections and some medicines. I was lucky that my son was one of the first diarrhoeal patients in the village who could get medicines. The disease was spreading and the stock with Debu doctor exhausted very soon. I had no money to give him. He allowed me to pay him Rs. 200 in a month's time. By evening my son felt better. But still drinking water remained a problem and cause of concern. After the water receded it took five more days to get the hand pumps repaired. And by that time my whole family started suffering from stomach trouble."

The practicing quack doctor in the village too had witnessed the same phenomenon as he recalls: Debabrata Sarkar, 35, is a Registered Medical Practitioner (RMP), who got his degree in 1998. Village Saspara is his maternal uncle's home. He got a proposal from his maternal uncle to start practicing in the village since there is no other doctor practicing nearby and the government sub-centre and PHC do not provide required services to the people. He started practicing from June 1999. It took little time for him to understand the types of diseases people suffer from in this village. "During the summer there is an increase in the stomach related diseases. In the rainy season this goes further up and during the flood in 1999, I got many patients of diarrhoea and in most of the cases they are viral and gradually get cured. The odd cases of bacterial diarrhoea are treated with the antibiotics. Here people insist on giving drips whenever the patients show some weakness or vomits a number of times". In the following year too he observed the same trend till the flood came. This helped him to keep some stock of drips, anti-biotic injections, ORS, etc. "Most of the villagers are poor here. They cannot pay for the treatment immediately even in the normal times", Sarkar told. After he started practicing in the village, he could attract many patients only because he has been very flexible in taking fees and provides service even going to the house of the patients at night. He said, "During the flood there was no doctor available in the nearby areas, even I thought of fleeing, after seeing height and force of the floodwater." However, because of his availability, the life of some of the serious patients could be saved. "In 2000, I had treated at least 100 patients during the high flood" he claimed. While speaking about the disease pattern of the area he said, "people generally suffer from dysentery, diarrhoea, fever, gastric trouble, etc. Since the people are poor and going to hospital or the other doctors would attract some immediate financial implications, therefore, people look for cheaper treatments and credit facility makes their life easier." He was very much concerned about the patients who come back from other places like Varanasi, Delhi, Mumbai, etc., "people come back with serious diseases, malaria and jaundice is very common with them. They come back to the village with serious conditions." On asking whether these migrant people also suffer from any sexually transmitted infections, he affirmatively said, "yes, do suffer from such diseases, but for the treatment they do not come to me, since I am located at the middle of the village and it would be embarrassing if others come to know about it. For the treatment of these cases they go to the private practitioners at Kandi. But I know many people of this village suffered from such diseases while working away from home."

There was no injury related death reported by the families of the respondents. This shows a relatively low level of injury related deaths at the time of floods. The respondents felt that they have lived with floods and so death in floods is what they expect the least.

Recurrent flooding leaves a definite impact on the livelihood of the people if the economy of the place is dependent on agriculture and related activities. This study shows that the recurrence of flood makes poorer households economically unstable and provides little scope to recover from losses. Eventually, a majority of the 'very poor' households have lost their land and turned into landless labourers.

The situation became further complicated since agriculture related jobs became scarce and the people now earn their livelihood as migrant labourers. The migrant labourers are generally exposed to harsh living conditions and suffer from a variety of health problems like malaria, typhoid, jaundice, gastric disorders and sexually transmitted infections (STIs). All the people interviewed for this study had suffered from either of these diseases at various points of time while on migration. Although the flooding has no direct relation with the diseases and sufferings of migrant labourers, recurrent flooding has been instrumental in pushing the people to migrate, which further led to health problems for them. The magnitude of the problem can easily be gauged from the family health survey conducted in February 2002, which shows that a total of 597 people were infected with STIs in the area. Out of these detected cases, a staggering 87 per cent (522 in absolute numbers) were women. This is because the male members of these families are generally temporary migrating labourers and the women in the families are vulnerable to be infected by them.

Health Problems of the Migrant Labourers

It was observed that the marginal agricultural landowners have become economically unstable after flood and a certain section of them were losing their hold over the lands and were then forced to look for other opportunities to earn the livelihood. This led to multi-pronged problems for them, on one hand they were becoming physically vulnerable coupled with inadequate intake from the homegrown stock and became more dependent on the market for basic foodstuff. On the other hand they were forced to migrate for their livelihood where they were facing harsh living conditions. This created further conditions of vulnerability for both the bread earner as well as the family left behind in the village. The case of Mantu Seikh, 35, was the testimony to the fact that to earn bread for the family, the person became seriously sick thereby endangering not only his life but the family as well.

Mantu Seikh is a resident of Namu—Para (Eastern Part) within the Saspara village. He has a family of six people, his aged mother, wife and four daughters of 11, 10, 8 and 6 years old. Mantu was an agricultural labourer in the beginning but had to enter into *kabari business* (purchase and sell of old goods) ever since jobs in his village became scarce from the beginning of 90s. He is the only bread earner for his family and for the purpose of the business he used to go to Asansole, Suri, Durgapur, etc., and stay out of the village almost 10 months in a year. The average monthly income was approximately Rs. 1200-1400. Three years back he suddenly developed fever and coughing with a chest pain. After coming back home he got treated for fever at Kandi SD Hospital, but the cough continued. He was directed to the DOT centre for Sputum microscopy and tested positive. He was advised to undergo DOT for the next six months. However, after having treatment for two months he started feeling better. Since Mantu was not earning and the family was suffering from poverty, he had to go back to his work place and discontinued the medicine after two and half months. The ailment aggravated after five months and when he went back to the same DOT centre he was scolded badly for not continuing the medicine in the earlier occasion. However, he enrolled himself to start the medicines again. This time again Mantu defaulted and due to the miserable family condition had to go back to his profession after three months. He looked for some jobs locally; floods racked havoc here, couldn't find one. "The living conditions is very harsh over there. We eat substandard food and stay in subhuman conditions. With my little income I cannot afford nutritious food, my family will starve then," he expressed with great grief. And this time the enemy came back even quicker. "I fell ill once again within one month. DOT centre refused me any further medicines and I had to go to the private doctor at Kandi. He advised me to go to Berhampore to see a chest specialist. There he did some tests and told me that some medicines will not work on me any more. He has prescribed some expensive medicines, which I can't afford. I have already taken loan of Rs. 1000 from one of my fellow villagers to conduct the tests and to see the doctor. People do understand my condition, so they will not give me any more loan." The radio-photography of Mantu was showing a huge patch over his lungs in the latest done x-ray. The x-ray report was taken to the SD Hospital for the confirmation of the state of the patient. He was indeed in the state of advanced infection. The booth representative of the panchayat was then informed about the case. Mantu Seikh's days are numbered, but "who will look after my children, I shall never die peacefully," tears came out of his eyes.

Mantu Seikh was not the only case that suffered to the extreme, but there are another 700 persons of the same village whose lives are badly affected. Being the part of unorganized sector, the life of these people has been very unsecured. From yet another example of Ajbahar

Seikh, the magnitude of the health related problems with the migrant labourers can be very well noticed.

Mahima Khatun, 44 is a widow for the last 14 years and illiterate. She has two sons and a daughter, who got married last year. Elder son Ajbahar 23, could study only upto primary level and had to quit school owing to his father's death in 1989, he was in class II and the younger son Mujibar 15 years was only one year old. The husband of Mahima used to pull rickshaw in the local areas and she often repeated that they had 3 bighas of land, which was used to cultivate rice during the monsoon season. At the demise of her husband the family got into trouble. There was no earning member in the family. She had then to take bold step to save the family, something she had never done before. She started handling the works of cultivation. During the cultivation season she started going to the field regularly. At the time of her husband's death she was hardly left with any saving. So, taking loans at a very high rate of interest (8 per cent per month) from the well off in the village is the other option and she had to look to this option only. Sowing was completed in time and a very good yield she got at the end. In total she got 36 maunds (1440 kgs.) of paddy. This was sufficient to meet the requirement of the staple food of the whole family. She started looking for other opportunities, so that the family got a monthly income. She started preparing per-boiled rice and started selling in the market. Till the August of 1990 things went well with arrangements she could manage within her limited capacity. Initially in 1990, she did not require any loan for the cultivation during monsoon. But there was a flood that year, which destroyed the crops. She lost her investment and also the reserve of staple food. Thereafter, flood continued in the alternative years. She could not stop investing in cultivation every year, "this was the only option left with me. Everyone in the village was taking chance and leaving the rest on luck. Thereafter, we never got good yield. Boro cultivation was very expensive with a low return. I just could not afford doing that." Losses could not be recovered, loan burden increased, over and above there was the pressure of high rate of interest. She gradually lost all her lands by 1998. "My elder son was only 17 years old then. We were in deep economic trouble. I just could not visualize the future of the family. One day my neighbour Akhai Sk. came and approached me to take Ajbahar to Varanasi for pulling rickshaw. He was not good at study, no work was available locally, so I gave my consent reluctantly", she thought that would be a relief for the family. Things got aggravated in the following year, "we lost our house in the flood. My son supported well. We constructed a small house. We observed in the last few years the flood frequency increased, so, we thought of constructing a pukka house later, after saving some money", she said while describing her plans. However, things did not go in her terms. In the year 2000, the magnitude of the flood was much fiercer and the family incurred much loss apart from the destruction of the house. Over this time her son, on whom she was depending for the recovery of the family, too fell sick. In the month of December he came back from Varanasi with Jaundice. It cost the family more than Rs. 1,500 for his treatment. His whole saving had gone and he took more than two months to get recovered. In the month of March he went back again to Varanasi, however, came back with malaria after two months. This time, the whole family was in trouble. Mahima had to take a loan of Rs. 4000 to meet the cost of the treatment. Ajbahar has become too weak to go back to his work for last one year. Presently the family has emerged in abject poverty and under tremendous pressure to pay back the loans. After losing the land she does not have any other asset left to be mortgaged. Mujibar, who was studying in class VII has dropped out of the school. Since no job is available in the village, he too is planning to migrate to some other cities to earn the livelihood of the family.

The diseases like malaria, typhoid, jaundice, gastric problems, which are visible and well discussed, but the problem of sexually transmitted infections generally go unnoticed. The researcher observed it during discussion with the migrant people that they generally avoid mentioning the problems of STI. When specifically asked about this everyone said many of their mates do suffer from it, however, this had never been a problem for himself. On asking their possibility of visiting sex-workers while staying away from home, Alim Sheik, who migrates to Kandla for rice packing work replied, "It is very common, most of the people go to such places, however, I have never been to". He further says, "After doing hard work throughout the week people generally relax in the week end. Going to movies and at times visiting such places is the only entertainment for the people who stay on migration for such a long time". On asking whether anyone of his known village fellows ever had an infection through the sexual intercourses, he replied, "Yes, I know at least three of my friends did have such infection some time ago". On further queries on their treatment seeking behaviour, he says, "Generally people get themselves treated there before coming back home. At times they even come back to the village and get themselves treated here". "However, they do not get themselves treated from the quacks practicing in the village. This is because they do not want their identity to get disclosed in this regard. This becomes embarrassing in the village situation," he adds further.

Dr. Chandan Mishra, a renowned medical practitioner in the Kandi sub-division town area too finds many patients with the diseases like syphilis, gonorrhoea etc. He also said that majority of those actually are migrant labourers. He thinks that when people are living alone without a family for such a long time, the tendency of getting into such acts of visiting the sex workers do increase. Earlier section of this chapter found that more than 75 per cent of the migrant people are married and stay on migration for 9-10 months in a year. Dr. Mishra also mentions that for the married migrant persons, who do not take family along, the problem becomes two pronged. Firstly, when the wives are left alone back home, the tendency of visiting the sex worker increases. Secondly, the chances of infecting the partner also gets doubled when the migrant comes back home with the disease.

No much statistical data was available in this regard both at Gokarna BPHC and the Kandi SD Hospital. However, a family health survey conducted in the month of the February 2002 shows the magnitude of the problem. In that single survey a total of 597 people were detected having STIs. Out of those a staggering 87 per cent (522 in absolute number) were women. And with all logic it can be said that the lower number of males detected with STIs to be attributed to their absence as a result of migration. It has become even more difficult to know about the exact number of STIs cases reporting to the PHC or hospital, ever since the STIs have been recategorized as 'Dermatological cases' from June 2000. "This has been done after receiving a Government Order (GO) from the State health department", explains the BMOH of Gokarna BPHC. This act of hiding the facts may lead to the further complication of social issues (Monthly Report sent to CMOH office from BPHC, Gokarna, February 2002).

Model for Direct and Indirect Impacts of Flood

To deal with the issue of the health impact of floods, different researchers have undertaken different approaches to identify and classify the impacts as direct/indirect, tangible/intangible, and primary/secondary (Penning-Rowsell, E.C. & Chatterton, J.B., 1977). However, these classifications are found to be overlapping and conceptually unclear. Application of these classifications was difficult and limited in the present study. A need was felt to reclassify the impact of floods in a comprehensive and non-overlapping manner. In this chapter, the impact of flood on health have been categorised into 'Proximate Impacts' and 'Consequential Impacts'. Based on this classification, a model for health impact assessment of floods has been conceptualised and is titled the 'Composite Health Impact Assessment Model (CHIAM)' (Parker, D.J. 1992; Islam, K.M.N., 2000; Pielke, R.A., 2000; Smith, K. and Ward, R., 1998; and Tapsell, S.M. and Tunstall, S.M., 2000).

CHIAM is designed to incorporate and measure both direct and indirect and short and long-term impacts of floods on health. CHIAM not only measures the 'Proximate Health Impacts' of floods but is also equally sensitive to the 'Consequential Health Impacts' of floods.

Proximate Health Impacts are defined as those which have occurred when the dwelling places and its surroundings are submerged and abnormally wet, including some buffer time caused by floods in a region. These would include impacts due to physical contact of human beings or property with floodwater. Such impacts could be direct or indirect but occur when the flooding was active. The classification of health impacts as direct and indirect, or primary and secondary can lead to non-clarity and sometimes overlapping. The analysis of proximate health impacts on the other hand removes these limitations.

Consequential health impacts are those which have their genesis after the offset of floodwater or which do not occur during direct contact of people and property with the floodwater. These consequential health impacts may include forced malnutrition resulting out of the damage caused to agriculture production after the onset of floods.

The Composite Health Impact Assessment Model not only measures the direct, primary or tangible flood impacts on health but also assesses the indirect, secondary and consequential health impacts, taking inter-sectoral interactions into account. The proximate health impacts, which include high mortality and morbidity rates, have a direct and high level of association with the following components of floods:

1. *Duration* of flooding at the living place as well as in the surrounding environment of the house;
2. *Speed* of the floodwater: (a) while entering the habitations, (b) in the subsequent period;
3. The *depth* of the water (this has been used to measure the impact of flood losses in economic terms as well); and
4. *Type of floods* (slow onset: rainfed, riverine etc.; Rapid onset: flash floods etc.).

So far, not many empirical studies have been conducted to highlight the impact of these four factors of floods on community as well as on individual health. However, studies point out that flood depth has direct consequence for humans and flood damage is associated with floodwater velocity. Low-velocity floodwaters of 1 m depth or more are usually considered to be a threat to humans and floodwater 1 m deep flowing at 1 m s^{-1} can be very destructive to the property.

The present study assessed the association between the duration of floods and its impact on the health of those affected by it. The study area has been generally more affected by river floods than flash floods. So the study and its findings are likely to have more relevance to river floods. The other two factors, i.e., the speed and the depth of the floodwater could not be considered due to the absence of statistical data.

The consequential impacts on health are very complex in nature. They not only require a very close understanding of inter-sectoral interactions but also need the identification of causal factors and effects. Also the importance of consequential health impacts compared to proximate health impacts needs closer examination and empirical evidence. Consequential impacts are of longer duration as compared to proximate impacts.

This model was further applied in analysing empirical data. However, some of the components of the model were not studied in-depth in this research study. Issues covered under the study and analysed based on this model are :

- *Proximate health impacts* :
  - Injuries
  - Accidental deaths
  - Water borne diseases that occurred at the time of the flood

- *Consequential health impacts*
  - Malnutrition
  - Migration induced health problems
  - Unemployment related health problems

Relief and the Issues of Cooperation

Flood or any other natural calamity in India is dealt with emergency relief and *ad hoc* compensation to the people through provisioning of basic services including supply of drinking water, food, medicine, health care, temporary shelter building materials, assistance to build dwelling units, etc., from various sources like government and non-governmental organisations. In most of the times the survivors of the disasters complain of insufficient and non-accessibility relief, partiality of choosing beneficiaries by the local authorities, inappropriate relief, pilferage, etc. The responses from the year 2000 flood victims were no exception. The in-depth enquiry into this aspect reveals the following :

1. Since doctors and medicines were not available in the local health centres along with the poor management of the services repelled people to either RMPs or self-medication over the counter. The poor quality of services offered by the nearest PHC of the study village was under severe criticism by the State media and a full length of report was published on the plight of the health facility offered.
2. 97 per cent respondents said no medical team had visited their village within 10 days after floodwater receded. This reflects that the bare minimum services from the State as an institution to reach out to the people to provide medical and health care services in emergency was not available.
3. Only about 13 per cent respondents received medical care from the NGOs in the village.
4. On the contrary, government departments seemed to have played a better role in regard to the disinfection of the tubewells, which are major sources of drinking water in the villages. About half of the respondents were of the opinion that government health department carried out disinfections of contaminated water in the tube wells or hand pumps very

quickly within 2 days when flood water receded. Another fourth of the respondents mentioned that it was the collective self-inflicted efforts of the villagers to carry out disinfections. The roles of Panchayats were highly dissatisfied in this regard and the members generally received people's flak for their inaction. In general, the role of Panchayats in distribution of relief items was often accused for partiality, motivation for petty political gains, corruption and pilfering of items, etc.

5. Panchayat members were not aware of Flood Contingency Plans drawn up at the district HQ; and they did not perceive a proactive role for themselves in flood preparedness or response.
6. All Gram Panchayats conducted a joint meeting with Block Development Officer (BDO) in mid July to exchange opinions, ideas and views on flood, but no action plan was drawn up.
7. Panchayats had very little executive powers to handle floods. For example, even they did not have powers for requisitioning boats in emergency.
8. Panchayat members themselves were part of the community and victims of flood. As a result it was difficult for them to act promptly to serve for the people whom they represent.

Coordinated Effort of INGOs, Government and People to mitigate Impacts of Floods

Experiencing the lessons from the Orissa Super Cyclone in 1999, a number of International and national voluntary organisations came forward with this idea of Community Based Disaster Preparedness (CBDP), under the leadership of UNICEF and in coordination with Government of West Bengal, a few local NGOs and international organizations like Oxfam, Caritas, etc. The aim of the programme was to make the disaster preparedness activities an integral part of the development programmes of the government. These were so far never considered together and the former as subset of the latter. The primary objective of this was to enhance the community's capacity to cope with flood disasters and thereby reduce the loss of life and livelihood and to involve the grassroots level institution like Panchayats in the activity.

The Government of West Bengal has designated the Relief Department as the State Nodal Agency for implementing the programme in the 10 selected districts of the State. Because Relief Department has well structured administrative set up having officer and staff till Block level. UNDP is supporting the initiative of the State Government where partnership has been made with the Panchayati Raj Institutions (PRIs)/Local Self-Government concerns like Departments, Administrative Training Institute (ATI), State Institute of Panchayat and Rural Development (SIPRD), NGOs. Relief Department has designated one officer as State Project Officer (SPO) as nodal officer to carry out DRMP in the State. In addition UNDP provided one technical human resource to support the State nodal agency.

Similarly, District Disaster Management Committee (DDMC) has been constituted under the chairmanship of District Magistrate. Relief section at the district level has been the focal point at the district level. The officer who is in charge of disaster management department was designated as District Project Officer for DRMP activities in the district. The Block Relief Officer is supporting Block administration for smooth implementation of the programme in consultation with the district administration.

Apart from State Steering Committee meeting which is mainly concentrated on policy matter issues, a State level monthly meeting is being held to review the physical and financial progress of DRM programme of each district, preparing action plan for the next month and also common issues and necessary actions. Either Secretary or Joint Secretary and State Project Officer of DRMP of Disaster Management Department leads the meeting in presence of all ADM (DM) and Deputy Magistrate (District Project Officers) of the DRM districts, PA and all DPOs-UNDP. The same way monthly district review meeting is held under the leadership of Additional District Magistrate to review the progress of DRMP and related issues.

A number of initiatives were undertaken, viz., development of user friendly IEC materials, training programmes for various stakeholders, formation of the committees in Block and Sub-Block levels, dissemination of early warnings and other important messages via radio broadcasting, preparation of contingency plans at the Blocks, involving academic and other specialised institutions to make comprehensive training and disaster management plans for the stakeholders, etc. in an effort to institutionalise to the disaster management activities within the government's administrative functions.

At the grass roots level, the target group for the programme had been the vulnerable sections of the community, especially women and children. The activities suggested in the programme are 'Participatory Learning and Action', 'Formation of SHGs', 'Participation in the group activities' and 'Attending Orientation/ Trainings', etc. The initialising activity carried out with the villagers in the programme is 'Participatory Learning and Action' in which the facilitator of the NGO after gathering some villagers, from all age groups, go for village survey followed by the social resource and vulnerability mapping of the village. The villagers draw maps on paper and specify the high, medium and low locations of the village, the area specific depth of the floodwater, speed of the water, various resources and infrastructure available within the village, and other details like direction of floodwater, possible exit points in case of emergency, monthly variation of the rains and possibilities of period of flooding, cultivation period of various agricultural produces, etc. This gives a fair amount of idea to the participants of the activity about issues related to flooding in the village and other details.

After that SHGs were formed by the female members of the families with the initiation of micro-saving. Orientation on the issues of flood response, health issues in emergency, early warning measures, preservation of the important household items for the emergency and preservation of the drinking water sources are given initially. Trainings on first aid, kitchen gardening, preparations of low cost life jacket, etc., are also imparted. Most importantly, during all these activities are government functionaries and PRIs are taken into confidence. Modest try was made to take up the issues in the Gram Sansad meetings (Village planning) to make CBDP an integral part of the planning. However, so far, the response from the PRI has been lukewarm as this is not considered as high in their list of priorities.

In the subsequent years in 2004, 2006 and 2007 floods inundated the study village and fresh informations were collected on the effectiveness of CBDP in terms of mitigating the impacts of floods by the community. The following observation was made :

1. Regular meetings of the women's groups to discuss on the issues of health, hygiene, community development and disaster preparedness.

2. Practice of gathering of food for emergency days on regular basis.
3. Systematic packaging of the materials and Family Survival Kit (FSK) that includes food items, medicines and important documents well before floodwater inundates the village.
4. Keeping in touch with the authorities of early warning system in the area.
5. Preservation of potable water during the time of emergency.
6. Better health care of children and vulnerable persons.

Informal discussion with SHGs in the area reveals that this initiative has number of other positive spin offs. These are as follows:

1. Women of the village have been more cohesive and collective decision-making has been possible through regular meetings.
2. Practice of Family planning and reduction in average size of family of the members of SHGs.
3. Better health of family members, particularly of the girls, who were hitherto considered to be lagging behind.
4. Better educational status of the both boys and girls of the families.
5. Reduction in the gender bias in providing foods to the girls in comparison to the boys.
6. Changes in the general attitude of the women who joined SHGs, in terms of dealing in family matters and outsiders.
7. Improvement in leadership quality among the women with enhanced mathematical calculation capacities.

Therefore, it should be noted that a visible improvement has been noticed both in terms of mitigating the impacts of the disaster also in the general empowerment of women in the area which is key to the community development as a result of this intervention.

Conclusion

The present study shows that the economic status of the households primarily determined the vulnerability or resilience levels of the community/individual to the flood hazard. The magnitude of flood losses was the highest among the economically 'very poor' class of households; they suffered from multiple impacts. On the one hand they lost their livelihood due to loss of agricultural land, and on the other, the loss of dwelling places, unstable occupational opportunities, poorer nutritional intake and a higher disease load made their conditions precarious. All these factors collectively multiplied the vulnerability levels of this class of households.

Structural solutions like construction of embankments, sophisticated meteorological weather prediction systems and water channel modification could not be a panacea for flood disaster mitigation. The need for strengthening of the capacities of the communities through non-structural measures including formation of sustainable self-help groups, alternative agricultural/cropping practices and improvement of resilience against floods at family level was felt. A small scale community based intervention in the area, which was mainly a NGO led initiative has shown greater impacts in mitigating the impacts of disaster at family level which are more community friendly and serves the dual purpose of community development in general. However, the initiative could not still be made an integral part of the system of development initiative of the government. The study further opens up the scopes to explore the areas like how to make the PRI members proactive on making these issues as part of their development planning, measurement of reduction in certain diseases through changes in practices of health and hygiene, changes in the cropping pattern and exposure of the SHGs to sustainable livelihood practices.

Although a number of initiatives have been taken by the government to reduce the impacts of flood disasters on the common people, however, institutionalization of the disaster management and preparedness activities could not be induced at all levels yet. Government departments still do not consider the disaster management activities as main stream activities, therefore, meet the hurdles of neglect. A serious effort from the government is needed to build capacities of the people, particularly who are at the grassroots and bears the brunt of the fury of natural disasters as the front line to minimize the early impacts. Women's groups in the villages with somewhat formal structures have great potentials to become frontline workers in wake of disasters. Emergency management in terms of health, hygiene, nutrition, security, distribution and management of relief etc. can be done efficiently through these groups. An orderly

support to the panchayats can be ensured through the involvement of the SHGs to ensure faster recovery of the victims of the disasters.

Acknowledgements

Prof. K.R. Nayar, Mr. (Late) Bankim Trivedi, Mr. Azad Singh Kalher, Mr. Subhasis Debnath of UNDP and Members and Employees of SPADE, Kolkata.

Acronyms

ADM (DM)	-	Additional District Magistrate (Disaster Management)
ARI	-	Acute Respiratory Tract Infection
ATI	-	Administrative Training Institute
BDO	-	Block Development Officer
BMOH	-	Block Medical Officer of Health
BPHC	-	Block Primary Health Centre
CBDP	-	Community Based Disaster Preparedness
CHIAM	-	Composite Health Impact Assessment Model
DDMC	-	District Disaster Management Committee
DGHS	-	Director General of Health Services
DOT	-	Directly Observed Therapy
DPO	-	District Project Officer
DRMP	-	Disaster Risk Management Programme
FSK	-	Family Survival Kit
GO	-	Government Order
GoI	-	Government of India
GoWB	-	Government of West Bengal
HHs	-	Households
IFRCRCS	-	International Federation of Red Cross and Red Crescent Societies
INGO	-	International Non-Governmental Organisation
NGO	-	Non-Governmental Organisation
ORS	-	Oral Rehydration Solution
PHC	-	Primary Health Centre
PRI	-	Panchayati Raj Institutions (Local Self-Government)
RMP	-	Rural/Registered Medical Practitioner

SDH	-	Sub-Divisional Hospital
SHG	-	Self-Help Group
SIPRD	-	State Institute of Panchayat and Rural Development
SSUP	-	Sanskriti-O-Samaj Unnayan Parishad
STI	-	Sexually Transmitted Infection
TB	-	Tuberculosis
UNDP	-	United Nations Development Programme
UNICEF	-	United Nations Children's Fund

References

Blaikie, P., T. Cannon, I. Davis, and B. Wisner, (1994): *At Risk, Natural Hazards, People's Vulnerabilities and Disasters*, Routledge, London.

Bureau of Applied Economics and Statistics (2001): *District Statistical Hand Book*, Murshidabad, GOWB, Kolkata, pp. 24-25.

Census (2001): Population Register (Provisional) of Block Development Officer's Office, Kandi.

Directorate General of Health Services, GoI, *Review and Planning Meeting on Disaster Preparedness—A Report*, 21-22 September, 1992, New Delhi.

Hovanitz, C.A. (1993): Physical Health Risks Associated with Aftermath of Disaster, *Journal of Social Behaviour and Personality*, 8, 5:213-254.

Hunter, W.W. (1876): *A Statistical Account of Bengal*, Volume IX, Districts of Murshidabad and Pabna, Trubner & Co., London.

International Federation of Red Cross and Red Crescent Societies (1998): *World Disaster Report 1998*, Oxford University Press, Oxford.

International Federation of Red Cross and Red Crescent Societies (1999): *World Disaster Report 1999*, Oxford University Press, Oxford.

International Federation of Red Cross and Red Crescent Societies (2000), *World Disaster Report 2000*, Oxford University Press, Oxford.

Islam, K.M.N. (2000): Micro and Macro-Level Impacts of Flood in Bangladesh, in D.J. Parker (2000) ed., *Floods*, Routledge, New York.

Legome, E., A. Robins, and D.A. Rand, (1995): 'Injuries Associated with Floods the need for an International Reporting Scheme, *Disasters*, 19, pp. 50-54.

Majumdar, S.C., (1941): 'Rivers of Bengal Delta', lectures delivered at Calcutta University as Special Reader of the University, in Biswas, K.R. (2001), *Rivers of Bengal*, Vol. I, West Bengal District Gazetteers, Higher Education Department, Government of West Bengal, Kolkata.

Malilay, J. (1997): in Noji, E.K. (ed.), *The Public Health Consequences of Disasters*, Oxford University Press, New York.

National Flood Commission (1980): *Guidelines and Instructions for the Implementation of the Recommendations of the Rastriya Barh Ayog*, Government of India, New Delhi.

O'Malley, L.S.S., (1914): Bengal District Gazetteers, 'Murshidabad', Reprint by Biswas, K.R. (1997), Govt. of West Bengal, Basumatiernment Corporation Limited, Calcutta.

PAHO (1981): *Emergency Health Management after Natural Disaster*, Pan American Health Organisation, Washington, DC.

Parker, D.J. (1992): The Assessment of the Economic and Social Impacts of Natural Hazards, Paper Presented at the International Conference on Preparedness and Mitigation for Natural Disasters, 28-29 May,1992, Rykjavik, Iceland.

Parker, D.J. (1992): The Assessment of the Economic and Social Impacts of Natural Hazards, Paper Presented at the International Conference on *Preparedness and Mitigation for Natural Disasters*, 28-29 May, 1992, Rykjavik, Iceland.

Parker, D.J., C.H., Green, P.M: Thompson, (1987): *Urban Flood Protection Benefits: A Project Apprisal Guide*, Grower Technical Press, Aldershot, UK.

Parker, D.J. (ed). (2000): *Floods*, Routledge, London.

Penning-Rowsell, E.C. & Chatterton, J.B. (1977): *The Benefits of Flood Alleviation: A Manual of Assessment Techniques*, Saxon House, Aldershot, U.K.

Pielke, R.A. (2000): Flood Impacts on Society—Damaging Floods as A Framework of Assessment, in D.J. Parker (2000), (ed.), *Floods*, Routledge, New York.

Roy, S. (2004): *Natural Disaster Management: A Case Study of Tornado*, Abhijit Publication, Delhi.

Rudra, K. (2001), Flood in West Bengal: A Collection from Newspapers, *Banbhashi*, Kolkata.

Rudra, K. (2002): 'Floods in West Bengal, 2000: Causes and Consequences', in Basu, S. (eds.), *Changing Environmental Scenario of the Indian Subcontinent*, ACB Publication, Kolkata, pp. 326–347.

Smith, D.I., J.W. Handmer, and W.C. Martin, (1980): *The Effects of Floods on Health: Hospital Admissions for Lismore*, Centre for Resource and Environmental Studies, Canberra.

Smith, K. and R. Ward, (1998): *Floods-Physical Process and Human Impacts*, John Wiley & Sons, Chichester, England.

SSUP (2000): *Situational Analysis of Life and Livelihood in Flood Prone Districts of West Bengal: Towards Holistic Flood Management*, SSUP, Malda.

Tapsell, S.M. and S.M. Tunstall, (2000): The Health Effects of Floods—The Easter 1998 Floods in England, in D.J. Parker (2000) (ed.), *Floods*, Routledge, New York.

Verley, A. (1994): *Disasters, Development and Environment*, Wiley, London.

West Bengal District Gazetteers (2003): Murshidabad Zilla Gazetteer, Department of Higher Education, GOWB, Murshidabad.

14

Bringing Together Diverse Stakeholders to Address Natech Risks

ANA MARIA CRUZ

This chapter provides an overview of Natech hazards (natural hazard/ disaster-triggered chemical accidents), their characteristics and the problems associated with Natech risk management. Because of its complex nature, addressing Natech risks requires bringing together a diverse group of stakeholders, including industry owners/operators, officials from government agencies in charge of industrial risk management, civil protection officials and first responders and policy makers as well as community members. Thus, the chapter presents the results of a Natech workshop which brought together participants from several countries and professional backgrounds with the objective to apply and test a Natech risk assessment methodology of a case study community. The workshop provided valuable lessons on communication and understanding among the diverse stakeholders.

Introduction

Regulations for prevention of chemical accidents during normal day-to-day plant operations have been introduced in many countries. However, there is evidence that existing regulations may not be sufficient if the particular conditions associated with chemical accidents triggered by natural disasters, also known as "Natechs," have not been factored in. Natural hazard forces often act on large areas increasing the likelihood of multiple and simultaneous chemical releases from one or more sources. Often, establishments that house large quantities of hazardous materials are located in highly industrialized urbanized areas. Thus, emergency response for Natech disasters can be particularly difficult because resources needed to attend to the natural disaster victims will have to be diverted to respond to the resulting chemical releases. Furthermore, government agencies in charge of natural disaster preparedness often work separately from those in charge of chemical accident prevention resulting in gaps in risk management and emergency response planning for these conjoint threats.

This chapter provides an overview of Natech hazards, their characteristics and the problems associated with Natech risk management. Because of its complex nature, addressing Natech risks requires bringing together a diverse group of stakeholders, including industry owners/operators, officials from government agencies in charge of industrial risk management, civil protection officials and first responders, and policy-makers as well as community members. Thus, the chapter presents the results of a Natech workshop which brought together participants from several countries and professional backgrounds with the objective to apply and test a Natech risk assessment methodology of a case study community. The workshop provided valuable lessons on communication and understanding among the diverse stakeholders which is needed for successful Natech risk reduction.

Natech Hazards and their Characteristics

Natech hazards refer to natural hazard triggered technological hazards. Although most research has concentrated on technological hazards involving the accidental release of chemicals in the form of toxic gases, liquid spills and fires or explosions from their containment vessels during and following a natural hazard or disaster, they may include other technological hazards such as country-wide power outages, disruption of lifeline systems, dam breaks, and others. In this chapter we are interested in Natechs involving accidental chemical releases and damage to lifeline systems that impede or hamper a region's capacity to provide emergency response both to the natural disaster victims and to the chemical accidents ensued.

Natech disasters can occur in areas subject to natural hazards and technological hazards. Thus, highly industrialized and urbanized areas subject to earthquake, tsunami, flooding and tropical cyclone hazards, among others, may be at risk of experiencing a Natech disaster. Thus, it is not surprising, for example, that the highest number of Natech events in the United States occur in the states of Louisiana, Texas, and California (Sengul *et al.*, 2005) which are heavily industrialized and are subject to earthquake, hurricane and flood hazards.

Some well documented Natech accidents occurred at an oil refinery in Kocaeli, Turkey, triggered by the earthquake of 17 August, 1999. The 7.4 magnitude earthquake hit one of Turkey's most industrialized and populated areas of the country. The earthquake triggered over 21 chemical releases with offsite (beyond the establishment's fence line) consequences to neighbouring residential areas. The multiple toxic hazardous materials releases and fires threatened residents and nearby industrial plants storing anhydrous ammonia, liquefied petroleum gas and ethylene, among other chemicals, posing an additional explosion hazard. Authorities were forced to order the evacuation of residents and emergency response personnel in at least two different municipalities less than 12 hours after the earthquake. The evacuation order resulted in the abandonment of search and rescue activities (Steinberg and Cruz, 2004).

Similar events have occurred in many parts of the world. In 2005, Hurricanes Katrina and Rita triggered over 300 chemical releases and more than 30.2 million litres of oil spills with harmful impacts to the surrounding communities and the environment in the United States' Gulf Coast. Besides the dramatic human suffering caused by the hurricanes, these Natech events represented an additional burden on emergency responders and remaining residents, and affected supply of much needed fuel for emergency response purposes. Furthermore, the chemical releases and oil spills resulted in huge direct and indirect economic losses due to lost product, prolonged facility shutdown periods, as well as liability issues (Cruz and Krausmann, 2008).

Cruz and Krausmann (2009) report that during the recent devastating Wenchuan earthquake on 12 May, 2008 in Sichuan Province in China hundreds of industrial facilities were completely destroyed or severely damaged. This resulted in multiple hazardous materials releases including ammonia and sulfuric acid from severely damaged industrial establishments in Honbai, and Yinghua, in Shifang City. Leakage of approximately 150 t of liquid ammonia and about 1000 t of sulphuric acid from damaged tanks were reported at a completely destroyed facility in Honbai (Hongliang, 2008). The Ministry of Environmental Protection of the People's Republic of China (MEP-PRC, 2008) reported that two facilities were destroyed or severely damaged in Yinghua, resulting in leakages of liquid ammonia and sulfuric acid. According to Hongliang (2008) stored sulphur at one of these facilities caught fire and burned for two days (on 14 May 2008, one to two tons of thousands had been consumed). Furthermore, the reporter found that liquid ammonia leaked because pipes connecting the pumps on two ammonia tanks (1,000 m^3 and 100 m^3) cracked leading to the release of all the liquid ammonia.

Awareness of the dangers posed by Natech disasters is growing. There is growing consensus in Europe, the United States and Japan, among other countries that government officials, industrial facility owners/operators, researchers and the public need to better understand the potential impacts of Natech disasters on nearby residents, the environment and other neighbouring industrial facilities.

The accumulated body of knowledge on Natech disasters indicates that :

- Natech disasters seem to be increasing in frequency (Showalter and Myers, 1994; Lindell and Perry, 1997).
- Flood related Natech disasters are more likely (in part because floods account for a much larger proportion of natural disasters; in the United States, floods represent about 80 per cent of all Presidential Declared Disasters) (Sengul *et al.*, 2005).
- Earthquakes are more likely to trigger a greater number of accidental chemical releases per event (Showalter and Myers, 1994).
- Older industrial facilities that handle hazardous materials are more likely to suffer damage which result in chemical releases during earthquakes (Cruz and Steinberg, 2005).
- Larger industrial facilities that handle hazardous materials are more likely to suffer hazardous materials releases during earthquakes (Cruz and Steinberg, 2005).
- The likelihood of multiple simultaneous releases from one or more sources is higher during a natural disaster (about 80 per cent of all Natechs which occurred in the United States between 1982-2003 involved at least two or more releases) (Sengul *et al.*, 2005).
- The consequences of Natech disasters can be far greater than either the natural disaster or chemical accident alone (Cruz, 2003).

Natech Risk Management and Emergency Response

Natural disasters cannot only trigger accidental chemical releases, but they can also hinder response to the chemical releases. In the case of a Natech disaster, the elements for emergency response to a natural disaster such as an earthquake must be joined with those for response to a chemical emergency. In an article published in *Natural Hazards Review*, Steinberg and Cruz (2004) write :

"Emergency response for a Natech is unlike ordinary response planning for chemical releases for a number of reasons including :

- The need to respond simultaneously to the natural disaster and the hazardous materials releases.
- More than one release may occur nearly simultaneously as the natural disaster will have a forcing effect over hazardous materials storage throughout the stricken zone.
- Lifeline systems expected to be available (e.g., water, power, and communications) may not be, chemical safety personnel are likely to be preoccupied, and mitigation measures (e.g., safety control panels, foam systems) may not function as anticipated due to upset from the natural hazard.
- Cascading events are more likely to occur during a natural disaster than during plant operation under normal conditions because the natural disaster increases the likelihood of multiple, simultaneous failures. If not taken into account during the planning process, emergency response needs are likely to overwhelm response capacity.

In addition, the response for the technological disaster will inevitably complicate the response to the natural disaster siphoning away resources, creating greater confusion among citizens and emergency personnel, and potentially reducing the capabilities of the natural hazard response effort. Furthermore, officials in charge of chemical accident prevention usually work independently from those in charge of natural disaster risk management. These unique aspects of response planning for natural disasters in conjunction with technological disasters make Natech disaster risk management especially complex and challenging."

There are various ways in which the risk of chemical accidents triggered by natural disasters can be reduced. These may include (Steinberg, 2004) :

- Design codes and standards.
- Chemical process safeguards.
- Combined natural hazard and chemical process safeguards.
- Land use planning (including analysis of domino effects).
- Disaster mitigation and response planning.

Steinberg (2004) observes that it is important to understand that these measures all help to reduce the threat posed by potential chemical releases to a certain extent but do not eliminate them entirely. Furthermcre, it is necessary to address each of these issues from a Natech risk reduction perspective. For example, it is not sufficient to carry out a seismic assessment of the processes of a plant that handle hazardous chemicals if the potential for damage caused by falling neighbouring equipment (that do not handle hazardous chemicals) or severe shaking and vibration from neighbouring structures are not considered. Civil engineers are called in to design and construct buildings and infrastructure to meet certain design wind loads or seismic codes at an industrial plant but another group of engineers and technical personnel is called in to construct metal storage tanks, piping and connections, and other accessories that may not comply with Natech specific design requirements. Land use restrictions are generally set based on the potential target populations that might be affected if a release occurs, but the triggering natural hazards are often neglected.

Although many countries have adopted regulations for chemical accident prevention and have taken steps to protect their infrastructure against natural hazard forces, these actions may not provide adequate protection if the particular conditions associated with conjoint events have not been factored in (Cruz *et al.*, 2004). Cruz (2005) compared Natech risk management practices in the United States, several countries in the European Community, Turkey and Japan. The author found that only a few countries had taken steps to prevent or prepare for Natech disasters. Although the United States' federal regulations do not address Natechs explicitly, the state of California does require a seismic assessment as part of the California Accidental Release Prevention (CalARP) Programme rule. Italy is addressing flood related Natechs by looking at ways to prevent flood-triggered chemical releases and to reduce potential losses caused by flooding. In 2003

France introduced amendments to its environmental law to reflect lessons learnt from past flood-triggered chemical releases and other industrial losses. In Kocaeli, Turkey, industrial plant owners and managers, as well as local government officials are well aware of the need to improve risk management practices to prevent Natech disasters in the future (Cruz *et al.*, 2006).

Natech Risk Reduction Strategies

In order to reduce Natech risk, there must be awareness that the problem exists, and the factors that contribute most to Natech risk must be identified and prevented or mitigated. Cruz *et al.* (2006) have pointed out the need to educate the public, policy-makers, and government officials on the risk of Natech disasters and what can be done to reduce it. Based on a workshop carried out with participation of civil protection authorities and researchers from more than 13 countries the authors summarize the following five strategies identified by the workshop participants key to Natech risk reduction:

- Education and awareness campaigns aimed at educating the public, government agencies, and decision-makers on the risk of Natechs and on the preventive and preparedness measures that can be taken to minimize risk.
- Emergency planning specific to Natechs. This included prevention and mitigation, and preparedness response planning for Natech at all levels of government.
- Public participation in Natech risk reduction planning. Natech risk reduction should incorporate: (a) the local population's perception of Natech risk, and (b) the level of Natech risk they are willing to accept.
- Modification of risk management regulatory requirements so that they specifically address the potential impacts of natural hazards at industrial installations.
- Land use planning, as an important technique for separating residents and facilities that use, produce or handle hazardous chemicals.
- Risk assessment, and risk mapping possibly tied to a centralized information database on Natech cases.

Indeed, one of the first steps to be taken by communities or regions that are at some degree of risk to natural hazards, and that are home to establishments that handle hazardous chemicals is to carry out a Natech risk assessment.

Covello and Merkfer (1994) define risk assessment as : "a systematic process describing and quantifying the risks associated with hazardous substances, processes, actions or events." The authors write that risk implies both the potential for adverse health and environmental consequences, and uncertainty with respect to the occurrence, magnitude, or timing of the consequences. A Natech risk assessment thus should involve the process of identifying possible adverse consequences that may result when establishments that house hazardous materials are exposed to natural hazards, as well as estimating their magnitude, timing and probabilities.

Cruz and Okada (2008) observe that there are limited studies available concerning risk assessment of Natech disasters. A few studies, primarily concerning earthquakes, have been published *(see* for example Kiremidjian *et al.,* 1985; and Werner, Boutwell and Varner, 1989; Salzano *et al.,* 2003; Campedel *et al.,* 2008). However, the above methodologies are intended for use by an industry owner/ manager to assess the risk of earthquake-triggered hazmat (hazardous material) releases at a facility, not to assess Natech risk to the community. Seligson *et al.* (1996) and Tierney and Eguchi (1989) described a methodology for estimating the risk of post-earthquake hazmat releases of anhydrous ammonia and chlorine in the Greater Los Angeles area. The methodology includes estimation of the number of potentially exposed people, and assumes the possibility of simultaneous releases from single or multiple sources. In their work, Seligson *et al.* established failure probability curves for industrial facilities versus earthquake magnitude. Furthermore, they present tables indicating probability of hazmat (hazardous material) releases versus ground shaking intensity values and damage scales. This methodology requires having probability estimates of the likelihood of hazmat releases for a given earthquake intensity, which is limited or non-existent for floods, tsunami, and other natural disasters.

To add to the problem, local governments often do not have the human or economic resources or expertise to carry out even an earthquake related Natech risk assessment. Cruz and Okada (2008) proposed a simplified Natech risk assessment methodology that allows experts as well as non-experts to easily and rapidly identify those areas of potentially high Natech risk. Once potentially high-risk areas are identified, resources can be directed for more in-depth analysis of these problem areas. The methodology serves as a screening tool and does not replace a full Natech risk assessment. It has the advantage that it provides a quick way in which local government officials and/or community members can identify those areas that pose the greatest Natech risk in their territory.

The following sections describe a workshop on the application of Cruz and Okada's Rapid Natech Risk Assessment (RNRA) methodology to two case study communities; and the workshop results. The workshop provided valuable lessons on communication and understanding among the diverse stakeholders present during the workshop.

The Natech Workshop

The workshop, entitled "Assessing and Managing Natechs (Natural-hazard triggered technological accidents)" was organised and hosted at the Joint Research Centre (JRC) of the European Commission on 17-18th September, 2007 in Stresa, Italy (*see* Cruz and Krausmann, 2007). The Natech workshop was attended by 25 participants from 16 different countries. The participants to the workshop came from a variety of institutions, including academia, government authorities and private enterprises; and from various professions, including engineering, urban planning, and sociology among others.

The participants worked together during the two-day workshop which involved discussion of key issues and problems in Natech risk management, presentation of new concepts, hands-on exercises, and the application of the RNRA methodology to two case study communities. Participants were divided into groups. Each group applied the risk assessment methodology to their case study, and presented the case study results and suggested possible Natech risk reduction strategies for their case study communities. At the end of the workshop, the participants proposed a set of key strategies for Natech risk reduction and discussed how they might be applied in their own country and context.

Case Studies

The objective of the case studies was to test the application of the

RNRA methodology by a diverse group of stakeholders coming from academia (e.g., professors and researchers), government authorities (e.g., Ministry of the Environment, Civil Protection Authorities, Regional and Urban Planning, Fire Department), and private enterprises (e.g., engineering, IT); and from various professions including engineering, urban planning, and sociology among others. The members of each group were selected so that there was a balance of professions and professional backgrounds in each group.

The case studies involved the application of the RNRA to two communities, *A* and *B*. The case studies were set up using real data. However, fictitious names were used for the communities to protect their identity. All workshop participants were given a step-by-step description of the RNRA methodology. Each participant received case study materials which contained a description of each case study community including information about the natural hazards and the hazardous materials present in each case study region. In addition, maps of the case study areas, tables used during the assessment process, and a spreadsheet used for calculations and results were also provided. All documents were made available in hard copy and digital form to all the participants.

Furthermore, the participants were presented with materials and tools that were needed during the assessment. The materials and tools included a method proposed by Campedel *et al.* (2008) to qualitatively estimate the likelihood of a hazardous materials release triggered by earthquakes and flooding; and presentation of open-access web software programs that can be used to model accidental chemical releases and fires or explosions.

The participants were assigned to groups of three. Three groups worked on case study *A*, based on data from a community in the United States, and two on case study *B*, based on data from a community in Turkey. All the case study materials were reviewed with the participants. Invited experts were made available to help with the exercise and to answer questions. Participants became familiar with the maps of their case study community identifying where each industrial facility was located and the location of storage tanks containing hazardous materials. They were asked to note areas of higher population density, location of residential areas near the industrial facilities, location of vulnerability centres (e.g., schools, Churches, stadiums), location of critical facilities (e.g., drinking water treatment plant, waste water treatment plant, electrical power station), location of emergency resources (e.g., fire departments, police departments, hospitals), and location of major transportation centres (e.g., airport, central train station, ports) and lifelines systems (e.g., water distribution systems, pipelines).

As was briefly discussed in the previous section, Natech risk assessment involves determining the likelihood of hazardous materials releases given a natural hazard occurring, and identifying possible adverse consequences to people, property and the environment that may result when establishments that house hazardous materials are exposed to the natural hazard forces. Due to the limited time available for the case study exercise, the natural hazards that each of the case study communities was subject to (and should concentrate their efforts on) had already been identified in the case study description as the "worst case scenario" natural hazard.

In the analysis, only the risks posed by storage tanks which contain hazardous materials were considered. Other parts of an industrial plant such as processing equipment and pipelines where hazardous materials are processed and transported were not included in the analysis. Furthermore, due to time limitations, not all the storage tanks containing hazardous materials that were actually present in each of the communities were included in the case study exercise. Instead, a sample of 20 storage tanks for each case study was selected for the purpose of demonstrating the application of the methodology.

The RNRA methodology involved estimating a Natech Risk Index (NRI) for each storage tank containing hazardous materials given the worst case natural hazard (which for both case studies involved a major earthquake), according to the following expression:

$$\text{NRI} = [\text{HRL}] * [D + Area\_sc + C] \qquad \text{... Eq. (1)}$$

where:

HRL: is a score that indicates the hazmat (hazardous material) release likelihood of each hazmat containing storage tank given the earthquake. It can take a value from 1-5, where 1 is low likelihood and 5 is high likelihood of release.

D: is a score that measures the potential consequences of the hazmat release on other hazmat containing storage tanks given the earthquake. It can take a value from 1-5, where 1 is low likelihood of consequences due to domino effects and 5 is high likelihood of consequences due to domino effects.

Area_sc: is a score that measures the potential consequences of the hazmat (hazardous material) release on the population given the earthquake. It can take a value from 1-5, where 1 is low likelihood and 5 is high likelihood of negative consequences on the population.

C: is a score that measures the potential consequences of the hazmat release on the environment and on essential facilities that are critical for the safety and well-being of the community given the earthquake. It can take a value from 1-5, where 1 is low likelihood and 5 is high likelihood of negative consequences on the *environment and essential facilities*.

The RNRA involved estimating HRL, and then estimating the potential consequences of the releases to people, property and the environment by estimating values for *D, Area_sc* and *C*. Then, applying Eq. (1) to obtain an estimate for NRI.

Estimating the Hazmat Release Likelihood (HRL)

The first step in the RNRA was to determine HRL of each storage tank in the case study due to the earthquake which could result in offsite impacts to the population. In determining HRL, each group considered information regarding the natural hazard, such as the earthquake magnitude and intensity, and the type of storage tank, the type of hazmat, type of storage conditions, presence or lack of safety and mitigation measures, as well as absence of these measures and other emergency response capacity due to earthquake damage. Furthermore, in estimating HRLs each group qualitatively estimated a score corresponding to the vulnerability of each storage tank due to the type of chemical contained (e.g., toxic gas, flammable gas, toxic or flammable liquid), and storage conditions (e.g., atmospheric, pressurized, refrigerated) when subject to the natural hazard forces. Common problems observed during previous earthquakes were discussed during the workshop to help estimate HRL. For example, intentional releases of refrigerated liquefied gases, such as anhydrous ammonia, have been reported in several cases due to prolonged power outages following earthquakes. Flammable and toxic liquids stored in atmospheric tanks are more likely to be released due to liquid sloshing with consequent damage to the tanks' shells. Flammable gases are often stored liquefied under pressure in spherical tanks, or in horizontal cylindrical tanks. Damage to tank support structures have been observed and may lead to rupture of connected pipelines resulting in hazardous materials releases. Nonetheless, pressure vessels are generally built to more stringent design standards, and with better quality materials and are, therefore, more resistant to external forces.

Other factors can influence the vulnerability of storage tanks containing hazardous materials. For example, the presence or absence of safety and mitigation measures during normal day to day plant operation may increase the risk during a natural hazard; as well as the performance of active and passive safety and mitigation measures during the earthquake. Groups were asked to make assumptions concerning risk management practices at the various industrial facilities in their case study communities and to use these assumptions to support their decisions.

Consequence Analysis

The next step involved carrying out a consequence analysis to determine the area that could potentially be impacted by each Natech event. The extent and consequences of each hazardous material release will depend on a number of factors including the type of chemical stored (e.g., toxic, flammable, explosive), storage tank type and storage conditions, the quantity present, and the potential to trigger secondary releases. The groups followed instructions on how to use one of the open-access software programmes available to estimate the extent (the area) of potential damages and health effects for each possible Natech event.

Estimating Potential Domino Effects, D

The consequences of a hazmat release could increase depending on whether it can trigger secondary, tertiary, or more events. For the purpose of the analysis each group considered only the potential for secondary chemical accidents (also known as domino chemical accidents) triggered by a fire or explosion of flammable gases liquefied under pressure. A primary event, such as fire or explosion, can trigger a domino chemical accident due to the blast overpressure wave, fire impingement and heat radiation, impact of fireball, and impact from missiles and projectiles on neighbouring storage tanks. For the purpose of the case study exercise, the groups were asked to assume that a domino chemical accident could occur only if the distance between a storage tank containing a flammable material and any other neighbouring storage tank containing another hazardous material was less than or equal to 1/2 of the maximum distance from the source where adverse effects would be observed (*see* Cruz and Okada, 2008; Cruz and Krausmann, 2007 for a complete description of the methodology and workshop). This value was used to demonstrate the application of the methodology, although it would be unlikely to observe domino effects at this threshold value.

In general, the closer other storage tanks containing hazardous materials are to the source, the more likely domino effects are, if an initial hazmat fire or explosion did occur. For further discussion on observed domino effects at various distances from the source *see* Cozzani and Salzano (2004), Birk (1998), and Birk *et al.* (2007). The higher the number of storage tanks within the area of impact of another storing flammable gases liquefied under pressure, the higher the risk. Even if nearby tanks are not affected during the initial Natech event, fires triggered by the earthquake will require that neighbouring tanks be kept cool to avoid over-pressurization and possible explosion. Keeping tanks cool becomes more and more difficult with an increase in the number of tanks exposed. The vulnerability of the population due to potential domino effects could also increase if a domino chemical accident increases the overall area affected by the primary technological accident.

Estimating an Area Vulnerability Score, Area_*sc*

Everything within the area of impact of each possible Natech event is potentially exposed and vulnerable. The next step involved determining vulnerability of exposed people and personal property. To calculate the Area_sc the groups considered factors such as the number of people exposed (or population density when population values were not known) following the earthquake, the distribution of the population during or immediately following the earthquake, presence of population centres (e.g., universities, large enterprises, shopping centres) or more vulnerable population groups (e.g., the elderly, the sick, children) who might have more difficulties in evacuating if needed, or who may be unable to take shelter during the earthquake. It was noted that those who live in low income housing may also be more vulnerable because their homes are more likely to suffer damage during the earthquake (e.g., due to lack of seismic restraints or use of lower quality materials) or are less likely to serve as a place for shelter.

Estimating Vulnerability due to Impacts on the Environment and Essential Facilities, C

The next step concerned estimating vulnerability due to impact on the environment and essential facilities, *C*. We include here any potential negative impacts of each Natech event on the environment, particularly water bodies that constitute sources of drinking water or other natural resources that constitute the livelihood for a community. Furthermore, we include here any potential negative consequences on essential facilities which are considered critical for maintaining the safety and well being of the public. These may include public utilities, lifeline systems, emergency resources, and emergency response capacity. Potential consequences on essential facilities from the Natech event can occur if these within the area of impact of the storage tank affected by the earthquake. For example, a toxic release might impede the passage of rescue teams trying to help trapped earthquake victims on the other side of the city, while at the same time blocked roads (due to debris from the earthquake) could delay arrival of hazmat teams to a contaminated area.

After estimating values for HRL, *D*, *Area_sc*, and *C*, each group used Eq. (1) to calculate the NRI value for each storage tank. Each group mapped the estimated NRI values for each storage tank using symbols proportional to their magnitude on their case study maps.

The groups were given time to carry out the RNRA, prepare a short summary of the case study results, and prepare a short 5-10 minutes presentation.

Results and Analysis

Due to the limited time available only two groups completed the analysis of the 20 tanks. The other three groups completed the assessment of 3 to 5 tanks. The risk assessment results for each case study are well documented by Cruz and Krausmann (2007), and thus will not be presented here. However, there were valuable lessons for future application of the RNRA methodology that are worth mentioning.

There were some differences in the interpretation of the various steps in the methodology. In part because of the different professional backgrounds and in part because the explanations were not sufficiently clear. This indicates that the methodology needs to be better explained, and new terms and concepts need to be better defined. Furthermore, some of the engineering concepts are difficult to understand. The use of look up tables and lists would facilitate and speed up the assessment process. It could also help to simplify the procedure and reduce errors in interpretation. Perhaps a few examples could be carried out before doing the actual RNRA. During the workshop, four out of five groups had at least one engineer. The question remains if an assessment team should include at least one engineer with some experience in industrial risk assessment or if the use of look up tables and lists would be sufficient. Having updated information and data is vital for a good assessment. The RNRA will only be as good as the data used to carry out the assessment.

Participants were asked to evaluate the case study exercise and the RNRA methodology. The following bullets taken from Cruz and Krausmann (2008) summarize the results of the discussions some of which have already been mentioned above:

- All of the participants agreed that the case study exercise was useful for them, and helped to improve their knowledge and understanding of the Natech problematic and its complexity.
- The participants felt that more detail was needed in order to estimate HRL values. They considered that in order to estimate HRL the assessment team needs more engineering/chemical processing knowledge, or more detailed guidance so that assumptions are correctly made and criteria correctly estimated. Thus, they questioned whether or not expert opinion was needed.
- A question was raised concerning the profile of the assessment team. For example, what disciplines are required at a minimum? Would it be possible for a non-chemical engineer or someone not having knowledge on chemicals to assess the risk to people regarding the release of chemicals? If not, what information would be useful to help understand the issue better?"

- The same applies to the earthquake structural vulnerability of the installations. What information is required to help chemical engineers or other non-engineering team members to understand this issue better? The same applies for other type of natural hazards.
- Many participants stressed the need to include the effects of the simultaneous natural disasters when estimating values for the various criteria particularly when calculating Area_sc and *C* scores. It is the conjoint natural disaster that makes the Natech situation so different and complex. It was noted that the groups often forgot this fact.
- The need to account for the operational capacity of local government to confront the approaching disaster in the Natech risk assessment was considered important. Physical exposure and vulnerability of emergency response resources are considered when estimating the *C* scores. Other criteria can be included to better capture the effect of local government's (as well as industrial or private citizen's) operational capacity.
- The workshop case studies both involved earthquakes. The participants suggested that an exercise involving cyclone, flood or other meteorological hazard be framed in addition to the earthquake one to give a broader background in doing calculations and appreciating the damage these can cause.

Individual and Group Activities

During the workshop individual and group activities were carried out in an effort to familiarize the participants with Natech risks, to promote communication and discussion between the diverse participants, and to raise awareness among the participants that there are other ways of defining terms and understanding concepts. This section summarizes the activities and their results.

Video Presentations and Discussion

As an introduction to Natechs, the first activity involved the presentation of two short videos. The first video (six minutes) concerned the large earthquake of magnitude Mw 7.4 on August 17,

1999 in Kocaeli, Turkey and the refinery fires that followed. The second video showed flooding and oil spills from a refinery in Coffeeville, Kansas on June 26, 2007. After viewing the short videos, the participants were asked to answer the following questions in groups: (a) what were the hazards in each case and if they thought these had been previously identified by government officials; industry owners/operators; and/or residents living in the vicinity of the industrial plants; and (b) what prevention and/or mitigation measures they thought had been taken before the Natech events to avoid damage or losses, and if they thought they had been successful or not.

All of the groups agreed that the natural hazards were a major earthquake and earthquake-triggered fires in the Turkey video; and major flooding and an oil spill from a refinery in the second video. The participants agreed that in both cases the natural hazard had combined with anthropogenic hazards. All groups agreed that government officials probably knew about the natural hazards, or they preferred to "not know" about them; industrial owners/operators knew about plant hazards in their day-to-day operation; the community may or may not have been informed depending on their daily activities, proximity to the plant, and emergency response planning. It was noted that often knowing that the hazard exists does not mean that you know or can imagine the possible accident scenarios.

In the case of the earthquake, the groups agreed that industry and government were probably aware of the potential consequences but the community was probably not aware. In the case of flooding the groups agreed that probably government, industry and the community were not fully aware of the hazards.

Based on images from the earthquake video, the groups thought it seemed that mitigation measures existed, but were not designed to current standards, or that the design of the equipment was not adequate for the magnitude of the event. In the case of flooding, they thought that the site was probably evacuated, but no measures to protect the installation had been taken. Furthermore, the groups proposed that probably the dikes around storage tanks had been designed to contain chemicals if released, but had not been designed to keep water out in the case of flooding. Other points that came out of the discussions included that mitigation measures that had probably been taken for internal day-to-day plant operation did not provide sufficient protection for a problem that became larger. Furthermore, mitigation measures that were in place likely failed due to the natural hazards. In the case of flooding, the groups agreed that if evacuation was ordered due to the floods, it also helped to reduce exposure to the hazardous-materials (hazmat) releases. However, contamination of property and homes in the affected area remained as was evident in the second video.

Concepts and Definitions

One important aspect of disaster risk management, particularly Natech disasters, is that it cannot be tackled by people working in one field alone but that it requires bringing in expertise from various fields and diverse backgrounds to solve problems. However, often even people working in the same field do not always agree on the meaning of certain concepts or their definitions. Participants were asked to define various concepts including hazard, vulnerability, risk, disasters, and Natech disasters. A summary of the different definitions provided by the workshop participants is presented in Table 14.1. Some definitions were similar and more general, others were quite specific. For example, one participant defined vulnerability as the probability of an item to have structural damage while another defined it as the ratio between number of casualties and the number of people in a given territory. This was not surprising as the two individuals come from different backgrounds; an engineer and a first responder, respectively.

Table 14.1: Concepts and Definitions

Concept	*Definition*
Hazard	— Something which is a potential threat to a person, community, environment or structure — A natural or technological phenomena which imposes risk upon a population — A characteristic condition of a system that can harm people, property or environment — A hazard is for example a characteristic of a plant which can generate an accident. A potential source of accident — Adverse effects resulting in loss of life, property, or causing environmental problems — A potential event that can cause harm
Vulnerability	— How able a thing or person/animal is to resist or recover from a particular hazard — Ratio between number of casualties divided by number of people in a given territory

(Contd.)

Concept	*Definition*
	— The susceptibility of people, property or the environment to harm from hazards — The vulnerability is the probability of an item to have structural damages — Degree of being affected by hazards — Degree to which an exposed element can suffer from the hazard
Risk	— Probability of something bad occurring — An action that could lead to something bad occurring — The order of hazard to hit a given population — The probability that harm can result from a hazard — The risk is a function which depends on frequency and on magnitude of an event — Possibility of a specific hazard to be realized — The probability of the hazard and its consequences
Disaster	— A change in the normal routine which changes temporarily or permanently in a person's life, the environment or the community — Death, injury, displacement of hundreds of thousands due to materialization of hazard — An event that can cause so much harm that it overwhelms the response capacity — Disaster cannot be measured by "response capacity" — A disaster is a situation of big magnitude and low frequency, like a major accident — Events that affect group of people or large extent of the environment beyond the coping capacity of the community — An event that overwhelms the capacity of a community to respond to it
Natech Disaster	— A technological disaster triggered by a natural disaster — The same as disaster, only caused by a chain of hazards — The natural hazard *causes* the technological disaster — A Natech disaster is a major [chemical] accident triggered by a natural event — A technological disaster as a consequence of a natural event, i.e. natural hazard or natural disaster. — A natural disaster triggered hazardous material release

The purpose of the exercise was not to find a common definition for each of the concepts. Rather, the exercise allowed participants to understand other participants' point of view, to be aware that we do not all define similar concepts in the same way, and that whatever definition is used needs to be clearly stated to avoid misunderstandings or confusion.

Probability of a Natech

Following the discussion of the case studies, participants were asked to write down what they considered to be the worst case natural disaster used for planning purposes in the region/jurisdiction where they live. Each participant was asked to specify the type of natural disaster, the expected magnitude, and location with his/her jurisdiction. Then, they were asked to give an approximate estimate from 0-100 per cent of the probability of a Natech occurring as a result of that disaster. Each participant was then asked to describe the potential consequences of the Natech event such as the type of industry affected, chemical released, extent of area impacted and number of people affected. All participants who lived in areas subject to natural and hazmat release hazards considered that Natechs were likely with probability estimates ranging from 1 per cen to 100 per cent depending on local conditions.

Strategies for Natech Risk Management

Each group was asked to propose strategies for Natech risk reduction for both community and for industry. Implementing risk reduction generally has a cost. Thus, each group was asked to discuss what would be the main problems and challenges in implementing each of the proposed Natech risk management strategies in their jurisdiction; by government officials and policy-makers in charge, and by industry owners/operators. Groups were asked to think about which of these strategies should be recommended; which should be mandated?

Following this exercise the groups then convened in a plenary session to identify those Natech risk management strategies that were considered priority key strategies to be recommended and /or mandated.

The following bullets summarize key Natech risk reduction strategies proposed by the participants for government agencies, and policy and decision-makers :

- Comprehensive hazard identification and analysis that considers Natechs.
- Natech risk assessment.
- Land use planning to reduce population exposure (e.g., relocation of people/hazardous facilities).
- Structural and non-structural measures specific for Natechs.

- Warning systems and evacuation plans that take into account Natech.
- Community Right to Know.
- Liability and compensation framework for Natechs.
- Enact and enforce enabling legislation (e.g., extra obligations for industry exposed to Natech hazards).
- Research to better understand Natech risk in the face of climate change.
- Educational and awareness campaigns.

The following bullets summarize key Natech risk reduction strategies proposed by the participants for industry owners/ operators:

- Use common cause failure analysis for system design.
- Structural safety measures and additional safety barriers (e.g., back up lifelines) for Natechs.
- Emergency planning that considers failure of emergency response equipment—"stand alone" plan—i.e. not relying on external lifelines.
- Adequate separation between critical elements for Natech scenarios.

The participants identified possible barriers to Natech risk reduction strategy implementation including :

- Industry resistance to additional regulatory burden.
- Effectiveness *versus* cost of implementation.
- Ignorance (not money).
- Land use planning is limited by existing development.
- Belief that nothing is going to happen, or that it will not affect them.

Conclusion

This chapter has provided an introduction to Natech hazards, their characteristics and problems. It has provided guidance on risk management and emergency response measures that can be taken to reduce Natech risk. Furthermore, key Natech risk reduction strategies have been proposed, among them the need to carry out Natech risk assessments of highly industrialized and densely populated areas. Thus, the results of a workshop on Natech risk assessment have been presented. The workshop provided a framework and practical tools for Natech risk assessment and management at the community level as well as valuable lessons for assessment teams made up of diverse stakeholders.

The Natech workshop was indeed a learning experience for all those who attended. The workshop provided an open atmosphere where people coming from diverse backgrounds and cultures could share experiences and knowledge on Natech risk management, and learn from each other. The various individual and group exercises and discussions helped to clarify the Natech problematic, and raise awareness among the participants that not all share the same point of view or define terms and concepts in the same way. The importance then of arriving at a workable agreed definition was stressed.

The workshop also provided lessons for the organizers. In any future workshop, more time should be allotted for discussion, awareness raising, etc., and more time for the presentation of the RNRA methodology, its application, presentation of examples, and discussion of results.

Acknowledgements

The author would like to thank all the participants and invited guests to the workshop: Assessing and Managing Natechs (Natural-hazard triggered technological accidents). The workshop was organised and hosted by the Major Accident Hazards Bureau (MAHB) of the Institute for the Protection and Security of the Citizen (IPSC) of the European Commission's Joint Research Centre (JRC) on 17-18th September, 2007 in Stresa, (Italy). The following people contributed to the workshop preparation and development: Elisabeth Krausmann, Laura J. Steinberg, Valerio Cozzani, and Michael Lindell.

References

AIHA (2007): *ERPG/WEEL Handbook*. American Industrial Hygiene Association, Emergency Planning Committee. < *http://www.aiha.org/webapps/taxonomy/portal.htm*> (22 Oct 2007).

Beem, H.; R. Fendler; W.B. Krätzig (2008): Impact of Storms and Earthquakes on Industrial Installations New Risk Control Approaches Required? Some Conclusions of a Research Project of the German Umweltbundesamt UBA. *Journal of Natural Hazards* (accepted, forthcoming).

Birk, A.M. (1998): *Propane and LPG BLEVE Incident Simulation for Plant Safety Analysis, Emergency Response Planning and Training*. Department of Mechanical Engineering, Queens University, Ontario.

Birk, A.M.; C. Davison; M. Cunningham (2007): Blast Overpressures from Medium Scale BLEVE Tests, accepted to the *Journal of Loss Prevention in the Process Industries*, March 1.

Campedel, M.; V. Cozzani; A. Garcia-Agreda; and E. Salzano (2008): Extending the Quantitative Assessment of Industrial Risks to Earthquake Effects. *Risk Analysis,* 28(5), DOI: 10.1111/j.1539-6924.2008.01092.x

Cozzani, V., and E. Salzano (2004): Threshold values for domino effects caused by blast wave interaction with process equipment. *Journal of Loss Prevention in the Process Industries*, 17(6), 437-447.

Cozzani, V.; M. Campedel; N. Buratti; B. Ferracuti; M. Savoia (2007): Development of a Framework for the QRA of Risk Related to Na-Tech Accidents Induced by Seismic Events. Presented at the 7th IIASA-DPRI Forum on Disaster Risk Management Coping with Disasters: Challenges for the 21st Century and Beyond, Stresa, Italy, 19-21 September.

Cruz, A.M. (2003): *Joint Natural and Technological Disasters: Assessment of Natural Disaster Impacts on Industrial Facilities in Highly Urbanized Areas.* Dissertation. Tulane University, New Orleans, LA., p. 212.

Cruz, A.M. (2005): Natech disasters: A review of practices, lessons learned and future research needs. Presented at the Fifth Annual IIASA-DPRI Forum on Integrated Disaster Risk Management: Innovations in Science and Policy. Beijing Normal University, Beijing, China, 14-18 September.

Cruz, A.M. and L.J. Steinberg (2005): Industry Preparedness for Earthquakes and Earthquake-Triggered Hazmat Accidents during the Kocaeli Earthquake in 1999: A Survey. *Earthquake Spectra*, 21(2): 285-303.

Cruz, A.M. and N. Okada (2008): "Methodology for Preliminary Assessment of Natech Risk in Urban Areas." *Journal of Natural Hazards*, 46(2), 199-220.

Cruz, A.M.; and L.J., Steinberg, A.L. Vetere-Arellano, (2006): Emerging Issues for Natech Disaster Risk Management in Europe. *Journal of Risk Research,* 9(5), 1-19.

Cruz, A.M., L.J. Steinberg; A.L., Vetere-Arellano J.P.; Nordvik, and F. Pisano (2004): *State of the Art in Natech (Natural Hazard*

Triggering Technological Disasters) Risk Assessment in Europe. Report EUR 21292 EN, DG Joint Research Centre, European Commission and United Nations International Strategy for Disaster Reduction, Ispra, Italy.

Cruz, A.M.; and E. Krausmann (2007): Results of the Workshop: Assessing and Managing Natechs (Natural hazard triggered technological accidents). *EUR Report 23288*. Joint Research Centre, European Commission, Italy.

Cruz, A.M.; and E. Krausmann (2009): Secondary Hazards following Natural Disasters: The Case of Natech Hazards. *China Emergency Management*, March.

EPA (2004): General Risk Management Programme Guidance. U.S. Environmental Protection Agency, Chemical Emergency Preparedness and Prevention. < http://yosemite.epa.gov/oswer/ceppoweb.nsf/content/EPAguidance.htm> (22 October 2007).

Fendler, R. (2008): Floods and Safety of Establishments and Installations Containing Hazardous Substances. *Journal of Natural Hazards* (accepted, forthcoming).

Hongliang, Ouyang (2008): Shifang's Chemical Fertilizer Plants Leak. *Caijing Magazine.* May 19, 2008, 18:11 (retrieved October 2008) <http://english.caijing.com.cn/2008-05-19/100063478.html>

Khan, F.I.; and S.A. Abbasi (1998): "DOMIFFECT (DOMIno eFFECT): user-friendly software for domino effect analysis." *Environmental Modelling and Software*, 13, pp. 163-177.

Kourniotis, S.P.; C.T. Kiranoudis; and N.C. Markatos (2000): "Statistical Analysis of Domino Chemical Accidents." *Journal of Hazardous Materials*, 71, pp. 239-252.

Lindell, M.K.; and Perry, R.W. (1997): Hazardous Materials Releases in the Northridge Earthquake: Implications for Seismic Risk Assessment. *Risk Analysis*, 17(2), 147-156.

MEP-PRC (2008): Ministry of Environmental Protection Releases Environmental Monitoring Information on Disaster Area: No Evident Change Found in Water Quality. *News Release.* Ministry of Environmental Protection, The People's Republic of China (MEP-PRC), May 14. (Retrieved October 2008) <http://english.mep.gov.cn/News_service/news_release/200805/t20080520_122693.htm>

Salzano, E.; Iervolino, I., and Fabbrocino, G. (2003): Seismic risk of atmospheric storage tanks in the framework of quantitative risk analysis. *Journal of Loss Prevention in the Process Industries*, 16, 403–409.

Sengul, H.; L.J. Steinberg; and A.M. Cruz, (2005): Hazard Characterization of Joint Natural and Technological Disasters in the United States. *Proceedings of the SRA 25th Annual Meeting*, December 4-7, Orlando, Florida, USA.

Showalter, P.S., and M.F. Myers, (1994): Natural Disasters in the United States as Release Agents of Oil, Chemicals, or Radiological Materials Between 1980-89: Analysis and Recommendations. *Risk Analysis*, 14(2): 169-181.

Steinberg, L.J. (2004). Natechs in the United States: Experience, Safeguards, and Gaps. In Vetere-Arellano, A.L., A.M., Cruz, J.P. Nordvik, and F. Pisano (Eds.), *Proceedings of the NEDIES International Workshop on Natech (Natural Disaster-Triggered Technological Disasters) Disaster Management*, Report EUR 21054 EN, Ispra, Italy, 20-21 October.

Steinberg, L.J.; and A.M. Cruz, (2004): When natural and technological disasters collide: lessons from the Turkey earthquake of August 17, 1999. *Natural Hazards Review*, 5(3): 121-130.

Warm, H.J. and K.E. Köppke (2007): Schutz von neuen und bestehenden Anlagen und Betriebsbereichen gegen natürliche, umgebungsbedingte Gefahrenquellen, insbesondere Hochwasser (Untersuchung vor-und nachsorgender Maßnahmen), UFOPLAN No. 203 48 362, German Federal Environment Agency, May. Available from http://www.umweltbundesamt.de/anlagen/publikationen.html (in German with English abstract).

15

Engaging the Media in Disaster Management

PATRALEKHA CHATTERJEE

Why do some disasters get more attention than others? The short answer is because media coverage of disasters is selective. To the media, where and who is affected by the disaster are critical. The level and intensity of coverage of the disaster depends on proximity, levels of interest of readers/viewers and the economic stakes involved, rather than the scale of the actual suffering. The challenge before the media is communicating the face of disaster beyond the immediate event. The challenge before disaster managers is to harness the power of media to reduce the vulnerability of communities to disasters. For this to happen, disaster managers must understand how the media operates, and its priorities. This chapter offers insights on how the media functions in the wake of a disaster and pointers to how its power can be harnessed to build safer and more resilient communities.

Introduction

As more and more people are caught up in a growing number of natural disasters, the market for 'disaster stories' is booming. Disasters offer high-impact images of devastated landscapes, faces of grief, a gripping narrative of thrills and tragic moments, of rescue and relief workers racing against the clock to save lives. Sometimes, the narrative can be pure Bollywood with the bad guys (the bureaucrats) and good guys (NGOs and community workers) slugging it out in front of flash bulbs and TV crews.

The stories that linger on in our memory, however, almost, always have a strong human interest component. Such stories are useful. Often, they catalyse action on the ground. The worst 'on-the-spot' stories from disaster zones are shoddy on facts, voyeuristic in tone, akin to disaster package tours. Carried repeatedly, such stories can breed compassion fatigue and reader/viewer resistance. Mainstream media worldwide carries a mix of both categories of stories. The challenge before the media is communicating the face of disaster beyond the immediate event. The challenge before disaster managers is to harness the power of media to reduce the vulnerability of communities to disasters. For this to happen, disaster managers must understand how the media operates, and its priorities. News coverage is typically more driven by 'events' and 'personalities' rather than the 'issues' behind the calamities.

> "Generally speaking, I would say that the main challenge in covering a disaster is not during the disaster itself. It is in doing those stories before the disaster that could mitigate the damage and harm, if people paid attention,"

Seattle Based Journalist Tom Paulson

Paulson, who has covered several small local "disasters" such as earthquakes, floods and food-borne disease outbreaks, cites the 2001 earthquake which struck Seattle as a case in point.

> "In 2001, Seattle experienced the moderately sized Nisqually earthquake–some buildings fell down, lots of minor and moderate damage but few injuries and only one indirect death (heart attack). In the early 1990s the media had begun to take our quake risk in the Pacific Northwest seriously as the scientific evidence showed that we were at risk of a major quake on the scale of something like the Sumatran quake that spawned the Indian Ocean tsunami. Before the 2001 quake, I wrote plenty of stories about how many buildings in Seattle (including schools and hospitals) would likely collapse during a good-sized quake. After the 2001 quake, officials promised to fix all these old buildings and change the law to require they be made safe. A year or two after that,

> little changed and soon the promise was forgotten. And the public does not care. The quake is a distant memory. So many of these unsafe buildings are still unsafe. Another problem has been that as state and local agencies work on disaster planning, the Bush-created U.S. Homeland Security department now has jurisdiction over such things and the feds always try to exclude the media for 'security' reasons. As a result, reporters are often excluded from a lot of these planning sessions or exercises—even though the media's role during a disaster is crucial."

Getting editors to continuously focus on such issues so that they remain 'alive' and act as warnings is a challenge.

Changing Contexts

This discourse on the coverage of disasters is taking place at a time of dramatic changes in the media and the natural landscape.

The risk of disasters occurring worldwide is increasing due to the expansion of slums, the increasing vulnerability of rural livelihoods to weather changes and deteriorating ecosystems. "Exacerbating this deadly trio is the established and omnipresent threat of climate change, impelled by greenhouse gas emissions generated by affluent societies and individuals, with the resulting burdens falling on developing countries and their poorest citizens," according to the first UN Global Assessment Report on Disaster Risk Reduction, launched in Bahrain in May 2009.

A key finding of the report is that even without climate change, disaster risk is still increasing worldwide. "If climate change is added to these disaster risk patterns, it will be a quite catastrophic picture," Andrew Maskrey, one of the report's authors, told IRIN (Integrated Regional Information Networks), a news agency focusing on humanitarian stories in regions that are often forgotten.

While hazards are largely unavoidable, especially with the growing threat of climate change, they only become disasters when communities' coping mechanisms cross a threshold, and they are unable to manage their impacts. The world's poorest and most vulnerable people, therefore, are those most at risk during disasters. Disasters not only destroy individual lives and families, they have an enormously debilitating impact on the development of resource-poor communities.

Technology has had a huge impact on how disasters are reported worldwide in recent years. Today, "news" goes online within seconds. Official response typically takes much longer. So, the first few reports from disaster zones inevitably focus on official neglect, mismanagement and so on. Time, public and media pressure fuel an improved response from government agencies. The situation on the ground looks better, generating more 'positive coverage'.

The combination of all these factors pose formidable challenges to governments, aid agencies, civil society and the media. It calls for more strategic partnerships in our preparedness and response.

To what extent is the media equipped to deal with the challenges? Proximity, politics and economics often determine the level of interest and extent of media coverage of a disaster rather than the scale of suffering. But alongside the constraints, there are new opportunities and new tools available to help a journalist or a development professional get information across to the public faster than before. This, in turn, has spurred the amateur, now called 'the citizen journalist', to provide independent reports and analyses on many areas of public interest, including post-disaster situations. Technology is one among many factors that can promote better coverage of a disaster.

An equally relevant issue in this context are the changes within the traditional media. While the number of disasters is increasing, newspapers are disappearing or reducing the number of pages, reporters are being laid off, and news gathering budgets are being slashed. India may have been less affected than many countries in the indusrialised world but it has not been immune to these shocks.

Against such a backdrop, field trips to disaster sites to do follow-ups, tracking nuances which may have been missed out in the hurry of reporting the immediate, are less likely. More likely are trips sponsored by aid agencies, NGOs and corporates with stakes in the disaster, and with an eye on publicity. The end result is 'positive coverage', not necessarily bad, and on occasions worthwhile as it draws attention to issues/personalities making a contribution. But there is a danger that this can lead to selective and stereotypical portrayal of a calamity, with preferential treatment towards those who have the resources to fund the roving reporter.

Despite these changes, the key issue is still information. Disaster-affected people need information as they need shelter, water, medicine and food. Information can save lives, livelihoods and resources. Yet aid organisations focus mainly on gathering information for themselves and not enough on exchanging information with the people they aim to support.

The media plays a critical role in disseminating information, and the media in turn needs timely and vital information. This is an opportune time, therefore, for officials and development practitioners and media persons to better understand each other's universe and collaborate with each other when it is in mutual interest.

How fast and accurately disaster managers can get information across to the media determines the images of the disaster that go out to the public. Logistics may not always permit offering as much information as the media seeks, But even amid constraints, a lot is possible.

I vividly remember my encounter with Gagandeep Singh Bedi, the District Collector of tsunami-ravaged Cuddalore district in Tamil Nadu in early 2005, a few months after disaster struck the district. I had arrived at Cuddalore on an assignment with The Lancet. After my visits to the field, I turned up at his office desperate for updated official information and insights about the ground reality. I did not have an appointment. There was a long queue of people outside his door waiting to meet the DC. He offered me a cup of tea, asked me to wait, and directed his secretary to put together a dossier of daily bulletins his office had been bringing out. This, he told me, would answer many of the questions I had. I was thrilled, not expecting such a positive response. After 15 minutes, I was ushered into his room. He wanted to know the focus of my article. In this instance, it was the psychological impact of the tsunami on communities. He readily shared his views on the subject, and then gave me references of NGOs working in his district and dealing with the topic. He did not give me too much time, but he made himself accessible, and was helpful. I remember the incident because it offers a valuable lesson of how officials, development practitioners and the media can work together.

Asian Tsunami, the Turning Point in Capturing the Face of Disaster

The December 26, 2004 Asian Tsunami marked a turning point in the history of disaster coverage. The tsunami struck just off Sumatra, Indonesia, in a fault line running under the sea. The rupture caused massive waves, or tsunamis, that hurtled away from the epicentre, reaching shores as far away as Africa. At least 230,000 people were killed and the livelihoods of millions were destroyed in over 10 countries. But Asia which has the largest TV audience in the world and fastest growing Internet and mobile phone markets failed to provide any public warning of the disaster. The tsunami communication failures triggered much soul-searching in the global humanitarian community and led to greater awareness about information as a vital form of aid in itself.

The media in Indonesia, Thailand, Sri Lanka, India and the Maldives—the countries worst hit by the 2004 Tsunami—did not do a good job of warning the people, but once disaster struck, traditional and new media did a good job of spreading the word.

An army of online citizen journalists quickly provided the world with essential first-hand accounts, photos, sounds and video of the earthquake and tsunami that devastated South Asia. Through the crisis, blogs like tsunamihelp.blogspot.com for example helped in generating participatory stories from the country on the issue. Many reported, through this blog, about their near-death experiences and the aftermath of the disaster that were not covered by the mainstream media at the start. Peter Griffin, a blogger and writer from Mumbai, India, set up a blog just hours after news of the disaster reached him. Two other bloggers, Rohit Gupta and Dina Mehta, also in Mumbai, helped him put the information in place. And very soon after, the blogging community around the world rallied to set up what has now become the South-East Asia Earthquake and Tsunami Blog.

The Asian tsunami also generated some excellent video stories of the recovery process. TVE Asia Pacific commissioned locally based film-makers in each country to keep revisiting these families every month for most of 2005. Local camera crews tracked the personal recovery stories of eight tsunami affected families in four countries—India, Indonesia, Sri Lanka and Thailand starting from 2005. This was done through monthly visits. Stories were led by surviving children aged between 8 and 16. This coverage resulted in five-minute monthly video reports on each child/family that were placed online, a 50-minute documentary released on the first anniversary of the disaster. This project, Children of Tsunami:The Journey Continues, gave a voice to the affected families, and also highlighted sociological, economic, ecological and other issues that warranted wider discussion during the recovery. Children of Tsunami is a good example of how to communicate the face of disaster. Through personal stories of anguish and survival, courage and resilience, it communicates the long and arduous journey back to normalcy for millions of Asians affected by one of the worst natural disasters of all time.

How does One Communicate the Face of Disaster?

There are many ways of capturing the face of disaster. The starting point, I emphasise, is to recognize that media is the vital link between the scene of disaster and rest of the world. Often once the media glare moves away from the site of the disaster, official concern also fades. But stories are embedded in events and processes leading up to the disaster and stemming from the disaster. This holds good no matter where the calamity occurs.

Indian Journalist Ammu Joseph in an insightful piece in Infochange (February 2005), a website, examines some of the critiques of the media's coverage of the 2004 tsunami and its aftermath. The calamity attracted huge international attention, she points out.

There was, for example :

> "excessive, if not exclusive, attention paid to post-disaster aid originating in Western nations, with little mention of inter-Asia assistance and, of course, scant reference to the tremendous outpouring of contributions in cash, kind, labour and expertise from civil society within the affected countries. Similarly, the relative coverage given to the impact of the disaster on different countries is fairly revealing—Somalia, for example, has barely been on the media radar whereas Thailand, where the maximum number of foreign tourists died or disappeared, was very much in focus."

Joseph also points out that Indian media also came under fire for :

> "sensationalism and voyeurism. And about the insensitivity with which grieving, traumatised survivors have been pursued, especially by television reporters anxious to feed the apparently insatiable hunger of 24-hour news channels for dramatic images and sound-bytes."

However, she points out that

> "journalists reporting from the affected areas were naturally scrambling to do the best they could to provide information about the unprecedented scale and scope of the devastation caused by the sudden, short-lived blast from the sea. Thanks to their energetic efforts, people elsewhere could at least try to imagine and understand the enormity of the calamity, and do whatever they could to help in a situation of such extensive death and destruction. It goes without saying, therefore, that any discussion on media coverage of the catastrophe is not meant to criticise as much as to learn."

In her article, Joseph makes the point that while the media tend to focus on women and children in any disaster situation, and this was no exception, they had been appearing primarily as victims (weeping, wailing, awaiting or availing relief), as mothers (faced with bereavement and/or difficult choices, especially in their attempts to save children), and as heroines (for example, the Swedish mother and the British schoolgirl holidaying in Thailand). "The question is whether or not such limited representations do justice to women's experiences, concerns and needs in the wake of the disaster", she asks.

This is a key issue in media coverage of disasters. Sometimes, unwittingly, we impose permanent victimhood on the disaster-affected. Disasters, like other crises, also throw up opportunities for empowerment. Examples of those who traversed the journey from being victim to survivor need to be told because they inspire and reassure at a time when reassurance is much-needed.

Stories need to be told about the dead, the injured and the missing. But there are also stories which also show that the disaster-affected can be agents of change. The images portrayed by the media have an impact that can be either empowering or disempowering. Disasters produce victims. But a victim does not remain in the same frame of mind for ever. Aided or unaided by external agents, tapping into inner resources, the 'victim' often times evolves into a 'survivor'.

Personally, I think the tale of such a survivor/survivors against the canvas of devastation, official action/inaction, volunteer rescue and relief effort makes a powerful "story". It is not the only way of telling a disaster story but a useful hook to explain and elaborate on other critical elements that build up to the disaster scenario or materialize in its aftermath.

Whose Disaster is it Anyway?

Why do some disasters get more attention than others? The short answer is because media coverage of disasters is selective. To the media, where and who is affected by the disaster are critical. The level and intensity of coverage of the disaster depends on proximity, levels of interest of readers/viewers and the economic stakes involved, rather than the scale of the actual suffering.

Some insights come from a 2006 report (Western Media Coverage of Humanitarian Disasters) by CARMA International, a US-based NGO. It examined Western media coverage of six humanitarian disasters: the earthquake in Pakistani Kashmir (October 8, 2005), Hurricane Stanley (October 1, 2005), Hurricane Katrina (August 23, 2005), the Indian Ocean earthquake/tsunami (December 26, 2004), the earthquake in Bam, Iran (December 26, 2003), and the humanitarian crisis in Darfur, Sudan (since February 2003).

This report analysed 64 daily and weekly publications in nine countries (UK, Germany, France, Spain, Italy, Netherlands, Pan-Europe, USA, and Australia). A total of 1,967 articles from 43 national and pan-national daily newspapers, four Sunday editions, and 17 weekly newspapers and news magazines were researched.

The researchers concluded that "Western self-interest is the pre-condition for significant coverage of a humanitarian crisis"; and that there appeared to be no link between the scale of a disaster and media interest in the story. For instance, of all the disasters, Stanley and Katrina suffered the fewest deaths, but Katrina got far more attention in the global media than any other humanitarian disaster studied. Further, according to CARMA, there was "a clear correlation between the perceived economic impact of a disaster on western markets and the quantity of media coverage: Where there is most economic interest (Katrina—USA), there is most coverage; where there is least, there is least interest (Stanley—Guatemala). To cite one example, 17 per cent of the articles on Katrina focus on its economic issues, the greatest for any disaster. In contrast, the Hurricane Stanley emergency had "no obvious significant economic or political interest. Consequently, there is virtually no coverage of any kind (25 in total) beyond the first few days, or coverage that focused on the humanitarian response."

In a disaster scenario, there are indeed many angles one can cover. Here are examples of two aspects which do not always get adequate emphasis: the psychological impact of the disaster and the survivors' own initiatives to get back to normal life.

Copied below is a report I filed for the *Lancet*, the British medical journal (*www.thelancet.com Vol. 365 March 5, 2005*). The story which was subsequently reproduced by the WHO India website (*http://www.whoindia.org/LinkFiles/NMH-News_and_Workshop_030505-Mental-health-care-for-india-tsunami-survivors.pdf*) focuses on South India's shattered coastal communities as tsunami survivors were just beginning to pick up the pieces of their lives. The spotlight was on psychological trauma among the disaster affected and the local initiatives to help survivors get back to normalcy.

> (More than two months after the sea swallowed her husband and destroyed her home, Chellamma sits quietly, thinking about the future of her three unmarried daughters. The 50-year-old widow and mother of seven from Muzhukuthurai, in tsunami-battered Cuddalore, Tamil Nadu, southern India, is only now starting to pick up the pieces of her life. "I used to sell fish. Now, there is nothing to sell, [because] no one is going to sea . . . My husband is gone. Who will look after my children and me?" she asks.
>
> All around is sand, a torn fishing net, and the remains of a thatched hut—once her home. But there is a glimmer of hope. Chellamma is one of 20 women in and around Muzhukuthurai who have formed a self-help group. The first step is a savings kitty, with each woman contributing Rs. 50 (around US$1). The savings, the women hope, will help them start income-generating enterprises and cope with future emergencies. The idea came from efforts by community-level workers recently trained in psychosocial counselling.
>
> Psychosocial care can be just as valuable as material assistance in disaster situations. And there is growing evidence to show that early diagnosis and timely interventions can make a significant difference to the recovery process. But few people who have experienced natural disasters view

themselves as in need of mental health care and are, therefore, unlikely to seek help. To help address the unique needs of such individuals, WHO recommends that health workers set aside traditional methods, avoid use of mental health labels, and use an active outreach approach.

In India, psychosocial care has changed a great deal since the Bhopal Gas Leak tragedy in December 1984. This disaster—the worst industrial disaster ever seen—left not only a trail of deaths and life-long illnesses, but also numerous mental disorders among survivors. Mental health workers were slow to respond, however, it was 6-8 weeks before psychiatrists became involved in the relief effort, a delay attributed to the fact that none of the five regional medical colleges had a psychiatrist on their faculty.

By contrast, psychosocial care was a key concern for local and national government immediately after the tsunami hit India in December 2004. One reason the situation is so different from that seen 20 years ago is the new generation of bureaucrats. In Cuddalore, for example, Gagandeep Singh Bedi, Cuddalore district's top government administrator admits that the "young generation of bureaucrats" like him are more responsive to new ideas. In Bedi's district, the Department of Medical and Rural Health Services and Family Welfare brings out a daily report about mental-health outreach sessions in different areas.

V. Sabeetha, a government psychiatrist who is overseeing mental-health outreach in the district, says counselling services are gratefully received. "My team and I have held counselling sessions in relief camps in all the 52 villages in the district... Most people we met appreciated being counselled on typical symptoms following any disaster, e.g., sleep disorders, nightmares, etc. No one had alerted them earlier about these symptoms," he says.

These sessions helped abate disaster stress in the early days.

But with most people now back in their villages, the big issue is follow-up, says Sabeetha.

Gauri, a community worker trained in psychosocial counselling by CREED, a local NGO affiliated with the Tamil Nadu Social Welfare Board, is trying to reintroduce some semblance of normality to the people of Muzhukuthurai.

She says active listening was the most valuable intervention immediately after the tsunamis. "We did not push [survivors] to speak if they did not want to. But we would ask them if they had eaten or bathed . . . With the man, the family breadwinner, gone, and with children to support, widows were nervous about the new, unfamiliar roles they had been pushed into."

Many whose homes were destroyed have been allotted temporary sheds. But most families prefer to stay with relatives. The women cook together and after the meal they sit around talking to each other. In many ways, the community bond compensates for the loss of the family support structure, explains Gauri.

"Though counselling is very important, we must be careful about not overdoing it. When we find someone can cope, then we have no role", says Koteshwar Rao, a psychiatric social worker with the Chennai-based Schizophrenia Research Foundation (SCARF), one of several agencies offering training in mental-health counselling for southern India.

"Many of the psychosocial interventions being used were instigated by the WHO regional office. "Within two weeks of the tsunami, WHO alerted medical schools and WHO collaborating centres. A group of people were identified to act as master trainers. Then, talks were initiated with the state Governments to drive the return to normalcy and mental health", says WHO official Cherian Varghese. He says the idea was to operate on a three-tier structure consisting of master trainers who would train local NGOs, and trainers at the district level who would, in turn, train community level workers.

"The primary need is not an overmedicalised approach. What most survivors need is empathetic listening and someone to show them a road map to the future", he adds.

A typical psychosocial counselling training session for NGOs and community volunteers, for instance, contains a lot of practical tools with which community level workers can assist tsunami survivors. SCARF trainer Koteshwar Rao stresses the importance of being up-to-date with latest government schemes and knowing details of agencies that are providing free services to tsunami-affected individuals. Other tools include innovative suggestions about income generation, such as those adopted by Chellamma and her community.

Given that most of those who come for training know little about mental-health counselling, the sessions are designed to be entertaining and interactive, with lots of games and opportunities to express one's creativity and concern. Most trainees also need a briefing about common symptoms of post-traumatic stress disorder and basic do's and don'ts of psychosocial counselling. "The idea is to expand the choices and options of the affected community so that they focus on the future," says Rao.

The Academy for Disaster Management, Education, Planning, and Training, an NGO helping to educate community workers, has trained nearly 200 elementary school teachers in tsunami-affected villages in southern India in providing psychological first-aid to children. Government school teachers who have undergone training are now experimenting with new ways of interacting with their students.

One government school teacher who had failed in her attempts to get a traumatised 6-year-old boy from a tsunami-affected village to open up took her class to a nearby nursery.

There, the child's interest was sparked by the plants and he began to ask questions. Taking the cue, the teacher bought him a few saplings. Since then, the boy and the teacher discuss the plants' progress everyday and the teacher has been reading stories about flora and fauna surviving adversity.

For the trainers, much of the work goes beyond classroom-style sessions. In the past few weeks, SCARF's Rao and his colleagues have travelled to villages to check whether the new community counsellors have taken on board the key principles of emergency psychosocial support. The cascade effect of the three-tier approach sometimes leads to partial comprehension of key principles—a Chinese whisper effect.

A key concern is monitoring vulnerable groups in the affected communities. This means not only children and widows but also widowers. A case in point is 60-year old tsunami survivor Kuppuswamy, who lost his wife and is now a single parent. Unfamiliar with domestic chores, the distressed man wonders who will cook for him when he moves out of the relief camp, and about the complexities of arranging a suitable bride for his 23-year old son.

Today, the immediate challenge is to extend counselling services to remote villages and reach those who have been neglected so far. But in the long-term, the challenge is to provide adequate mental health care with only small numbers of mental-health professionals. There are less than 4,000 trained psychiatrists in India, and even fewer clinical psychologists. Predictably, most are located in major cities. As a result, the majority of people living in rural areas have virtually no access to mental-health facilities, so for them recovery is likely to be long and slow.)

Another story focuses on earthquake-struck Gujarat in 2001 and one local newspaper's valiant struggle to carry on with its work in the disaster site.

(Ground still rumbling, journalists in quake-ravaged Indian city soldier on)

By Patralekha Chatterjee
Special to freedomforum.org
03.06.2001

For the journalists at the *Kutch Mitra* newspaper, the pressures of the job go beyond those usually associated with chasing stories and tracking down sources.

Four or five times a day, the ground beneath them shakes and rumbles. "We feel aftershocks and get a little nervous," said Nikhil Pandhya, a reporter for *Kutch Mitra*. The 52-year-old mass-circulation newspaper is published in Bhuj, the city in western India near the epicentre of a devastating earthquake six weeks ago.

Aftershocks still ripple through the region, which is slowly recovering from the disaster that killed an estimated 30,000 people. Three employees of *Kutch Mitra* were killed in the earthquake, but the newspaper soldiered on.

Journalists visiting Bhuj in the earthquake's immediate aftermath marvelled that *Kutch Mitra* was so quickly up and running. A reporter for the Associated Press wrote that staffers "tended their wounded, buried their dead and went back to work".

For a time after the magnitude 7.7 temblor on January 26, the *Kutch Mitra* staffers worked from makeshift tents and wrote their articles longhand. The newspaper's printing press escaped damage.

"Now, we are back at our desk, inside our office," says Pandhya, the reporter. "It is like any other newsroom." But the hours logged everyday tend to be longer than before the quake—14 instead of 8, said a colleague, Navin Joshi.

Pandhya noted that "most of our stories focus on the rehabilitation" efforts in Bhuj, a walled city of 150,000 people in Gujarat State. Bhuj is in the Kutch district of Gujarat.

Kutch Mitra (which means Friend of Kutch) sells for the equivalent of 4 cents a copy and circulates in the damaged neighbourhoods and among the many homeless in relief camps.

In an article several years ago, the newspaper had warned about the dangers of earthquakes in the region, a warning that went largely unheeded.

End Notes

Social media has been a game-changer impacting disaster management and disaster reportage. Journalists are on Facebook and Twitter. So are humanitarian agencies such as Médecins Sans Frontières (MSF). A striking example is the massive global rapid response to the devastating earthquake in Haiti on January 12, 2010 when a 7.0 quake killed an estimated 200,000 people and levelled the city of Port-au-Prince in 15 seconds. Within hours of the earthquake, organizations engaged in disaster management had launched full-fledged online campaigns to inform the world of the actions they were taking to support the victims in Haiti and how the public could help. Non-Governmental Organizations tapped their supporters through Facebook, and followers on twitter, subscribers on RSS feeds and text messages.

Technology has made it easier for the government and non-governmental institutions engaged in disaster relief and management to tell their tale. This narrative, whether transmitted through glossy booklets or on the you tube, contains valuable information. But it is easy to miss the emerging concerns in the flood of statistics. It is the media's job to remain vigilant, ask the right questions, and turn the spotlight on the gaps, alongside the stories of individuals who see opportunities when faced with barriers, and institutions who forge partnerships to build a strong, lasting change.

Index